Adventuring in *Hawaii*

The Sierra Club Adventure Travel Guides

Adventuring in *Hawaii*

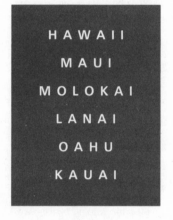

HAWAII

MAUI

MOLOKAI

LANAI

OAHU

KAUAI

RICHARD McMAHON

SIERRA CLUB BOOKS · SAN FRANCISCO

LIBRARY OF CONGRESS CATALOGING-IN-PUBLICATION DATA
    McMahon, Richard, 1928–
        Adventuring in Hawaii : Hawaii, Maui, Molokai, Lanai, Oahu, Kauai / by Richard McMahon.
            p.   cm. — (The Sierra Club adventure travel guides)
        Includes bibliographical references and index.
        ISBN 0–87156–428–9 (alk. paper)
        1. Hawaii—Guidebooks.   I. Title.   II. Series.
    DU622.M38   1996
    919.6904'4—dc20   95–42683
                                                                  CIP

Production by Robin Rockey
Cover design by Bonnie Smetts
Book design by Amy Evans
Maps by Christopher McMahon
Composition by Wilsted & Taylor

Printed in the United States of America on acid-free paper containing a minimum of 50% recovered waste paper of which at least 10% of the fiber content is post-consumer waste.

10   9   8   7   6   5   4   3   2   1

Contents

Acknowledgements

M ANY PEOPLE CONTRIBUTED time and effort to this book, or provided information which has made it a better work than it otherwise would have been. I am indebted to Audrey Sutherland and Lorin Gill, who were kind enough to read the manuscript and make corrections and numerous suggestions. Bobby Owens gave me fresh insights into surfing and surf spots. Ed Petteys, Curt Cottrell, Michael Baker, and Rodney Oshiro of the State Forestry Division provided up-to-date information about trails and access. Daniella Laau and Alice Santiago, two very helpful ladies at the State Parks Division, have cheerfully furnished me with camping information and assistance over the years, and Sherrie Samuels kept me apprised of the latest park developments. My son, Christopher, was responsible for reproduction of all graphics, and Gina Lambert did a fine job on the maps. Iris Wiley reviewed my suggested reading list.

At Sierra Club Books, my thanks to Jim Cohee for taking on the project, to Heidi Reinberg for her conscientious, expert copyediting and many useful suggestions, and to Amy Evans for shepherding the book's graphics. Last, but far from least, my wife, Ann, mowed the lawn, washed the cars, and performed many of my other household chores while I was busy writing and researching the book.

Author's Note

IN SELECTING ADVENTURES for this book, I felt obligated to respect the wishes of property owners who, while allowing small numbers of local people to cross their property, are unwilling to open these properties to the larger numbers that might come from the publication of a book such as this one. The State of Hawaii has also closed several trails that make great treks for the adventurous, but that, as we went to press, needed improvement or better marking. Though knowledgeable local hikers use them, visiting hikers might face a real danger of getting lost or injured.

Finally, if you know of an adventure that you feel should be included in this book, please let me know. Any information you contribute will be gratefully acknowledged in subsequent editions of *Adventuring in Hawaii.*

CHAPTER ONE

Islands of Adventure

WHEN MOST PEOPLE think of Hawaii, adventure is probably not one of the things they have in mind. Swaying palm trees, lovely girls dancing the hula, sunbathing on Waikiki Beach, mai tais at sunset—romantic images all, but adventure doesn't seem to be part of the picture. Yet for those seeking it, the Hawaiian Islands can provide more adventure than almost any other similar destination.

In fact, the islands have attracted adventurers for more than fifteen hundred years. It was the Polynesians, perhaps the greatest seagoing adventurers of all time, who first came to these islands. Setting forth in double-hulled sailing canoes, they cast off to explore an unknown sea, guided by ancient navigational techniques that utilized the ocean swells, currents, and stars. We will never know how many men and women perished as these canoes made the perilous trip across 2,000 miles of open ocean to establish a new homeland. Eventually these travelers found an island they were to call *Havaii*, which they then colonized, bringing the plants and animals they would need to sustain themselves.

More than a thousand years passed before another adventurer, Captain James Cook, set eyes upon the world's most isolated inhabited island chain. This was a meeting of cultures that was to cost the Hawaiians their birthright—and Cook his life. Adventurers of another sort followed Cook: Yankee traders arrived to strip the sandalwood, taking it to the Orient and returning with silks and spices. Then came New England whalers—rough and ready men who hunted leviathans at sea—and women and rum ashore—leaving disease and disorder in their wake.

Missionaries came to do good, entrepreneurs to do well. Fortunes were made in land speculation, cattle ranching, and sugar, but not by the Hawaiians, who watched helplessly as others took over their land and their power. And then their very heritage was usurped by an adventurous cabal of Caucasian businessmen who overthrew the ancient regime and arranged the annexation of the islands by the United States. Finally, early one December morning, adventurers from the Land of the Rising Sun flew out of the dawn, risking everything on one great throw of the dice, to try to gain an empire.

Though war thrust Hawaii into the spotlight, peace brought an ever-increasing influx of tourists less interested in adventure than in the sybaritic pleasures of the South Seas. But the adventure is still here. It waits in the soaring green hills and the cobalt blue sea, the lava-spewing volcanoes and the waterfall-filled valleys, the lush rain forests and the parched deserts. This book will show you how and where to find it.

How to Use This Book

The purpose of this book is to offer a different and exciting way to enjoy the Hawaiian Islands, to provide the reader with an adventure, rather than the usual tourist visit. This first chapter, "Islands of Adventure," contains important information that will make you a more informed traveler as well as enhance your enjoyment. Following this introduction are chapters devoted to each of the islands of Hawaii, describing the adventures that await you. While most of these activities can be enjoyed on every island, a few are unique to one particular island. With the exception of skiing, every adventure listed can be undertaken at any time of the year. The section below gives general information about these activities. It is important to read this section, as well as the one pertaining to a given activity in each island chapter, in order to gain an overall view of what's available.

Adventuring by Car

These sections, while covering the more frequently visited common attractions, also lead to lesser known and out-of-the-way points of interest rarely seen on the usual vehicle itinerary. Basic information about each island is provided here. Even if you don't plan to do much driving *it is important to read, or at least browse, these sections.* There is information here that is not provided elsewhere, and you will need to refer back to these sections if you are traveling the same route by bicycle, or driving to a trailhead. And if you are planning to enjoy some of the other adventures in this book, but would like to do some sightseeing in between expeditions, these sections will highlight what to see and how to get to a particular sight.

Backpacking Adventures

Some of the finest adventures in the islands require only a backpack and the stamina to carry it. Most of the trips simply require that you be a reasonably experienced backpacker in fairly good physical condition. You should be capable of walking up to 12 miles per day with a pack weighing up to 30 pounds. Trail-finding skills are not required, as most routes are well marked. Special guides are not necessary; this book should give you all the information you need to plan and complete your trip. However, you may find it rewarding to take any of these trips with a group. The Sierra Club Outings Department (85 Second Street, San Francisco, CA 94105; phone 415-923-5522) offers backpacking trips in Hawaii throughout the year. Several adventure travel companies also organize the same sort of excursion. And, of course, there are Hawaiian companies that offer guided backpacking trips. Check with your hotel or consult the free handouts available at Hawaiian airports.

Day Hiking

It is not necessary to backpack in order to enjoy some of the best hiking in the islands. One of my "Hawaii's Best Adventures" is the Nualolo-Awaawapui Loop, a day hike on Kauai. If you like to hike

Iao Valley and its famous "Needle" are accessible by car and bicycle. Photo by Richard McMahon.

and are in reasonably good physical condition, you should have no trouble with any of these trips. A day pack large enough to carry water, rain gear, lunch, and any personal items is all that you should need. There are many more hikes and hiking trails in the islands than are listed in this book, but I've winnowed them down to some of the best. If you plan to do extensive hiking, see the Suggested Reading section, Appendix I, at the end of the book.

Snorkeling and Diving

These sections describe excellent trips you can make from shore without the use of a boat. Boat diving in Hawaii is expensive, and, unfortunately, only becoming more so. In this book, I mention only a few, very special, boat dives. There are lots of commercial dive operations that go to great places, but the shore excursions described here go to great places too, and they won't cost you anything. If you are interested in boat diving, free handouts are available at area airports, or your hotel activities desk should have all the information you need.

If you plan to do much snorkeling, bring your own mask, snorkel, and fins, or buy them when you arrive. (You'd pay as much to rent these items as you would to own them.) Scuba divers should, at the very least, bring a regulator and wet suit. If you plan to do any extensive diving, you may want to bring along everything but your tanks. However, if you're thinking of making just a few boat dives with commercial operators, many of them furnish all equipment as part of their packages.

For the most part it is possible to dive or snorkel in Hawaii anywhere you can safely get into and out of the water. In this book, only the better, more popular spots are mentioned, places where visibility is usually good and where there is something interesting to see, such as coral formations, caverns, arches, or lots of tropical fish. Of course, exploring on your own may reveal other fine spots, and the excellent *Beaches of . . .* series of books by John Clark (see Suggested Reading, Appendix I) lists many more places where you can snorkel and dive.

All dive and snorkel adventures described here assume good weather, low winds, and calm seas. Even the normally calm leeward beaches can be hazardous when high winds prevail, or when heavy surf pounds the shore. Unpredictable currents can occur at these times, and visibility is usually poor, making snorkeling and diving pointless as well as dangerous. The summer months have the most consistently good ocean conditions, but on the leeward beaches you will find many fine days any time of the year. On the north and windward sides, good conditions are less frequent outside the summer months, and even then there are many periods of high and dangerous surf. At any time of the year, snorkeling and shore diving are usually best in the morning, before the wind and the waves come up. Each entry is coded to indicate the activity you can enjoy there: A (D) is a scuba diving site, (S) indicates snorkeling, and (D/S) shows that both activities can be enjoyed. Note: Some dive sites are also popular surfing areas. Do not compete with surfers. When they are out, the waves are up, which means poor visibility and dangerous diving.

Hawaii has many marine conservation areas, where such activities as fishing, netting, spearing, and collecting of any marine life, including coral and shells, are prohibited. These areas are usually posted to inform you of restrictions. Generally, it is best to assume that nothing may be disturbed or taken from the water in such places. The individual sections in the book will let you know if you are entering such an area.

Surfing

Depending on who you talk to, Hawaii is either the best—or one of the best—surfing sites in the world. But all Hawaiian islands are not equal when it comes to surfing. An experienced surfer arriving from the mainland would rarely head to Hawaii or Molokai. The big waves are on Oahu and Maui, and the sections on these two islands will tell you where to find them. However, for those surfers who find themselves on the outer islands, or for those determined to get off the beaten wave, the specific island sections will also show where the good surf is elsewhere.

There is a big difference between summer and winter surfing in Hawaii. While summertime surfing is fun, winter surfing is serious. (Incidentally, in surfing, the terms "summer" and "winter" coincide with summer and winter surf conditions, not the exact calendar months. Therefore, in the Surfing sections of this book, summer refers to April through September, while winter is September through April.) No beginner or casual surfer should even consider riding Hawaii's winter waves without a clear knowledge of a particular site and a realistic assessment of his own surfing capabilities. Even in winter there are places where surfing is usually safe, if not spectacular, such as Chun's Reef on Oahu, which has a break similar to Sunset's. Wherever they decide to surf, however, casual surfers should not compete with the experts for space on winter's monsters. Experts come from around the world to challenge these waves and they will not appreciate novices cluttering up the lineup and getting in their way.

There are more surfing locations in Hawaii than can be mentioned in this book. One guide lists thirty-three surfing spots on Oahu alone; another lists ninety-six! Each surfing location listed in this book is coded to indicate the type of surfing that takes place there: (S) = shortboard surfing; (L) = longboard surfing, (B) = bodyboarding, (BW) = bigwave boarding, and (BS) = bodysurfing. If you are planning what is primarily a surfing vacation, refer to the Suggested Reading section, Appendix I, at the end of the book.

Finally, if you are a surfing visitor to the islands, there is the decision of whether to bring your own board with you or to rent or buy one in Hawaii. There are pros and cons to each course of action. If you already own your own board, the $50-each-way charge to bring it with you seems reasonable. But after arriving, many surfers find that their home boards are not suitable for Hawaiian waves, and the boards wind up either stashed in a corner or smashed on a reef. Hawaii is on the cutting edge of surfboard technology, and its board shapers produce the latest, state-of-the-art boards. If your surf sojourn will be an extended one, the advantage of buying a board in Hawaii is that you will be getting one of the most advanced surfboards made, specifically designed for the Hawaiian waves you will be riding. Renting may sound like an attractive way of trying out one or more of the latest boards; however, many rentals are beat-up older boards, or the big tankers that tourists ride at Waikiki. If you can find a good one, renting could be the way to go. But do bear in mind, too, that good used boards can usually be found for sale at reasonable prices.

Windsurfing

As with board surfing, Hawaii provides the setting for some of the world's best windsurfing conditions. By far, the prime locations are on Maui and Oahu, but the Windsurfing sections of this book will let you know where you can sailboard on the other islands as well (though there is no appreciable windsurfing activity on either Molokai or Lanai). Windsurfing is a year-round sport in Hawaii, so intermediates and flat-water sailors can come at any time; more experienced surfsailors seeking high-performance winds will be happiest in spring and summer. And even those wanting to escape the cold at home can still find good sailboarding during the winter months, although they may have to look harder.

The prevailing winds in the islands are the northeast trades, which blow about 75 percent of the time. In winter, however, the trades are sometimes replaced by windless days or kona winds blowing from the southwest. Each surf spot requires either adjustment to these conditions or packing up and moving to a different area. The best sailboarding locations are those where geographic features create greater-than-average wind velocity. These can be found at island points, offshore from downsloping valleys, or in or near channels that funnel the wind.

Many of the prime windsurfing sites in Hawaii are also favorite surfing spots. Even though differing wind requirements usually keep the two sports from mixing, there are times when surfers and sailboarders will be competing for the same waves. In such a situation it is important to remember that surfers have the right-of-way. Surfers have been on the scene longer and sometimes resent the intrusion of sailboarders into what has always been surfing territory. Courtesy and giving way when required should allow you to avoid most unpleasantness.

As to whether to bring your own equipment or not, most authorities recommend that you rent windsurfing equipment in Hawaii rather than bringing your own from home. There are four very good reasons for this: your home equipment is probably not suitable to the big wave and high wind conditions here; if your equipment is longer than 9 feet it will have to be boxed and shipped air freight at considerable expense; renting will allow you to try out the latest innovations in sailboard technology; and good used equipment is for sale in Hawaii at cheaper prices than anywhere else in the world.

There is a continuing argument about which island offers the best windsurfing, Maui or Oahu. Many claim that nothing beats Maui's north shore. Others swear that Kailua Bay on Oahu offers the best all-around windsurfing found anywhere. Expert sailboarders rave about Hookipa on Maui, while other equally accomplished sailors insist that Backyards on Oahu is *the* place. While it probably boils down to personal choice where winds and waves are concerned, when it comes to après-surf ambience, Maui definitely has the edge. Paia (Maui) is a surfer's town, while Kailua (Oahu) is a residential community. At Lahaina or Kihei (both on Maui), a sailor need only cross the street after beaching the board for the day to find digs, a restaurant, or a watering spot; at Mokuleia (on

Oahu), he or she has a fair way to go to find either accommodations or any sort of nightlife. But, diversions aside, the windsurfing is great on both islands. Which is best? If you have time, why not try them both and decide for yourself?

Biking

Hawaii is a favorite destination for cyclists. Fine, year-round cycling weather, magnificent scenery, good campgrounds, and world-famous places to visit combine to provide the cyclist with virtually everything he or she could want. Many bicycle tour companies offer trips in the islands, but it is just as easy to plan your own with the help of this book. Some islands are more bike friendly than others, and you will learn how to deal with that. It costs $50 each way to bring a bike with you from the mainland to Hawaii, and $20 each way to do so from one island to another within the islands. If you are planning to bike on Maui or Hawaii, you can save the interisland charge by flying directly to Kahului or Kona (see the Public Transportation section, later in this chapter). Bicycles may be shipped unboxed at the owner's risk, in which case handlebars must be turned sideways and protruding parts (pedals, mirrors, etc.) must be removed. But keep in mind that good bicycles can be rented on all of the islands, and Honolulu has bicycle shops that carry all the latest racing, touring, and mountain models.

Hunting

Hunting is permitted on all six of the main islands of Hawaii, though specific hunting areas are established for each island. Public hunting is not permitted on Niihau, which is privately owned, nor on Kahoolawe, uninhabited and recovering from years of abuse as a site for military target practice. Currently, six species of animal and fifteen species of bird are open to hunting. Pronghorn antelope, feral cattle, and wallaby (!—see the Mammals section in this chapter) are closed to hunting, as are all water birds, including ducks and geese, and certain other birds. Lotteries are held to hunt some animals, such as deer, feral sheep, and mouflon, all of which can only be taken during a very restricted season. Seasons and bag limits vary by island, species, and hunting area. Some of this information is provided in the various chapters of this book, but regulations do change and are too complex to cover in detail. Complete information is furnished with a hunting license.

To hunt anywhere in the islands, including private land, a valid hunting license is required, and this creates a problem for visitors. In order to obtain a license, an applicant must attend a state-operated hunter education program. This free twelve-hour course is offered twice monthly on Oahu (less frequently on other islands), and is usually given over the course of a Friday and Saturday. Once the class is successfully completed, a license can be purchased at the Division of Forestry and Wildlife (see Appendix II), or at certain outdoor supply stores. The cost is $10 annually for residents and $95 for nonresidents. Licenses are free to residents sixty-five years of age or older. For further information, or to register for the course, call 587-0200.

Despite the presence of some exotic species on the hunting list, the most often hunted animals in Hawaii are goats and pigs. They are hunted primarily by local residents and primarily for meat, although sport definitely enters into the picture. Both animals cause destruction of habitat—pigs endanger native plants in the forest, and goats cause erosion on ridges and open hillsides. In the most threatened areas, goats and pigs can be hunted year-round, and there is no bag limit.

The Hawaiian feral pig is a cross between the domestic animal that arrived with the early Polynesians and other introduced pigs, including a European boar brought in specifically for hunting. While in other parts of the world you may go boar hunting, in Hawaii you "hunt pig." And this is hunting in a class by itself. Since feral pigs live mostly in the thick, mountainous rain forest, there is rarely enough open space to shoot one with either a rifle or a shotgun. Local residents usually hunt pigs with dogs to run down and corner the animal; then, while the pack holds the beast against a bank, constantly nipping at its legs and ears, the hunter closes in with a knife and slits its throat. It is not a sport for the fainthearted.

Another (safer) method of pig hunting is to reconnoiter trails that they are known to inhabit and find a spot where they have really rooted up the place. Bivouac there overnight, or mark the spot and return well before daylight, then wait for the pigs to show up at first light and blast away. If you do hunt like this, however, don't go out and brag about it; just go home and quietly enjoy your feast. No self-respecting local nimrod would hunt in such a fashion.

Goats first came to the islands with the adventurers Cook and Vancouver, who left the animals with the hope that they would multiply and provide a meat supply for future ships calling on the islands. They did. By the turn of this century the goats had multiplied so fast and were causing so much damage to the ecosystem that rigid controls had to be imposed. Later, eradication programs were put into effect in Hawaii Volcanoes and Haleakala national parks, and on the island of Kahoolawe. Hunting goat is in many ways the opposite of hunting pig: goats favor open areas and mountain ridges where firearms can be used to advantage. Dogs are not so effective when hunting goats, though, as the goats can retreat to cliffs and rocky ledges where the dogs cannot follow.

The Division of Forestry and Wildlife maintains a list of guides who lead hunting trips on all of the islands. Some will furnish weapons and ammunition, and some have access to private lands where game is supposedly more plentiful. Most rifles, shotguns, and bows and arrows may be used; when hunting with dogs, spears and knives are permitted. All firearms and ammunition brought into the state must be registered within forty-eight hours with the Chief of Police of the county concerned.

Fishing

Deep-sea fishing is extremely popular in Hawaii, and Kailua–Kona, where record marlin catches are made, is considered one of the world capitals of the sport. But you can also take ocean fishing trips from Maui, Oahu, and Kauai. Freshwater fishing is possible on Kauai, and, to a more limited extent, on Oahu. Though licenses are not required for saltwater fishing they are required for fishing for freshwater species in Hawaii. Licenses can be obtained from the state Department of Land and Natural Resources on any island, or from selected sporting goods stores statewide. They cost $3.75 for residents and $7.50 for nonresidents. A special tourist license, good for thirty days, costs $3.75.

Skiing

That's right—and I'm not talking about water skiing. Real downhill snow skiing takes place in Hawaii on Mauna Kea, the state's
highest peak, usually from January through March. Mauna Kea
can offer great long runs of a mile or more; you can do the mountain
on your own or join a group. If you plan to ski in Hawaii, you will
need to bring all equipment with you: Currently there is no place
to buy or rent snow ski equipment in the islands. To learn how to
set up your own mile-long ski tow for five people for only $100 a
day, turn to the Skiing Mauna Kea section in the "Hawaii" chapter.

Other Adventures

In general this book avoids commercial enterprises, primarily because you can have all the adventure you want in Hawaii for free,
except for the cost of whatever equipment is required and transportation to get to where you need to go. But some people enjoy
adventures that require commercial assistance.

*Note: No person, commercial enterprise, or other organization
paid any fee or provided any other inducement to be mentioned in
this book.*

Submarines with large portholes for underwater viewing operate from Waikiki, Lahaina, and Kailua–Kona. You can also find
parasailing outfits on these three islands, though on an erratic
schedule. Helicopter tours are offered on all islands. Glider rides
and parachute jumping are available at Dillingham Airfield on
Oahu. Horseback trips on all islands range from half-day jaunts to
overnight expeditions. An overnight horseback trip into Haleakala
Crater on Maui is offered by the Kaupo Store, Kaupo, Maui 96713;
phone 248-8209. For information on any of the above, check with
your hotel or consult any of the free airport handouts.

Places to Stay

This book does not include a list of major hotels or luxury resorts,
since such information is readily available elsewhere. A good
source of such data is the *Hawaii Visitors Bureau Accommodations
Guide*, which lists HVB member hotels on all islands, their amen-
ities, price ranges, etc. It also includes information about bed-and-

breakfasts. It is available free from the Hawaii Visitor Bureau, 2270 Kalakaua Avenue, Honolulu, HI 96815; phone 924-0266. Free airport advertising handouts also provide limited hotel information and restaurant listings.

You will find, however, a few suggestions in this book for places to stay near some of the adventure spots, especially where lodging might otherwise be difficult to find. Lodging at adventure spots is usually moderately priced and includes campgrounds and cabins, where available. Although there may be other accommodations available that will do just as well, I could not check them all.

Maps

It is important that you have good maps to refer to in conjunction with this book, both in planning your adventures and for later reference in the field. The University of Hawaii Press publishes an excellent series of reference maps for each island. Each map costs $2.95 (Molokai and Lanai are combined on one map) and can be purchased in Hawaii's bookstores, airport newsstands, or supermarkets, or directly from the University of Hawaii Press, Order Department, 2840 Kolowalu Street, Honolulu, HI 96822; phone 956-8255. In the Backpacking, Day Hiking, and certain other sections of the book, reference is made to the appropriate U.S. Geological Survey 1:24,000 quadrangle series (Quad) map sheets. These may be purchased directly from USGS Map Sales, Box 25286, Denver, CO 80255; phone (800) 654-4966. In Hawaii they are available from Pacific Map Center, 250 Ward Avenue, Suite 220, Honolulu, HI 96814, phone 591-1200; or The Hawaii Geographic Society, 49 South Hotel Street, Honolulu, HI 96813, phone 538-3952. Other useful maps mentioned in the text are available from Earthwalk Press, 2239 Union Street, Eureka, CA 95501, phone (800) 828-6277; and Trails Illustrated, P.O. Box 3610, Evergreen, CO 80439, phone (800) 962-1643.

The Land and the Sea

Creation of the Islands

Millions of years ago, as the tectonic plate under the Pacific Ocean inched its way along the earth's crust, a great undersea mountain range began to form. As the plate moved slowly northwest, it passed over a "hot spot," a fissure in the ocean floor, allowing massive amounts of magma to flow upward from deep within the earth's mantle. Over the centuries these lava deposits grew into huge mountains, which drifted with the Pacific plate. In time, most of the mountain peaks rose above the surface of the sea and became islands.

No sooner had these islands appeared than they were assaulted by wind, rain, and waves intent on battering them back into the sea from which they had come. Eons passed and the first islands finally subsided into the ocean, worn down by the elements and by their own great weight. But new islands took their place as uncountable tons of lava spewed forth.

Today the hot spot continues its work. Volcanic eruptions on Hawaii Island increase that island's size while, offshore, Loihi, a new mountain, is forming under the sea. Someday it, too, will break the surface to gain life as a separate island in the chain, or perhaps to attach itself to its big neighbor.

Geology and Geography

Because of their volcanic birth, the Hawaiian Islands consist almost exclusively of basaltic rock, with only a fringe of sedimentary rock along some shorelines and in valleys once penetrated by the sea. The basalts are rich in magnesium and iron, and it is the iron that gives Hawaiian soil its characteristic red color. The islands are young by geological standards, ranging from almost six million years (Kauai), to 3 million (Oahu), to about 700,000 (Hawaii). Although these figures may sound old, they are less than a blink in geologic time. *Homo habilis* was walking the earth before the island of Hawaii broke the ocean's surface.

What is commonly referred to as the "Hawaiian Islands" actually consists of 132 islands, islets, reefs, and shoals stretching more than 1,500 miles southeast–northwest across the Pacific Ocean. Midway Island, scene of one of the major naval battles of World War II, is part of the island chain, although it is administered separately by the U.S. Navy. More than 99 percent of the state's land area of 6,425 square miles lies in the eight main islands, which are, in order of size, Hawaii, Maui, Oahu, Kauai, Molokai, Lanai, Niihau, and Kahoolawe. Hawaii is by far the largest of these—bigger than all of the others combined—earning it the nickname "Big Island."

Despite its image as a South Seas tropical paradise, Hawaii is actually located in the north Pacific; in fact, the state just barely falls within the Tropic of Cancer. Hawaii lies almost 2,400 miles from California and 3,850 miles from Japan, on the same latitude as Mexico City, Hong Kong, and Calcutta. Hawaii is the fourth smallest of the United States, larger only than Rhode Island, Connecticut, and Delaware. But the island of Hawaii is the nation's largest island, including territories such as Guam and Puerto Rico.

Climate

Hawaii's climate is one of the best in the world. Although technically there are only two seasons, summer and winter, in Hawaii, there is less than 9 degrees of temperature change between them. The warmest months in Hawaii are August and September, the coolest, February and March. A sampling of approximate average temperatures at various island locations is shown below.

Upland temperatures are lower than those at sea level, as can be seen by comparing temperatures for Waikiki, Manoa, and Lanai City above. The temperature drops 3 degrees for every 1,000 feet of altitude, which can have a considerable impact in the mountains, particularly if it is windy and raining.

Water temperature varies about the same, seasonally, as air temperature does, but it is much steadier throughout the day. The average ocean temperature in September is 80 degrees; in February it is 73. Freshwater streams and pools are usually colder.

Rainfall in Hawaii is heavier in winter than in summer, but there is never enough differential to have a true "rainy season." In many locations most of the rain comes at night or early morning, and outdoor activities are not usually inhibited. But Hawaii does have rainy days, sometimes several in a row, just like anywhere else. Whether you see rain in the islands depends more on where you are than when you come. Most rain falls on the windward (eastern) side of the islands, and mountains stop much of it before it can

Location	Summer	Winter
Oahu		
Honolulu	78	72
Waikiki	80	72
Manoa	75	69
Kaneohe/Kailua	79	73
Maui		
Lahaina	78	71
Hana	77	71
Haleakala (summit)	50	42
Molokai (Airport)	77	72
Lanai (Lanai City)	73	66
Hawaii		
Hilo	76	71
Kailua–Kona	77	72
Waimea (Kamuela)	67	62
Mauna Kea (summit)	42	31
Kauai		
Lihue	78	70
Poipu	79	72
Kokee	66	55

reach the leeward (western) areas. It rains more upland than it does on the beaches. So if it is raining where you are, go somewhere else, usually toward the leeward side of the island, or move from up-country to the coast. Approximate average annual rainfall for selected locations is shown below.

Generally, rain increases with altitude up to about 6,000 feet, where it then begins to diminish sharply; Mount Waialeale, at 5,148 feet, is one of the wettest spots on earth.

Humidity tends to remain at a fairly steady range between 60

Location	Inches
Oahu	
Honolulu	25
Waikiki	27
Upper Manoa	158
Kaneohe	70
Kailua	35
Maui	
Lahaina	15
Hana	70
Haleakala (summit)	50
Molokai (Airport)	30
Lanai (Lanai City)	38
Hawaii	
Hilo	133
Volcanoes Nat. Park	103
Waimea (Kamuela)	40
Kailua–Kona	25
Mauna Kea (summit)	8
Kauai	
Lihue	44
Poipu	36
Kokee	72
Mount Waialeale	451

and 80 percent throughout the islands. Even when humidity is higher, its effect is usually tempered by the trade winds.

Air quality in Hawaii ranks among the highest in the nation. Though the major air pollutant is automotive traffic, particularly in Honolulu, industrial pollution in Hawaii is negligible. Fortunately, in Hawaii, air pollution does not tend to settle in over an area, as it does in such cities as Los Angeles and Denver; trade winds normally disperse the pollutants and blow them out to sea. A recent source of natural pollution is the Kilauea volcano, which has been in constant eruption since 1983. Under certain wind conditions volcanic pollution, called *VOG* locally, affects the Kona coast of the island of Hawaii, and sometimes carries as far as Oahu.

Length of Day

Hawaii's proximity to the equator makes for a relatively minor change of daylight hours between summer and winter months. The longest day in Hawaii is thirteen and a half hours, the shortest is eleven; night falls quickly once the sun is down. The state does not switch to Daylight Savings Time in the summer, but remains on Standard Time year-round.

Flora and Fauna

The Most Endangered Place on Earth

Because of their isolated location, the Hawaiian Islands have nurtured many unique species of plants, birds, and insects found nowhere else in the world. But today Hawaii's native forest is under siege by development, goats and pigs, and introduced plants that crowd out and strangle indigenous species. Hawaii has lost more of its native birds than any other place on earth. With less than one-quarter of 1 percent of the land area of the United States, Hawaii has 40 percent of the nation's endangered bird and 34 percent of the nation's endangered plant species. Hawaii's only two native mammals are both endangered species, and all sea turtles in Hawaiian waters are either endangered or threatened. Even the most popular visitor to the island, the humpback whale, is on the endangered species list.

Attempts to reverse this march toward extinction have been only partially successful. Efforts are being made to control or eradicate predators of plants and birds, and artificial propagation is being employed. But when preservation of habitat clashes with development interests, the forest and its inhabitants usually come out second best. Ecologically oriented organizations, such as the Sierra

Club and The Nature Conservancy, wage a good fight, but it is a constant one.

Hawaii's Beleaguered Plants

Depending on whose taxonomy you accept, Hawaii has between 1,000 and 2,500 kinds of plants that exist nowhere else, yet few tourists or residents ever see them. The swaying palms, sprawling banyans, colorful flowering shrubs, and fields of sugarcane and pineapple—all are introduced species. Many native plants have been eliminated in the lower elevations by loss of habitat and introduced plantings. Native flora is now normally found only in the upland forests and deep valleys, and on mountain ridges. Even in these spots, these plants are under assault from rampant introduced plant pests like blackberry, guava, banana poka, and clidemia, and from feral pigs and goats.

Hawaii's Endangered Birds

At one time more than 110 kinds of birds existed exclusively in the Hawaiian Islands. The isolation of the islands and the absence of predators, the benign climate, and an abundant food supply allowed them to evolve and prosper. With the coming of the Polynesians, however, the situation changed drastically. The clearing of forests for primitive agriculture reduced the birds' habitats, they became prey to dogs and rats, and Hawaiians hunted certain species of birds for their colorful feathers or for food.

By the time of Captain James Cook's arrival in the islands in 1778, at least forty of these species were already extinct. They have been identified solely by fossil remains. Of the seventy or so species that remained, another twenty-three have become extinct since the arrival of Westerners, and thirty-one are currently on the endangered species list. The outlook is not bright, and Hawaii's endemic bird population continues to decline. Continued human encroachment further reduces habitat, new predators (cats and mongooses) attack nests, mosquitoes transmit avian malaria, pigs and goats destroy native forests, and introduced birds compete more aggressively for food and living space. Artificial propagation efforts have had mixed results. The *nene,* the Hawaiian state bird, does well at propagation sites, but when reintroduced to the wild its reproductive rate is poor. The *alala* (Hawaiian crow) is so scarce that inbreeding of captured *alala*s has caused some infertility among the species, and live hatchlings are rare. In 1993 it was estimated that only thirty-two of them remained in the wild. Unless there is a major turnaround, the species could be extinct by the turn of the century.

Hawaii's Threatened Sea Life

The Hawaiian monk seal is one of the world's last two surviving tropical seals (the other is the Mediterranean monk seal). Almost extinct by the 1900s, it is slowly making a comeback under protected status. The monk seal resides almost exclusively in the uninhabited northwestern Hawaiian islands, although in recent years individual animals have come ashore on Kauai, Oahu, Maui, and Hawaii. In 1992 a seal gave birth to a pup on the north shore of Oahu, while another seal delivered a pup at Maalaea Beach on Maui in 1993.

Three species of sea turtle are found in Hawaiian waters. None of these migratory species are native to the islands. The Pacific green sea turtle is the most common of the three. Favored for its meat, and for making turtle soup, its numbers have been severely depleted, and it is now on the threatened species list, with "protected" status. The Pacific hawkbill sea turtle, prized for its "tortoise shell," is on the endangered list. Both turtles are known to come ashore to lay eggs in Hawaii. The rare Pacific leatherback sea turtle, largest of the three, is an infrequent visitor. It is also endangered.

At least sixteen species of whales, the most common of which is the humpback, have been observed in Hawaiian waters. All are protected while in U.S. waters. The humpbacks migrate to the islands between December and April to mate and give birth, then return to Arctic waters in the spring. Killer whales (orcas) have been noted in Hawaiian waters on a very infrequent basis. Seven kinds of dolphin (porpoise), including the Pacific bottlenose and the spinner, inhabit the seas surrounding the islands.

Hawaiian sharks include the whitetip reef shark, gray reef shark, tiger shark, and hammerhead. Until 1991 shark attacks on humans were rare. From 1991 through 1994, however, there were twelve attacks, three of them fatal. Most of these assaults were against surfers, and there is speculation that sharks might mistake them for turtles or seals, both of them regular items in a large shark's diet. Even with these increased occurrences, however, the over-all incidence of shark attacks is low considering the amount of year-round aquatic activity and the large number of people in the water.

Insects

Nearly 10,000 species of insect are found in Hawaii, and about 98 percent of these exist nowhere else. These include 3,000 varieties of beetle, 1,500 types of fly, 1,250 varieties of wasp and bee, and 1,250 classifications of moth and butterfly. Half of the world's cricket species are Hawaiian. Recently about 35 types of cave-dwelling insects, all of them having lost such attributes as eyes, pigmentation, and wings, have been discovered living in lava tubes.

The islands also have their fair share of insect pests, introduced mainly since Western contact. The mosquito arrived with a whaling ship that dumped mosquito larvae into a Maui stream while refilling its water casks. Soon afterward missionaries in Lahaina noted that people were complaining of a new "singing, stinging fly." Cockroaches, bedbugs, fleas, and lice followed soon after. Biting and stinging insects such as wasps, spiders, scorpions, and centipedes inhabit most islands. Black widow and brown widow spiders have also been spotted, but cases of them biting humans are rare.

Reptiles

There are no snakes in Hawaii, except for a small, rarely seen blind snake that lives mostly underground. A real threat to Hawaii, how-ever, is the brown tree snake, which has devastated the bird population of Guam. Seven of these snakes have been found on Oahu since 1981, brought in by aircraft or their cargo, but the snake is not believed to have become established in the islands. The state Department of Agriculture has instigated a vigorous control program to keep such an eventuality from happening. Three species of frog and one of toad are found here, as are several varieties of lizard, chameleon, and gecko. None are native.

Mammals

The previously mentioned Hawaiian monk seal and the hoary bat are the only mammals native to the islands; all land animals, wild or domestic, have been introduced. The most common animals existing in the wild today are feral pigs and goats, found on all of the populated islands except Lanai. Small numbers of feral sheep are found on Hawaii, as are smaller numbers of mouflon both there and on Lanai. Pronghorn antelope were introduced on Lanai, but their survival rate has been poor. Black-tailed deer have become established on Kauai, as have axis deer on Molokai, Lanai, and Maui.

The brush-tailed rock wallaby provides an interesting example of unintended animal introduction to Hawaii. A pair of these animals, native to Australia, escaped captivity in 1916 and established a small colony in the upper reaches of Kalihi Valley on Oahu. On the other hand, a deliberately introduced species, the mongoose, has proved to be an ecological disaster for Hawaii. The mongoose was brought in to control rats in the cane fields, and while the animal does make inroads into the rat population it has virtually wiped out all ground nesting birds on all of the islands except Kauai, where it was never introduced in the first place.

Hawaii and Its People

The Polynesians

According to the most prevalent theory, the ancestors of the Polynesians began migrating from Southeast Asia into the Pacific thousands of years ago. By 1500 B.C. they had reached Samoa and Tonga; by the second century A.D. they had settled Tahiti and the Marquesas. Somewhere between the third and seventh centuries, at a time when European sailors hugged their own coastlines and looked upon the open sea with fear and superstition, Polynesians set out from eastern Polynesia in double-hulled sailing canoes and discovered the Hawaiian Islands 2,400 miles away.

We do not know whether it was war, famine, or simply curiosity that prompted these people to abandon their homeland and embark upon one of the great ocean adventures of all time. Carrying dogs, pigs, and chickens, and seeds and live plants such as banana, coconut, and sugarcane, they established themselves in the new land. For a time, contact with the home islands was maintained, and new immigrants arrived. About the eleventh century canoes from Raiatea, near Tahiti, reached the islands, bringing new immigrants, some cultural changes, and perhaps a new social order. Then, sometime after 1350, all communication with the outside world ceased, and Hawaii became the world's most isolated island community.

The Sandwich Islands

It was the preeminent English explorer Captain James Cook who "discovered" the islands for the West more than a thousand years after the Polynesians had settled them. Cook was en route from Tahiti to the North American continent, where he was under orders to seek the elusive "Northwest Passage" that other distinguished explorers had failed to find. On January 18th, 1778, he sighted Oahu and Kauai. Cook spent two weeks exploring Kauai and Niihau and then continued on his way, but not before naming his discovery after his patron, the Earl of Sandwich.

Unsuccessful in his efforts to find a sea passage through the North American continent, Cook returned to winter in the Sandwich Islands. After sighting Molokai and exploring the windward shores of Maui and Hawaii, he dropped anchor at Kealakekua Bay on Hawaii's leeward coast, almost a year to the day after his first sighting of the islands. Less than a month later he was dead, killed in an altercation with the natives over a stolen boat.

Napoleon of the Pacific

One of the young chiefs who came aboard Cook's ship in 1778 while it was anchored off the east end of Maui was Kamehameha, a nephew of one of the high chiefs of the island of Hawaii. Ruler of the Kohala and Kona districts of that island, Kamehameha began a war in 1782 against his fellow chiefs that lasted for ten years, and ended with Hawaii, Maui, and Molokai under his control. In 1795 Kamehameha landed at Waikiki and Waialae with a large army. Marching inland, he defeated the Oahu forces in the battle of Nuuanu, in which many soldiers of the losing side were driven over the cliffs of the *Nuuanu Pali* and killed on the rocks below.

A year later Kamehameha attempted the conquest of Kauai, but his war canoes became dispersed and were destroyed by a heavy storm. He then turned his attention to consolidating his rule and restoring prosperity on the other islands, which had been ravaged by years of warfare. In 1804 he tried to invade Kauai again, only to be thwarted when his army was stricken with cholera. It was six years before his gaze once more focused on the only island to elude his grasp. In 1810, as he was readying another attack, the chief of Kauai acknowledged the rule of Kamehameha, and the island passed under his sway.

Kingdom of Hawaii

Kamehameha would reign for nine more years, bringing his government in line with some Western principles but maintaining the old feudal control of the land and its people, and adhering to the ancient Hawaiian religion. At the time of his death in 1819, he had established the dynasty that would succeed him. But with the passing of the old king, the ancient religion could not survive the assaults of the modern era. Within six months of his death, his son and successor, Kamehameha II, ordered all idols and *heiau*—great stone platforms upon which were arranged idols, altars, and other religious structures—destroyed. The following year the first missionaries from New England arrived in the islands, now ripe for the introduction of a new religion.

Kamehameha's successors lacked the stature and the toughness of the old warrior. Pressured by missionaries with religious interests and by businessmen with commercial ones, they were often hard pressed to protect the interests of the kingdom and their subjects. Over the years, many of the day-to-day affairs of the kingdom fell into the hands of advisors and ministers, many of whom were Americans or other Caucasians. Some of these officials saw little or no need to separate their own financial interests from those of the government, so along with power they accumulated land and wealth.

As the population of native Hawaiians declined due to the introduction of Western diseases, the number of foreigners increased, as did their commercial and political influence. By the middle of the nineteenth century, the king had been persuaded to end the feudal system of land control, and land could be purchased for the first time. Unfortunately, as a result of the subsequent collapse of the economy, many of the chiefs who now owned land were forced to sell it; even the king had to sell land to pay his debts. Other large tracts passed into foreign hands through marriage into Hawaiian chiefly families.

With the first arrival of Western ships in the islands, a small industry, centered around resupplying these vessels, had been born. This was later followed by the sandalwood trade, which lasted only as long—less than twenty years—as it took avaricious chiefs to strip the forests. Servicing the whaling fleet became the next industry, with almost 600 ships anchored in the islands in 1846. The Land Reform Act of 1848, which allowed the sale of land, permitted the formation of large plantations for the growing of sugar, and the face of Hawaii changed forever.

By 1875 the plantation economy was firmly established. The sugar business prospered, and by 1890 the population, which had been declining for a hundred years, was on the upswing. Hawaii was the only group of islands in the Pacific other than Tonga that had maintained its independence during the 1800s, a period of imperialist and colonial expansion. This was due less to the skill of Hawaii's diplomats than to rivalry among the major powers, including the United States, who did not want to see Hawaii pass under the control of any other. But the island's political state was about to change.

In 1890 the U.S. Congress enacted a tariff that was detrimental to the importation of Hawaiian sugar, plunging the economy of the islands into a depression. Sugar planters realized that only annexation by the United States would ensure a good price and a reliable market for their product. Shortly after Queen Liliuokalani assumed the Hawaiian throne in 1891, a group of influential Caucasians formed a secret society that began to work toward Hawaii's annexation. Spurred by what they viewed as autocratic and destabilizing actions by the queen, a Committee of Safety, composed of many of these same Caucasian businessmen, and aided by U.S. Marines and the American consul, took possession of the government and forced the queen to surrender her authority.

From Territory to Statehood

Almost the first act of the Provisional Government of Hawaii was to dispatch ministers to Washington, where a treaty of annexation was written. However, after sending his own representative to the islands to see things for himself, President Grover Cleveland concluded that the overthrow of the Hawaiian kingdom had been an illegal act, and he refused to resubmit the treaty to the Senate. With the route to annexation barred, at least temporarily, the Provisional Government, led by Sanford Dole, established itself as the Republic of Hawaii.

When the Spanish American War ended in 1898, the role of the United States in the Pacific changed drastically. For the first time a distant colony, the Philippine Islands, came under American control, and Hawaii, lying between Manila and California, achieved a new strategic importance. With a new party and a new president in power in Washington, arrangements were concluded quickly, and on August 12, 1898, the Republic of Hawaii surrendered its sovereignty to the United States.

The years prior to World War II were uneventful in the new territory. Annexation achieved most of the economic objectives of Hawaii's business interests, and sugar, pineapple, and other commercial enterprises flourished. United States military forces began the fortification of the islands, and Pearl Harbor, Fort Shafter, and Hickam Air Base were constructed. After World War I, Honolulu became a regular port of call for ocean liners bringing well-to-do tourists to Waikiki's two luxury hotels, the Moana and the Royal Hawaiian.

The Japanese attack on Pearl Harbor on December 7th, 1941, propelled Hawaii onto the world stage. After the war, a large military presence remained on Oahu, as the Korean War and the Vietnam War drew large groups of American forces into conflict in Asia. With Hawaii's admission to the Union in 1959 as the fiftieth state, tourism exploded, reaching one million visitors in 1967, doubling that in 1972, and doubling the number again in 1979. The year 1990 saw nearly seven million visitors to the islands, and tourism is now firmly established as the state's major industry.

Things You Should Know

Culture

The Polynesians who colonized Hawaii brought with them their mythology, their beliefs, and their laws. Over time, isolation from their former homeland brought changes peculiar to their new circumstances, but they remained essentially a superstitious, subsistence culture. Hawaiian society was dominated by a rigid caste system headed by the *alii,* or chiefs, at the top, and the *makaainana,* or commoners, at the bottom. In between these poles stood the *kahuna,* experts in various skills. The highest of these, the priestly *kahuna,* were advisers to the *alii,* keepers of their genealogy, and interpreters of the ancient religion. Some of the *kahuna* were *alii* themselves.

Order was maintained by a pervasive and complex series of laws, or *kapu,* which controlled many actions of daily life. Women, for example, could not eat pork, coconuts, bananas, or certain kinds of fish, and they were forbidden to eat with men. *Makaainana* were required to prostrate themselves before *alii,* and were in fact forbidden to gaze upon the chiefs; a commoner could even be killed if his or her shadow fell across the person of a chief. A *makaainana* child could be put to death if it cried aloud while an *alii* was ill.

The Hawaiian religion contained many gods and spirits, both good and evil. The four major gods were *Kane,* god of creation and light; *Lono,* god of the harvest; *Ku,* the god of human activities and war; and *Kanaloa,* ruler of the wind, the sea, and the underworld. Among the lesser gods were *Pele,* goddess of fire, and *Maui,* the catcher of the sun, who dragged the Hawaiian Islands up from the bottom of the sea. Religious rituals were held at *heiau,* and sacrifice was an important rite; at certain *heiau* human sacrifice was prac-

ticed. Although Kamehameha II ordered the *heiau* destroyed, many
of their stone foundations survive, and can be seen throughout the
islands.

In ancient Hawaii, all land belonged to the high chief either of a
large district or of the particular island. In a manner similar to European feudalism, the high chief apportioned most of the land to
his lesser chiefs, keeping certain parcels for himself. These, in turn,
would allow the commoners to work the land in exchange for services or produce, some of which the lesser chief would keep for
himself, and some of which he would pass up to the high chief. All
who lived on and worked the land were free to gather its resources
for their own use—wood and thatch from the forest for dwelling
construction and for cooking fires, shellfish and seaweed from the
beaches, and fish from the sea. Thus, the early Hawaiians had no
concept of private land ownership. When such ownership was finally allowed, misunderstanding of its principles cost the Hawaiian
people their heritage. After Kamehameha's conquest, all land was
ceded to him and his heirs.

Over the years people of many races came to the islands, most
to work on the plantations, but some to establish businesses and
conduct trade. Chinese, Japanese, Filipino, and Portuguese immigrants brought their traditions to Hawaii, sometimes retaining
their own identity, sometimes blending with local customs. The
Chinese, perhaps because they were the first to be brought to Hawaii, are the only ethnic group to have originally settled a specific
locale after leaving the plantation. Thus Honolulu, like New York
and San Francisco, has an area known as Chinatown. But there is
no "Japantown" or "Filipinotown," although there are neighbor-
hoods and parts of the islands where such ethnic communities are
more prevalent than others. Hawaii is the only state in the union
where Caucasians do not represent a majority of the population.
As of the 1990 census, Caucasians comprised 33.4% of the population; persons of Japanese ancestry 22.3%; Filipino 15.2%; Hawaiian and part Hawaiian 12.5%; Chinese 6.2%; and other races
comprising the remainder. One reason for the relative racial harmony that exists in Hawaii is that all of its citizens are members of

a racial minority. No one group can dictate to another. People must cooperate—socially, politically, and economically—if they want to accomplish anything.

Language

Hawaiian is not spoken on the islands except by a very few older persons, and it is rarely heard other than in songs, chants, or hula performances. Only on Niihau, which has a population of less than 250, is Hawaiian spoken regularly. But place names and street names are mostly Hawaiian, as are the common names of many plants and fish, and many Hawaiian words have entered the everyday conversation of people of all races. (For a glossary of Hawaiian words used in this book, please turn to page 40.)

Hawaii had no written language until American missionaries gave it one. They established an alphabet of only twelve letters, five vowels, and seven consonants. That this selection was somewhat arbitrary is evidenced by spellings given by earlier visitors, who apparently heard "Owyhee" for Hawaii, "Honoruru" for Honolulu, and "Tamehameha" for Kamehameha. Despite the frequency of these earlier spellings, the missionaries decided not to include the letters *Y, R,* or *T* in the alphabet.

Although it appears formidable, Hawaiian pronunciation is surprisingly easy once you know the rules. The seven consonants *H, K, L, M, N, P,* and *W* are pronounced as they are in English, except that *W* sometimes has the sound of *V.* The vowels *A, E, I, O,* and *U* are pronounced as in Spanish instead of English. Thus *A* is pronounced as in *father, E* as in *they, I* as in *machine, O* as in *oboe,* and *U* as in *Zulu.* The language also has eight diphthongs, the four most common of which are shown below. They are always stressed on the first letter, and the two letters are not as closely joined as in English. They are pronounced approximately as follows: *au* is pronounced like the *ow* in *how, ae* and *ai* as *eye,* and *ei* as the *ay* in *day.*

Basically, all Hawaiian letters are pronounced. Thus the town of Kaaawa on Oahu is pronounced Ka-a-a-va (four syllables). Various diacritical marks are used, mostly in scholarly or reference works, to aid in meaning and pronunciation. You will usually not find such marks in newspapers or guide books. A possible exception is the backward apostrophe, which indicates a glottal stop, a break in a word similar to the break in *oh-oh* in English.

You may hear a foreign language being spoken by residents of Hawaii. Most often this will be Japanese or Ilocano (a Philippine language), because many residents have such a background. Occasionally you may hear Chinese or Samoan for the same reason. Another "language" you may hear is pidgin. Although certain guide books encourage it, I advise you not to try to speak pidgin to anyone. Although pidgin probably originated with immigrants who had difficulty learning English, that is no longer its main purpose. Pidgin is spoken today by persons who share certain cultural interests and values. It is often spoken deliberately, especially by people of Asian/Pacific background who are capable of speaking conventional English but use pidgin as an "insiders'" language to set themselves apart from a Caucasian-dominated culture. I have lived in Hawaii for twenty-five years and still can't speak pidgin without sounding patronizing or phony.

Government Structure

Unlike most of the mainland, Hawaii has a two-tiered, rather than three-tiered (city, county, state), governmental structure. City and county governments are combined in the islands, and mayors are county, not city, officials. There are four counties: Hawaii, Maui (which includes Molokai, Lanai, and Kahoolawe), Oahu, and Kauai. Hawaii differs from its mainland counterparts in that the state's public schools and libraries are unified and controlled at the state level, but there are no state police.

Cost of Living

Hawaii has the highest food and housing costs in the United States, and this drives prices up for many other commodities as well. Depending upon where you live, you will probably be shocked at prices in the supermarkets here. However, it is not at all difficult to find good hotels and excellent restaurants that cost no more than similar facilities in other parts of the country, and quite a few that, in fact, cost less. The airports are awash in free advertising hand-outs listing hotels and restaurants in all price ranges on all of the islands. Many of these pamphlets provide good maps and other useful materials. With that in mind, there is no need to list a great deal of such information in this book.

Public Transportation

Most of the major airlines, foreign and domestic, fly to Honolulu. In addition, United Airlines has direct flights from San Francisco and Los Angeles to Maui and Kailua–Kona on the Big Island, and American Airlines has direct flights to Maui from Dallas and Los Angeles. Unless you have your own boat, travel between the islands is almost exclusively by air. At present a daily passenger ferry runs between Kaunakakai on Molokai and Lahaina on Maui, primarily to provide commuter service for workers, but there is no other passenger surface transportation. Hawaiian Airlines provides scheduled jet service among all islands except Niihau, and Aloha Airlines flies scheduled jet service to Kauai, Maui, and Hawaii. Both airlines offer many flights per day, each flight averaging 20 to 40 minutes. Mahalo Air offers scheduled prop-jet service to all of the outer islands except Niihau. Commuter airlines (Island Air, Air Molokai) service the smaller airfields such as Wailea, Princeville, and Hana. Some of them also fly to the major airfields. Since these smaller planes fly at lower altitudes than the main carriers, they offer more of a sightseeing trip between the islands, and they sometimes cost less than the bigger planes.

Only Oahu has a full-fledged bus service covering the entire island on a regular schedule seven days a week. There is a bus service on the island of Hawaii, connecting major towns on a once-per-day schedule, five or six days per week depending on location. Kauai has a county bus service, operating hourly in both directions from Lihue six days a week. Maui has no bus service, but a commercial shuttle operates between the airport and the Lahaina-Kaanapali area. See the appropriate island chapters for more information.

Taxi service is available on all islands, but you usually must call for one or find a taxi stand, and, with the exception of Waikiki, taxi stands are normally found only at the airports or major hotels. Even in Honolulu taxis do not cruise for fares as they do in most mainland cities.

All major car rental agencies have offices in Hawaii; it is possible to rent a car on all of the islands, and a van or four-wheel-drive vehicle on most of them. Rental is at a flat rate, and there is normally no mileage charge. However, in addition to the standard 4 percent general excise tax, the state has slapped a $2 per day tax on rental cars. If you plan to rent a vehicle on one of the outer islands you should make reservations as early as possible. Renters of four-wheel-drive vehicles need to be especially careful to ensure they are getting what they need and are paying for. Many car rental agencies, including the most well known, rent Jeeps and other ostensibly four-wheel-drives, which sometimes turn out to be two-wheel-drive versions, or vehicles that have had their four-wheel-drive trains disconnected.

Telephone Service

The area code for the entire state is 808. A telephone call on any island to any other point on that island is considered a local call. A call from one island to another, or to any other location outside the islands, is a long-distance call. Many hotels add a service charge for phone calls from their rooms, including local calls. Local calls placed from a public phone cost 25 cents, with no time limit—which is both good and bad. It's good because you don't have to go fumbling through your pockets for change when an operator cuts in to ask for more money. But it's bad because the person on the phone you need to use has no financial incentive to stop talking.

Beach Access

Often visitors walking down the main street of Waikiki or driving along the Kaanapali coast of Maui express dismay at the long line of hotels and condominiums that seems to take up every inch of space, forming a wall against public beach access. They might be less concerned if they knew that all beach-front land in Hawaii is considered public property. While no landowner is required to allow you to cross his property to reach the beach, if you arrive there by another route he or she cannot tell you to leave. And, despite the bumper-to-bumper appearance of buildings at Kaanapali, there is still a reasonable amount of public access to the ocean.

In order to obtain zoning and building permits, the newer developments at Kaanapali, Wailea, and the north Kona coast of Hawaii have been required to provide public beach access. Instead of grumbling about these mandates and cutting corners, most builders have done an excellent job of constructing and maintaining clean facilities and parking areas, in some cases even restoring and preserving archaeological features in the public areas. To find such public access on Maui, for example, watch for small square blue-and-white "Beach Access" signs along the road. An exception is Wailea, where larger signs, such as "Wailea Beach," indicate access. On the Big Island, you usually must drive into a resort and look for the signs. If you have trouble finding access, you are perfectly within your rights to drive up to a hotel and ask where the public access is. You will be politely directed to the beach, which usually sits to one side of the main hotel grounds. But you should not expect to use the hotel's lobby or grounds to go back and forth unless you plan to use some of its services, such as the bar or restaurant.

Hiking and Camping

Hiking, like all other outdoor sports except skiing, is a year-round activity. The islands boast hundreds of miles of hiking trails— through dense rain forests, across parched deserts, along deserted coastlines, into uninhabited valleys, and up high mountain peaks. Surprising to most visitors is that Oahu, which has more buildings, more roads, and more overall development than any of the other islands, also has more forested hiking trails than any of them, including Hawaii, which is four times Oahu's size. Some of the finest hikes in the islands are described in detail in this book.

The standard "uniform" for hiking in Hawaii is shorts and a T-shirt, with a jacket for rain protection carried in your day pack. Some hikes, because of heavy brush along the trail, may be more comfortable in long pants. If you have sensitive legs, you may want to start out in shorts and carry a pair of long pants in your pack. Jogging shoes will do for many hikes, but hiking boots are the best all-around choice, and are essential on lava and on the high mountains. Warm clothing is a must in the mountains. Sun protection is also important while hiking, especially along open coastal trails and at the higher altitudes. A wide-brimmed hat and sunscreen should be part of such hikes.

It is important to stay on established trails when hiking in Hawaii. Not only does this protect fragile forest systems, but it will protect you—from getting lost, and from possible serious injury. Much of the forest off the trail is almost impenetrable, choked with brush, vines, and *hau*—the branches of this sprawling, ground-hugging tree will stop anything but the smallest of animals. Deep volcanic fissures, especially prevalent on the islands of Hawaii and Maui, are often so overgrown with vegetation that they are invisible until after a hiker takes that fatal step. Rock climbing should not be attempted anywhere in the islands. The aging volcanic rock is unstable and can crumble under very little pressure.

There are hiking trails on all of the islands that go through hunting areas, and there are usually signs at trailheads warning of this fact. Some of these areas permit hunting all year round. Be alert when hiking, and if you stay on established trails, as recommended, you should have no trouble. It may be disconcerting to suddenly see a pack of dogs charging down the trail in your direction, and if that happens, keep cool and stand still. The dogs are after pigs, not you.

Carry sufficient water with you, or be prepared to treat or boil water if you plan to fill your canteen along the way. Water from all surface sources can contain organisms that cause giardiasis, leptospirosis, and other gastric illnesses. And if you intend to resupply your water along the way, make sure there are sources available. Many long hikes have no sources of water, including some backpacking trips. The hikes mentioned in this book will provide the water information you need.

A lot of scare stories have been heard about hikers in Hawaii being threatened or shot at by marijuana growers. I have not been able to document any of them. Much of what has been written about growing pot in Hawaii has been speculative and highly inaccurate. After all, how many growers are going to talk publicly about their operations? There is no doubt that for many years growing marijuana was big business in the state. But the crackdown, when it came, was overpowering. More than two million marijuana plants were uprooted in 1987, and in 1990 the state destroyed more than $7.7 billion worth of marijuana. In 1993, the value of plants destroyed had dropped to $995 million. The weed is still being grown, of course, but its halcyon days are over. Hawaii, which once supplied the world with "Maui Wowie" and "Kona Gold," has now been reduced to importing the stuff.

Always lock your car at any trailhead, campground, or point of interest, and leave nothing of value inside. Chain bicycles to immovable objects. Take everything with you that would cause problems if stolen—money, airline tickets, credit cards, cameras, binoculars—anything that would ruin your trip if lost. Breaking into cars is almost a cottage industry in Hawaii, and its more experienced practitioners can have your locked car open in 30 seconds. An obviously empty car is less of a temptation for them. And keep in mind that many of today's rental cars have a lever inside the car that opens a locked trunk.

There are more than 120 campgrounds in Hawaii, ranging from beach sites to forested glens to the summit of Mauna Loa, 13,677 feet high. Though most require permits, many are free, while others charge a fee, which is usually small. State campgrounds are free, but permits are required. County campgrounds require permits, and all but Honolulu (Oahu) charge a small fee. Camping is permitted along all trails under the jurisdiction of the state Forestry and Wildlife Division, except the Makiki/Tantalus routes. A free permit is required. Throughout the book, when campgrounds are mentioned, the authority that controls the campground is cited. In the case of county, state park, and forestry campgrounds, addresses for permits are given in Appendix II. For others, addresses are shown directly in the text.

If you are going to camp you should plan to pitch a tent, even on the beach. Much of the island's rain falls at night, and you will want something to keep the mosquitoes away—and to prevent the centipedes and scorpions from sharing your bed. A camp stove is also important. Firewood is usually scarce, and what there is, is often wet. Live trees or bushes may not be chopped down or trimmed for firewood. In the mountains you will need a sleeping bag and a ground pad, and warm clothing.

If you plan to do extensive camping in the islands, my book *Camping Hawaii* (University of Hawaii Press, 1994) provides detailed information on all Hawaiian campgrounds and inexpensive backcountry state cabins and lodges, as well as nearby points of interest, activities, and hiking trails.

Local Issues

Hawaii has been touted as a place where people of all races live in harmony and with respect for one another. While this is generally true, the situation is not quite that blissful, and never has been. As is the case anywhere, friction does sometimes develop. And people on the lower end of the economic ladder tend to resent those higher up. Soon after Western contact, Hawaiians and Caucasians occupied the upper level of the ladder, while Chinese, Japanese, and Filipinos—all originally brought in as plantation laborers—found themselves at the bottom. Over the years the Chinese and Japanese moved "up," and Hawaiians and part-Hawaiians moved "down," to be joined in recent years by newer arrivals, mainly from other Pacific islands such as Samoa and Tonga.

There is a saying in the islands that succinctly condenses their social history. As a result of the arrival of the Caucasian missionaries and members of other races to Hawaii, it is said that "the Caucasians got the land, the Chinese got the money, the Japanese got the political power, and the Hawaiians got religion." This is not far from the truth—and the Hawaiians don't like it.

Recently, a "sovereignty" movement has sprung up in the islands, with goals ranging from financial compensation, for what is viewed as an illegal takeover of the islands by the United States, to demands for total national independence. The movement gained momentum from the hundredth anniversary of annexation, and as the result of an apology for that action by the U.S. Congress. But the movement suffers from splintered organizations with conflicting objectives. And it is probably safe to say that the sovereignty movement is fueled, at least in part, by the fact that Hawaiians find themselves so economically disadvantaged in their own homeland.

All that being said, people do tend to get along with one another better in Hawaii than in most places. And, as a visitor, you will normally find a friendly reception and be made welcome by people of all races.

Hawaii's Best Adventures

Shown below are my choices for the best adventures in the Hawaiian Islands. If your time is limited, or you just want to experience the very best that the islands have to offer, choose from this list. All of these adventures are covered in detail in the appropriate chapters.

Hawaii

MAUNA LOA TRAVERSE: This three- or four-day climb of the world's largest active volcano, with stays at cabins along the way, traverses a fantastic landscape of moonscape lava formations, culminating in a day on the rim of a huge, active caldera.

HAWAII VOLCANOES NATIONAL PARK COASTAL LOOP: Visited infrequently, the shoreline of the national park offers seclusion and delightful small beaches—oases in a desert of lava. Beginning and ending in a high dryland forest, this trip makes use of a cabin and overnight trail shelters.

WAIMANU VALLEY: This isolated and uninhabited valley lies at the end of a 7-mile forested trail that starts at Waipio Valley, a larger neighbor to the south. A beautiful waterfall with a deep pool lies about an hour's hike from the mouth of the valley.

SKIING MAUNA KEA: If you are a skier who has been everywhere and you think you have done it all, a downhill run between giant cinder cones—and a view to infinity—will change your mind.

Maui

HALEAKALA—FROM THE SUMMIT TO THE SEA . . . : This two- or three-day trip begins at the 10,027-foot peak of Haleakala, one of the largest dormant volcanoes in the world, and ends at the coast 22 miles away. One naturalist has called this trek the botanical equivalent of hiking from Alaska to Mexico. Traversing shifting volcanic sands, lava flows, dry desert, and lush rain forest, and affording magnificent views all the way, this is one of the premier adventures in the islands.

MOLOKINI ISLAND SNORKEL/SCUBA DIVE: A small, crescent-shaped island 3 miles offshore of Maui, Molokini offers wonderful underwater scenery and sea life. An added bonus during the winter and early spring is the opportunity to spot whales during the cruise to or from the island.

Molokai

KAYAKING THE NORTH SHORE: Pristine, isolated valleys, magnificent waterfalls cascading into the ocean, and the highest sea cliffs in the world await the kayaker on this unequaled water adventure ending at the Kalaupapa settlement. Here, for more than a hundred years, victims of leprosy were segregated from the rest of society. Kalaupapa was made famous by the Belgian priest Father Damien, who worked and died here.

HIKE TO KALAUPAPA SETTLEMENT: This short, 2-mile hike, to the once-forbidden colony where leprosy victims were confined, offers striking views of Molokai's wild north shore and a tour of the secluded settlement.

Kauai

BACKPACKING THE KALALAU TRAIL: Traversing some of the most magnificent country anywhere, this 11-mile-long ancient foot trail crosses mountain streams, passes through verdant valleys, winds around sheer sea cliffs, and ends at Kalalau Valley's marvelous beach.

KAYAKING THE NA PALI COAST: The ocean equivalent of hiking the Kalalau Trail, this water journey visits lovely beaches, enters dramatic sea caves, and anchors over almost virgin snorkeling spots, with fantastic scenery all the way.

NUALOLO–AWAAWAPUI LOOP: This 12-mile hike packs more spectacular scenery into one day than any other hike in the islands. Starting in a rain forest, the hike descends to the open, windswept ridges of the Na Pali coast with their incredible views into two of Kauai's dramatic "hanging" valleys, and returns through some of the best dry-mesic forest left in Hawaii.

CHAPTER TWO

Hawaiian Words Used in This Book

.

THIS IS NOT a typical list of "useful" Hawaiian words, but rather those that you will come across in this book, and will need to understand. I assume you know where to place a *lei* and what to do at a *luau*.

a'ā–one of the two types of lava flows, *a'ā* has a rough, clinker-like appearance.

ahu–stone cairn, usually used to mark a route or a trail.

aina–land, earth.

alaloa–ancient highway, or main road, usually around the coastal circumference of an island. Sometimes called the "King's Highway."

ali'i–chief, noble, member of the ruling class in old Hawaii.

aloha–I only include this word because its pronunciation is often abused. It is one of the most used words in the language and its meanings are many. Often used as a greeting (hello, good-bye), it can also mean love, affection, compassion, mercy, pity. It is pronounced with the accent on the second syllable, never on the third. The abuse of its pronunciation is the habit of many tour guides and entertainers, who greet a large group by shouting ah-loooo-HA, drawing out the second syllable and barking the third. The group, or audience, then dutifully responds in the same manner. This is garbage. Don't do it, and maybe the practice will die out as it deserves to.

hala–a coastal tree, also known as the *pandanus* in other parts of Polynesia. Its leaf was used for weaving hats and bowls, and its seeds served as a brush for daubing dye on tapa cloth.

hale–house, structure.

haole–originally a foreigner, now a Caucasian, whether foreign or not.

hapuu–a native Hawaiian tree fern.

hau–tree, member of the hibiscus family. Low-growing *hau* makes a virtually impenetrable obstacle in the forest.

heiau–a temple or place of worship of the old Hawaiian religion. Nothing remains of most *heiau* today except their stone foundations.

holua–an ancient Hawaiian slide, and the sled used on it.

iki–little, such as Kilauea-Iki ("Little Kilauea").

kahuna–priest, expert.

kai–sea, seawater.

kamaaina–accurately, a person born in Hawaii, but sometimes used to denote a longtime resident.

kapu–taboo, forbidden. When seen on a sign, it means "keep out," or "do not touch."

kiawe–a dry area tree, member of the mesquite family. Introduced as fodder and to reforest dry, lowland areas.

King's Highway–an old Hawaiian road or trail, usually around the outer circumference of an island (see *alaloa*).

kipuka–an island of vegetation surrounded by a lava flow.

koa–an important native tree, used for making canoes in ancient Hawaii and still used for bowls, furniture, and floors.

kona–leeward, particularly the leeward side of an island. Kona winds blow toward the leeward side, as opposed to the customary trade winds, which blow toward the windward side of the islands.

kukui–the state tree of Hawaii, also called the candlenut tree.

koolau–windward, usually refers to the windward side of an island.

kuamoo–a trail of single smooth stones across a rough lava field, allowing easy, barefoot travel.

local–not a Hawaiian word, obviously, but it has a specialized meaning in the islands. A "local" bus driver is not the guy who drives the bus that makes all the stops. A "local" person in Hawaii is not simply a resident. "Local" has ethnic connotations, referring to persons of mixed race, usually of Polynesian/ Asian background. It is not pejorative or insulting. When a TV news announcer states that a "local male about thirty years old" was injured in a car crash, he is using the word as a means of identification, in the same way as if he had said "Caucasian male."

makai–toward the ocean. In Hawaii, directions are sometimes given in relation to a geographic reference. You may be told that where you want to go is "*makai* three blocks, then go Diamond Head two more blocks."

mauka–toward the mountains (see *makai* above).

mauna–mountain, as in Mauna Kea ("white mountain").

moana–ocean.

ohia–the most common native tree in Hawaii. Thousands of acres of *ohia* forest still exist, particularly on the island of Hawaii. *Ohia* grows at elevations from 1,000 to 9,000 feet and, depending on growing conditions, can appear as anything from a bush to a forest giant. It and the *hapuu* are among the first plants to regenerate on new lava fields.

pahoehoe–one of the two kinds of lava flows, *pahoehoe* has a smooth surface when unbroken.

pali–cliff, precipice.

Pele–goddess of fire and the volcano.

puka–hole, depression.

puu–hill, rise.

ti–an important plant. Its leaves are used to make hula skirts and to wrap food for cooking.

wai–fresh water, liquid.

CHAPTER THREE

Hawaii
Volcanoes from the Sea

H AWAII IS NOT only the biggest of the Hawaiian Islands, it is the largest island in the United States. Its 4,034 square miles make it larger than all the other islands of Hawaii combined. It is the youngest of the islands, between 650,000 and a million years old and still growing. The Big Island is "big" in many aspects. Mauna Loa is the world's biggest mountain in volume, and Mauna Kea is its highest peak when measured from its base at the ocean floor. The Parker Ranch is the largest privately held ranch in the United States. Mauna Kea houses the world's largest telescope and the world's foremost collection of astronomical observatories. Mauna Loa is the world's largest volcano and Kilauea is its most active—in constant eruption since 1983.

Hawaii is 93 miles long and 76 miles wide. Mauna Kea, at 13,796 feet, is not only the island's highest peak, but the highest in the state as well. Almost half of Hawaii's 121,000 residents (ranking it second in population behind Oahu) are of Japanese descent—a percentage higher here than on the other islands. Tourism, sugar production, and cattle ranching are Hawaii's major industries, although the sugar industry is declining dramatically. Hamakua Sugar, one of the largest plantations in the state, ceased operations

HAWAII

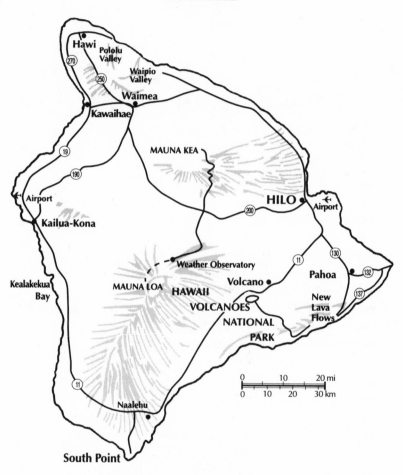

in 1994. Agriculture will continue to play an important role in the island's economy, however; macadamia nut orchards are expanding into some former sugar lands, and Hilo continues to be the anthurium and orchid growing capital of the state.

Tourism is centered on the warm and sunny Kona coast, and at Hawaii Volcanoes National Park. But the Big Island is giving Oahu a run for its money with the recent proliferation of plush resorts along its "Gold Coast," the area that runs north from Kailua–Kona to Kawaihae. Self-contained in a way that Waikiki hotels can never be, these expensive watering holes have their own golf courses, beaches, and water activities, as well as the usual spas, restaurants, bars, and shops. And, expensive though they may be, these spacious resorts are beautifully designed and lie lightly on the land, bearing no resemblance to the congested, concrete mass that is Waikiki.

There is minimal public transportation available on Hawaii. The Hele-On bus service has five buses arriving in Hilo each morning from Pahoa, Kau, Laupahoehoe, Kailua–Kona, and South Kohala; these buses return each afternoon. They run Monday through Saturday for the first three locations; Monday through Friday to Kona; and seven days a week to South Kohala. It is best to call 935-8241 for the latest schedule. Hitchhiking is permitted on Hawaii.

Adventuring on the Big Island can take you from tropical beaches to subarctic mountain heights, and from lush rain forests to parched deserts. You can ski down a snowy slope in the morning and swim in a warm sea that same afternoon. If the volcano cooperates, you may see a lava flow cross a road, setting fire to the asphalt with its heat, or watch it plunge into the sea, exploding with a roar of hissing steam. You can hike where few people have gone before and be alone when you get there. You can snorkel and scuba dive right offshore at dozens of places and find abundant and colorful coral and tropical fish. This book will show you how to do it all.

Adventuring by Car

Note: This section is designed to be used with a good road map at hand, such as the full-color topographic map of Hawaii (University of Hawaii Press, $2.95).

If you can spend a week—which is not an unreasonable amount of time for a place with as many attractions as Hawaii—this section will show you how to have a Big Island adventure in a way that few visitors ever enjoy. Even if you can't spare a week, you can prepare your own itinerary with the help of this section. Though the adventure begins and ends in Hilo, making a loop by heading south, you could just as well start by heading north and do the loop in reverse. Or you could begin and end the trip in Kailua–Kona on the coast opposite Hilo. A consideration here is that some flights from the mainland fly into Kailua–Kona, while flights to Hilo start in Honolulu or other interisland airports. Finally, if you need to make a shorter trip, you could begin in either town and drop your rental car off in the other, paying an extra drop-off charge. All major car rental companies have offices at both airports, or furnish frequent shuttle buses to nearby locations. Be sure to make reservations in advance, as available cars frequently sell out.

Hilo and Vicinity (75 miles round-trip)

Hilo, with a population of 40,000, is the Big Island's largest town, as well as its county seat. Hilo is also Hawaii's rainiest town, with an average annual rainfall of 133 inches. All that rain has one good side: Hilo is lush, the orchid and anthurium capital of the islands. To the first-time visitor to Hilo, the city's waterfront seems strangely configured. To the west, old buildings and storefronts line the bay, while to the east new hotels and government buildings have sprouted. In between, on what seems to be the most desirable economic land, a wide green space, devoid of any large structures, meets the eye. In 1946 and 1960 Hilo was struck by devastating *tsunami*s (tidal waves) that wiped out this section of the town and caused more than 200 deaths. After the second one, a decision was made not to rebuild this area.

A good place to start your Hilo adventure is at Rainbow Falls or Boiling Pots, both located in Wailuku River State Park on the northwestern outskirts of town. Situated in a tropical setting, the falls can be viewed directly from the parking lot, or from a viewpoint to the left of the lot atop a short stairway. The falls are 80 feet high and discharge more than 300 million gallons of water each day.

Rainbow Falls lies within the city limits of Hilo. Photo by Richard McMahon.

To reach Rainbow Falls from the Hilo waterfront, drive west on Highway 19 (Kamehameha Avenue), turning left on Waianuenue Avenue. After it passes Hilo High School on the right, the road will fork; take the right fork and watch for a sign, about a quarter of a mile on the right, that will lead you into the parking lot for the falls. To reach Boiling Pots—which gets its name from water cascading into a series of pools, swirling and rolling as it flows—continue on

Waianuenue Avenue for about 1.6 miles to Peepee Falls Street and turn right to the parking lot. There is no trail, but when the stream is not too high it is possible to walk out to some of the pools. One caution: Do not swim here. Some of the swirling waters lead to underwater tunnels into which swimmers can be sucked. Upstream from Boiling Pots you will be able to see Peepee Falls.

If, while driving from town toward the falls, you take the left fork instead of the right, you will reach Kaumana Caves, 2.6 miles farther on. Here, a collapsed roof allows you to enter a lava tube. (Lava tubes are formed by lava flows that cool and harden on the surface but continue flowing underground. When the flow finally ceases, the tube empties, leaving an underground passage. Many ancient Hawaiians used lava tubes as burial chambers.) A stairway descends some 50 feet down a fern- and vine-filled pit leading to two entrances. To explore these tubes you will need a good flashlight, but if you are satisfied with a peek, you can wander in 20 feet or so.

Back in town, the Lyman Mission House and Museum (276 Haile Street; phone 935-5021) is worth a visit as an example of an early missionary home. The adjoining museum features exhibits pertaining to Hawaii's diverse ethnic groups.

Driving south out of Hilo on Highway 11, watch for signs on the right for Panaewa Rain Forest Zoo, which features lush plantings as well as denizens of the rain forest and other animals, some of which are housed in open habitats. Continuing on Highway 11 you soon reach Keaau, where Route 130 branches off to the left and Route 11 continues to Volcano. Turn on Route 130 for now, which will bring you to the small, funky town of Pahoa, providing you don't take the bypass around it. Pahoa is little more than a series of clapboard-front buildings, rickety and tired, but charming in a washed-out sort of way.

If you stop for lunch at Paradise West, a small restaurant at the edge of town, some residents may tell you that Pahoa was formerly the marijuana capital of the Puna district, with some of the lawless aspects of the stateside Wild West. The town is quieter now, but old habits linger. The Hemp Store, which sells clothing and other prod-

ucts made from hemp cloth, touts literature advocating the legal-
ization of marijuana: For instance, one leaflet proclaims that if
all Hawaii's sugar acreage were devoted to hemp (read "pot"), it
would provide enough biomass for all the state's energy needs.

At the south end of Pahoa the road forks, with Route 130 bearing right. Take the left fork, Route 132, for about 2.5 miles to Lava
Trees State Park. Here, some 200 years ago, a lava flow swept
through a forest of large *ohia* trees. When the lava receded, it left
large "molds" where it had surrounded the trees and burned them
out. Now these grotesque shapes stand among new growth, and it
is possible to peer down into many of them and see the imprint of
the trees that burned long ago. The park has a covered picnic area,
drinking water, and rest rooms.

If you are interested in snorkeling, refer now to Wai Opae Ponds
in the Snorkeling and Diving section of this chapter, for a unique
experience both scenic and close to shore. Otherwise, continue east
along Route 132 until it meets Route 137 coming in from the right.
Turn right, and the road will soon narrow and begin to follow the
sea. You will find no tour buses and few other tourists here, but that
is their loss and your gain. This is rural Hawaii as not many people
see it. Rain forest, coconut groves, mango trees, and a scattering of
modest homes prompted a friend to remark that this is as close as
Hawaii comes to Tahiti. And more development is not likely. This
is the East Rift Zone of Kilauea Volcano, and homes and residents
here are at the mercy of Pele, the goddess of fire, as you will soon
see for yourself.

Stop at Isaac Hale Beach Park and you may find Pohoiki Springs,
a freshwater pond heated by volcanic action. From the caretaker's
house, walk toward the head of the bay along the shore, and then
follow the short path that leads into the vegetation. If you can't find
it, someone may be able to direct you. If you choose to continue
southwest along Route 137, you'll pass Mackenzie State Recreation Area, a pretty picnic area in a forested grove overlooking the
sea. Watch for Milepost 19, and a small parking turnoff. A short,
rocky path leads to the unmarked Kehena Beach, one of the best
beaches on this coast. Nude bathing is common here.

KALAPANA LAVA FLOWS: About 9 miles past MacKenzie is the former junction of Highways 137 and 130. The junction was once covered by lava flows, but a paved connection has been reestablished. Stop your car for a moment and stand facing the ocean. To your front lies a field of hardened lava and toppled palm trees that was once the town of Kalapana, destroyed in 1990. Kaimu Black Sand Beach, considered by many to be the prettiest beach in the state, once curved gracefully on your left. It now lies buried forever under the same flow. Several small subdivisions used to dot the hillsides here, and the town contained two picturesque churches, two beach parks, and a funky country store. A well-known local attraction, "Queen's Bath," a freshwater pool in a lava depression, was reputed to be a place where high Hawaiian chiefesses bathed. In 1986, Kilauea's eruption, which had started back in 1983, began nibbling at Kalapana. By 1990 everything was gone, buried under 1.2 billion cubic yards of lava. Nearly 300 homes and other structures were destroyed here and in adjoining communities, with the cost of the damage exceeding $130 million. Though the flows that destroyed Kalapana have now cooled, and it is a fascinating place to explore, the active lava flows have now moved west into the national park, and could return at any time.

Drive the remaining few hundred yards on 137 to its end at a newly paved parking area, which includes a new store and a snack bar. Walk up on the lava rise. From there you will be able to get an idea of the vast extent of the volcano's destructive force. If you would like to explore the lava fields themselves, a tour over the lava in this area that has been done by enough people to indicate that it *may* be safe is described in the Day Hikes section of this chapter, under "Kalapana Lava Flows." Please read this section before venturing out on the flows, as the section contains important information and safeguards.

You're now ready to rejoin Highway 130, but instead of proceeding north toward Pahoa, turn left and drive to the barrier across the road. You may meet someone coming or going around the barrier, carrying supplies. Pele is capricious; she did spare a few homes in the area, though they are now completely surrounded by lava and cut off from all utilities. But some of their owners still use them, if only on a part-time basis. If you have a four-wheel-drive vehicle, you can drive around the right side of the barrier on the rough bulldozed road that generally follows the old lava-buried Highway 130, which formerly led into the park. You will be able to drive on four segments of this road as you pass over a moonscape of miles of new lava. The road ends after 3.5 miles, and to exit you must retrace your steps.

When you have finished exploring, turn north on Highway 130 for the uphill ride back to Pahoa. You will find that you have this wide highway virtually to yourself. After about 5 miles, begin watching for a pullout on the right, from which you should be able to see steam rising over the trees a short distance from the road. Park, and take the trail that leads to the source of the steam, a small hill. You can climb to the entrance of the vent, descend inside a rock chamber, and enjoy a natural steam bath. Once you reach Pahoa, return to Hilo the same way you came, or head for the volcano, as described below.

Places to Stay. Most of the modern hotels in Hilo are located on Banyan Drive, a picturesque peninsula lined with large banyan trees. Cheaper, more modest hotels can be found closer to the center of town. Several attractive B&Bs operate in Hilo and the vicinity. Consult the *HVB Accommodations Guide* for a listing of such facilities. Camping permits can be obtained for Onekahakaha and James Kealoha Beach parks, but inquire at the county permits office about their desirability: the campgrounds are sometimes overrun by homeless people.

The Village Inn in Pahoa is what a very small South Pacific hotel must have looked like in Robert Louis Stevenson's day. It has only five rooms, each individually furnished with period pieces. Prices are very reasonable (P.O. Box 1987, Pahoa 96778; phone 965-6444). Three small restaurants are located across the street. Several B&Bs also operate in the subdivisions near Pahoa. Inquire locally.

Camping in the Puna area is limited to three sites, Kalani Honua Conference and Retreat Center, Isaac Hale County Beach Park, and MacKenzie SRA. Neither of the last two has any water, and Kalani Honua is expensive—$15 per person, $25 per couple per night. Kalani Honua also offers rooms, dormitories, and vegetarian food ser-

vice. Both the county and the state campsites require permits (see
Appendix II).

Hawaii Volcanoes National Park

Covering over 229,000 acres and stretching some 35 miles from an
altitude of 13,677 feet to sea level, Hawaii Volcanoes probably traverses more vegetation zones than any other park in the national
system. Kilauea Caldera, which is the center of most of the park's
activity, lies at an elevation of 4,000 feet and receives an annual
rainfall of 102 inches. Days are usually warm, but they can be cool,
especially when it's raining or windy. Nights are usually cool, in the
40- to 50-degree range, but they, too, can be colder. The park contains more than 150 miles of trails, and even if you have limited
time at your disposal, you should try one or two of the shorter ones.
There is an admission charge of $2 per person or $5 per car, good
for 7 days. Golden Age and Golden Access Passports are honored.
To reach the park, follow Highway 11 from Hilo, a distance of 28
miles.

The vehicular tour of the park described below requires two
days. The first day takes in points of interest along Crater Rim
Drive, and the second day explores Chain of Craters Road and the
currently active lava flows along the seacoast. If you have more
time, please refer to the Day Hikes section in this chapter. One of
the best ways to see and feel this park is to set out on foot.

*Day 1—Crater Rim Drive (15 to 22 miles, plus 28 miles if you
start from Hilo).* Your tour of the park should begin at the visitor
center, where you will find maps, brochures, displays, and a film on
the volcano. This, too, is the place to get the latest information
about current volcanic activity. Cross the highway to the Volcano
House Hotel for a spectacular view of Kilauea Crater.

Leaving the visitor center, turn right on Crater Rim Drive. You
may want to make short stops at the Sulphur Banks on the right and
the Steam Vents on the left. In a little over a mile you will pass Kilauea Military Camp, an R&R center for military personnel and
their families. Watch for Kilauea Overlook on the left, which affords a fine view across the caldera. Stop at the Volcano Observa-

tory and Jaggar Museum for an interesting and informative exhibit on the volcano and the surrounding area. There is another caldera overlook here, offering a good view into Halemaumau Crater.

Continuing around Crater Rim Drive, you will pass the beginning of Kilauea's southwest rift. After driving another mile, park at the large lot on the left and take the short walk to the Halemaumau Overlook. If you are mystified by flowers, fruit, and the bottle or two of Gordon's gin that may be perched on the rim of the crater, they are offerings to Pele, goddess of fire, who resides in Halemaumau. (Pele reportedly has a taste for gin, with a preference for Gordon's.) After you pass Keanakakoi crater, you'll enter an area where a cinder eruption from Kilauea Iki in 1959 blanketed the forest up to a depth of several feet. The forest has returned, but the layer of cinders is still visible.

One mile past the crater you'll reach the intersection of Chain of Craters Road on the right. Turn left, into the Devastation Trail parking lot. Twenty years ago this short walk was a striking tour through hundreds of fallen trees, victims of the Kilauea Iki eruption, strewn like giant matchsticks across the barren, cinder landscape—a smaller version of the present-day Mt. St. Helens area. The walk is much less dramatic now, although some guidebooks will lead you to expect otherwise by reproducing old photographs of the area. The forest has grown back and most of the fallen trees have rotted away or been covered by new undergrowth. A fifteen-minute walk along a boardwalk brings you to a sudden viewpoint overlooking Kilauea Iki. The brown hill on your left is Puu Puai, the cinder cone formed by the 1959 eruption, its huge lava fountain reaching an incredible 1,900 feet. If someone in your party is willing to forgo the walk, he or she can drive a car here and pick up the walkers at this end. Otherwise, return to the parking lot the way you came.

Exiting the Devastation Trail parking lot, turn left, continuing along Crater Rim Drive to Thurston Lava Tube. The Thurston Lava Tube trail descends into a large fern-choked pit, enters the illuminated lava tube from a collapsed roof, and exits from a second collapse. Although this is the official exit, the tube continues, and

if you have a flashlight and sturdy shoes you may explore farther
on your own (and at your own risk—parts of the ceiling might be
about to fall).

The last stop on your circular tour of the crater rim is Kilauea
Iki Overlook, where you can view the crater from the side opposite
Puu Puai. After you've seen that view, you'll want to return to the
visitor center. There you may want to browse the Volcano Art Center, where many local artists display their wares. If you still have
time, you can visit Kipuka Puaulu, a pretty 1-mile loop through a
native forest island, cut off from its surroundings by an ancient lava
flow. Kipuka Puaulu lies between the park entrance and Namakani
Paio Campground on the Mauna Loa Road, which turns off Highway 11 to the right. A short detour takes you to a series of tree
molds, formed when a lava flow burned out a forest of large *ohia*
trees. If you prefer, you can visit this area on your way to Kona.
Even if you are not camping, Namakani Paio makes a nice rest or
lunch stop, a green and shaded place affording an oasis amid all the
black lava.

Day 2—Chain of Craters Road (56 miles round-trip). One of the
highlights of a visit to the park is a trip to the end of Chain of Craters Road in the coastal area, where lava flows have overrun the
road on their march to the sea. This is a constantly changing area.
Prior to 1986 Chain of Craters Road became State Highway 130
when it left the park boundary, continuing on to Hilo. On November 26th of that year, lava crossed the highway for the first time,
and the connection between Hilo and the southern section of the
park was severed. Since then a 7-mile segment of the road has been
blanketed by thick lava flows. In the ensuing years Kilauea has destroyed the park's visitor center and museum at Wahaula, overrun
Kamoamoa, one of its prettiest campgrounds and picnic areas, and
claimed Lae Apuki, the ruins of an old fishing village. At this writing the lava barrier stands west of the Kalapana Trailhead, which
has also been overrun by lava.

Since the main attraction of the trip is the active lava flows along
the seacoast, inquire about the latest activity at the visitor center
before you leave. If you are some distance from the park, you may

call 967-7977 for a 24-hour recorded message about eruption status. You may want to plan to be at the flows at sunset, which can be the best time if they are active. Hillsides that appear black during the day glow dull read as the light fades, and, if the flows are active, rivers of bright orange spill down the slopes. Bring a flashlight and wear walking shoes or boots, not thongs. There are no facilities of any kind on this trip, so bring plenty of water and food, and make sure you have enough gas for at least a 60-mile round-trip.

To begin the trip from the visitor center, return to Chain of Craters Road. You will pass three craters along the road at which you may stop to look, but make sure to stop at Pauahi Crater on the left. Leave the car in the lot and walk up to the wooden platform for a view into the crater and of Mauna Ulu (Growing Mountain), an imposing lava shield to your front. Resembling a miniature Mauna Loa, Mauna Ulu was formed by a large eruption that lasted from 1969 to 1974 and is responsible for the huge cascades of black lava plunging to the sea that you will soon be driving across.

Pull off the road again into the Mauna Ulu parking area and drive to the far end of the lot. Walk toward Mauna Ulu and you will see a remnant of the old Chain of Craters Road, which was covered by the 1969–1974 eruption. If it is a clear day, take the short, 1-mile hike to Puu Huluhulu, the brown, hump-backed hill to the left of Mauna Ulu. From there you can see Puu O'o, a solitary, smoking cone, and the source of most current activity. Be sure to take this hike if Puu O'o is fountaining. It has been known to spout streams of lava hundreds of feet in the air. The grotesque lava shapes along the trail are tree molds, formed when lava ponded against trees and then receded. You can look down into some of them and still see the outlines of tree trunks.

Your next stop should be Kealakomo Picnic Pavilion, about 7 miles farther down the road, its peaked roof easily visible off to the right. From here you'll have an expansive view of the Puna coastline and lava fields. This is a good spot for a coffee break, or lunch if you got a late start. A resident mongoose may appear on the rocks below the right side of the pavilion, sniffing for a handout. Beyond the pavilion, the road descends more steeply, making a long hairpin turn as it drops over the Holei Pali. At the bottom of the turn is a pullout where you may want to stop for a picture of the "black Niagara" made by Mauna Ulu's lavas pouring toward the sea.

Don't miss the opportunity to see the ancient petroglyphs at Puu Loa—they may not be there much longer; the lava flows are moving closer. The trail, 0.7 miles long, begins from a large pullout in the road, on the left as you face the sea. The petroglyphs—among them human figures, sails, circles, and dots—can be viewed from the circular boardwalk. No one knows the significance of these rock carvings, or who made them, or why. They have been found on all islands, but the Big Island has far more than any other.

About a mile past the Puu Loa pullout, the road reaches the sea and follows the coastline until it stops at a barrier manned by park rangers. You will be directed to turn around and park the car along the side of the road facing the direction from which you came. From here you can usually walk to where the road is cut by the latest lava flow. It is 7 miles before Highway 130 appears again. In the space between, Kilauea's fury has destroyed the town of Kalapana, a state park, the famed Kaimu Black Sand Beach, the Royal Gardens subdivision, the National Park Wahaula Visitor Center, and several other park features.

What you see depends on what Pele is up to on the day you visit, and what the rangers feel is safe. One day I stood in the parking lot of the Wahaula Visitor Center with two of my young granddaughters and watched a lava flow burn the building to the ground. One night I sat on the black sand beach at Kamoamoa with dozens of others and saw slow-moving rivers of bright orange overrun the campground, toppling palm trees and setting fire to the surrounding forest. At other times I've seen nothing at all but tons of cooling black lava. It all depends on Pele . . . perhaps an offering of Gordon's gin at the edge of Halemaumau before you drive down?

In the past, park management has done an excellent job of balancing public safety with the natural desire of people to get as close to the volcanic activity as possible. Unfortunately, in 1992 a visitor was killed when a lava ledge collapsed into the sea. This was the first death due to volcanic action in the park since 1924, but it seems to have had an effect on park policy. Since the accident, park rangers now appear less willing to allow people to get so close to volcanic activity, in some cases keeping spectators as far away as a quarter of a mile. Sad, because one of the main attractions of the park has always been the opportunity to witness a volcanic eruption close up. I, for one, hope it can stay that way.

Places to Stay. *Volcano House* (P.O. Box 53, HVNP, HI 96718; phone 967-7321) is the only hotel within the park. It has a spectacular location right on the rim of Kilauea Caldera. There are a lodge and several B&Bs in Volcano, only a mile from the park entrance. One of these, **My Island,** also provides a B&B referral service for the rest of the island (P.O. Box 100, Volcano, HI 96785; phone 967-7216). The state park division also runs a low-cost cabin in Volcano. There are two drive-in campgrounds in the park, Namakani Paio, on Highway 11 about 3.5 miles past the park entrance, and Kipuka Nene, on Hilina Pali Road, off Chain of Craters Road. Both have rest rooms, covered picnic shelters, and drinking water. Permits are not required and there is no charge for camping, which is limited to seven days in a given year. The Volcano House also operates a few rustic cabins at Namakani Paio, each of which contains only a double or two single bunk beds. A picnic table and grill are outside each cabin, and bedding is provided. Community rest rooms and showers are in a separate building. **Kilauea Military Camp** (KMC, HVNP, HI 06718; phone 967-8333) offers an excellent place to stay for military personnel, active or retired, their families, and certain government civilian employees. Or, if you prefer, it is also possible to stay in Hilo, if you don't mind driving 45 minutes each way.

National Park to Kailua–Kona—via South Point

From Hawaii Volcanoes National Park to the town of Kailua–Kona is a distance of 96 miles. While it can easily be driven in one day, if you want to undertake most of the sightseeing and enjoy one or more of the described excursions along the way, the excursion will probably require an overnight stop. If this is what you plan to do, refer to Places to Stay at the end of this section.

Leaving the national park, turn west on Highway 11, toward Kailua–Kona. Now the great bulk of Mauna Loa's eastern slope will loom on your right for the next 40 miles, its summit 16 miles distant and more than 13,000 feet high. The road begins a long, gradual descent from 4,000 feet to sea level, which it reaches at Punaluu, about 30 miles from the park entrance. Watch for the turnoff to the last remaining easily accessible black sand beach on the Big Island, as Kilauea has now claimed Kaimu and Kamoamoa. Rest rooms and drinking water are available. Swim with caution: The wave action and strong currents are sometimes dangerous here. After Punaluu, the road begins to climb again, and 8 miles farther on you will enter the sleepy little town of Naalehu, which bills itself as the southernmost town in the United States.

The turnoff to South Point is about 5 miles from town, where you turn left onto a paved but narrow road. On your way you will pass a large wind farm, windmills churning to produce electricity from the stiff winds that almost continuously sweep this area. Permanently bent trees and billowing waves of grass attest to their force. South Point, called Ka Lae by Hawaiians, is the southernmost point in the fifty states, and is an area of archaeological importance. The ruins of an ancient fishing shrine lie here, and the surrounding near-shore rocks exhibit circular holes drilled by ancient fishermen. The Hawaiians drilled these holes to provide secure tie-downs for lines tied to their canoes, allowing them to fish safely where it was too deep to anchor but impossible to remain motionless otherwise. The waters off South Point are rich fishing grounds swept by strong currents and fierce winds. Modern-day fishermen employ the same technique by winching their boats out from moorings at the base of the steep cliffs.

A 3-mile walk along the coastal Jeep road leading east from the parking lot leads to Green Sand Beach, its color formed by olivine crystals washing out of a shoreline cone. The cone is now about half eroded, forming a pretty, curved beach. Access is from a lava shelf on the southwest side of the beach. Attempting to reach the shore from the upper part of the cone is dangerous due to unstable conditions, and causes further erosion of the hill. There is no water or shade in the area and swimming should be attempted only with caution and only on calm days. The bottom drops sharply off shore, and rough water and waves will make return to the beach difficult.

Returning to Highway 11 from South Point, the road now circles the south end of Mauna Loa and turns north. Ten miles after returning to the highway, at the western end of Hawaiian Ocean View Estates, a cinder road turns off to the left. This is the Road to the Sea, one of the few public accessways to the shoreline in the Ka'u District. It is 7 miles from the highway to this coast, where cinder cones and green sand beaches lie in total isolation. By proceeding slowly, an ordinary vehicle can normally drive all but the last section of this road. However, road conditions change, and if it appears too rough at any point, stop and continue on foot.

The Manuka State Wayside offers an opportunity for a walk in a typical dry *ohia* forest. *Ohia,* a native tree, is the most common tree in the islands. An easy 3.5-mile loop trail leads upward from the picnic area, the walk taking no more than two hours. At the top of the loop a short trail leads to a collapsed lava tube crowded with ferns, trees, and other vegetation.

About 8 miles from Manuka, a steep, narrow road turns off to the left toward the fishing village of Milolii. This small collection of modest houses may be the last truly functioning fishing community in the state. It is not a tourist attraction. There are no shops, restaurants, or hotels—just residents engaged in their day-to-day work. The citizens, most of them of Hawaiian ancestry, of this close-knit community follow a way of life established by preceding generations. But don't expect grass shacks and hula skirts—tin-roofed houses and jeans and T-shirts are what you will find at Milolii.

If you have some extra time, an interesting 4-mile hike along the coast south from Milolii leads to the Ahole Holua, the best preserved ancient slide in the Hawaiian Islands. Hawaiians lined these structures with *pili* grass, and then raced down them on sleds with wooden runners. Pele, the goddess of fire, was said to disguise herself so she could compete with young chiefs in these events. En route to the *holua* you will pass lovely, palm-lined Honomalino Bay and sections of a *kuamoo,* a single line of smooth stones embedded in the rough lava (also called the "King's Highway") so that barefoot travelers (and the king's tax collectors) could walk from village to village along the coast. *Kuamoo* also means "backbone" in Hawaiian: These paths were given the name because of their resemblance to a skeletal backbone stretching across the lava. Watch for a prominent grove of *kiawe* trees on the shoreline, which marks Okoe Bay, a pretty and completely hidden gray sand beach. When you're ready, return the way you came.

Back on Highway 11, the next turnoff is for Puuhonua o Honaunau National Historical Park, the most frequented stop on the south Kona coast. Look for a turnoff to the right that leads to St. Benedict's Painted Church, just a short distance off the park's access road. In ancient Hawaii a *puuhonua* was a place of refuge, a sanctuary for persons who had broken a *kapu,* one of the strict rules that regulated Hawaiian society prior to the arrival of Westerners. After certain cleansing ceremonies were performed, the *kapu*-breaker was free to leave without penalty.

Once you've reached the 6-acre Honaunau Park you'll find a mausoleum, a *heiau* site, tide pools, a canoe landing, and interpretive displays. A one-dollar admission fee is charged, and Golden Age and Golden Access Passports are honored. Honaunau Bay is an excellent snorkeling site. Snorkelers should not enter the water from the park, but from the vicinity of the boat ramp adjoining the park or the picnic area, reachable via the dirt road leading from the left end of the parking lot.

After your visit, do not return to Highway 11 on the wide access road, but instead strike out across the narrow paved road that goes north across the lava fields to Kealakekua Bay, where Captain James Cook dropped anchor and came ashore on the Big Island. At the end of the road is the Hikiau Heiau, where Cook was honored at his arrival, some say as the god Lono. (Less than a month later Cook was killed while trying to take a chief hostage in exchange for the return of a stolen boat. A vivid account of this event is given in O. A. Bushnell's *The Return of Lono.*) A white obelisk in memory of Cook can be seen across the bay on its northern shore, not far from where the adventurer was killed; you can rent a kayak at the boat ramp and paddle over to the monument. A school of dolphins will usually escort you partway, cavorting and leaping out of the water right beside you. If you are a snorkeler, be sure to bring your gear. The landing at the monument is one of the best snorkeling spots on the island (see the Snorkeling and Diving section in this chapter).

The road from the bay leading up to Highway 11 passes a coffee mill, one of several that process locally grown Kona coffee. The mill offers free tours and free coffee, and you can purchase a supply of the stuff if you wish. Until recently, this part of the Hawaii coast was the only place in the United States where coffee was grown; now it is being grown commercially on Kauai, Maui, and Molokai.

If you did not make the kayak trip to the Cook memorial, it is possible to make a 4-mile round-trip hike to the white obelisk you saw across Kealakekua Bay. If you would like to do so, please see the Day Hikes section of this chapter. Resuming the drive to Kailua–Kona, you may wish to detour upslope to Holualoa, a small town that looks like a Pahoa with art shops. Turn off Highway 11 at Route 180, which forks to the right. You can also visit here later as a side trip.

Kailua–Kona is really the town of Kailua. *Kona,* in Hawaiian, means "leeward," and all the major islands have a leeward coast. To prevent confusion with Kailua on the *windward* coast of Oahu, the post office christened the Big Island's town "Kailua–*Kona.*" Most people now simply refer to this city as Kona; however, you may hear it referred to by any of the three names.

Kailua–Kona is the deep-sea fishing capital of the islands, and some people consider it the marlin capital of the world. It is also a haven for "snowbirds" from the mainland who have purchased winter homes or condos here, seeking a sunny escape from ice and snow. The town itself is small and touristy, but attractive nonetheless. It has only a few beaches, and these are quite small, a fact that usually surprises first-time visitors. The big Kona coast beaches lie farther to the north.

The Hulihee Palace, a two-story structure at the north end of town, was the summer residence for King Kalakaua. Built in 1838, from lava and coral, it contains furnishings of the period. It is located almost across from the Mokuakaua Church, also built from lava and coral.

A great way to see all kinds of tropical fish is to snorkel at Kahaluu Beach Park (see Snorkeling and Diving in this chapter). Even if you have never snorkeled, it is well worth your time to rent equipment at the beach for an hour or so and try it out at this shallow and very safe location. Green sea turtles are almost always there, amazingly undisturbed by all the human activity.

Still under development is Kaloko-Honokohau National Historical Park, just north of town opposite the Kaloko Industrial Park. Some accounts say that Kamehameha I is buried in a secret cave somewhere within the national park grounds. Rugged, barren lava covers much of this coastal area, yet it was once a thriving settlement. Two ancient fishponds and a fish trap, as well as the remains of several *heiau*, all have major archaeological significance. The runway of an unusually wide *holua* and a section of *alaloa* ("King's Highway") are also preserved in the park. The small freshwater pool encircled by harsh black lava is known locally as the Queen's Bath. The lava platforms surrounding the pool were sentry posts, where guards protected the queen's privacy. A long sandy beach fronts the park, much of it strewn with lava rocks and fragments. The frequent nudists who visit this beach are tolerated as the beach is out of the way and not heavily used.

Places to Stay. There are few accommodations between the national park and Kailua–Kona, and since the trip is only 96 miles, most people make it in one day. But if you are exploring along the way, you may want to make an overnight stop—or even two. **Seamountain Lodge** (P.O. Box 70, Pahala, HI 96777; phone 488-8301) is located on the coast 28 miles south of the national park, at Punaluu, the site of the previously mentioned black sand beach. Seamountain offers condominium accommodations, with a two-night minimum, though exceptions are made. The lodge is convenient to South Point, as is the **Shirakawa Motel** (929-7462), on Highway 11 in Waiohinu. The Shirakawa, which claims to be the southernmost motel in the United States, is a clean, no-frills place, with plain rooms and budget prices. Some units have kitchenettes.

Rounding the corner into the district of South Kona, you will find the **Manago Hotel** in the town of Captain Cook, a reasonably priced, small hotel with simple rooms—some with great views of the ocean—from its 1,400-foot elevation. This is a great starting point for exploring Kona coffee country, for visiting Puuhonua o

Honaunau (Place of Refuge) and Kealakekua Bay, or for hiking down to Cook's monument. A little farther down the road, at Honalo, lies **Teshima's Inn,** smaller, quainter, also reasonably priced, with views of a Japanese garden rather than the sea. As both of these hotels are close to Kailua–Kona, you can easily drive on into town if you prefer more upscale accommodations.

There are lots of hotels and condos in Kailua–Kona, ranging in price from moderate to expensive. Some B&Bs can be found along the route, as well as in Kailua–Kona and the surrounding vicinity— consult the *HVB Accommodations Guide.* There are no campgrounds in or near Kailua–Kona, though campgrounds are located at Punaluu, Whittington, and Milolii Beach parks; county permits are required (see Appendix II). Of the three I prefer Whittington, a quiet, lovely spot.

The Gold Coast—Kailua–Kona to Pololu Valley (58 miles)

North of Kailua–Kona, on the ocean side of the Queen Kaahumanu Highway (Route 19), stretches the Big Island's Gold Coast, so named for the proliferation of lush, super-expensive resorts that have sprung up there in recent years. At first, it is hard to imagine any kind of development at all in this hostile landscape. Miles and miles of lava appear to blanket every inch of land from the mountains to the sea. But the developers seem determined to prove that if you have the sun, the sea, and the money, anything is possible. The lava has been pulverized, topsoil and trees have been brought in, and lava fields have been made to bloom with golf courses, swimming pools, and luxury hotels. Tourists not wealthy enough to stay here drive by in a rush, seeing nothing to detain them. But this coast has much beauty to offer—if you know how and where to find it.

Some 2.6 miles north of the turnoff to the Kailua–Kona Airport, a sign for Kona Coast State Park marks a road leading seaward across the harsh lava to Hawaii's newest jewel, a 4-mile stretch of coastline that includes some of the finest white sand beaches on the Kona coast. Purchased from estates, and wrested from developers under the power of eminent domain, several parcels of pristine shoreline have been combined to form the most recent addition to the state's public parks system. Beginning just south of Mahaiula, including Makalawena, and encompassing the Maniniowali Beaches, a treasure trove of swimming, snorkeling, diving, surfing, and fishing sites has been secured by the state and protected from development, all destined to become a marvelous, unspoiled shoreline park.

The 4.3-mile-long road into the park is narrow and in poor condition, but it can be driven slowly in a conventional vehicle. Just before the road ends in a parking lot, a historic *alaloa* crosses it from north to south. An *alaloa* was a main road, or belt road, around an island, and, like the *kuamoo* mentioned earlier, was often referred to as the "King's Highway." Remnants of these roads still exist on several islands. This one, which once stretched from Kailua–Kona to Kawaihae, is particularly well preserved.

Right beside the parking lot is a small *kiawe* grove with picnic tables fronting a wide beach. By walking north along the beach and rounding a small point, you'll reach Mahaiula, a fine beach with an abandoned beach house at its north end. This beach is on the former estate of a well-known *kamaaina* family. From the beach house it is possible to walk a mile north on the *alaloa* to an even prettier spot, Makalawena, where there's another white sand beach and a lovely, ironwood-backed cove. Just behind the beach is Opaeula Pond, once an ancient Hawaiian fishpond but now an important water bird sanctuary.

After you return to the highway, you'll see a large cinder cone on the left side of the road 1.5 miles north of the park entrance. A few hundred yards past the cone a rough dirt road heads toward the sea, reaching Maniniowali, another great white sand swimming beach, and the north end of the park. Drive this road only if you have either a high-clearance or a four-wheel-drive vehicle. If you have neither, make the 1-mile hike down to the beach. (Even if you drive, you will have to go the last few hundred yards on foot.)

Another lovely spot off the beaten track is Kiholo Bay, with its lagoon and freshwater pools. Twelve miles from the airport entrance you will reach another dirt road heading seaward. (You will be unable to drive on this road, as there is a locked barrier.) Park the car off the highway and walk down the road about a mile to the shoreline. Three sand and pebble beaches stretch along the bay; the lagoon and most of the pools lie to the north, past the private houses fronting the beach.

Anaehoomalu Bay and its curved, palm-lined beach are good spots for swimming or sunbathing. Turn off Highway 19 on the road to the Royal Waikoloan Hotel and follow the Public Access signs to the south end of the beach and the public parking lot. Here you will find rest rooms, outdoor showers, and beach access. A private beach park for use of Parker Ranch employees will be on your left as you face the water, and the hotel off to your right. Two large fish ponds lie between the beach and the hotel, amid the palm trees. There is also an extensive petroglyph field on the resort grounds, as well as a section of the *alaloa* seen earlier to the south.

Farther up the coast, the Kalahuipuaa Fishponds are one of the most archaeologically significant sites on the north Kona coastline. Thanks to the efforts of the Mauna Lani Hotel, these ponds have not only been preserved, but are still in production. The hotel has incorporated the ponds into its landscaping plan, and afforded public access to them, as well as to the beach. Other ancient coastal sites on the hotel grounds have also been preserved. To reach the ponds, turn off Highway 19 at the entrance to the Mauna Lani Hotel, and follow the signs to the public coastline access. The paved path crosses an ancient lava flow with several interesting features, such as a cave inhabited in prehistoric days.

Also accessible now from the grounds of the Mauna Lani are the Puako Petroglyph Fields. The former trail from Puako Road to these fields of nearly three thousand carvings has been closed. The new trail from the hotel leads to the largest grouping.

(The Mauna Lani has shown what can be accomplished when a hotel works willingly, rather than reluctantly, with mandated public access requirements. Its neighbor, the Mauna Kea Hotel, fought the public access issue in court for seven years before finally giving in and providing public passage to its beach. Paradoxically, once the issue was settled, the Mauna Kea also did a fine job of providing beach facilities and parking for the general public.)

If you are ready for a beach day, or just a couple of hours in the sun and surf, Hapuna Beach State Recreation Area is only 5 miles north of the Mauna Lani Hotel. A well-maintained park with extensive facilities, this area has the widest white sand beach on the island. Two hundred yards across and half a mile long, Hapuna slopes gently enough so that its waves are almost always safe in the summer. Care should be taken in winter months and during any period of storm or high surf, as there are no lifeguards at this beach, and drownings have occurred here. A luxury hotel and golf course opened in 1995 on the north end of the beach. In a turnabout from the way things usually operate in Hawaii, the hotel shares access to the state park beach at Hapuna.

At the junction of Highway 19 and Route 270, bear left on 270, toward Kawaihae and Hawi. One of the most important *heiau* in Hawaiian history lies a little over 2 miles north of Hapuna. Puukohola Heiau, built by Kamehameha in 1791, is now a national historic site overlooking Kawaihae Bay. At war with other chiefs of the Big Island, Kamehameha was told by a *kahuna,* or priest, that if he built a *heiau* at this spot he would become ruler of all the Hawaiian Islands. As the *heiau* was being completed, Kamehameha invited his chief rival to the site to discuss peace, only to kill him and sacrifice his body to the gods he would worship at the *heiau.* Nineteen years and many battles later the prophecy was finally fulfilled.

After Kawaihae the road follows miles of dry, uninhabited coastline, where parched grasses and *kiawe* trees are the predominant vegetation. The shores are rocky and the sea cobalt blue. Eleven miles past the original junction you will reach Lapakahi State Historical Park, the site of an abandoned fishing village. It is hard to imagine a settlement prospering in this inhospitable place, but a community existed here for five hundred years. A self-guiding trail brochure is available, featuring a map keyed to various archaeological remains, but it takes a good deal of imagination to visualize the village from that which is left.

According to genealogical chants, Mookini Heiau was built in 480 A.D. and used exclusively by Hawaii's kings and ruling chiefs for worship and human sacrifice. *Heiau* were usually constructed atop huge stone platforms (such as the one at Puukohola), but Mookini is a walled enclosure almost the size of a football field. Legend says that the entire structure was built in one night, from stones passed hand-to-hand from Pololu Valley, more than 10 miles away—a feat that would have required 15,000 to 18,000 men. To reach this legendary *heiau*, turn left off Route 270 about 7 miles past Lapahaki Park, at the sign for Upolu Airport. Just before reaching the airfield, turn left again onto the narrow dirt road that runs parallel to the shore, and proceed about 2 miles. The *heiau* will appear on a rise to your left.

Located half a mile past the *heiau*, a fenced enclosure is reported to be the spot where Kamehameha I was born. The large rocks within the enclosure are said to be his birthing stones. From this historic spot you can return to the highway either by retracing your route or proceeding around the enclosure and through an abandoned Coast Guard Loran (Long Range Navigation) station.

As you continue along Route 270 en route to Kapaau, note the statue of Kamehameha on your right as you pass through the small town of Kapaau. In the late 1870s the city of Honolulu commissioned a statue of the king from a sculptor in Florence, Italy. The ship bringing the statue to Hawaii sank on a reef and a duplicate statue, which now stands in the famous square opposite the Iolani Palace, was ordered. Later the original statue was recovered from the wreck and placed where you now see it, commemorating the king's birth nearby.

The road ends at Pololu Valley Lookout, where a dramatic view of the windward Kohala coast unfolds. Pololu is the northernmost of seven beautiful valleys separated by high sea cliffs along this shore. Only Waipio, the southernmost, is inhabited. A path leads to the bottom of Pololu Valley, a descent that takes about fifteen to twenty minutes. The valley itself is private property, but you are welcome to stroll the beach, or swim if the water is calm. A trail at the far end of the beach leads to the next two valleys, both of them uninhabited but both private property.

Places to Stay. Most of the hotel resorts north of Kailua–Kona are in the ultraluxury category, with rates to match—after all, that's why it's called the Gold Coast. One exception is the moderately expensive Royal Waikoloan (885-6789) at Anaehoomalu Beach. The ultraluxury resorts, in case you have the money or just want to splurge, are all listed in the *HVB Accommodations Guide*.

You might consider the Hilton Waikoloa Village, another "bargain." It is a fantasy hotel, appealing to those who would enjoy rooming at Disneyland, with trains and boats pulling up to the lobby to take guests to their rooms or other destinations on the hotel grounds. I like to be critical of hotels like these, but I have to admit the place is beautiful. It recently went through a financial reorganization, and rumor has it that it was sold to its new owners for about twenty-five cents on the dollar of original investment. In an effort to regain profitability and attract customers, it has reduced its prices.

At the opposite end of the spectrum, in both facilities and price, is the Kohala Lodge (889-5433) in Hawi, with plain, clean rooms at budget prices. B&Bs are few in this area. Hapuna Beach has six A-frame shelters for rent at $15 per night, each housing up to four persons. These are very basic accommodations, nothing more than a screened-in space, two long wooden platforms for sleeping, and a small table. You must provide your own bedding. A central shared-use dining hall includes a small kitchen; rest rooms and showers are in separate buildings. When I last checked, the whole facility was pretty run down, but you can't beat the location. For further information about these facilities, contact Hawaii Untouched, at 329-2944.

There are four campgrounds I'd recommend in Kohala, all at county beach parks: at Spencer, near Kawaihae; Mahukona, and Kapaa, just north of Lapakahi; and Keokea, near the end of the road and close to Pololu Valley Lookout. These require county permits obtainable for a nominal $1 per person per day (see Appendix II) charge. The best of the four are Spencer and Keokea.

Waimea and the Hamakua Coast (72 miles)

Returning to Hawi from Pololu Lookout, watch for the junction with Route 250 (Kohala Mountain Road) on the left. The twenty-mile drive to Waimea passes through upcountry ranch land and forests, and provides sweeping views over the entire north Kona coast. As you enter Waimea, the green, rolling slopes of the extinct Kohala volcano rise on your left, the foothills reaching right down into the town.

Spencer Beach Park Campground. Photo by Richard McMahon.

Waimea is also known as Kamuela, another attempt by the post office to avoid mixups, this time to distinguish the town from Waimea on Kauai. Waimea has long been the headquarters of the Parker Ranch, and more recently for the many astronomical activities on Mauna Kea. The Parker Ranch is the largest privately owned cattle ranch in the United States, currently controlling over 250,000 acres of land. It runs over 50,000 Hereford cattle, plus other breeds, a dairy herd, sheep, and horses. The ranch maintains a visitor center in town, and it is possible to tour its historic ranch homes. There is an admission charge.

As you drive east from Waimea after rejoining Highway 19, both sides of the road afford views over rolling grasslands and grazing cattle. Much of what you see is part of the Parker Ranch empire. As you approach the coast, a high forest takes over, and a weather change is possible as the dry Kona coast gives way to wetter Hamakua. At Honokaa, turn left, and drive through the town to the end of the road at Waipio Valley Lookout. Here the largest valley on the island spreads before you, with its mile-long, black sand beach. A thriving Hawaiian community once populated this lovely valley, but only a few people live here today. Most of its residents left for the cities by the turn of the century, and the remainder were driven out by the two devastating *tsunami*s of 1946 and 1960.

Waipio looms large in Hawaiian legend and history. It was supposedly a favorite place for some of the most powerful gods of the ancient religion, and the demigod Maui is believed to have died in the valley. Many powerful chiefs were born here, and it was at Waipio that Kamehameha received his war god, putting him on his path of conquest. More recently, Waipio Valley figured prominently in a theft from the Bishop Museum in 1994 of two sacred relics, caskets containing the remains of two of ancient Hawaii's most renowned chiefs. It is believed that the relics were returned to a secret, sacred burial place in the valley.

The road down to the valley, although paved, is for four-wheel-drive vehicles only. It is not so much the four wheels driving that is needed; it is the low gear-shift ratio: The 25 percent grade is far too steep for the brakes and transmission of a standard car. Several tour companies offer trips into the valley by four-wheel-drive Jeep or van. Try Waipio Valley Shuttle and Tours (775-7121). It takes about twenty to thirty minutes to walk down the road to the valley floor, and about thirty to forty-five minutes to walk back up. It is a strenuous trip, but well worth it if you have the time and the stamina. If you are interested in exploring the valley on foot, please refer to the Day Hikes section, later in this chapter.

Leaving Waipio Lookout, return to Honokaa and rejoin Highway 19, heading south. After about 2.5 miles, watch for a small sign reading "Kalopa Park." A narrow, paved road leads up to Kalopa State Recreation Area, an immaculately maintained park within a rain forest at an elevation of 2,000 feet. Continue to watch for more small signs, showing you where to turn along the way. At the park, several trails wander through the forest, the easiest and most interesting of which is a forty-five-minute loop with numbered stakes explaining the trees and plants on the trail. Trail guides are available from a box at the beginning of the loop. If you plan an extensive exploration of Waipio Valley you may want to overnight at Kalopa (see Places to Stay at the end of this section).

Do not miss the turnoff to Akaka Falls State Park, twenty-six miles past the Kalopa road. Rising steeply through cane fields, the road leads to a half-mile paved loop trail through a beautifully lush, botanical garden–like setting to two waterfalls, Kihuna Falls and Akaka, which plunges 442 feet into a narrow gorge. It is 14 miles to Hilo from the falls turnoff.

Places to Stay. Because places to stay between Waimea and Hilo are few, more entries than usual are included here to aid in finding accommodations. Two motels are located in Waimea, **The Parker Ranch Lodge** (885-4500) and the **Kamuela Inn** (885-4243), both on Kawaihae Road, and both in the moderate price category. The **Hotel Honokaa Club** (775-0678), on the main street in Honokaa, is a plain, budget priced facility, with both clean rooms and a dormitory, a restaurant, and ocean views. There is also a "hotel" of sorts in Waipio Valley. It has five simple rooms, but no electricity or gas; light comes from kerosene lanterns. There is no food service, but guests have access to a kitchen. Rooms are budget priced, at $10 per person, per night as of this writing. Call 935-7466 or 775-0368 for reservations.

There are several B&Bs in the Waimea–Hamakua area: **Island's End** (889-5265), located in Waimea; **The Log House** (775-9990), three miles from Honokaa on the old road to Waimea; **Hamakua Hideaway** (775-7425) in Kukuihaele, less than a mile from Waipio Valley Lookout (it also has a wonderful scenic view). Camping and cabin rentals are available at Kalopa State Park; there are campgrounds at Laupahoehoe and Kole Kole Beach County parks.

Mauna Kea Summit

Before ending your car tour of the Big Island, there is one more adventure you might like to undertake. If you have a four-wheel-drive vehicle, or are willing to rent one, driving to the summit of Mauna Kea is an experience you should not miss. Mauna Kea, at 13,796 feet, is the highest mountain in the state and the highest in the Pacific, easily topping Japan's Mount Fuji (12,388 feet). It is the highest mountain in the world when measured from base at the ocean floor. The world's leading astronomical complex is located on Mauna Kea; the facility will have 13 major installations in operation by the turn of the century. The world's largest telescope, the Keck, and nine others are already functioning. Five nations have instruments on Mauna Kea, and the Large Earth–based Solar Telescope (LEST) is under construction by an international consortium. Mauna Kea's last eruption probably occurred about 3,600 years ago, and its summit caldera is gone, a victim of collapse and erosion. Still, numerous large cinder cones dot the summit area, creating a surreal background for the observatories.

For any trip to the summit you must have warm clothing: hat, windbreaker, sweater, long pants, gloves, and shoes. This is not the place for shorts and thongs. Sunglasses and sunscreen are also important. To reach Mauna Kea you will have to use the Saddle Road (Route 200), which goes from Hilo to the Kona side of the island. Most rental car companies do not allow their vehicles, even four-wheel-drives, on this road, the one exception being Harper's Car Rental (969-1478), which does allow its four-wheel-drive vehicles to use it. You will need a four-wheel-drive for the trip to the summit anyway. Don't let the rental car restriction worry you if you have a rental that permits you to use the road. The Saddle Road is a two-lane, paved highway, narrow and curvy in spots, but better than some other roads in the state where there are no such restrictions. After all, a large astronomical workforce drives the road every day.

Drive west on Kamehameha Avenue through downtown Hilo to the junction with Waianuene Avenue (Route 200) on the left, just outside of town. Bear left at the fork, continuing on the Saddle Road for about 25 miles, watching for a hunter check-in shack on the left. Across from the shack, on the right side of the highway, a wide, paved, unmarked road begins. This is the Mauna Kea Road. If you are coming from Kailua–Kona or Waimea, take Highway 190 to the junction of Highway 200, and watch for the hunter check-in shack, about 25 miles from the turn onto Highway 200. Following this road for 6 miles brings you to the Onizuka Center for International Astronomy (961-2180) at 9,300 feet. This is as far as you can go in a regular car. *Do not go farther unless you have four-wheel drive. Even if your car could manage the very steep*

Three of ten astronomical observatories on Mauna Kea, at 13,796 feet, the highest point in the Hawaiian Islands. Photo by Richard McMahon.

road—most can't—conventional transmissions and brakes cannot stand the strain of the long, steep descent.

The Onizuka Center is only open Friday through Monday, and there are no gas, food, or other supplies available for purchase. Rest rooms are available. The center offers some programs on weekends, including slide shows and stargazing. Call them for details. Be sure to see the young silverswords growing in an enclosure behind the center. These rare, high-altitude plants grow only here, on Mauna Loa, and on Haleakala on Maui.

After leaving the center, the road becomes unpaved for almost 5 miles, with the pavement beginning again 2 miles before the summit. When you reach the top of the mountain, you will find a flat parking area beside a large observatory. You can expect snow, and sometimes lots of it, between December and April. To your right you will notice a cinder peak about 300 yards away, with a footpath leading to a metal pipe at its top—this is the true summit of Mauna Kea. You can explore the summit area either on foot or by driving the limited road system. Views from here are spectacular in all directions, but there are no tours of any of the observatories on a walk-in basis. If you would like to visit the summit area but prefer not to drive yourself, Waipio Valley Shuttle and Tours (775-7121) offers tours of the mountain.

It is possible to experience some symptoms of altitude sickness at this elevation, especially if you drive directly up from Hilo; this quick trip affords the body little opportunity to acclimate to the thinner air at the summit. Headache and nausea are the most common symptoms, with shortness of breath and perhaps dizziness accompanying any exertion. A mild headache may be treated with aspirin or a similar medication, but the only treatment for serious symptoms is to descend the mountain.

When you are ready to go down the mountain, remember to engage the low gear–ratio lever on your vehicle, to give all your gears a "double low." You should stay in this low ratio all the way down to the visitor center, and for the steep 2 miles beyond.

The University of Hawaii offers free tours of the Mauna Kea summit every Saturday and Sunday at 2:30 P.M. You must provide your own transportation and check in at the Onizuka Visitor Center at least forty-five minutes before the tour begins.

Places to Stay. One way to avoid or reduce the effects of altitude sickness is to allow time for your body to acclimate to the altitude. Some travelers do that by overnighting at Mauna Kea State Recreation Area before driving up the mountain. The park, at an elevation of 6,500 feet, offers inexpensive cabins, but no tenting is allowed. The cabins have kitchens, hot showers, and rest rooms; rates include bedding and kitchen utensils. Reservations can be made through any state parks office (see Appendix III).

Backpacking Adventures

The Mauna Loa Traverse (24 miles, 3–4 days; strenuous)

Maps: USGS topo quads—Kipuka Pakekake, Puu Ulaula, Kokoolau, Mauna Loa. Trails Illustrated Topo Map, Hawaii Volcanoes National Park. Mauna Loa Back Country (free park handout).

Mauna Loa is both the world's largest mountain and the world's largest active volcano. With a volume of 10,000 cubic miles, it has more than 100 times the mass of Mt. St. Helens. Mauna Loa and its sister mountain, Mauna Kea, are the two highest mountains in the Pacific Ocean area, both of them higher than Japan's Mount Fuji. Climbing Mauna Loa (Long Mountain) is one of the world's most unusual hiking experiences. The hiker is alone in a moonscapelike environment devoid of vegetation or any other sign of life, the silence broken only by the crunch of boots. Yet this is a landscape possessed of a stark, awesome beauty.

Mauna Loa has erupted 39 times in the last 150 years, most recently in 1984. Although Kilauea has caused far more damage in recent years, an eruption of Mauna Loa usually causes more concern. The direction of Kilauea's lava flows is generally predictable, restricted to its caldera and the Puna coast area, both sparsely populated locations. Mauna Loa, however, has threatened Hilo to the northeast, sent lava pouring southwest, where subdivisions now stand, and also to the northwest, where the plush resorts of the Kohala Gold Coast have sprouted. Because of its great height, and the huge amounts of lava it has historically spouted, Mauna Loa's potential for destruction is much greater than Kilauea's.

We know that early Hawaiians climbed Mauna Loa, possibly to make offerings to Pele, the goddess of fire. A member of Captain James Cook's crew attempted to climb the Kona side in 1779, but failed. The first successful climb by a Westerner was made fifteen years later by a crew member of explorer George Vancouver's expedition, using a route from the national park side of the mountain (see below). A large U.S. exploring party under the command of Lieutenant Charles Wilkes reached the summit by the same route in 1841 and spent almost a month mapping its craters. The present trail was constructed by a company of U.S. Army engineers in 1915, at the suggestion of Thomas Jaggar, founder of the Hawaiian Volcano Observatory. The Red Hill Cabin was built in the same year, but it was not until 1934 that the Mauna Loa Cabin was constructed at North Pit. Threatened by an eruption, the Mauna Loa Cabin was moved to its present location on the rim of the summit caldera in 1940.

There are three approaches to the mountain, one from Hawaii Volcanoes National Park, one from Highway 11 just south of the park border, and one from the Saddle Road between Mauna Loa and Mauna Kea. This section describes the approach from the park, with a descent via the Saddle Road route; it offers the Highway 11 route as an alternative down the mountain. The ascent from the Saddle Road is covered in the Day Hikes section of this chapter. To get the most from the trip, you should allow four days, giving you a day to explore the summit area. Without the free day at the summit, however, the trip can be made comfortably in three days.

If at all possible, try to arrange the trip as a traverse, as described here, with a dropoff on one side of the mountain and a pickup on the other. If you don't have an available nonhiker in your group, contact Harper's Car Rental (1690 Kamehameha Avenue, Hilo, HI 96720; phone 969-1478). They will deliver your party to the trailhead in the park and pick you up at trail's end on the other side. An alternative is to hike to the summit and return the way you came. This way, you need make no special arrangements; you simply leave your car at the trailhead and it is waiting for you when you return.

A climb of Mauna Loa requires careful preparation. Although weather on the mountain is generally good, you must be ready for adverse conditions. Despite its location in the tropics, snow, blizzards, and driving rain can occur at any time of the year. Temperatures drop below freezing at night, and the upper elevations can be covered with snow any time between November and May. (One year, on May 31st, a friend testing a new sleeping bag slept between snowbanks at the summit. The temperature registered 12 degrees at midnight.) Warm clothing is essential, including rain- and wind-protection gear. If the weather is fine, you may be able to hike in a shirt and shorts, but if it changes you will need long pants, a windproof jacket, and even gloves. You will also need warm clothing in the cabins at night.

Mauna Loa is no place for sneakers or running shoes. Good, sturdy hiking boots are required for stability on rough, uneven lava and to withstand its sharp, jagged edges, which can easily cut through sneakers. A hat is also a necessity, or, better yet, two of them: a wide-brimmed model for sun protection during the day and a soft, wooly pulldown cap for cold and for sleeping in at night. You will also need a warm sleeping bag, a cooking stove, fuel, and utensils, a first aid kit, a flashlight, and sunglasses. Food should include emergency provisions, and you should carry two quarts of water per day per person while hiking.

Permits are required for climbing Mauna Loa, and can be obtained at the park's visitor center. Permits are free and issued on a first-come basis no earlier than noon on the day before your climb. Cabins are shared by all permitees. A total of eight persons is allowed at Red Hill Cabin, twelve at the Mauna Loa Cabin; stays are limited to three nights per site. Both cabins have bunks and mattresses for the prescribed number of people, attached water catchment tanks, and pit toilets. Check the status of the water level at the cabins when obtaining your permit, and be sure to pick up a free trail map. Water found along the route or from the tanks at the cabins should be boiled or treated before drinking.

Trail markings on Mauna Loa consist of rock cairns placed prominently along the route. Sometimes the trail disappears entirely, and you will be dependent upon these cairns. For this reason it is important to always keep the next marker in view. Since these cairns are made from the same black lava as the rest of the mountain, it can be almost impossible to see them at night, so be sure you start your day early enough to reach your destination before dark. Snow in the winter months can obscure the trail, as well as any dangerous cracks and fissures that might be present. Use extra caution so as not to lose the trail in such conditions.

It is critically important to remain on the trail on Mauna Loa. Hikers have been seriously injured breaking through unstable lava crust in off-trail locations, and one hiker who left the trail to examine a distant snow field has never been found. The mountain is so huge and so featureless that disorientation is a real danger if you stray far from the trail. If this happens to you, and you cannot find the trail, make your way cautiously downhill, detouring around areas that appear fragile, broken up, or otherwise unstable. Yours will be a long, slow trip, but if you have the clothing and equipment described above and don't panic, you will make it down. If night comes while you are still on the mountain, stop, find a sheltered spot if you can, get in your sleeping bag, and wait until daylight. Under no circumstances should you try to travel at night.

It is possible to experience altitude sickness on Mauna Loa, al-

though the long, slow approach from the park and the overnight at
Red Hill Cabin should allow your body sufficient time to acclimate
to the thinner air on the mountain. Headache and nausea are common occurrences, and can be treated with aspirin or a similar medication. With sudden or prolonged exertion, shortness of breath
and perhaps a slight dizziness can be expected. More serious symptoms, such as severe nausea, disorientation, or chest pain, require
immediate descent.

SUGGESTED ITINERARY: I suggest you allow four days, as follows, for this trip: one day to hike to Red Hill Cabin, one day from
there to the Summit Cabin, a day free to explore the summit, and
a day to hike to the end of the trail at the weather observatory. The
details of this trip are outlined below.

Day 1—Trailhead to Red Hill Cabin (7.5 miles). Whether you
are coming from Hilo or Kona, or overnighting in the park, you will
need to drive to the junction of Highway 11 and Mauna Loa Road,
about 2.5 miles west of the national park entrance. Note that you
do not need to enter the park or pay the entry fee unless you need
to pick up your permit at the visitor center. The Mauna Loa Road
winds its way 13.5 miles to the trailhead. After passing Kipuka
Puaulu, the road enters a pretty upland forest where *koa* trees predominate. Although paved all the way, this road becomes narrow
and winding, and one-way in places, with several blind turns. Go
slowly and honk your horn at the worst spots. The road ends at
6,662 feet at a picnic shelter and lookout; the trail begins here.
There is a small parking lot and pit toilets, but no water. Red Hill
Cabin, at Puu Ulaula, lies 7.5 miles ahead, at 10,025 feet.

The first part of the trail is relatively level, making its way over
2,000-year-old, reddish-brown lava flows. After an hour or so of
walking you should have come about two miles; you'll be at about
7,500 feet. You will have left the forest behind, and it is at this point
that remaining vegetation decreases sharply. In another hour you
will be at about 8,200 feet, the vegetation line, where the last *ohia*
trees disappear. Just before the 5-mile mark (2.5 hours), you will
have your first glimpse of your destination. Puu Ulaula, a prominent reddish-brown spatter cone, can be seen 2 miles to the north-

west. You are now at 8,900 feet. The cabin, which lies at the cone's western base, does not become visible until you are almost upon it. The trail now follows a collapsed lava tube, and finally crosses onto the rust red lava flows of Puu Ulaula, where the cabin finally comes into view.

Puu Ulaula gets it color and its name ("Red Hill" in English) from the iron content of the lava oxidized by years of weathering. A short climb to Puu Ulaula's peak affords a fine view over most of the island, including Puu O'o, the source of Kilauea's current eruption. A stone platform at the peak has a plaque citing major points of interest. If you watch and listen around dusk, you may hear and see hoary bats, one of only two native Hawaiian land mammals, flying about.

Day 2—Red Hill to Mauna Loa Cabin (11.6 miles). Your destination today is 13,250 feet, and the Mauna Loa Cabin on the rim of the crater. Plan to leave early for this long hike, with its 3,225-foot altitude gain. Expect to feel the effects of exertion more than you normally would, especially as you go higher on the mountain. This is not altitude sickness, but a natural reaction to reduced oxygen intake. Be sure to pack out your trash as you leave Red Hill Cabin.

As the trail leaves the rust-colored lava of Puu Ulaula, you will feel as if you are entering a world of black. It will soon be apparent, though, that lava comes in many different colors—during the day you will see a variety of shades: brown, red, green, gold, and blue. After 2.6 miles, the trail crosses onto the 1984 lava flow, the most recent eruption. You will now be at 10,970 feet; you will cross this 1984 flow two more times. After 4 miles you'll reach a cone formed by an eruption on July 4th, 1899, two months after the Battle of Manila Bay in the Spanish-American War. If the sign is still there, it will tell you that this is Dewey Cone, named in honor of Commodore George Dewey, the victor in that battle. You will now be at 11,320 feet.

A water hole is located about 100 feet south of the trail, in a collapsed lava tube at the 11,845-foot level, 5.6 miles into the hike. However, if the sign along the trail is missing, it will be almost impossible to find the hole. After hiking 9.5 miles (about 5 hours), you will reach North Pit, a large crater now filled with lava from the 1984 flow. Elevation at the crater is 13,000 feet. This is your first view of Mokuaweoweo, the immense caldera of Mauna Loa. Jaggar's Cave, a small pit with an overhanging ledge, was used for shelter by volcanologist Thomas Jaggar during his observation trips to the crater, and by hikers to the summit before the cabin was built in 1930. If you follow the direction of the sign, Jaggar's Cave is less than 400 feet away.

Be careful when reading the signs here. Do not take the trail to the *summit,* but to the *cabin* (they lie on opposite sides of the crater). The cabin is now two miles ahead, the longest 2 miles in the state—or maybe it just seems that way. You may be able to pick out two large rock cairns off in the distance on the eastern wall of the caldera, on your left; they are not far from the cabin. The trail drops to the floor of North Pit, crosses its eastern side, passes the sheer drop into Lua Poholo on the left, and then makes its way to the top of the caldera wall. The cabin, set back from the caldera rim about 100 feet, is in a spectacular setting. Even the outhouse has a fantastic view.

If there is a water shortage in the cabin's catchment tank, there is a water hole, marked by a large cairn, about a quarter mile south of the cabin. It is possible to see the cairn from the window in the cabin's kitchen. I have always found water here, although it might be frozen in winter. When the sun goes down the temperature will fall rapidly, possibly dropping to as low as 10 degrees Fahrenheit. Step outside anyway. You have never seen the night sky as you will see it from here. This is one of the few places in the northern hemisphere where the Southern Cross is visible. Look for it on the southern horizon in late spring. On a clear night you can see the glow of Hilo's lights to the east, and the summit of Mauna Kea to the north. It is easy to get the feeling that you are not on Earth, but rather somewhere in outer space.

Day 3. This is a day to relax and explore the summit area. First, take a good look at Mokuaweoweo. This huge caldera is more than 3 miles long, a mile and a half across, and 600 feet deep. Its floor is now covered to a depth of 6 feet by lava from the 1984 eruption. The cairn at the caldera edge in front of the cabin was put there by the Wilkes expedition of 1841, and just south of the cabin are remains of the rock walls built as windbreaks for the group's tents. On the opposite (west) side of the caldera, you can see the summit of the mountain at 13,677 feet. A possibility for this exploration day is a 9.5-mile round-trip hike to the summit, on the other side of the caldera. But you can save nearly half this distance by making the summit hike en route to the observatory on your descent tomorrow.

The path leading south from the cabin soon forks. (The left fork is the beginning of the Ainapo Trail, which will be discussed later.) Take the right fork and continue south along the caldera rim. About 1.7 miles from the cabin you will reach South Pit, a deep cut in its wall joining it to the main caldera. Lava from the 1984 eruption spilled into the south end of the pit and beyond. Two additional pit craters, Lua Hohonu and Lua Hou, lie a quarter-mile and a half-mile, respectively, south of South Pit. The 1984 flows barely missed Lua Hohonu, nor did they enter Lua Hou.

Another option is to descend into Mokuaweoweo Crater by climbing down a steep rockslide roughly parallel to the water hole, and exploring its still steaming floor. According to Stuart Ball, in *Backpacking Trips in Hawaii,* it is possible to cross the crater floor and climb out via the 1949 cinder cone (I have not done this). You could then turn right and hike along the rim to the summit cairn, and return to the cabin by way of the Summit Trail and the Cabin Trail. This would be a great adventure, but keep in mind that the altitude will take its toll on you during the uphill portions of the trip, particularly the ascent from the crater floor.

Day 4—Mauna Loa Cabin to Mauna Loa Weather Observatory (6 miles). This downhill hike, which should take about 3 hours, leads you to the opposite side of the mountain, where the trail ends at 11,000 feet. If you plan a side trip to the summit cairn, add 5.2 miles (round-trip) and 3 more hours.

You begin by retracing your route back through North Pit to the intersection of the summit and observatory trails. From there it is 3.8 miles to the observatory and 2.6 miles to the summit. Continuing toward the observatory, the trail crosses a rough Jeep road, used for access to the former location of the weather observatory.

You are at 12,860 feet. In just over another 0.5 miles the trail intersects the Jeep road again, this time following it for about a quarter of a mile before turning off to the left. Watch for a small sign marked "Trail." You are now at 12,425 feet.

After leaving the Jeep road the trail virtually disappears, and the route, marked by rock cairns, continues over smooth black boulders. Watch for two large cairns positioned near a wide, collapsed lava tube. At this point you are at 11,800 feet, with a mile and a half to go: You will now be able to see the white dome of the weather observatory. After you have gone a total of 4.7 miles (2.6 miles from the start of the observatory trail) you will cross the Jeep road for the last time. You are now at 11,685 feet. The trail ends at the Jeep road, at which point you turn right and enter the parking lot where, hopefully, your ride is waiting.

ALTERNATE DESCENT VIA THE AINAPO TRAIL:
(18.2 miles, 1–2 days)

The Ainapo Trail was the path used by ancient Hawaiians to climb Mauna Loa; Ainapo was the main route up the mountain until construction of the Mauna Loa Trail in 1915. The first ascent of the volcano by a Westerner was made along this trail when Archibald Menzies, the surgeon of the Vancouver expedition, made the climb in 1794. After the Mauna Loa Trail was built, the Ainapo slowly fell into disuse, and portions of it disappeared. State Forestry and Wildlife crews reestablished the trail in 1993. At that time, a new trail shelter, about midway between the summit and Highway 11, was constructed.

You must have a permit if you plan to overnight on the trail, and camping is only permitted at the shelter. (This permit is in addition to the one required from the National Park for use of the cabins on the Mauna Loa Trail.) You may make reservations for use of the Ainapo Shelter not earlier than one month in advance by calling 933-4221. The written permit may then be obtained from the Forestry and Wildlife office at 1648 Kilauea Avenue, Hilo, HI 96720. Although the descent can be made in one long, downhill slog (providing your knees are up to it), a more enjoyable trip can be had by overnighting at the Ainapo Shelter. It is also possible to ascend the mountain via the Ainapo Trail, but because it is considerably steeper than the Mauna Loa Trail route, the Ainapo descent makes for an easier, quicker trip.

It is 7.5 miles from the summit to the Ainapo Shelter, which lies at 7,750-feet elevation. The 5,500-foot descent transits alpine stone desert terrain, devoid of vegetation until the trail reaches lower elevations. The shelter is a fully enclosed cabin containing six bunks with mattresses and a table with six stools. Water, which should be treated before drinking, is available from a catchment tank, and a clean, odorless composting toilet is on the cabin's porch. A separate structure even houses a stall shower and a dish-washing area. It is 2.7 miles from the shelter to the lower end of the trail, which passes first through a subalpine shrub/*ohia* forest, then a mesic *koa/ohia* forest. The trailhead is marked by a gate at the entrance to the Kapapala Forest Reserve at an elevation of 5,650 feet. Here, you can be picked up by a four-wheel-drive vehicle, if you make the arrangements, saving an additional 8-mile hike to the highway.

If you continue on foot, an additional 2.3 miles will bring you to another gate, which marks the end of the forest reserve. Beyond the gate lies private land belonging to Kapapala Ranch, from which the state has obtained a right-of-way for access to the Ainapo Trail-head. This access applies during daylight hours only, and deviation from the access corridor constitutes trespassing. At this point, you should have another 5.7 more miles to go before you reach the end of the trek. On your way down, you will pass the Ainapo ranch house and two corrals before reaching Highway 11 midway be-tween mile markers 40 and 41.

Finally, if you would like to make the Mauna Loa Backpack with a group, the Sierra Club usually offers the trip among its annual outings, which often include hikes to other features of the island such as the coastal area loop mentioned in the next section. You could thus enjoy two adventures for the price of one. For more in-formation, write: Sierra Club Outings Dept., 85 Second Street, San Francisco, CA 94105; phone 415-923-0636.

Hawaii Volcanoes Coastal Loop

Except for the portion along the Chain of Craters Road, the coastal area of the national park is seldom visited. For the most part the area has been left to occasional backpackers and a few sturdy day hikers. At first appearance it may seem that there is good reason for this isolation, for this is stark landscape, dry and windswept, with scant vegetation and little protection from the elements. Despite over 30 miles of coastline, only a few locations permit entry into the refreshing cool of the sea. But these sites are jewels, oases in a desert of hard, black rock. And sweeping views of dark cliffs against a bright blue sea create a wild, unforgettable beauty.

This little-traveled part of the park lies southwest of the Chain of Craters Road. A brief glance at the Coastal & East Rift Backcountry strip map, which can be obtained free from the Visitor Center, will show that many itineraries are possible over its seven connecting trails. Several loop trips are possible, but, as is usually the case, the best itineraries are those where you can be dropped off at one point and picked up at another. Overnight stops are possible at five locations. All of these except Apua Point have shelter of some sort, with additional tent camping permitted. Each site has a pit toilet, and all but Apua have catchment water, which should be boiled or treated before drinking. A free permit, required for overnight stays, is available at the visitor center. Be sure to check on the water level in the catchment tanks where you will be staying. Also pick up the free map of the coastal area trail system.

Pepeiao Cabin contains three beds, three extra foam mattresses, a table, and counter space. Located in a thinly forested *kipuka* at about 1,700 feet, it is the only overnight site not situated on the coast. Kaaha, Halape, and Keauhou have identical three-sided roofed shelters with gravel floors and simple outdoor grills. But beware: All three campsites have healthy roach and ant populations, which may make you decide to opt for a tent. Of the three, only Halape and Keauhou afford access to the ocean; Halape is the nicer and safer of the two.

The itinerary below is designed to show you the best features of this striking, lonely coast. You can also use the free strip map mentioned below to plan your own shorter or longer trip.

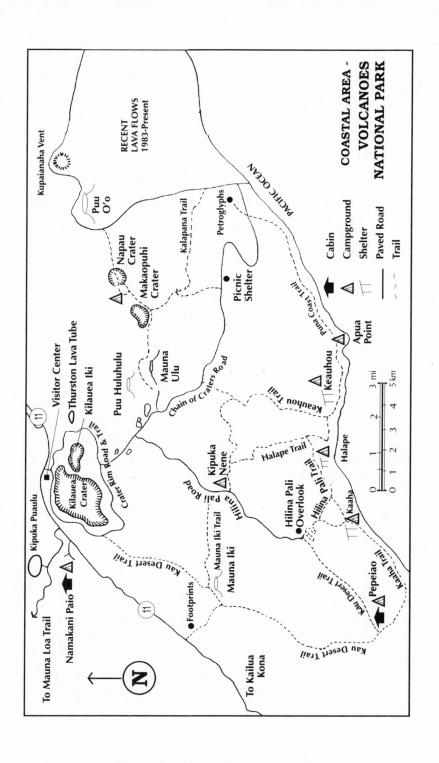

COASTAL AREA -
VOLCANOES
NATIONAL PARK

Kipuka Nene–Pepeiao–Halape–Kipuka Nene Loop (27.6 miles, 3 days; moderate to strenuous)

Maps: USGS topo quads—Kau Desert, Makaopuhi Crater, Naliikakani Point. Trails Illustrated Topo Map, Hawaii Volcanoes National Park. Coastal & East Rift Backcountry strip map (free handout at park).

This trip drops from 2,900 feet to sea level, and then makes its way back up again, passing spectacular, if stark, scenery. The trek's only drawback is the beginning 3.4-mile walk on the road to Hilina Pali. If you have a nonhiking driver, you can be dropped off at Hilina Pali, saving the road walk. Kipuka Nene, the start and end of the hike, is a drive-in campground, with a pavilion, picnic tables, rest rooms, and catchment water.

Day 1–Kipuka Nene to Pepeiao Cabin (8.2 miles). Park at Kipuka Nene and continue on foot on the Hilina Pali Road to the overlook, about 3.4 miles. Two trails begin there, the Hilina Pali and the Kau Desert Trail. Make sure you take the Kau Desert Trail, which veers off to the right. The trail descends gradually for the next 4.8 miles, passing through meadows and thin forest, and over old lava flows. Shortly after Pepeiao Cabin comes into view, you will reach a junction with the Kaaha Trail, where a left turn brings you to the cabin. The Kaaha Trail was formerly known as the Kalue Trail, and you may find signs for one or the other; rest assured, however, that they are the same trail. The cabin sits in an attractive clearing with a few trees nearby. Other hikers have been bothered by ants and roaches here, but I have never found either in the cabin as long as the screen door is kept closed.

Day 2—Pepeiao Cabin to Halape Shelter (12.2 miles). As you leave the cabin on the Kaaha Trail, vegetation becomes more sparse as the trail descends toward the sea. When the trail enters a rugged *a'a* flow the descent steepens, and footing becomes tricky on the loose rubble. From here on it is sometimes difficult to distinguish the cairns marking the trail, so take extra care in looking for them: The problem is that some of the natural lava formations in this area look very much like cairns. At the bottom of the *pali* the trail turns northeast and follows the sea. This is a rugged coastline, with waves crashing against low lava cliffs. The prominent hill on the coast to your front is Puu Kaone, which lies between Kaaha and Halape, and which you will pass behind tomorrow. Attention is required to stay on the trail, which meanders over alternating *a'a, pahoehoe,* and dusty sand. Just after the trail turns inland toward a sharp cliff, you will reach Kaaha Shelter, a good place to stop for lunch. Water should be available from the catchment tank, and you can cool off by stretching out in the shallow, water-filled depression about a quarter of a mile seaward of the shelter.

Resuming the hike, the trail proceeds uphill from the shelter and soon forks. Take the right fork, which intersects the Hilina Pali Trail after 1.4 miles. The footing is more even here than on yesterday's trip, at least relatively speaking, but the trail is sometimes obscured by tall grass. Three miles farther on, you reach an intersection with the Halape Trail. A right turn will bring you to the Halape Shelter in less than an hour.

Halape is a stunning change from the landscape of the past two days. Its small, crescent-shaped cove is the only white sand beach for miles, and young palms and milo trees offer shady campsites directly on the beach. Swimming is safe in the relatively shallow cove, and in the open ocean when conditions are calm, but strong currents are possible any time of the year. Halape was struck by a severe earthquake in 1975, which caused a collapse of the shoreline, killing two campers. Dead palm trunks offshore still provide a grim reminder of that event.

Day 3—Halape to Kipuka Nene (7.2 miles). Since this is a relatively short day, you might want to take a side trip to Keauhou Shelter, a 3.2 mile round-trip. Keauhou is second only to Halape as a scenic oasis on this otherwise barren coast. Instead of a single white sand beach, at Keauhou a rocky point is dotted with small, gray sand pocket beaches within a shallow inlet. But the beach here lacks Halape's shade, and the inlet is too shallow for swimming, though snorkeling is good. As with Halape, caution should be exercised in the open ocean.

Today's hike is all uphill, regaining the 2,900 feet lost at the beginning of the trip. The first 1.6 miles retrace the route to the junction of the Hilina Pali Trail, and then the Halape Trail rises steeply as it zigzags over the Puueo Pali. A wide, grassy lava plain, sloping upward, leads to a series of terraces divided by steep scrambles. A wire fence parallels the route on this section. The foot trail turns into an old, overgrown Jeep track, and soon thereafter intersects a larger dirt road. Turn left and proceed through the dry upland forest for two more miles to Kipuka Nene.

VARIATIONS: A study of the park's Coastal District map will suggest many variations of the above trip, so only a few will be mentioned here. The above hike may be shortened by one day by taking the Hilina Pali Trail instead of the Kau Desert Trail at Hilina Pali Overlook, and proceeding directly to Halape, rather than overnighting at Pepeiao Cabin. This route also bypasses Kaaha, and increases the first day's distance to 11.4 miles. Hilina Pali Overlook may also be used as the base of a shorter loop, which takes hikers by Pepeiao Cabin and Kaaha Shelter. Another loop may be made from Kipuka Nene to Halape and Keauhou, with a return via the Keauhou Trail and the road connecting it with Kipuka Nene. And, for those who don't like ups and downs, Keauhou and Halape can be reached by the Puna Coast Trail, which begins at the Puu Loa parking area. It is a flat, relatively uninteresting 11.3 miles one way.

(The Sierra Club sponsors an annual backpack trip into the coastal area, often in conjunction with a Mauna Loa excursion. For details, see the end of the Mauna Loa section.)

Mauna Ulu to the Sea (18.2 miles, 2–3 days; moderate)

Maps: USGS topo quads—Makaopuhi Crater, Volcano, Kalapana. Trails Illustrated Topo Map, Hawaii Volcanoes National Park. Coastal & East Rift Backcountry strip map (free handout at park).

This trip affords a great introduction to the moonscape lava terrain of Kilauea's east rift zone—massive lava flows, steaming fissures, huge craters, plus a unique exploration of Puu O'o, the source of much of the current volcanic activity. No map or guide issued by the Park Service will tell you how to reach Puu O'o.

Special Note: Between the time of the completion of the writing and this book's publication, lava flows closed the lower end of the Kalapana Trail, making it impossible to complete this hike. But even if the Kalapana Trail is closed, this trip is more than worthwhile because most of the spectacular scenery is on the first portion of the route, and you still have the opportunity to hike to Puu O'o. In the event that you make the trip while Kalapana is closed, you can exit via the Naulu Trail (see Day Hikes, later in this chapter), or return via the same route if you only have one vehicle.

Because this is such a varied hike and because the landscape is so dramatic and unusual, the trail will probably be rebuilt once the current phase of Kilauea's eruption ceases. For that reason I am leaving the trip in the book, even though the volcano has been in constant eruption since 1983. Pele has to get tired someday.

This trip requires either two vehicles, or someone to pick you up at the trail's end. Although it can conceivably be made in one long day, there is so much of interest along the way that a single day would not do it justice. Traversing more varied landscape than any other in the park, this hike crosses huge lava fields, skirts giant craters, enters thick rain forests, and finally descends over wide, grassy slopes to the sea.

You will need a camping permit, which can be obtained at no charge from the visitor center, where you should also pick up the free trail map of the coastal district. Inquire as to where the trail currently ends while you are there. Note that there is no water anywhere on this trail; you will have to pack it all in.

Day 1—Mauna Ulu to Napau Crater via the Napau Trail (7 miles). To reach the trailhead, take the Chain of Craters Road to the turnoff for Mauna Ulu, 7 miles from the visitor center. Park at the far end of the parking lot. (If you are using two vehicles, position the other wherever the Kalapana Trailhead is resurrected, somewhere near the end of the Chain of Craters Road.) Walk toward Mauna Ulu, looming in front of you. You will be walking on a remnant of an older Chain of Craters Road, covered by Mauna Ulu's 1969–1973 eruptions. Watch for the trailhead on the left. At its start, the trail crosses a lava field containing many tree molds, some of which still have the burned-out trunks of trees lying nearby.

Peer inside the molds carefully to avoid damaging them, and you will see the impressions the trees left as the molten lava surrounded them.

In about a mile, you'll reach Puu Huluhulu, a swaybacked green knoll surrounded by lava. Take the path to the top for a look into its crater, as well as sweeping views of lava fields, distant forests, Mauna Ulu, and steaming Puu O'o, the source of the current volcanic activity, which you will explore tomorrow. Be sure to climb Puu Huluhulu if you are lucky enough to be there when Puu O'o is fountaining. Descending the hill, the trail continues in an arc around Mauna Ulu and then climbs a smaller dome on its eastern flank. The lava turns from black to reddish brown as the trail follows a line of steaming fissures.

Descending once more to black lava fields, you'll advance right to the rim of Makaopuhi Crater, the largest crater in Kilauea's East Rift Zone. The trail skirts the south rim of the crater and then enters a forest, with the crater's edge still on the left. Watch for the Kalapana Trail junction coming in on the right. The sign may read "To Naulu Trail" or "To Kalapana Trail": in any event, this is the only other trail in the vicinity. Note the spot; you will return to it tomorrow. From this point it is two more miles to Napau Crater, the end of the day's hike.

Before you reach Napau Crater, you will come to the ruins of a former *pulu* factory. *Pulu* is the downy fiber found in the *hapuu*, or tree fern. For a brief period in the mid-1800s *pulu* was used as a filler for pillows and mattresses, and this factory was established in the middle of a thriving fern forest to harvest the *pulu*. Once it was discovered that *pulu* disintegrated after a few years, its use was discontinued, and the fern was saved from probable extinction.

Not too far from the factory, a sign on the trail points to the left to Napau Campsite. For now, stay on the main trail and proceed to the rim of Napau Crater, its huge expanse framed by steaming Puu O'o nearly 3 miles away. Then return to the campsite to find a suitable place for your tent. Much of the ground is uneven, sloping, and jagged enough to ruin most tent floors. Interpret the boundaries of the campsite liberally, and choose a comfortable location.

Day 2—Hike to and Explore Puu O'o (6 miles round-trip). (If you are making this trip in two days, you can do this hike on Day 1 after setting up camp, or before leaving on Day 2). The route to Puu O'o is over relatively new lava, which can be unstable. Its surface is often a thin crust that can break under a hiker's tread, causing your foot to drop as much as 8 inches or even more. Long pants may provide some protection here. The trail is poorly defined and unmaintained, but it is important to stay on it wherever possible, as it gives some assurance that it has supported hikers who have preceded you. Although most of the activity has moved farther east, Puu O'o is still active, and lava might flow or fountain from its vent at any time. Exercise care around any active lava flows, steaming vents, or areas of intense heat, and be ready to beat a hasty retreat if Madame Pele begins to act up.

Take the trail through the campsite to a wide lava flow at the edge of the campground. Turn right on the flow, following the line of rock cairns. When you reach the rim of Napau Crater, descend to its floor over a steep *a'a* flow. Look for a faint trail, marked by small cairns, that crosses the crater and then exits between two small cones. Once you're out of the crater, the trail will begin to climb. When you reach a fork, bear right. You will pass some banked lava to the left, and then go through a jumbled mass of broken lava before beginning a gradual descent to Puu O'o. Just before the base of the cone the trail will disappear, and you are on your own—reread the warnings in the previous paragraph. Return to the campground via the same route.

In November 1992, Puu O'o was the scene of a drama worthy of an Indiana Jones movie. On that day a helicopter containing a camera crew filming shots for the Paramount film *Sliver* lost power and plunged into Puu O'o's steaming crater. Though the hapless photographers huddled on the rim of a lava lake for two days, a daring rescue effort by another helicopter finally succeeded in lifting the crew out of the maw of the volcano (the pilot had climbed to safety earlier). Even the downed helicopter was later recovered.

Day 3—Napau Crater to the Sea at Lae Apuki via the Kalapana Trail (11.2 miles). Begin today's hike by returning to the trail and retracing your steps to the junction of the Kalapana Trail. Turn left and you'll soon enter a deep forest of giant tree ferns and other rain forest plants. Watch for orange metal tabs, which mark the trail on this section, on trees. After 1.2 miles the trail leaves the forest, at which point the Naulu Trail begins. This is a confusing junction, so be careful to take the correct route. (If the Kalapana Trail is closed, you will need to exit via the Naulu Trail—See Day Hikes in this chapter.) Both trails go over paved remnants of the old Chain of Craters Road at this point, the Naulu heading south to the present road and the Kalapana veering east (left). Make sure to stay on the Kalapana.

The route now alternates between forest and open areas, the open spaces often covered by tall grasses and large stands of *uluhe,* a native fern that can make going difficult. More colored tabs on trees mark the forested parts of the route. About 3 miles past the Naulu Trail junction, the ocean comes temporarily into view, and the route begins to drop steeply. The trail enters a dense forest and then emerges in sweeping fields of grass, which continue all the way to the trail's end at the road (which is also now the end of the Chain of Craters Road, thanks to the lava flows). If you have time, and if you have not been here before, explore this area, especially if lava is flowing into the sea nearby, as it frequently does (see "New Coastal Lava Flows" in the Day Hikes section of this chapter).

Waimanu Valley (16 miles round-trip, 3 days; strenuous)
Maps: USGS topo quads—Kukuihaele, Honokane.

This hike crosses picturesque Waipio Valley, ascends its north wall, and traverses a lovely coastal forest that ends in a beautiful, isolated valley. Waimanu is a miniature version of Waipio, except that it is uninhabited, so it is possible to explore its reaches. Much of the valley floor is wetland, and five major waterfalls keep it that way. The largest of these, complete with a wonderful pool, is only an hour's hike from the campsite.

A permit, required to camp in Waimanu, can be obtained from the Division of Forestry and Wildlife, 1643 Kilauea Avenue, Hilo, HI 96720; phone 933-4221. The number of permits issued is limited, and specific campsites are assigned to each party. The maximum stay is 3 nights. Reservations are made on a first-come basis no earlier than one month in advance.

This trip begins from Waipio Valley Lookout, about 50 miles north of Hilo. Driving north on Highway 19, turn onto Route 240 at Honokaa, and follow the route to the end of the road. The lookout provides one of the most dramatic views in the islands. An emerald green valley enclosed by sheer, thousand-foot walls, a mile-long black sand beach, and a bright blue sea all combine to make an unforgettable picture. Note the long switchback on the opposite wall of the valley: It is the start of the Muliwai Trail, which you will follow to Waimanu. Park at the small lot, or, if it is full, along the side of the road. The road from the lookout down to the valley floor is for four-wheel-drive vehicles only. Its 25 percent grade is well beyond the braking and transmission capacities of conventional vehicles.

Day 1—Waipio Lookout to Waimanu Valley (8.5 miles). As you walk down the road, give way to all vehicle traffic in both directions. When you reach the valley floor, turn a sharp right on the dirt road toward the sea and follow it to Waipio Stream, which enters the ocean. Observe the stream carefully before deciding where to cross. If the water is high and flowing rapidly, it is usually easiest to cross at the mouth, where the stream meets the sea. The stream is shallower there, and its force is dissipated. If the stream is flowing strongly, try the ponded area just behind the beach, but test it without your pack to make sure it is not too deep. Even so, you will probably have to carry your pack over your head. Heavy rains farther up the valley can make the stream impassable; do not cross the stream if it appears unsafe to do so. High water sometimes abates in a few hours. It is worth waiting rather than risking a dangerous crossing. A stout stick is always a good aid when crossing a swift-flowing stream.

Once across the stream, a trail just within the treeline heads for the opposite valley wall and is a better choice for hiking—especially with a backpack—than the soft sand of the beach. When you reach the forest at the base of the wall, watch for a fork in the trail. Normally there is a Forestry sign there, but it is sometimes vandalized. If this is the case, the metal pole may be standing; if so, take the trail indicated by the pole. Otherwise, choose the trail that seems to go uphill (to the right). If you make a mistake, it will be obvious soon enough. The wrong trail leads to the back of Waipio Valley, while the switchbacks on the correct trail begin almost immediately.

The trail soon breaks out into the open, where the advantage of an early start soon becomes evident as the sun bears down. It is hard, hot going, but the footing is firm and the views are spectacular. Within forty-five minutes to an hour you'll reach the welcome shade of a cool ironwood forest where there's also an abundance of huge eucalyptus, monkey pod, and Norfolk Island pine. The trail levels out, and remains fairly level until the descent into Waimanu. About twenty minutes after reaching the forest, and just after the second stream crossing, you will come to a delightful pool, with a small waterfall, directly off the trail on the left. This is the perfect place for a dip to cool off from the climb, followed by lunch.

The trail continues to wind its way in and out of a series of gulches (fourteen in all), and crosses several small streams. A two-hour trek from the lunch pool brings you to a roofed, open-sided trail shelter with a wood floor. It measures about 17×25 feet, and has a high bench along one side, which could be used for cooking or sleeping. Since you are now within 2 hours of Waimanu, I do not recommend you overnight here, unless bad weather or other problems force you to do so. Three more gulches, requiring another forty-five minutes, and you should reach the top of Waimanu Valley, which appears through the trees on your right. From there it is an hour and fifteen minutes to the valley floor.

The path into Waimanu requires caution. Many small, loose stones make footing difficult, and the trail is subject to washouts. At the bottom you'll have one more stream to cross. Again, choose your crossing site carefully, and do not cross if the stream seems too high. You are permitted to camp on the near side of the stream, if necessary, until the water level recedes, and then proceed to your designated campsite. The campsites stretch along a black sand and boulder beach, in a wooded rise between the beach and a marsh. There are ten marked tenting sites, each of which has a rustic fireplace. Two composting pit toilets provide sanitation. Water is available from a spring-fed stream descending from the north wall of the valley. To find it, walk to the far end of the beach, watching for a faint trail heading up to the valley along the north wall. You will reach a small, rushing stream in about ten minutes. Even though its source is a spring, the water should be treated before use.

Day 2. This day is for relaxing, exploring the beach and the valley, and hiking to Waiilikahi Falls. Depending on the time of year, there may or may not be a sandy beach. Swim in the ocean only if you can find a sandy entrance, and then only if the water is calm. Entering or exiting the water over the boulders can cause injury even under medium wave conditions. You can explore the valley from trails on either side, but they both peter out quickly and you will have to make your own way. Expect to get wet. The front of the valley is mostly wetland, which dries out as the land rises toward the head wall. Marijuana was grown in the upper reaches in the 70s and 80s, and some may still be there.

To get to Waiilikahi Falls, about 2.3 miles away, start on the trail leading to the water source. Cross the stream, watching for faint signs of the trail that follows the base of the valley wall. It will soon become hard to see, but ribbons tied to trees help mark the route. If you lose sight of the ribbons, stay close to the valley wall, and you will reach the pool at the base of the falls. The water plunges into the pool with a sheer drop of 320 feet. Be sure to take a refreshing swim. It is possible to explore farther up the valley, but, as already noted, there will be no paths to guide your way.

Day 3—Return to Waipio Valley Lookout.

Day Hikes

Day-hiking opportunities on the island of Hawaii are probably more varied than in any other area of comparable size in the country. Hike an active volcano more than 13,000 feet high, or descend into the crater of another one. Walk across misty lava plateaus hundreds of years old, or onto flows so new their surfaces still radiate the heat of their eruptions. Climb up an alpine peak or down a steep canyon wall. Trek over deserts where plants struggle to survive and into rain forests where they prosper in jumbled profusion. All of this and more is possible in an area smaller than the state of Connecticut. The best of these adventures is described below.

Hawaii Volcanoes National Park

Although lava—and you will see plenty of it—is its main attraction, day hikes in this park also include coastal beaches, dusty deserts, and rain forests.

CRATER RIM TRAIL: (11.6-mile loop, 6–7 hours; easy)

Maps: USGS topo quads—Kilauea Crater, Volcano. Trails Illustrated, Hawaii Volcanoes National Park.

This trip is second only to the "Mauna Ulu to the Sea" backpack excursion for variety of scenery, landscape, and vegetation. Completely encircling both Kilauea caldera and Kilauea Iki, this trail features forest paths, desert sands, and lava tracks, steaming bluffs and deep craters, and a walk-through lava tube. It begins at Volcano House, across from the visitor center, but if you are staying at Kilauea Military Camp (KMC), or camping at Namakani Paio, you may start at either of those two locations. This itinerary begins and ends at Volcano House.

From the visitor center, cross the road to Volcano House and walk through the lobby to the terrace for a spectacular view overlooking Kilauea Crater. With the crater on your left, walk to the end of the terrace and the hotel grounds, where a hiker symbol marks the beginning of the trail. The path is paved here, and descends into a forest of trees, ferns, and ginger. As you proceed, watch for signs to the observatory and Jaggar Museum. Your first two turns should be to the right, after which your direction will be pretty straightforward. The path is no longer paved, and it soon begins to follow the crater rim, with more great views. You'll pass the Steaming Bluffs, and a little over 2 miles from the start you'll reach the Volcano Observatory and Jaggar Museum. You can either stop now or see it another time, but there is a good view here of Halemaumau, Kilauea's fire pit.

Leaving the observatory, the forest begins to thin out, and the ground underfoot takes on a sandy quality. After 1.4 miles, the Kau Desert Trail branches off to the right. Stay left, and the trail soon crosses a large surface crack. This is the beginning of Kilauea's Southwest Rift. At about 1.4 miles from the Kau Desert Trail junction, the Halemaumau Trail comes in from the left. You are now standing on the lava flow of 1982, the latest activity at Kilauea's summit. You have a choice here of making an extra 1.5-mile round-trip to the fire pit overlook, or saving it for another hike or visit by car. About a mile and a half beyond the Halemaumau Trail junction the route skirts the edge of Keanakakoi Crater, and just over half a mile later it crosses Chain of Craters Road.

The forest deepens now, with tree ferns and large *ohia* trees the predominant vegetation. Nearly two miles from the road crossing, the trail intersects a dirt "Escape Road" and turns left, joining this road to the Thurston Lava Tube. This is a good opportunity to visit the quarter-mile loop through an illuminated lava tunnel, unless you want to have more time (and a flashlight) to explore its inner reaches. To resume the hike, cross the road (Crater Rim Drive) and the parking area to the paved path on the opposite side. Turn left, and follow the pavement a short distance until it enters the trees and begins a stepped descent. For the next mile and a half the trail hugs the rim of Kilauea Iki, offering dramatic, drop-off views into its crater. It also crosses the former Waldron Ledge Lookout, where most of the road and the parking lot plunged into the crater during an earthquake in 1983. The trail follows this road remnant a short distance, and takes you back to Volcano House.

KILAUEA IKI LOOP: (5.7 miles, 3–4 hours; moderate)
Maps: USGS topo quads—Kilauea Crater, Volcano.

One of the most interesting trips in the park, this half-day excursion begins at Volcano House, crosses a corner of Kilauea Crater, traverses the floor of Kilauea Iki (Little Kilauea), emerges at the Thurston Lava Tube, and then joins the Crater Rim Trail to return to the starting point. It begins at the same point as the previous trip, at the trail sign to the right of the Volcano House (as you face it from the road). Descend on the same paved path, but bear left at the sign for Halemaumau Trail. You are now descending into Kilauea Crater through a lush forest that includes native plants, several varieties of ginger and ferns, and *ohia* trees. Watch for several large fissures just off the trail, which are almost hidden by vegetation, a perfect example of just how dangerous off-trail hiking can be in a volcanic environment. The large rock fall you will see on your left was caused by a 1983 earthquake; it is part of the Waldron Ledge Road and parking area, which collapsed into the crater. You will cross this site on the return part of the loop.

Near the end of the descent, the crater floor comes into view, and Halemaumau Trail, marked by rock cairns, is clearly visible stretching across the crater floor. Bear left almost immediately from the Halemaumau Trail onto the shorter trail, also marked by cairns, that stays close to the crater wall. Notice that even on this inhospitable lava surface, ferns and even small *ohia* trees have established themselves in the cracks where moisture accumulates. The trail will soon leave the crater floor to ascend Byron Ledge, the divide between Kilauea and its smaller namesake. Follow the signs to Kilauea Iki and Thurston Lava Tube. Lots of *ohelo* berries grow along this section of the trail. *Ohelo,* a relative of both the blueberry and the cranberry, is an orange or red berry that grows on a small shrub. Considered sacred to the goddess Pele, Hawaiians would not eat the berry without first offering some to the goddess of the volcano. In 1824, High Chiefess Kapiolani, a recent convert to Christianity, approached Kilauea and defied Pele by eating the berries without offering any to her. This was taken by many Hawaiians as a sign that the old gods could not stand up to the powerful new one, and the act was considered one more blow to the traditional religion of the islands.

When Kilauea Iki's caldera comes into view, watch for a trail junction on the right, dropping steeply on a stepped, rocky path to the crater floor. The path makes its way first across *a'a* and then *pahoehoe* flows, reaching a pit at the base of Puu Puai, a large cinder cone formed during the eruption of 1959. The pit was the source of a spectacular fountaining eruption in November 1959 that lasted for days and spewed lava a record 1,900 feet into the air. From this point the trail continues across the center of the steaming crater floor. At the far wall, the path climbs through a forest similar to the one at the beginning of the trip, reaching Crater Rim Drive and Thurston Lava Tube. If you have already visited the lava tube, do not cross the road but bear left on the paved path. The trail quickly enters the forest again, and for the next mile and a half it hugs the rim of Kilauea Iki, providing sheer, dramatic views into its crater. The trail then crosses the former Waldron Ledge Lookout, mentioned earlier, where most of the road and the parking lot plunged into the crater during a 1983 earthquake. The trail then follows this road remnant a short distance to Volcano House.

A shorter loop trip (about 4 miles) is possible by parking at Kilauea Iki Overlook, just north of Thurston Lava Tube. From there, you may head in either direction on Crater Rim Trail, descending to the crater floor from either the same trail described here, or at Thurston Lava Tube if you prefer to do the trip in reverse.

MAUNA ULU TO NAPAU CRATER: (12.2 miles, 6–7 hours; moderate)
Maps: USGS topo quads—Makaopuhi Crater, Volcano. Trails Illustrated, Hawaii Volcanoes National Park.

This trip requires either two vehicles or someone to pick you up at trail's end, which is on the Chain of Craters Road across from the Kealakomo Picnic Shelter. If you can't arrange this, you may go back the way you came, which is not a bad option because there is so much to see, and the scenery does look different on the way back. (In that case, the distance covered would be 14 miles.) The route winds around massive Mauna Ulu (Growing Mountain), crosses huge lava fields, skirts giant craters, and passes through thick rain forests. There is no water anywhere on this trail, and I recommend you carry at least two quarts per person. The hike is a shortened version of the Mauna Ulu to the Sea backpack trip in the previous section; please refer to that trip for the first part of this hike, to the Napau Crater, where you may want to stop for lunch.

When you're ready, return to the trail and retrace your steps to the junction with the Kalapana Trail. If you are returning the way you came, keep going. Otherwise, turn left and you'll soon enter a deep forest of giant tree ferns and other rain forest plants. Watch for orange metal tabs, which mark the trail along this section, on the trees. After 1.2 miles, the trail exits the forest, at which point the Naulu Trail begins. This is a confusing junction, so be careful to take the correct route. Both trails go over remnants of the old Chain of Craters Road, the Naulu heading south to the present road, and the Kalapana veering east (left). Make sure you are on the Naulu Trail.

The next 2 miles to the road are mainly over *pahoehoe* lava flows, interspersed with some *a'a* and occasional isolated clumps of trees. The picnic shelter at the end of the trail provides sweeping views over the coastline. A resident mongoose that makes its home below the right seaward corner of the pavilion may appear there to forage for your leftovers.

KIPUKA NENE TO HALAPE BEACH: (14.5 miles round-trip; moderate to strenuous)

Maps: USGS topo quads—Kau Desert, Makaopuhi Crater. Trails Illustrated, Hawaii Volcanoes National Park. Coastal & East Rift Backcountry strip map (free handout at park).

Halape is a stunning oasis in the midst of a black lava landscape, a lovely, palm-lined cove on an otherwise hostile shore. Maybe I think it is so beautiful because it is so unexpected, so out of place, so welcome in this bleak region. As previously mentioned, Halape was ravaged by a 1975 earthquake that killed two campers. The quake caused Halape's shoreline to sink over six feet and destroyed its pretty coconut grove. However, the beach has recovered nicely, and is as attractive as it used to be, only in a different way. Admittedly this is a long day hike, better done as an overnight trip, which I recommend if at all possible.

The hike begins at Kipuka Nene Campground, 10.5 miles from the visitor center on the Hilina Pali Road. A dirt road behind the picnic pavilion leads through a gate, bearing east, first through former pasture land, now mostly molasses grass, and then through a dry, upland forest of *ohia,* guava, and shrubs. After 2 miles, turn right at the junction with another dirt road, which soon turns into a rocky trail. This trail descends over a series of terraces divided by steep scrambles, and for a time it runs parallel with a fence on the left. It then traverses a broad, grassy lava plain, culminating in a steep switchback down the Puueo Pali. Shortly thereafter, the Hilina Pali Trail joins from the right, and another 1.5 miles should bring you to the Halape Shelter. There is nothing to interest you at the shelter except catchment water, which should be treated before you drink it, and an open-air pit toilet. Head for the delightful beach for lunch and a swim. Swimming is safe in the shallow cove and in the open ocean when conditions are calm. If you are like most other visitors to this unique place, when it's time to go back you won't want to leave.

NEW COASTAL LAVA FLOWS

Maps: USGS topo quads—Makaopuhi Crater, Kalapana. Trails Illustrated, Hawaii Volcanoes National Park.

Depending on current activity, visitors are allowed to explore the cooling lava, and can hike over it under certain conditions. Distances will vary, and the hikes are usually fairly easy, though footing is sometimes difficult. If they feel it is safe to do so, park authorities often mark out trails across the lava fields. These trails are not permanent, and they come and go with Pele's whims. Check at the visitor center or with the rangers at the end of the road for the latest flow status. To reach the new flows, and for exploring along the way, please refer to "Chain of Craters Road" in the Adventuring by Car section of this chapter.

Other Day Hikes on the Big Island

KALAPANA LAVA FLOWS: (4 miles round-trip; easy)
Maps: USGS topo quad—Kalapana.

Although the hike described here begins only seven road miles from the New Lava Flows (above) in Hawaii Volcanoes National Park, that road now lies buried under thousands of tons of lava. This excursion requires a 66-mile detour to reach the Kalapana area from the coastal park boundary. It is easier to reach from Hilo or during a tour of the north Puna area (see Adventuring by Car in this chapter). To reach the lava flows, drive south from Hilo on Highway 11 to the junction with Highway 130, about 6 miles. Turn left on 130 and follow it until you reach a barrier where lava flows have covered the road. Park off the road.

Before you start out on the hike described below, there are some things you should keep in mind. New lava is rough and unstable. Although it may appear hard and feel firm underfoot, there is nothing to prevent the crust from breaking, or even the roof of a lava tube from collapsing under your weight. And, although it seems totally useless and probably is, much of this land is still private property—you may be walking over someone's former home, and the land still belongs to him or her. Should you come upon an undamaged house or plot of land, do not trespass on the property, but instead treat it with the same respect as you would the property of any other.

To begin the hike, cross the barrier across the road. You should soon find a rough, bulldozed road approximating the buried highway. If you look seaward, you will see a scattered line of trees in the distance. Head out across the lava field toward the right side of this tree line. You will have to pick your way. The surface is rough and jumbled in places, and you will need to detour around cracks and fissures. Look back from time to time, to establish reference points for your return trip. As you approach the tree line, you will come upon a bus trapped in the lava and the remains of a house, marked by a scorched sink, a refrigerator, and metal roof paneling: heavy objects all, but afloat on an even heavier river of lava.

Upon reaching the tree line you will discover that the lava flows spared a long strip of vegetation along the coastline. This is called a *kipuka*, an island of untouched land surrounded by lava. There are several homes within this *kipuka*, some with cars still parked nearby or swings and seesaws in the yards. Make your way over the raised lava bench, near the right end of the tree line, into the trees. Some searching should reveal a path leading seaward that will take you to a lovely small, sandy cove. Swimming there is safe only on calm days, and then only within the cove itself, but this is a great spot for lunch or for just relaxing. When you are ready, retrace your route, guided by the reference points you picked out earlier.

WAIPIO VALLEY: (2–6 miles, half to full day, depending on activities; strenuous)
Maps: USGS topo quad—Kukuihaele.

For a description and background information about this beautiful valley and directions for getting to it, please see the Adventuring by Car section of this chapter. This hike begins at the Waipio Valley Lookout, one of the most scenic spots in the state. It is not possible for a conventional car to manage the 25 percent grade on the road leading down into the valley, so unless you have a four-wheel-drive vehicle, park at the overlook and proceed on foot. It takes about 20 to 30 minutes for the downhill trip, and 30 to 45 minutes to climb back up. The grade is very steep, as your legs will soon tell you.

Once on the valley floor, turn right to go to the beach, or stay left for an exploration of the near part of the valley. If you choose the valley, the first turn in the road will reveal a magnificent amphitheater side valley, featuring Hiilawe's twin falls making a sheer drop of 1,200 feet. Unfortunately, an irrigation project above the valley uses Hiilawe's water, and sometimes only one of the falls is flowing, sometimes neither. The dirt road meanders by a few houses and rock walls, and crosses two fords where you will get your feet wet. Eventually you will have to retrace your steps. The upper reaches of the valley are fenced off by private property.

As mentioned earlier, in February 1994, two woven sennit caskets containing the remains of ancient Hawaiian high chiefs were stolen from the Bishop Museum in Honolulu. Although the caskets have never been found, evidence suggests that they were taken so that they could be returned to Waipio Valley, the ancestral home of the chiefs, and reburied in a secret place.

Turning toward the coast instead of the valley will bring you to Waipio's windy black sand beach, which is backed by a long grove of ironwood trees. The beach stretches almost a mile to your left, while a boulder-strewn shoreline greets you on the right. The switchback trail you can see ascending the north wall of the valley leads to isolated Waimanu Valley, a backpacking adventure mentioned earlier. If you stand far enough out on the beach you will be able to see a waterfall, plunging over a cliff and into the sea, about half a mile off to the right. You can reach these falls by rock-hopping along the coast. If you opt for this, exercise caution, as some of the rocks, in slide areas, are unstable.

If you prefer the beach, wade Waipio Stream if the water is not high, or follow the pretty path through the ironwoods as far as you like, strolling back along the beach on your return. If you are hardy enough, the ascent of the switchback takes about 50 minutes, reaching a deep forest containing some of the largest Norfolk Island pines, eucalyptus, and monkey pod trees in the islands. If you continue for another 20 minutes or so, you'll cross two small streams, which will bring you to a lovely trailside pool with a small waterfall. This is the perfect place for a dip and lunch before you turn around.

MAUNA LOA SUMMIT FROM THE SADDLE ROAD: (12.8 miles round-trip, 9–12 hours; strenuous)

Maps: USGS topo quads—Kokoolau, Mauna Loa. Trails Illustrated, Hawaii Volcanoes National Park. Mauna Loa Backcountry strip map (free from park).

This is a strenuous hike by anyone's definition. Beginning at the weather observatory in the saddle between Mauna Kea and Mauna Loa at an elevation of 11,000 feet, this trek rises steeply over lava boulders, cinders, and *a'a* and *pahoehoe* fields, reaching Mauna Loa's summit at 13,677 feet. Altitude sickness is a possibility, primarily because of the high start, which gives the body little opportunity to acclimate to the altitude. Despite these disadvantages, this is a dramatic and rewarding hike, providing sweeping views, including a look into the crater of one of the world's largest active volcanoes. And it provides an alternative for those who would like to climb the mountain but cannot spare the three to four days necessary to make the backpack trip from Hawaii Volcanoes National Park. Make sure you carry long pants, a warm windbreaker, and a hat in your pack if you are not wearing them. I do not recommend this hike in the winter months if snow is on the mountain—and it usually is. Snow can obscure the trail, and hide cracks and fissures that can cause serious injury if stepped in unawares, as has happened to hikers in the past.

One difficulty in reaching the trailhead is the previously mentioned problem of most rental car companies not allowing their cars on Saddle Road (Highway 200). Unless you choose to ignore the restriction (some drivers do), I suggest you rent a four-wheel drive from Harper's Car Rental (969-1478), an agency that will permit you to use the Saddle Road. This will also give you the opportunity to drive to the summit of Mauna Kea (see Adventuring by Car in this chapter), in which case you could stay in the cabins at Mauna Kea State Recreation Area. In any event, I recommend staying in the cabins the night before the hike up Mauna Loa. This stopover not only gives you an earlier start, but more important, the cabins are at 6,500 feet, which provides good overnight acclimatization, reducing the possibility of altitude sickness on the climb.

You must get an early start for this hike, preferably at the trailhead no later than 7 A.M. It is long and steep, and the altitude will slow you down. You cannot afford to still be on the mountain after dark, in part because the lower portions of the trail are marked by rock cairns the same black color as the lava on which they stand. They are almost impossible to pick out at night, even with a powerful flashlight, and there is no foot trail impression to follow. If you are starting from Hilo, you should allow yourself 90 minutes to reach that site, or 30 minutes from the state park cabins.

Coming from Hilo, leave the north end of town on Highway 200 and drive for about 25 miles, watching for a small hunter check-in shack on the left. A paved road leads to the right at this same point. Do not take this road, but turn around and head back toward Hilo the same way you came. (I have deliberately taken you too far, since the road you want is hard to see, while the shack is an easy landmark.) Less than half a mile back from the shack there is a large hill on what is now your right; immediately after is a dirt road leading off to your right. Turn here. (If you are coming from Mauna Kea State Recreation Area, or from the Kona side of the island, simply slow down when you spot the shack, then follow the rest of these instructions). Follow this narrow dirt road for about 8.2 miles to several antennas and satellite dishes. Make a sharp right turn, and the road soon becomes paved, though it remains narrow. Another 9 miles brings you to a small parking lot with a weather station above it. A sign guides you a short distance down a rough Jeep road, passing in front of and below the observatory to the trailhead.

The first part of this trail is characterized by boulders and cairns rather than a foot trail. Some of the natural lava formations resemble the cairns, so you will have to watch carefully in order to keep to the trail. (For some reason, this seems more of a problem on the way down.) At 1.2 miles, you cross the same Jeep road you started on, and you will also cross it 2 more times. Incidentally, this road was built in 1951 for access to the original weather observatory, which at the time stood at 13,450 feet. Logistics proved too difficult over this very poor road, and in 1956 the observatory was moved to its present location.

At 1.5 miles, the trail reaches two large cairns that mark a collapsed lava tube at 11,805 feet. This is the last point from which you can see the observatory, and the first place from which you will be able to see it on your return. A small sign, reading simply "Trail," points to the left at 2.2 miles, and less than a quarter of a mile farther you'll meet the Jeep road for the second time. Another "Trail" sign directs you to follow the road for about 0.3 miles to a point just before a locked gate appears across the road, at which point you'll turn off the road to the right marked by a sign and a large cairn. You are now at 12,500 feet.

Here the trail becomes a cinder pathway until it crosses onto a shiny *pahoehoe* flow in about half a mile. At 12,860 feet you'll cross the Jeep road for the last time. You will have now hiked 3.3 miles. Half a mile farther are signs pointing to the Cabin Trail, the Mauna Loa Trail, and the Summit Trail. Make sure you take the Summit Trail, but before you do, move forward a short distance for a view of North Pit and Mokuaweoweo, the immense crater of Mauna Loa that looms before you. Also look for Jaggar's Cave not far off the trail to the right as you face the crater. This shallow pit, reinforced by rock walls, was used as a shelter by volcanologist Jaggar during his overnight stays on the mountain, and by hikers until the summit cabin was built. You will be at 13,020 feet—with 2.6 miles and 650 feet to go.

The trail then follows the western rim of North Pit and then the main crater itself, although the crater is not always in view. But when you finally reach the summit cairn, the entire caldera will stand open before you—3 miles long, a mile and a half across, and 600 feet deep. Mauna Loa's last eruption, which lasted for 21 days, was in March 1984. According to its recent activity cycle, the mountain may erupt at any time, although it normally gives warning of the event. Take time for lunch and a well-earned rest and be sure to sign the log book in the cairn before you leave. But also be sure to start down early enough so as not to get caught on the mountain after dark, which usually happens no later than 6 or 7 P.M.

MAUNA KEA SUMMIT: (8.7 miles up, 6.3 miles [or less] down, 8–10 hours; strenuous)
Maps: USGS topo quad—Mauna Kea.

Mauna Kea, at 13,796 feet, is the highest point in the state, the highest peak in the Pacific, and the highest mountain in the world if measured from its ocean-floor base. For those reasons alone it is a magnet for "peak baggers." But the mountain is a worthwhile climb apart from these statistics. The view from its summit is awesome, and its surreal combination of observatories and cinder cones is unique. For a description of the mountain and its summit, please see "Mauna Kea Summit" in the Adventuring by Car section in this chapter.

As with the previous hike, you will need long pants, a warm windbreaker, and a hat. Even gloves will be welcome.

The trailhead begins at the Onizuka Center for International Astronomy, a small visitor center at 9,300 feet. The center was named for Ellison Onizuka, a native of Hawaii who was one of the astronauts killed in the *Challenger* explosion. Although a foot trail leads up the mountain, a short distance from here, this itinerary uses the road for the climb, and the trail (or a variation of it) on the way down. The trail, steep and alternately rocky and sandy, is more suitable for downhill movement than uphill, and too much time would be spent ascending it to make this a realistic day hike. Also, if you want to make this trip in the winter months the road is your only option, both up and down, as most of the trail will be covered by deep snow.

Like Mauna Loa, this hike requires an early start. You should arrive at the center no later than 7 A.M. As with the Mauna Loa Summit day hike, I recommend you start this trip by overnighting in the cabins at Mauna Kea State Recreation Area. They are only 7.5 miles from the junction at Route 200, and sleeping at 6,500 feet will help your body acclimate to the altitude.

To reach the center from Highway 200, follow the instructions for Mauna Loa (see the preceding section). When you reach the hunter check-in station, turn off the highway onto the good paved road leading directly to Mauna Kea. There is no sign, as casual traffic is not encouraged. The road is steep, but paved all the way. It is 6.3 miles to the center. Park in the lot in front of the building, which will be closed if you are here as early as you should be, although the rest rooms may be open—they are the last you will find; there are no public facilities of any kind on the summit. Before you leave, you may want to walk through the gate at the end of the lot into the sloping field where some small silverswords are growing.

As you begin your trek up the road you will pass several buildings on the right—these are support facilities for observatory personnel. Note the large reddish-brown cinder cone across from the center, as well as the dirt road coming in on the left. You will need to guide on the cone if you return by the trail, and you'll be ending the hike at this road. As you ascend, the trees will soon give way to scrub, grasses, and spikelike plants growing along the shoulders of the road. These are not silverswords but mullein, a biennial weed. A look back at the saddle area reveals green meadows, cinder cones, huge lava fields, and an awesome view of Mauna Loa, its massive profile filling most of the panorama. The pavement ends about a mile from the center, and does not begin again until about a mile from the summit. As you go higher, and as you look back, you will be able to see the outline of the crater on Mauna Loa's summit.

After a series of switchbacks, the road becomes relatively straight, curving now and then and ascending steeply over a broad rock and cinder slope. The high brown hill that you can see in the distance, far ahead and slightly to the right, is the peak. You'll reach the steepest part of the road about a mile before a sharp hairpin turn, which begins the final switchback at the base of the summit cone. You will almost certainly feel the altitude here. Go slowly, breathe deeply, and stop as often as you need to. Just before the hairpin turn look for a trail off to the left, leading around the north (right) side of a large cinder cone. This is an old Jeep track, blocked off by boulders. It is also the end of the Mauna Kea Trail, which you may want to hike on the way down. You will also pass the first observatories here, at a height of about 13,300 feet.

The final climb up the switchback leads you to a plateau on which stand two large observatories. The first building, on the left side of the road, houses the University of Hawaii's 88-inch telescope. On the opposite side of the road and separated from the plateau by a small saddle is Puu Wekiu, the mountain's actual summit. Climb over the guardrail, descend to the saddle, then climb up a path in the cinders (or make your own) to "bag the peak." You may even find a path already existing in the snow. Even if the peak is covered with snow, it is usually possible to reach the summit. There you'll enjoy the highest view in the islands. Lunch will have to be in the lee of one of the buildings where you'll be protected from the wind, which is usually strong. The observatories are not open to visitors, and doors are kept locked. The university building has a small inside viewing room from which you can view its instruments, but there is really not much to see.

For the return trip you have three choices. In descending order of time required they are: retracing your steps on the road; hiking the trail; or following the road, but cutting off the switchbacks by cross-country shortcuts. The weather will be a major factor in which route you choose. If there is snow on the mountain you will be limited to the road, at least until you get below the snow line. By then it will probably be too late to intersect the trail, but you may be able to shortcut the last series of switchbacks. If there is heavy fog, you will not be able to do the switchback shortcuts since you cannot see where you are going, and you would also be better off not using the trail.

No matter which route you take, you should swing by Lake Waiau, which, at 13,020 feet, is the highest lake in Hawaii, and the third highest in the United States. To get to the lake, take the Mauna Kea Trail, which, as you noted on the way up, begins just past the last hairpin turn after descending the summit, and is marked by large boulders blocking the way to vehicles. Follow the trail around the right side of Puu Hau Kea, the large cinder cone, and in about half a mile you'll reach an intersection. Take the right fork and you'll soon reach the lake, which covers about 2 acres and has a maximum depth of 10 feet. Returning to the intersection, proceed straight across the trail if you are descending via the road, which you will re-join in about 0.3 miles. If you are going down the trail, turn right and continue on down.

DESCENDING VIA THE TRAIL: The trail soon begins to descend steeply, and a conglomeration of metal poles and rock cairns mark the route at irregular intervals. After about a mile you'll reach an ancient adze quarry, Keanakakoi, which was in use as early as the fifteenth century. There are many basalt flakes and chips in the area, including partially finished adzes, but please don't take anything. This is part of the Mauna Kea Ice Age Natural Area Preserve, and everything is protected by law. Mauna Kea was the only place in Hawaii where a glacier existed during the Great Ice Age, perhaps as recently as 8,000 years ago.

The trail continues down a wide, barren valley toward a reddish-brown cone, circles its base, and turns toward a smaller cone with a fairly deep crater. Passing to the right of that cone you'll reach an area where a wide view of the saddle opens up for the first time. Soon an indistinct junction appears where the main trail curves to the right, toward a white pole. If you wish to re-join the road, you can now do so, by turning left toward the red pole that marks the less distinct trail leading to the road. On the trail route, there are no more cairns or posts to follow, and you must now guide on the track of the trail itself and the reddish-brown cone near the Oni-zuka Center, which soon comes into view. After crossing the a'a field and a rough ridge, the trail meets a dirt road. Follow this road downhill until it meets the main road.

DESCENDING BY ROAD: This is the fastest way down the moun-tain, shortcutting the switchbacks, but you must have good visi-bility to take advantage of it and you must be reasonably surefooted. This is a "pick and choose" route, in which you make several straight cross-country descents between the switchbacks. Accordingly, you should never leave the road unless you can see the portion of the road below you that you have selected as your next destination. You will be walking steeply downhill, often on loose rock and cinders, and even a routine fall can have nasty conse-quences on the sharp, jagged lava.

The first opportunity for a shortcut comes almost immediately after you leave the summit, and it will save you almost a mile of travel. As the road makes a gradual arc to the right where it drops from the peak, the hairpin turn at the bottom of the summit cone will come into view. This is the spot where the Mauna Kea Trail begins, which you noted on the way up. Select a point on the road near the hairpin turn and "launch" yourself off the road. This is a steep but exhilarating drop, similar to running on a downhill scree slope. You can go as fast or as slow as you want—the slower, the safer. (I would not recommend you do this if the slope is snow covered.) Once back on the road, there is no reason not to visit Lake Waiau. It is a short detour, and there are no more opportunities for shortcuts for another 4 miles. Follow the directions above.

After re-joining the road from Lake Waiau, proceed for about 3.5 miles until you are once more on a series of switchbacks. You are now on your own. How and when to shortcut the switchbacks is entirely up to you. Just remember: Always have another segment of the road below in sight as your goal. And once Hale Pohaku's support buildings come into view, you can use the principle that the shortest distance between two points is a straight line—usually. You will find enough steep gullies and washes to go around to make you wonder.

PUU O'O TRAIL: (14 miles round-trip, 7–8 hours; moderate)
Maps: USGS topo quads—Puu O'o, Upper Piihonua.
This is a very special hike traversing several of the most beautiful and isolated *kipuka* on the islands as it wends its way along the northeastern slope of Mauna Loa at the 6,000-foot level. It is not to be confused with the Puu O'o vent of Kilauea Volcano (which is covered in the Backpacking Adventures section in this chapter). Like the two preceding trips, you must use the Saddle Road (Highway 200) to reach the trailhead. The trail remains relatively level along its entire length; there are no major ups or downs. The trail is in the saddle's "mist belt," which means it can be foggy or raining. While the fog can lend an ethereal quality to the landscape, it may also obscure trail markings, which even under the best conditions are sometimes difficult to see.

The trail gets its name from a nearby large cinder cone on the slopes of Mauna Kea. At one time the trail extended to the town of Volcano, and from there to Keauhou Landing, now a coastal campsite in the national park. Cattle were driven from the Puu O'o Ranch down the trail to Keauhou, where they were swum out to ships and taken to market. Today it is possible to follow the trail farther than I describe in this book, but it is swallowed up in private land before it reaches Volcano. There is some talk at the state level of extending trail access at some future date.

The trailhead is on the left side of the Saddle Road (Highway 200), 22.4 miles from Hilo. As you near that mileage point, slow down and note a Jeep road on the left. This is the Powerline Road, so named because it follows a line of poles no longer in use. Some poles are standing; some are not. You may choose to return on this road, a route that is quicker and more direct than the trail; it will also bring you out on the highway less than a mile from your car. Continue on the highway for 0.8 miles until you see a wooden sign on the left reading "Puu O'o Horse and Foot Trail"; pull off the road and park in the small, rough lava lot. The trail begins on a lichen-covered *a'a* flow, with *ohia*, ferns, *pukiawe,* and *ohelo* the predominant vegetation. If fog is present, the whole setting seems eerie and mysterious. At times the trail is hard to follow. When it crosses the old lava fields the beaten track vanishes, and the small rock cairns are difficult to spot. Watch for colored ribbons—pink, orange, or sometimes blue—on the shrubs.

The trail widens as it passes over the *a'a* flow, and at about the two-mile point a small water-filled crack appears beside the path. The footpath, easy to follow in the forested *kipuka*, continues to be hard to pick out whenever it crosses the intervening lava flows. Keep watching for ribbons and cairns. At just under four miles, the trail enters one of the largest and most beautiful of the *kipuka*, where you are greeted by giant *ohia* and tree ferns and lovely miniature moss-bordered ponds. Look for the rare *akala*, the native raspberry, which grows only in Hawaii. Its berry looks exactly like the normal variety, but much larger, and the bush itself generally has no thorns. Unfortunately, blackberry has begun to intrude here as elsewhere along the trail.

Two more miles will bring you to a soggy meadow crossed by a Jeep track. Soon after entering another large, very wet *kipuka*, the foot trail disappears. Retrace your steps to the Jeep track, turn right on it (or left if you did not enter the *kipuka*), and it will quickly bring you to an intersection with Powerline Road, mentioned earlier. Turn right and proceed until the road is cut by a huge, rough *a'a* flow, from the eruption of 1984. Although the road ends here, the trail has been reconstituted as a rough path, marked by pink and blue ribbons on narrow poles, over the flow. After about a mile on this flow, the trail will once more enter an *ohia* forest. This is as far as you should probably go on a day hike considering you must retrace your steps, which you may do, or you can return via the quicker Powerline Road. If visibility is deteriorating, I recommend you use the road.

CAPTAIN COOK MONUMENT: (4 miles round-trip; moderate)
Maps: USGS topo quad—Honaunau.

This white obelisk stands on the north shore of Kealakekua Bay, south of Kailua–Kona, near the spot where Captain James Cook was killed by the Hawaiians in 1779 in a dispute over a stolen boat. There is an extra benefit to this hike. If you carry a mask and snorkel in your day pack, in addition to a hike with sweeping coastal views you will be able to enjoy one of the best underwater views anywhere in the islands.

From Kailua–Kona take Highway 11 south about 12 miles to the turnoff for Kealakekua Bay. About 50 yards or so from the highway, a rocky dirt road turns off to the right. Make the turn and then pull off and park on the edge of this road. (A good spot is on the left under an avocado tree.) Walk straight down the road for about 50 yards, watching for a Jeep track to the left. Do not enter the gate in front of you; the Jeep track is just before it. Once you identify the Jeep track, you will either be in luck or you won't: If you are in luck, the track will have been recently cleared and will be easy to see. You can then follow it easily downhill, an ascent that features sweeping vistas of the coast until you come to the Cook monument. If you are out of luck, the track will be overgrown with grass and weeds as high as or higher than your head. In this case it will be necessary to push or fight your way through the growth, hoping it doesn't get bad enough to make you turn back.

For about a mile the trail is bordered by tall grasses and vine-choked trees, papaya, mango, and avocado among them. These soon give way to *koa haole,* and then to low grasses and shrubs as the trail passes over old *a'a* flows. You'll have a great view of the coast and the sea, and as you descend you'll begin to see into the head-wall area of Kealakekua Bay on the left. At the bottom of the slope another Jeep trail joins from the right, and you'll walk be-tween rock walls on both sides of the road until you reach the shore-line, where the Jeep track ends.

At the shoreline a poorly defined trail heads left through the woods. Before taking it, however, walk out on the smooth, flat rocks on the shoreline and look for a bronze plaque, sometimes high and dry, sometimes covered in about six inches of water. The plaque will inform you that this is the spot where Cook met his death. It is a monument that few people see or know about. Make your way along the path, keeping the water in view on your right, and you will very quickly come to the white obelisk, the official Cook monument. This is a good spot for lunch—and time to break out the mask and snorkel. You can jump in the water directly from the jetty in front of the monument, but you may have the company of one or two large tour boats from the town of Kailua–Kona, whose snorkelers will join you in the water. The underwater scen-ery is wonderful (see the Snorkeling and Diving section in this chap-ter). Many kinds of fish, coral, and urchins crowd the water, which ranges in depth here from three feet to sheer dropoffs. Don't remove anything from the water here, though, as this is a protected under-water preserve. Relax and enjoy yourself, but allow enough time for your return—it is a long, hot hike—ascending 1,400 feet in 2 miles.

Snorkeling and Diving

The Big Island offers the finest snorkeling and diving in Hawaii, al-most all of it on the Kona coast. Old lava flows that poured into the sea for centuries have created hundreds of submerged caves, un-dersea canyons, and sheer dropoffs. There are no rivers bringing runoff from the land, the weather is almost always fine, visibility is excellent, and there are lots of easy entries to the water. The windward coast, on the other hand, has dozens of streams pouring silt from the cane fields into the ocean, killing coral and clouding visibility. The windward weather is much rainier, and the coastline is mostly rugged and rocky—hazardous to people struggling with tanks and other gear. This is a good time for you to review the warning comments under Snorkeling and Diving in the How to Use this Book section.

There are three locations on the windward side where you *can* snorkel, if you happen to be in the area. Two are in Hilo, James Kealoha Beach Park and Richardson Ocean Center (Leleiwi Beach Park), both accessible by driving east on Kalanianiole Avenue, 2.2 and 3.5 miles, respectively. And there is one place on the windward side that is so marvelous that it is worth a trip in itself. Few guidebooks know of it; no tour buses come calling.

WAI OPAE CORAL POOLS (S): Tucked away on the Puna coast, just south of Cape Kumukahi, are a series of tidal pools that showcase coral that you would normally have to go much deeper to see. Put away your tanks. Coral gardens bloom here in 5 to 10 feet of water, and the smaller varieties of reef fish dart in and out, ignoring your presence. Snorkeling here is like swimming in a tropical aquarium. At no other location in the islands can you see so much coral with so little effort. Some of the ponds are interconnected so you can swim between them, while others require hopping out of the water, taking a few steps and jumping in again.

To reach this unusual spot, drive south from Hilo on Highway 11, turning left at Keeau on Route 130. Stay left again on Highway 137 just past Pahoa, remaining on the road as it makes a sharp right turn before the lighthouse road. After about a mile watch for a straight dirt road to the left named Vacationland Drive. (If the sign for Vacationland Drive is down, take any of the relatively straight dirt roads leading to the left and through the small development near the shore.) Follow this road to the shore, watching for a wide *pahoehoe* flow, in which you should be able to see the nearer, smaller ponds. Waves will be breaking on a reef about 500 yards offshore. Park and walk out on the smooth lava flow—you will be able to see the coral as you walk, it's so close to the surface. Then choose your pond, and dive in.

The remainder of the Puna coast, from the national park to South Point, is mostly inaccessible to the public. Punaluu and Whittington Beach parks are exceptions, but these are not particularly good either as dive or snorkel sites. At least one scuba authority recommends Whittington as a good place to see turtles and big fish, particularly among the piers of the old wharf. But the water is almost always rough and he suggests diving with a shoreline. I have never tried it: Swimming around underwater pilings in rough water trailing a line from shore is more adventure than I need.

The rest of this section is devoted to locations on the Kona coast. The town of Kailua–Kona is a good base for exploration, since it is centered between the northern and southern sites. For convenience I have listed the dive sites in two groups: those north of town, then those to the south.

OLD KONA AIRPORT (D): Now a beach recreation site, divers will find interesting rock formations, coral, and lots of reef fish here. Bigger fish, such as *ulua,* can often be seen out near the edge of the reef, which drops in a coral wall from 60 to about 120 feet. One good entry is from the north end of the runway. Park as close as you can to the end of the lot and look for a cove with a small beach. You can either stay shallow by swimming along the coastline, or head out toward the dropoff, which is fairly close to shore. An easier entry, over a stepped lava shelf, can be made from the south end of the runway. Park at the south end, near the tennis courts, and follow the sandy path to a small inlet where two shelves lead into about eight feet of water. (Note: The slope is deceptive and it is easy to get into deep water quickly.) Rest rooms, showers, and picnic tables are available. To reach the Old Airport, drive north on Kuakini Road, the next road toward the mountains from the King Kamehameha Hotel.

HONOKOHAU HARBOR (S): To avoid boat traffic from the harbor, snorkelers should hug the south coast to reach this area of underwater rock ledges and reef fish. Once in the water, follow the lava point on the left side of the beach, which leads to an area of large underwater rocks. To reach Honokohau, head north from Kailua–Kona on Highway 19, turn left at the sign for Honokohau Harbor (about three miles), and follow the road to a parking area near the harbor entrance on its south side. Walk across the lava flow, looking for a small beach inside the cove almost due south from where you parked. There are rest rooms back at the harbor.

ANAEHOOMALU BAY (S): It is almost always easy to get in the water in this beautiful protected bay, although the water is often murky close to shore. Much of the bay's bottom is sand, with frequent coral heads thrusting upward. Look for sand paths through small reefs, where the fish congregate. To reach the bay, drive north from Kailua–Kona on Highway 19 about 25 miles, turning left at the large Waikoloa Beach Resort–Anaehoomalu Bay entrance. Turn left at the sign for the public beach and park in the large paved lot. The entrance to the beach is straight ahead. Enter anywhere along the sandy beach. Swim left along the shoreline, or head straight out, where visibility is usually better. Rest rooms, showers, and water are available.

MAKAIWA BAY (MAUNA LANI HOTEL) (S): This would be a good diving spot except for a half-mile walk from the parking lot loaded down with diving gear. Driving north from Kailua–Kona on Highway 19, turn at the entrance to the Mauna Lani Hotel, about 27 miles. Make a left turn into a small parking lot, following the signs for shoreline access. From this lot a paved trail leads over an old *pahoehoe* lava flow, featuring several marked archaeological sites, before reaching the Kalahuipuaa Fishponds on the left and the hotel condos on the right. Take the path to the left, along the coastline, around these ancient and still functioning ponds. Where the ponds end, near the south end of the bay, look for a protected cove and enter the water there. Swim to the left along the rocky shore, where you will soon see lots of fish and black lava rocks covered with coral.

PUAKO (D/S): Divers will see the most colorful scenery here, but snorkelers can also enjoy the near-shore seascape. Puako's reef is noted for its close-to-shore caves and arches, as well as plenty of deep-water coral. The underwater landscape is really exceptional here; canyons and tunnels abound. Turtles often come by, and you will find lots of reef fish. Depths can be anywhere from 10 to 120 feet. Puako is a place that you can keep coming back to because you still don't feel you've seen it all. About 30 miles from Kailua–Kona on Highway 19, turn left at the sign for Puako. Follow Puako Beach Road to its end, where a sand road enters the trees and continues for a short distance. Park anywhere along the road, and walk over the rocks to the small cove, a good entry point.

WAIALEA BAY (D/S): Although difficult to get to, this is a good spot for both snorkelers and divers who don't mind a relatively shallow dive of no more than 30 feet. Two separate reefs extend out to sea almost four hundred yards from the beach, yet the depth here is only about 20 feet. Coral heads and lots of fish line the route. Driving north on Highway 19, proceed as to Puako, turning off the highway on Puako Beach Road but making the first right, on the paved but very rough Old Puako Road. At the second dirt road, between telephone poles 69 & 70, turn left on the rough dirt road leading to the beach.

KANEKANAKA POINT (D): This dive is somewhat difficult to get to, but it offers an interesting seabed of arches, ridges, and valleys close to shore. There is an abundance of reef fish, and the bigger ones often come in close to shore. If you are with a mixed party of divers, snorkelers, and swimmers, the group can set up base at the nearby Hapuna Beach (see the next entry), which has rest rooms, showers, and picnic facilities. To reach the dive site, follow the directions above for Waialea Bay, but continue on Old Puako Road to telephone pole 67, where the third left turn heads seaward. Follow the dirt road to its end, overlooking Waialea Bay. Look for a trail leading down the cliff to a small beach. Enter the water at the north end of this beach, snorkel out to the point before submerging, then follow the coastline.

HAPUNA BEACH STATE RECREATION AREA (S): Primarily a swimming and body-surfing spot, Hapuna is the largest white sand beach on the Big Island. Snorkeling is good along the rocky shore at the south end of the beach. The farther out you go, the more coral and fish you will see, but be sure conditions are calm. Hapuna is a good place to spend the day swimming, snorkeling, picnicking, and exploring the beach trail to the north, which leads to lovely Kaunaoa Beach (see the next entry). Divers in the group can go to either Kanekanaka Point or Waialea Bay, both previously mentioned. Hapuna is about 32 miles from Kona on Highway 19. Turn off at the sign for Hapuna, following the road to the parking lot.

KAUNAOA BEACH (S): Snorkeling here can be enjoyed as part of a day at Hapuna Beach (above) or on its own. Kaunaoa is the site of the Mauna Kea Hotel, the oldest of the luxury hotels on the Kohala Coast. The beach can be reached via coastal trail from Hapuna (about 25 minutes), or by driving onto the hotel grounds and parking at the south end of the parking lot in spaces reserved for public access, and then following a path to the south end of the beach. Rest rooms and showers are provided. Mauna Kea Hotel is the next turnoff on Highway 19 after Hapuna, about a mile farther north. The best snorkeling is off the south end of the beach along the rocky point. There are lots of fish there, as well as some small reefs and fairly large coral heads.

SPENCER BEACH COUNTY PARK (S): Ease of entry and a long, shallow coral reef directly offshore are the attractions at Spencer, which also offers rest rooms, showers, drinking water, and picnic and camping facilities. The beach is wide and sandy, with a very gentle shore break, but the water is sometimes murky due to silt and runoff from nearby Kawaihae Harbor. This is a worthwhile snorkel when the water is clear, especially if you are camping here. From Kona, drive north on Highway 19 to the intersection of Highway 270. Turn on 270, then continue for just under a mile to the turnoff on the left for Spencer Beach Park. Enter the water from anywhere on the beach, or from the rocky area below the pavilion.

NORTH KOHALA COAST (D): A cobalt blue sea beckons allur-
ingly along a rocky coast from the town of Kawaihae north to
Lapakahi State Historical Park—there is excellent diving almost
anywhere along the stretch. Caves, arches, trenches, and ledges provide great scenery, hiding places for lobsters, and a backdrop for
game fish such as *ulua*. The problem is finding access to the shoreline, and then a safe entry to the water once you get there. For divers
with a four-wheel drive and a sense of adventure, this is a great
coast to explore. For starters, here are two places that can be
reached with an ordinary car, although a four-wheel drive will
mean less walking.

About a mile north of Kawaihae is an industrial area off the right
side of the highway. A stop sign is located on a road where it joins
the highway from that area. Park off the highway across from the
stop sign and look for a trail leading to a point on the water's edge.
Follow the trail and choose your entry.

Another good spot is Kaiopae Point, about a mile farther north.
Watch for a sign on the highway reading "District of North Kohala." You should see a Jeep track on the ocean side of the road.
Park, and follow the Jeep track to the edge of the cliff, where you
will have to climb down to the rocks below. This sounds like a lot
of effort, but it is worth it. Enter the water and follow the rocks
straight out to sea. You will find caves, ledges, and coral-filled valleys, as well as big fish.

LAPAKAHI STATE HISTORICAL PARK (S): The site of an ancient
fishing village, Lapakahi combines an archaeological experience
with a refreshing snorkel in clear water. Large black boulders containing coral patches are the main feature at Lapakahi, a marine
conservation area. The best place to enter the water is from the
white stone and rubble beach in what remains of the village. Then,
follow the shoreline. The turnoff to the park is on Highway 270,
about 12 miles north of the Highway 19 intersection.

MAHUKONA BEACH COUNTY PARK (D/S): Mahukona was formerly a small port facility operated by the Kohala Sugar Company
to ship its raw sugar. The company stopped using the port in the

late 1950s and the plantation itself ceased production in 1975. This is an "artifact" dive—all kinds of junk litters the bottom of the sea here. Easily visible are a large anchor and anchor chain, railroad wheels, cable—even a sunken ship, complete with boilers and propeller, in 30 feet of water. Maximum depth here is about 60 feet, although most of the dive will be in shallower water. The best place to enter is from the old concrete pier, which is a short walk down the road from the beach park. Once in the water, swim right, toward the north end of the bay. Another possibility is to enter from the rocky shore at the beach park itself, where a reef heads straight out. The Mahukona turnoff is on Highway 270, about 13 miles from the Highway 19 intersection. Rest rooms, showers, and picnic tables can be found at the park.

KAPAA BEACH COUNTY PARK (D/S): Lava ledges, black boulders, and some coral are the key features here. Divers will see more than snorkelers, as the coral and fish get better at the 60-foot drop-off farther out, but this is still a good place for both activities. Entry can be made at a small cove at the south end of the park, or from lava ledges north of the rest rooms. Start at one end and finish at the other. Although there are picnic tables at Kapaa, there is no water. The turnoff for Kapaa is about a mile north of Mahukona.

The following sites are located south of Kona, beginning with those closest to the town.

KAHALUU BEACH PARK (S): This is by far the easiest and safest place to snorkel on the Big Island. Children learn to snorkel here because it is very shallow—2 to 10 feet. The water is crowded with people, yet the fish hang out here in droves. (Don't be put off by all the people standing in knee-deep water. The fish are there, swimming around their ankles.) Even turtles cruise in to graze, and they'll let you swim right along beside them. If someone in your party has never snorkeled before, this is the place to learn, but even experienced snorkelers can enjoy themselves at Kahaluu. Even if you don't own equipment, you can rent it, at reasonable rates, from a van right on the beach.

To reach Kahaluu, drive south from Kailua–Kona on Alii Drive for about 4 miles, watching for the sign to the beach and the parking lot on the right. Rest rooms, showers, drinking water, and picnic tables are available.

KEALAKEKUA BAY (D/S): One of the most historic places in Hawaii, Kealakekua Bay, a marine conservation area, also offers one of the prettiest snorkeling and dive locations in the islands. Kealakekua Bay is the spot where Captain James Cook first came ashore on the Big Island. The white obelisk erected to his memory on the bay also marks a great dive and snorkel site. There is no road to the monument. You reach it either by boat or by renting a kayak at the boat ramp at the bay and paddling across, or via a 2-mile hike (see Day Hikes in this chapter). You may also reach the site by commercial tour boat from Kailua–Kona (see the end of this section). Unless you own or have access to a boat, I recommend the kayak— if you are lucky, a school of porpoises will escort you partway to the monument. And if you plan to dive, the kayak is your only choice as you can't lug your scuba gear up and down the steep, hot trail.

Regardless of how you arrive, enter the water from the small concrete jetty in front of the monument. A rainbow of colors spreads before you: Fish and coral of all types and colors pop up immediately. The gradually sloping ledge quickly leads to a sharp coral-encrusted dropoff of 90 feet, but there is plenty to see along the shallow reef, which reaches depths of 6 to 15 feet. On my most recent trip here I found a whitetip reef shark resting on the bottom of a cave in only 10 feet of water, with weekend snorkelers thrashing all around. Once discovered, the shark patiently, without leaving its lair, tolerated a series of snorkelers diving down and gawking at it. Whitetips are one of the few shark species you will see resting in caves. Unlike most other sharks, it does not need to keep moving to force water through its gills.

To reach the bay, take Highway 11 south from Kailua–Kona about 18 miles to the Kealakekua Bay turnoff. Drive to the shoreline and turn right to the parking area at the end of the road. In case you don't have time to kayak to the monument, a second dive and snorkel site can be accessed by going straight instead of turning right when you reach the water; enter the bay from the boat ramp. Snorkelers should follow the shoreline in either direction, though divers may head straight out. Depth here varies from 5 to 30 feet. A third option for divers is to drive south, in the opposite direction of the beach park on the narrow road, until you reach telephone pole 5. Turn right and drive as far as you can, then look for a good point of entry. Coral, ledges, and fish abound here.

HONAUNAU BAY (D/S): This bay is the site of Puuhonua o Honaunau National Historical Park (see Adventuring by Car in this chapter). The area is well protected all year round. Divers can enter the water from flat lava rocks to the immediate right of the boat ramp, where coral begins immediately in about 12 feet of water; a steep dropoff to 100 feet is not much farther out. Snorkelers will enjoy archways and canyons close to shore, and can also explore the south side of the bay along the park shores. To reach Honaunau, drive south from Kailua–Kona on Highway 11 about 20 miles. Watch for the large sign and wide paved turnoff to the park. Take the road after the park entrance to the boat ramp, and enter the water from a spot along the flat *pahoehoe* flows.

Another place from which to snorkel and dive is the park's picnic area. To reach that spot, drive to the far end of the park's parking lot and follow the small sign to the picnic area. Once you reach the tables, park and select an entry point. Flat *pahoehoe* flows along the shoreline afford easy entries and exits.

HOOKENA BEACH COUNTY PARK (D/S): This location provides an easy dive with lots of ledges, coral heads, large boulders, and reef fish, especially from the lava flows north of the park. There is very limited parking at the beach park, where the south end offers a good place for snorkeling. Watch for the turnoff to Hookena about 20 miles south of Kailua–Kona on Highway 11. Turn left, and if you are diving, proceed 2.3 miles, turning right on a dirt road that leads to the lava flows. Park wherever it looks like you can find a good point of entry. Depths here range from 10 to about 40 feet. If you can't find parking at the beach, this is not a bad place to snorkel. If you do go to the beach, enter the water at its south end, or at the north end near the ruins of the old landing.

MILOLII BEACH PARK (D/S): The small settlement at Milolii is the last working fishing village in the Hawaiian Islands (see Adventuring by Car in this chapter). Considering the myriad other dive options and its out-of-the-way location, it's probably not worthwhile coming to Milolii only to dive or snorkel. But if you are going to be here anyway, say to make the hike to the *holua* (see Adventuring by Car), you might as well bring mask and fins along to cool off afterward. The best entry point is at the beach park near the far end of the village. Climb over the small sea wall and swim south over the shallow rocky ledges. When you reach the dropoff, you can dive if you have tanks, or snorkel along the valleys that taper toward the edge of the reef. Snorkelers will be in 5 feet–plus deep water, while divers can descend over the dropoff to 60 feet. The turnoff to Milolii is about 35 miles south of Kailua–Kona on Highway 11; watch for the sign. It is another 5 miles down a paved but narrow road to the village.

SOUTH POINT (D): This is primarily a "prestige" dive for experienced divers who would like to be able to say they dived the southernmost site in the United States. It is a difficult entry, the bottom close to shore is littered with fishing and boating debris, and there can be strong currents with which to contend. But South Point offers large caves, including some directly under the boat hoists, big fish, and, of course, that brag factor. Make a careful reconnaissance of the point before deciding where to enter the water: One possibility is a small cove north of the navigation light; another is to climb down the rocks east of the last hoisting platform. You might also climb down one of the hoists, if you can handle your equipment on the long steel ladder. The ocean bottom, made up mostly of boulders, starts at 20 feet, but it deepens quickly to 100 feet and more. If the seas are anything but calm here, go somewhere else. To reach South Point, head south from Kailua–Kona on Highway 11 about 53 miles to South Point Road on the right. It is another 10 miles to the end of the road. Park and find the boat hoists on the right (west) side of the point.

SNORKEL AND DIVE BOAT TRIPS: There are many excellent diving areas off the Big Island's Kona coast that can only be reached by boat. If you do not own your own boat, you might want to try some of the interesting commercial ventures listed below. There are many dive operations on the Kailua–Kona coast (eighteen at last count) about which you can find out more from your hotel or a tour agency in Kailua–Kona. These commercial outfits normally provide all equipment, lunch, and, in some cases, even an open bar.

Two boats make daily trips from Kailua–Kona to Kealakekua Bay, the *Fairwinds* and the *Captain Cook VI*. For an unusual dive adventure, you can Swim with the Mantas, make a night snorkel, or dive off the Kona Surf Hotel, where large manta rays are attracted to the area by the hotel's powerful lights. You can enter the relatively shallow water right from the hotel's grounds and see the show free of charge. If you would rather don scuba gear, most of the dive shops in the area offer nightly tours when conditions are right. *The Kona Aggressor* is a luxury live-aboard that plies the Kona coast between Kailua–Kona and South Point, visiting some of the best dive sites. The vessel offers seven-, five-, and four-day tours, and carries a maximum of ten persons.

Surfing

There is some very good surfing on the Big Island—but surfing Hawaii does present some unique challenges. First, surfing areas on the island tend to be far apart. If you find the surf is flat in Hilo but hear it's up in Kailua–Kona, it's a 90-mile drive to confirm that fact. Another problem is access. There are lots of waves on the Big Island that have never been surfed because they are too difficult to reach, or they are fronted by large tracts of private land. Then there is Madame Pele. In 1990, lava flows obliterated two of the best surfing areas on the island, Drainpipes and Kaimu, and the community of Kalapana was left without a surfing spot. It turned out not to matter much, because a short time later the residents of Kalapana were left without a community as well. Today, Kalapana and its surfing areas are just a wistful memory. If you don't live on the Big Island, surfing there makes the most sense if you plan it in connection with other activities. Come for the volcano—but bring your board along.

Leeward Coast Surfing Areas

On the Kona coast the boards are in action year-round. Ideal off-shore winds make for good conditions any time, except during kona storms—those that come from the southwest. South swells in the summer bring good tubes, and west and northwest swells assure powerful walls in winter. While the Kona coast does not have the consistency of Oahu's wave height, when a major swell does arrive it provides fine surfing. There are three surfing areas in or near the town of Kailua–Kona, and several minor ones to the south. A unique feature of leeward surfing is the schools of tropical fish that glide beneath your board in the crystal-clear water while you're waiting for a wave.

Honls (also known as Haddos) (S/L/B) is an excellent small-wave spot, offering both left and right breaks as the waves hit the reef. Honls is usually crowded at high tide; when the tide is low, the reef can be dangerous. Honls is located just south of the Hilton Hotel on Alii Drive.

Banyans (S/L/B) is considered the best surfing spot on the Big Island. Left breaks give the best rides in summer, while rights dominate in the winter. (A shallow reef requires caution riding rights at low tide.) Surfers coming to the Big Island to avoid the crowds and the hassles of Oahu will not be happy at Banyans. Surf bullies are known to hog all the good waves, sending the easily intimidated ashore. As you might infer, Banyans is named for a large tree near the entry point, which is behind the Kona Bali Kai condominium, 76-6246 Alii Drive.

Lymans (S/L/B) is of interest in summer primarily to beginners and intermediates perfecting their skills. Winter provides challenging waves for the more experienced surfer. Left breaks are best then. A shallow reef off Kamoa Point requires caution. Lymans is located about 0.4 miles south of Banyans on the north side of Kamoa Point.

Three fair surf spots well south of town will take you far from the crowds. *Kealakekua Bay* has two spots which work best during south swells. *Hookena* has left-breaking waves during the summer. *Milolii* has right and left breaks during south swells.

Windward Coast Surfing Areas

The best windward surfing is found at *Honolii Beach Park* (S/L/B), just north of Hilo. This is a beautiful arena, one of the prettiest surfing areas anywhere. Although there are breaks all year, and summer waves are fun, winter surf at Honolii is for experienced surfers only. In November 1994, a surfer died here when high waves knocked him off his board and the currents pulled him out to sea. Honolii offers mostly left breaks, but short rights are possible. Other surfing spots in the Hilo area are much more dependent on conditions than Honolii. *Hilo Bay*, a winter spot, needs a big north swell, and is best with Kona winds. *Three Miles* and *Richardson Bay*, both east of Hilo, are also winter spots that need large north swells.

Farther up the Hamakua Coast, at the end of the road, *Waipio Valley* (S/L/B) is almost a cult spot, surfed by only a few hardy insiders, almost all of them local residents. Waipio has right and left breaks all year round, although much of the winter surf is not rideable. This is one spot where you can be sure of surfing alone or with one or two others at most. The catch is that the road into the valley is for four-wheel-drive vehicles only, and hiking down and back on the road's 25 percent grade is a killer—even without a surfboard.

Windsurfing

No one comes to the Big Island to windsurf: There are far better spots and conditions on Oahu and Maui, or even Kauai. Access to the water is a major problem, and with heavier equipment, sailboarders have even more problems than surfers trying to find places to launch. Rocky coastlines on the windward shore, and the large wind shadows of Mauna Loa and Mauna Kea on the leeward shore, further restrict sailboarding activity. But one of the good things about Big Island sailboarding is that at least there are no crowds.

If you happen to be on Hawaii and would like to test the wind, one place to try is *Anaehoomalu Bay,* 25 miles north of Kailua–Kona on Highway 19. This would be particularly appealing for someone staying at the Sheraton Royal Waikoloa Hotel who wanted to take beginner lessons, which are available at the beach. Boards can also be rented at Anaehoomalu. The water is usually flat, and the sheltering action of the bay keeps the wind at a light 3 to 6 knots. When trade winds are strong, and during kona storms, beginners have to head for the beach, but more experienced sailors will enjoy slalom and chop-jumping action. The Sheraton is the cheapest of the hotels along this expensive coast. There is a fine, oceanfront campground 9 miles north at Spencer Beach County Park; otherwise, it's back to Kailua–Kona.

A true windsurfing adventure can be found at *Kaalualu Bay,* considered by many to be the best sailboarding spot on the Big Island. Intermediate to experienced surfers can have fun here all year round except when big south swells are running. Launching is a water start from a lava ledge. Kaalualu is miles from anywhere, and part of the adventure is getting there. You will need a high-clearance vehicle, such as a four-wheel drive. Although the four-wheel feature is not required, a conventional car will have difficulty at several places on the narrow, rutted dirt road. From either Kailua–Kona or Hilo, drive south on Highway 11 to South Point Road. Go south for 4 miles, then turn left onto unmarked Kipuka Maheo Road. This is a gravel road, just north of the windmill farm, that leaves the highway at about a 45-degree angle. You'll soon reach an unlocked ranch gate, and then another (please close both gates after passing through). After another 4 miles you will reach a T intersection with another dirt road. Turn left and travel half a mile to reach the bay, or go right to a very pretty picnic spot on a small sheltered cove. Weekend windsurfers often camp here. The **Shirakawa Motel** is the only nearby accommodation, about 10 miles back toward Naalehu. Whittington Beach County Park, 2.5 miles east of the town, is a very good oceanfront campground. There is a food store and a small snack bar in Naalehu.

Biking

The main thing to remember when planning a bicycle trip of the Big Island is that it is bigger than all the other Hawaiian Islands combined. Even if you have cycled on Maui, for example, you'll need to keep in mind that Hawaii is over five times larger. Distances between points of interest are greater than on the other islands, and campgrounds are farther apart. Maui has a huge mountain that towers 10,000 feet into the sky; Hawaii has two much bigger mountains, both of them well over 13,000 feet. The Big Island is famous among cyclists for its Ironman, a grueling triathlon held annually in October. Some come to compete, others to test themselves against the route, and still others come simply to watch and have fun. At least two bike touring companies run regular trips on the island.

Except in and around the towns of Hilo, Kailua–Kona, and Waimea, traffic is relatively light, and roads are generally wide and well maintained. Vistas on and above the Kona coast can extend for miles. If the volcano is performing, it can stop your bike in its tracks. The windward side of the island can leave you drenched with rain; the leeward side can soak you with sweat. (Everything about the Big Island is big.) It is ideal for cyclists who enjoy long rides and sweeping views.

Below are three suggested bike tours. The first two visit places of high interest, and the third takes in some of the best scenery that the island has to offer. Following the tours are suggestions for those who wish to plan longer, round-island trips.

Tour 1: Hilo–Kalapana Lava Flows Loop (88 miles round-trip)

This tour of the Puna District passes through some lovely coastal scenery, quiet rain forests, and the volcanic devastation at Kalapana. There is a long, gradual rise from Hilo to the other side of Pahoa, and then a downhill glide to the coast. The route rises again on the return trip, between Kalapana and Pahoa. On the outbound leg, Pahoa is the last stop for food and drink unless you overnight at Kalani Honua (see below), and Lava Trees State Park is the last stop for water.

Please refer to Adventuring by Car (Hilo and Vicinity), earlier in this chapter, for a detailed description of this route, maps, and other important information.

Tour 2: Kilauea Crater Rim Loop (11 miles)

This ride, on a two-lane paved road, completely circles Kilauea Crater in Hawaii Volcanoes National Park, an awesome experience in a landscape unlike any other in the islands. The road must be shared with tour buses and tourists in rental cars, which can be a fair parade, especially on weekends. But this is such an unusual ride that it is worth the trouble. If you are coming to the park from Hilo, it is a 28-mile continuous uphill push, from sea level to an elevation of 4,000 feet, but it is mostly a good, wide road, and traffic diminishes a few miles past the Hilo Airport.

Starting at the visitor center, and turning right (when facing the crater and Volcano House), there is a short downhill, followed by a gradual incline to the observatory and the Jaggar Museum. Then it's a curving, downhill swoop to the Halemaumau Overlook parking lot followed by a long, gradual uphill to Devastation Trail, Thurston Lava Tube, and, finally, back to the visitor center. Please refer to Adventuring by Car ("Hawaii Volcanoes National Park"; "Crater Rim Drive") for detailed route and other information.

Other Rides in Volcanoes National Park

CHAIN OF CRATERS ROAD: (50 miles round-trip)

For cyclists with excellent uphill skills and endurance, this is an outstanding ride, often highlighted by active lava flows plunging into the sea. If the volcanic activity is your main reason for making the trip, be sure to check with the visitor center about the current status of the eruption before you start out—just like the rest of us, Pele occasionally takes a day off. From the time you leave the visitor center, the ride is almost all downhill, dropping from 4,000 feet to sea level in 24 miles. This is a long, exhilarating run with the most sweeping coastal views in the Hawaiian Islands. However, keep in mind that all that downhill soaring must be made up. There are no facilities of any kind on this trip, so bring plenty of water and food. Please refer to Adventuring by Car, "Chain of Craters Road," in this chapter for a description of the route and points of interest along the way.

MAUNA LOA ROAD: This access road for hikers climbing to the summit of Mauna Loa is strictly for uphill fanatics and downhill freaks. It rises 2,600 feet, in a series of switchbacks, in a little over 13 miles. The road is paved all the way, but it is narrow, mostly one-lane, and has many blind curves. Although traffic is minimal, be cautious, especially on the downhill. You will pedal through a pretty, upland forest distinguished by lots of young *koa* trees. There is a fine view from the end of the road, where there is a picnic shelter and pit toilets, but no water.

Tour 3: North Kohala Loop (48 miles)

This trip starts and ends in Waimea, headquarters of the Parker Ranch, the largest privately owned cattle ranch in the United States. More recently, Waimea has also become the support center for the many astronomical activities on Mauna Kea. There is nothing trop-ical about Waimea. Its green hills and rolling pastures proclaim the ranch country that it is. At an elevation of 2,600 feet, Waimea can be a cool, welcome oasis from the hot Kona coast below. There is no food or water available on the outward leg of this trip until Hawi, and none on the return until Kawaihae. There is a long climb at the beginning of the trip, and another at the end.

Riding west from town on Highway 19, turn right on Route 250, toward Hawi. Almost immediately the road will begin to climb; it will continue to do so for the next 6 miles. The road is narrow as it winds through this rolling ranch country, but there is little traffic, and the sweeping views over the coastline are fantastic. As you con-tinue to ride through upcountry ranch land and forests, the road levels out and then begins a long descent that ends when you roll into Hawi. You can replenish your supplies here. At Hawi you have the option of a side trip to Pololu Valley Lookout, at the end of the road (16 additional miles round-trip). It's a nice ride through rural Hawaii, but there is nothing special about it except the lookout, which *is* scenic and quite dramatic. You can camp at nearby Keokea Beach County Park, a very pretty, secluded spot.

If you opt to continue your journey without visiting the lookout, turn west on Highway 270. If you don't mind riding a couple of extra miles on an uneven dirt road, you can visit Mookini Heiau, one of the oldest *heiau* in Hawaii, built in 480 A.D. For directions and information about the *heiau,* and the nearby Kamehameha

Birthing Stones, please see Adventuring by Car, "The Gold Coast to Pololu Valley."

If you continue on Highway 270, in about 5 miles you'll reach Lapakahi State Historical Park, the site of an abandoned fishing village (for a description, see above reference). There are campgrounds nearby, at Kapaa and Mahukona County Beach parks. From Lapahaki to Kawaihae, the road follows miles of dry, uninhabited coastline, with parched grasses and *kiawe* trees the predominant vegetation. The shore is rocky and the sea cobalt blue. Spencer Beach County Park, just past Kawaihae, is one of the best campgrounds on the island, with a large pavilion and a very nice beach. The large *heiau* overlooking the water nearby is Puukohola, one of the most important *heiau* in Hawaiian history. It has a small visitor center. You may want to spend the night at Spencer, but if you don't plan to camp you are ready to undertake the 10-mile, 2,600-foot climb back up to Waimea.

Other Big Island Rides

THE IRONMAN ROUTE: This 112-mile course runs from Kailua–Kona to Hawi via highways 19 and 270, and then returns on the same route. The only reason I can think of to make this trip is to be actually involved in the event. The first 33 miles, between Kailua–Kona and Kawaihae, comprise a hot, boring ride through miles of black, inhospitable lava. There are no trees, no grass—almost no vegetation of any kind to provide relief from the unrelenting black sea of rock. The stretch from Kawaihae to Hawi is better, but you soon hit head winds. You can ride over this section of the route as part of Tour 3, above, but you will be riding downwind. Also, you should note that once you leave Kailua–Kona, the only places to get food or drink are Kawaihae and Hawi.

KAILUA–KONA TO PLACE OF REFUGE: (42 miles round-trip)
This is a pretty trip, through upland coffee country, enhanced by great views of the Kona coast but marred by relatively heavy traffic and narrow stretches of road. Food and drink are available pretty much all along the route, with the exception of the section off

the main highway between Kealakekua Bay and Puuhonua o Honaunau.

The trip begins with a steep uphill climb at the south end of Alii Drive to Highway 11, where a right turn continues the climb for another 2.5 miles. There is fairly heavy traffic, but the road is wide until you near the town of Kealakekua. There the road narrows and there is almost no shoulder, and the traffic does not abate very much. Once you reach the town of Captain Cook, watch for a sign indicating a road on the right to Kealakekua Bay. Bear right and descend the steep hill to the coast, where a right turn brings you to the bay where Captain James Cook dropped anchor and came ashore on the Big Island. Also at the end of the road is the Hikiau Heiau, where Cook was honored upon his arrival. A white obelisk in his memory can be seen across the bay on its northern shore.

After leaving the bay, do not return to Highway 11, but instead strike out across the narrow, paved road that goes south across the lava fields to Puuhonua o Honaunau National Historical Park. (Please see Adventuring by Car, "National Park to Kailua–Kona," in this chapter for a description of this park.) After your visit, take the wide road, that rises steadily uphill for 3.5 miles, to re-join Highway 11, where you turn left for the ride back to Kailua–Kona. Before reaching the highway, you can stop to see St. Benedict's Painted Church. Turn left off the main road and follow the sign a short distance.

CIRCLING THE BIG ISLAND: It is not really possible to completely circle the island of Hawaii, but you can come pretty close. You can circle the south end of the island, but you will need to take a side trip to get to Ka Lae, the island's southernmost point. As for the north end, on the windward side, the road ends at Waipio Valley. Paradoxically, the road on the leeward side also ends on the windward side, bending around the north point of the island from Hawi and ending at Pololu Valley Lookout. In between the two roads is a 12-mile isolated, roadless coastline, where six lush, uninhabited valleys run from the mountains to the sea.

There is no particular advantage to circling the entire island by bicycle. The distance is considerable, and your cycling time can be better used. Also, most of the island's volcanic origin is still very much in evidence, and hours will be spent pedaling through many miles of monotonous lava. One way a circle-island ride may be worthwhile is by exploring along the way, rather than simply racing down the asphalt. Even some of the worst stretches of lava hide secret beaches and tide pools, if you know where to look. In this respect, the Adventuring by Car section of this chapter is a good guide for the cyclist determined to complete a circumnavigation of the island.

MAUNA KEA KAMIKAZE: Finally, taking a page from the long-established downhill run on Haleakala on Maui—and topping it by over 3,500 feet, **Mauna Kea Mountain Bikes** (P.O. Box 44672, Kamuela, HI 96743; phone 885-2091) offers a bus ride to the top of the state's highest peak, followed by what might be the highest downhill bike run in the world. See the Adventuring by Car section of this chapter for a description of the route.

Hunting

You can hunt more species of animals and birds on Hawaii than on any other island. You may hunt goat, pig, feral sheep, and mouflon. There are ample public hunting areas, well spaced throughout the island. Many of them permit daily, year-round hunting of goat and pig with no seasonal limit. At one time a special permit was required to hunt mouflon and feral sheep, the season was short, and the limit was one animal per season. Some years ago a suit was filed by the Sierra Club and others, on behalf of the *palila,* a small, endangered native bird whose habitat was threatened by the sheep feeding heavily on the *mamane* tree. The suit resulted in a court order directing the eradication of mouflon and feral sheep on Mauna Kea (Hunting Area A). Because of this order, a special permit is no longer required, hunting may take place year round, and there is no bag limit. However, feral sheep hunting is also allowed in other areas where restrictions may apply: You will need to check the latest regulations. In some ways, it is sad to see the elimination of mouflon on Mauna Kea. The mouflon is a handsome animal, always imposing as it stands proudly on a ledge high on the mountain. But as an introduced species, one that exists elsewhere, it does not have the importance of our endangered native birds. The *palila* is found nowhere else in the world.

You may hunt fourteen different kinds of bird on Hawaii: ring-necked, green, and Kalij pheasant; California Valley and Japanese quail; Chukar partridge; gray, black, and Erkel's francolin; Indian sandgrouse; barred, spotted, and mourning dove; and wild turkey. With the exception of wild turkey season, the bird hunting season normally lasts from the first Saturday in November through the third Sunday in January, weekends and holidays only. For wild turkey, the season is the first three weekends in January. Although it is in the same general location as the hunting area for mammals, the public bird hunting area is more restricted.

Skiing Mauna Kea

Mention skiing in Hawaii to most people and they think it's a joke. Or they think you are talking about water skiing. But snow skiing on Mauna Kea is no joke. Winter snow on the mountain can provide excellent conditions and long runs. Schussing around the base of giant cinder cones is a unique experience, as is winding in and out among the premier astronomical observatories of the world. If you are a hot-shot, dedicated skier, there may be better places to spend your limited vacation time. But if you like the idea of skiing in the morning and swimming at a tropical beach in the afternoon, or if you are going to be in Hawaii in the winter months anyway, bring your snow skis along—you will not be disappointed.

At 13,796 feet Mauna Kea is the world's highest mountain when measured from its base on the ocean floor. You have probably never skied at this altitude before, and you may feel some adverse effects. Most people experience some shortness of breath when exercising at this altitude, particularly when moving fast or uphill. Some get headaches or a slight feeling of nausea. These are normal occurrences at this elevation, and you can safely take aspirin or whatever painkiller you prefer to alleviate the symptoms. However, if the discomfort persists or gets worse, you may have no choice but to descend the mountain; this is the only cure for altitude sickness.

One way to minimize these effects is by acclimatizing to the altitude. You can do this, at least in part, by staying at Mauna Kea State Recreation Area the night before you go up the mountain. The altitude there is 6,500 feet, and an overnight stay will lessen your chances of problems higher up the mountain. The state offers very reasonably priced cabins there, complete with bedding, kitchen utensils, a heating stove or fireplace, and hot water. This is the best place from which to base your ski trip. Not only is the rec area the closest lodging to the mountain, but by not descending below 6,500 feet your body will continue the acclimatizing process. For reservations, write Division of State Parks, P.O. Box 936, Hilo, HI 96720; phone 961-7200.

Although you will need a four-wheel-drive vehicle to reach the summit of Mauna Kea, you will also need one to use as your "ski lift" (see below), so it will actually do double duty. As mentioned earlier, most car rental companies do not want their cars driven on the Saddle Road (Highway 200), which you must use to get to Mauna Kea. One company that will rent you a four-wheel drive without the restriction is Harper's Car Rental, phone 969-1478. When renting your vehicle, be sure that all members of your party are listed as drivers (see below).

To reach Mauna Kea State Recreation Area from Hilo, take Highway 200 (Saddle Road) west 28 miles, watching for a sign to the park on the right. If you are coming from Kailua–Kona, take Highway 190 north about 33 miles to the junction with Highway 200. Make a sharp right turn, then follow 200 for another 17 miles, watching for a sign to the park on the left.

To reach the summit of Mauna Kea from the Mauna Kea State Recreation Area, take the Saddle Road east toward Hilo about 8 miles until you see a wide paved road on the left. There is no sign, but the road can be identified by a hunter check-in shack on the right side of the highway (There is no other structure for miles.) The road is steep, but paved to the visitor center, at which point the pavement continues for another mile or so and then becomes gravel until about a mile from the summit, where the road is paved once more. You may encounter snow on the road in the summit area, but the road should be open unless you are driving up in a blinding snowstorm—in which case you should turn around.

Once you reach the snow line on the mountain, watch for the lowest point at which the snow is deep enough so that a skier can comfortably ski to the road. This will be the bottom of your "ski lift." As you continue up the mountain, try to pick out the best downhill run—if there are other skiers present, they are probably already on it. (Once you reach the top of the mountain, it is usually best to ski down from the right side of the road as you face downhill, as this normally provides the longest run. However, conditions differ from year to year.) You should now be the top of your "ski lift." To put it into operation, have one member of the group drive down to the snow line, pick up the others, bring them back up; someone else takes over driving for the next run. You now have your own private ski lift, with no lift lines. If you have a large group, Harper's also rents four-wheel-drive pickup trucks, which can carry a lot more people and skis.

Do not come to Hawaii expecting to ski in a bathing suit—Mauna Kea is cold. The average mean low temperature from December to March is 28 degrees and the mean high is 38. A bright sun can make it feel much warmer (wear sun protection); a high wind, much colder (bring a jacket). If you would like to ski the mountain with a congenial group, the Ski Association of Hawaii (1389 Queen Emma Street, Honolulu, HI 96813), maintains a list of its members interested in teaming up with others for skiing on Mauna Kea. At the present time there are no sporting goods stores in Hawaii that sell skis, ski equipment, or clothing, so you will need to bring your own.

Finally, skiing in Hawaii is like anywhere else: it depends on the snow. There are great years, good years, and bad years. If you are coming here mainly to ski, get as much information as you can in advance to avoid disappointment. For most people, it's a long trip to Hawaii's ski slopes.

CHAPTER FOUR

Maui
House of the Sun

LONGTIME RESIDENTS of Maui will tell you that the place has
gone to hell. There are too many hotels, too many cars, and too
many tourists. And, after a drive from Kahului through Lahaina to
the Kaanapali coast, you might well agree. Oahu, with 80 percent
of Hawaii's population and with most of the state's tourist traffic,
has more undeveloped sandy beachfront than Maui. Yet despite
all the waterfront hotels and condos, Maui still has many miles of
unspoiled beaches and shoreline—and its interior is almost all
wilderness. Real adventures are waiting on Maui; you just have to
know where to find them.

Maui is the second youngest island of the Hawaiian chain, its age
estimated to be between 800,000 and 1.3 million years. Its 729
square miles make it the second largest of the main islands, though
it was once much larger: At one time the island of Maui also included the now separate islands of Molokai, Lanai, and Kahoolawe
in one large mass that geologists refer to as *Maui Nui* (Big Maui).
Today the island is 48 miles long and 26 miles wide, and the two
volcanoes that gave it birth are its most prominent features. They
separate the island into two distinct geographic divisions: West

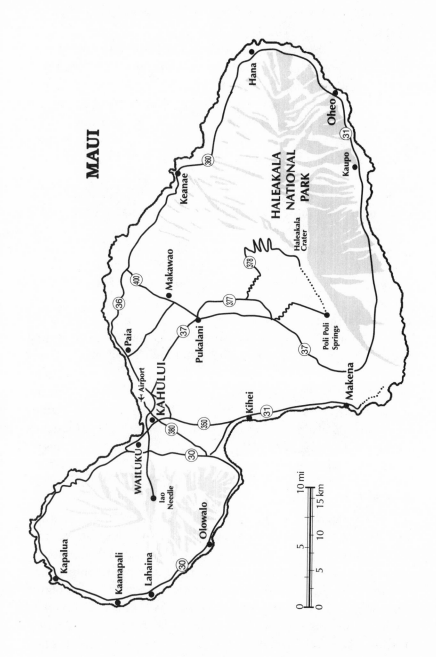

Maui and East Maui. Haleakala, at 10,023 feet, is the island's highest point.

Puu Kukui, West Maui's peak, is one of the wettest spots in the world, with more than 400 inches of rainfall per year. On the other hand, East Maui's summit, Haleakala, rarely receives more than 30 inches of rain in a particular year. Virtually all of Maui's beach resorts are located on the island's leeward side, Kihei and Wailea on East Maui and Kaanapali and Kapalua on West Maui. And although West Maui's favorite tourist town, Lahaina, is leeward, Hana, East Maui's Mecca, is windward.

Maui's main industry, like the other Hawaiian islands, is tourism. Sugar and pineapple are the island's main agricultural crops, and agriculture seems destined to survive here longer than on the other islands. Most of Maui's population of 91,000 people works in either the tourism or agriculture industries, or for state or county offices, which also administer functions for Molokai and Lanai. There is no public transportation on the island, but Trans Hawaiian (877-7303) operates an hourly shuttle service daily (7 A.M.–7 P.M.) from Kahului Airport to the Lahaina-Kaanapali hotels, with a courtesy shuttle north to Kapalua. Hitchhiking is illegal.

Adventuring by Car

Note: This section is designed to be used with a good road map at hand, such as the full-color topographic Map of Maui, University of Hawaii Press, $2.95.

The Hana Highway–South Shore Loop (111 miles, plus travel from Hana)

The Hana Highway is the most popular tour on Maui after Haleakala. In only 52 miles it manages to make over 600 curves, cross 56 one-way bridges, pass numerous waterfalls, and take in an overwhelming amount of beautiful scenery. Unfortunately, most tourists miss the best part of the adventure by driving to Hana and returning on the same day. I always feel sorry for the folks I see who emerge from buses at Hana Beach Park, eat a quick picnic lunch, and then get back on their buses for the long ride back. There is much adventure to be had on this trip along the way, and in side trips from Hana, and you are not going to experience much of it from your car. If at all possible I urge you to stay at least one night in Hana, so that you will have time to do more than simply drive a very demanding road and at the end buy a T-shirt that says "I Survived the Hana Highway." You may have survived it, but you won't have experienced it.

This itinerary allows two nights in Hana, not because there is that much to do in the town itself, but so you'll have ample time to enjoy the side trips that help make the long journey worthwhile. If you cannot spare that much time, modify the itinerary to suit your own schedule.

One of the best adventures on Maui is to continue around the south end of the island from Hana, on Highway 31, through Kaupo, rather than drive back the way you came. Some car rental companies do not want you to do this, except in a four-wheel-drive vehicle. This restriction is a holdover from the days when the road between Kipahulu and Kaupo was in poor condition—a rocky dirt track frequently closed by washouts. Some years ago, before this road was paved, a torrential rain caused a landslide on the Hana Highway that marooned quite a few touring motorists in Hana, myself included. After two days of unrelenting rain, and no opening of the highway, most people (especially those with planes to catch) elected to attempt the southern route. Despite the weather, all made the trip safely and without incident, including some very low-slung, four-door sedans. Today the entire highway is paved except for a 4-mile stretch at Kaupo. Although narrow and winding, this piece is no worse than the road from Hana to Oheo (Seven Pools), and rental car companies have never restricted that road (if they did, they wouldn't rent many cars).

So, if you plan to take advantage of this great way to complete your Hana adventure, be sure to rent from a company without the restriction, or rent a four-wheel drive. One word of warning: If you should break down along the way, there is little traffic on the road and nowhere to phone for assistance, and it will cost big bucks to get a tow truck out there to bring you back.

The following itinerary assumes you will spend two nights in Hana. If you decide instead to make the round-trip in one day, you can select one or two of the side trips that appeal to you, but you won't be able to spend much time on them. If you intend to return by the same route, rather than continue around the south side of the island, you can take some of the side trips on the way out and some of them on your return. This is a good option if you haven't gotten around the driving restriction.

Day 1—Kahului to Hana (52 miles). To reach the Hana Highway from Kahului, take Highway 36 east from town. You should allow three hours' driving time to Hana, adding in whatever time you spend at stops along the way. You might want to take note of your odometer reading before you leave Kahului. I will refer to various side trips and trailheads by their distance from Kahului, as well as mileage markers when possible.

After first passing the airport, the road crosses extensive sugar cane fields and then follows the ocean. You'll first enter the small town of Paia, its pastel, false-front buildings typical of former plantation towns now trolling for tourist dollars. Three miles past the town is Hookipa Beach Park, a world-famous windsurfing site. If the winds are up, and they usually are, you may want to park and watch the action for a while. At the intersection of Highway 36 and 365, the road becomes Highway 360, the official Hana Highway. Mile-posting signs start over at this point.

Just past the 2-mile marker you will reach Hoolawa Bridge, easily identified as it is a double bridge, with separate oncoming traffic lanes. The mile-long trail to Twin Falls begins at Hoolawa Bridge. This is a pretty spot for lunch and a swim, or from which to gaze at the falls. Park off the road near the red gate located just before where the road crosses the bridge. There is a stile to help you climb over the gate, and a No Trespassing sign to make you wonder if you should. Local residents pay no attention to the sign, and you will meet folks coming and going on the trail. In fact, the first time I was looking for the trail, a policeman directing traffic around a construction site pointed me toward the fence. Once on the other side of the fence, proceed directly down the Jeep road in front of you. At a point 0.4 miles from the gate, a trail to the left leads to a large pool fed by a small waterfall. If time is short and you just want to take a quick dip, you might want to stop here; otherwise, return to the road, which soon fords a stream. Shortly after reaching a clearing, faint trails branch off to the left and right. Go straight ahead, and the trail makes a slight turn to the right and then reaches an irrigation ditch. Follow the path along the ditch until you reach the first waterfall. A trail on the right side of the pool leads to a group of second smaller falls. Even on weekdays you will probably not be alone here as this is a popular spot. You may also encounter skinny dippers either at the falls or at the first pool.

Stop next at Waikamoi Ridge Trail Nature Walk, a loop trail a little over a mile long that gives a good glimpse of the rain forest upslope of the highway. Between mile posts 9 and 10 there is a large turnout on the right side of the road, just below the ridge. A turnstile at the beginning of the forested slope marks the trailhead. The trail leads up to a lookout covered by tall eucalyptus and paperbark trees. From the lookout you may make a loop, return to your car, ending with a walk of about 0.3 miles, or you can continue up the ridge through a small bamboo forest to a second lookout and picnic area. You can return via the Jeep road for a round-trip of 1.2 miles. Since much of the land upslope of the highway is in private hands, Waikamoi offers one of the few opportunities to walk in the rain forest, although there are no native plants in this particular location.

Just a short distance from Waikamoi, at mile marker 11, the highway crosses Puohokamoa Stream, where two waterfalls tumble into a pool that can be seen from the road. There is a small pullout, with a picnic area, just before the bridge. A very short trail leads through dense overhanging vegetation to the pool and a picnic table, this one covered but missing its benches at my last visit. If you have the time to explore, a trail from the left side of the pool leads to an upper falls. Another 1.2 miles down the highway is Kaumahina State Wayside, a rest stop with drinking water, rest rooms, and picnic tables. Note the attractive plantings near the rest rooms, and take a few minutes to walk to the lookout for a fine view of the Keanae Peninsula. You will be about halfway to Hana, and the best scenery—and the slowest part of the road—lie ahead.

At the 16-mile marker (30 miles from Wailuku), the state maintains Keanae Arboretum, a free botanical garden featuring dozens of tropical plants, shrubs, and trees. There is a whole section of palms, and one dedicated to plants introduced by the original Hawaiian settlers, including functioning taro paddies. There is also an upper section of the arboretum, accessible by a rough trail, devoted to native and introduced rain forest plants. There are no rest rooms or drinking water available. Just around the curve from the arboretum you will come to a white bridge with a pretty pool below it. There is a gravel pullout on the right, and a short trail descends to the pool just before crossing the bridge. This is a good spot for a dip. After you return to the highway, watch carefully for the Wailua Wayside Overlook, 0.4 miles past the turnoff to the town of Keanae. Park and take the very short trail through the *hau*, for a long view of the Koolau Gap, a huge, ancient lava path now completely covered by vegetation. The nearby staircase leads to a sweeping view of the coast and Keanae Peninsula.

Waterfalls are the main attraction on the next section of the road, which runs between Keanae and Puaakaa. Drive slowly and watch carefully, as some of them appear suddenly and very close to the highway.

Puaakaa State Wayside, at milepost 22, is a perfect spot to stop for lunch if you get an early start; it's also a wonderful place to just relax and swim at one of two little pools connected by the small falls. Picnic tables, rest rooms, and drinking water are provided. This spot, including the pools, is practically *on* the highway, yet it feels secluded. This is the last stop on this itinerary before Hana. Watch for the sign to Waianapanapa State Park, off to your left; you will be returning there to continue your adventure tomorrow. For now, unless you are camping here or staying in the cabins, drive on into Hana. I am assuming that you have had a full day, and are now ready for a break.

Places to Stay. There are no hotels or B&Bs along the Hana Highway. If you want to overnight en route, your only choice is to bunk in a dormitory at the YMCA's Camp Keanae (242-9007), a little over halfway to Hana. This is not an attractive option. The dorms, one for each sex, are small, narrow rooms, with bunks and nothing else. If at all possible you should overnight in Hana (which includes Waianapanapa). Hana is the ideal base for the things to see and do that are described in the next section.

If money is no object, the premier hotel in Hana is the **Hotel Hana Maui** (248-8211), which offers plush rooms, cozy cottages, and large bungalows overlooking the ocean. **Heavenly Hana Inn** (248-8442) has a very attractive Japanese-style setting on the highway about a mile north of town. Prices are not cheap, but they are much less than those at the Hana Maui. **Aloha Cottages** (248-8420) features five two-bedroom units on a hillside overlooking Hana Bay, complete with kitchens and baths. **Hana Kai Resort** provides studio and one-bedroom units in a lush setting on a rocky beach; its rates are fairly high. For B&Bs in the Hana area, or elsewhere on Maui, contact **Bed & Breakfast Maui Style** (879-7865), or refer to the *HVB Accommodations Guide*.

Camping options around Hana are fairly limited. Waianapanapa State Park, about 3 miles north of town, has low-cost state cabins and a free campground. See Appendix III for cabin reservations and camping permits. The only other place to camp in the Hana area is Oheo Gulch, the coastal portion of Haleakala National Park. Located 10 slow, winding miles south of town, Oheo is an alternative primarily for those wanting to spend more time exploring the Oheo area, or as an overnight stop en route around the south end of the island. The campground has toilets, but no drinking water. Camping is free and a permit is not required, but a stay is limited to 3 nights.

Unless you are staying at the Hana Maui Hotel, accommodations with a kitchen are important in Hana. Only that hotel's restaurant is open every night for dinner, and though the food is gourmet class, it is very expensive. The Hana Ranch Restaurant serves a buffet lunch, but offers dinner only on Fridays and Saturdays. A fast-food style stand at Hana Bay, Tutu's, offers breakfasts and lunch. Two stores in town, the Hasegawa General Store and the Hana Ranch Store, are stocked well enough to keep you cooking good meals for a few days. The original Hasegawa store, well known to old-time Hana travelers, burned down several years ago, and the store now occupies new quarters. This more-modern version is nowhere near as picturesque or as interesting as the old store, though, which stocked everything from matches to machetes.

Day 2—Hana and vicinity. Despite all the hype in the tourist brochures, Hana is a very ordinary small town, much like any other in Hawaii. It has a nice beach park, a small museum, a couple of stores, a luxury hotel and a few other places to stay, and that's about it. The attraction of Hana is its isolation and the things to see and do in the surrounding area. Start your tour by driving to Hana Beach Park on Hana Bay. A short trail from the end of the road leads to a cave where Queen Kaahumanu was born. Kaahumanu, one of the wives of Kamehameha, was regent during the reign of Kamehameha's two successors, and became the most powerful woman in the kingdom. Opposed to Christianity at first, her conversion gave a major boost to the religion's establishment in the islands. At the time of her birth, a war between rival chiefs forced Kaahumanu's mother to hide in the cave.

You can swim at Hana Beach Park, but the water is usually murky and the beach is not particularly attractive. A better choice is either Koki Beach Park or Hamoa Beach, both of them reachable from Haneoo Road, about a mile south of town. The Hotel Hana Maui uses Hamoa for its guests; there are separate facilities for the public. But the best beach of all is Kaihalulu, better known as Red Sand Beach, a secluded, dramatic setting accessible via a narrow trail. Leaving Hana Bay, turn left at the first crossroad, pass the school, and park at the end of the road just before the hotel cottages. On your left as you face the sea is an open grassy field. Walk diagonally across this field, toward the water, until you reach the corner of the hotel fence. A trail leads steeply downhill from this point, then turns left and follows the shoreline. The short trail is narrow and precipitous but it soon reaches a marvelous cove where red cinders have washed from the hillside to form a unique beach. Although the surf is usually rough here, a natural breakwater protects the beach and forms a pool that is usually safe for swimming. Because of its isolation, nudists sometimes frequent this beach.

When you have had your fill of Red Sand Beach, return to the Hana Highway and retrace your route to Waianapanapa State

Park, about three miles north of town. There you will find an over-look over a cove with a black sand beach, segments of an *alaloa* (King's Highway) running north and south, and the Waianapanapa Caves, collapsed lava tubes partially filled with fresh water. (Legend has it that a jealous Hawaiian chief murdered his wife in the upper cave, and sometimes its water turns red as a result.) Stairs leading down allow you to swim in this cave for what is a rather eerie experience. For the more intrepid, a short underwater passage on the left side of the cave leads to inner sections where it is possible to walk and swim, if you have a waterproof flashlight—as well as a spare. The lower cave is also water filled, but its shallow pool is usually stagnant and uninviting.

The black sand beach is accessible by a short path from the picnic area, but swimmers should exercise caution at all times due to strong currents. No attempt to enter the water should be made during periods of high surf. The coastal trail leading south to Hana from the park traverses a dramatic section of the shoreline, and portions of the *alaloa* are clearly visible. The surf pounds thunderously against this coast, often spraying the trail and those hiking it. The trail will take you all the way to Hana (about 3 miles), but there are places where it meanders and becomes hard to follow. Watch carefully for small rock cairns, footprints, and other signs, and if you lose the trail, retrace your steps until you pick it up again.

Another great side trip from Hana is Blue Pool, a freshwater coastal pool fed by a waterfall. Other than local residents, few people know about this lovely spot. From Waianapanapa Park, return to the highway and turn right, toward Kahului. In a little over half a mile you will reach the road to Hana Airport on the right; stay on the highway for another 0.2 miles to Ulaino Road and turn right. After a mile and a half you will reach Kahanu Gardens, worth a visit in its own right.

For now continue past the gardens, either on foot, or, if the weather is dry, you may drive the last 1.4 miles, parking where the road ends at a rocky stream on the coast. Ford the stream and follow the coast north for about 150 yards to one of the prettiest spots on Maui. A lovely pool nestles at the base of a fern-encrusted lava wall. All across this rocky face, water trickles over ledges and through cracks to fall into the deep blue pool below. The temptation to dive in is irresistible.

On your return, you may wish to visit Kahanu Gardens (248-8912), with its more than 120 acres of tropical plantings. Piilanihale Heiau, the largest *heiau* in the Hawaiian Islands, is located on the grounds. There is an admission charge and the gardens are only open on certain days and at specific times. Call for information.

If you have visited all or most of the places on this itinerary, the day should be drawing to a close, and you will welcome a return to your accommodations. Tomorrow another adventure begins.

Day 3—Hana to Ulupalakua Ranch (37 miles). Today you will drive south 10 miles from Hana to Oheo Gulch, still erroneously called "Seven Sacred Pools" on some maps. This is a name apparently invented to attract tourists to the Hana area. The pools were never sacred and there are a good deal more than seven of them. Oheo is part of Haleakala National Park, which runs to the sea via Kipahulu Valley. The entire upper part of the valley is a scientific reserve, closed to the public. For those continuing around the south shore of the island the itinerary will continue; for those returning the way they came on the Hana Highway, the itinerary ends after exploring the Oheo Gulch area. If you are going around the south shore to Ulupalakua, fill your gas tank in Hana and ask the attendant about the condition of the road—sometimes there are washouts. Later you can also check the bulletin board at the ranger station at Oheo, which posts up-to-date information about road conditions.

Shortly after leaving Hana the road becomes narrow and winding. Drive slowly and with care. Despite its condition, the road is heavily traveled. You may have heard that quite a few celebrities own homes and estates along this road. They do, but you will not see them. Almost all of these mansions lie well off the road, protected from curious tourists. About two-thirds of the way to Oheo the road crosses a bridge where Wailua Falls drops behind it into a gorge below. Traffic is likely to jam up here as people try to view or take pictures of the falls where there's little room to pull off the road. If you are able to park, take the short trail just before the bridge to view or swim in the pool at the base of the falls.

You will know you have reached Oheo Gulch when you cross another bridge where a series of pools and small cascading falls appears on both sides of the road. Continue to the parking lot on the left, from which a path leads to the lower pools. On a clear day Mauna Kea and Mauna Loa, on the island of Hawaii, are clearly visible across the Alenuihaha Channel. Swimming in the pools is safe except during periods of heavy rain or very high water, but ocean swimming in this area is dangerous. The two parallel pools closest to the sea have a tunnel connecting them about 8 feet below the surface of the water. If you dive down in whichever pool allows you to look toward the sun, you will see light coming through the tunnel. (If you are a confident underwater swimmer, you can terrify unsuspecting tourists or friends who watch you dive into one pool but don't see you come up in the other.)

Across from the parking lot a trail leads uphill to Makahiku Falls Overlook and Waimoku Falls, and a thrilling side trip swimming up a steep-sided gorge to another lovely falls and a deep, secluded pool (see Day Hikes in this chapter).

Once you've had your fill of the pools, continue your journey from Oheo; in just over a mile, on the left side of the road, you'll see Palapala Hoomau Church, the burial place of Charles A. Lindbergh, the man who made the first trans-Atlantic flight. The famed "Lone Eagle" was a longtime resident of Kipahulu, and personally selected this isolated spot as his last resting place.

At this point those returning via the Hana Highway should turn back. For those continuing on, the next 6 miles to Kaupo require attention. Traffic will be almost nonexistent, but the narrowness of the road requires slow, careful driving. If you do meet another car on this mostly one-way stretch, one of you will more than likely have to back up. Just hope it isn't you. You will, however, see some magnificent coastal scenery on this part of the trip, and pass isolated houses that will make you wonder who lives in this wild place. Four miles after leaving Oheo the pavement ends, and you will be on a rough gravel road for the next 4.5 miles. When you reach Kaupo, you will find its store the sole structure on the highway. The store keeps erratic hours and will probably be closed, but this is a good place to pull over and take a breather. The Kaupo Trail begins about 1.5 miles up the road just east of the store, and ascends 8 miles to Haleakala Crater. Look upslope and you will be able to see Kaupo Gap, a giant rent, in the wall of the crater, that spilled huge lava flows all the way to the coast. You will be driving on those flows for the next 5 miles, continuing to see the gap from different perspectives.

After Kaupo the road is still very narrow for another 2 miles. Then the pavement finally begins again, the road widens, and most drivers breathe a long sigh of relief. When you have driven about 16 miles on the paved road, the highway will curve north; at this point you will have climbed more than 2,000 feet on the flank of the mountain. Stop here for a sweeping view of the ocean and four islands: Molokai to the north; Lanai and Kahoolawe to the west; and the islet of Molokini, close offshore below. Also visible from this point, directly downslope, is the stark landscape of La Perouse

Kaupo Gap as seen from Maui's seldom traveled shore road. Photo by Richard McMahon.

Bay, and the lava fields from the last eruption on Maui, which took place in 1790.

When you reach Ulupalakua Ranch, you have only driven 37 miles from Hana, but it will seem much longer. You may stop and visit the tasting room of the Tedeschi Winery, which produces red and white wines, champagne, and pineapple wine. Until recently this was the only winery in the islands, but another has now opened in Volcano, on the Big Island. This day's itinerary ends with a pretty drive through upcountry Maui, its green pastures rolling toward the sea.

Places to Stay. There are no accommodations between Hana and Ulupalakua Ranch. Since the next itinerary will take you to Haleakala National Park, the ideal arrangement would be for you to overnight somewhere upcountry, especially if you plan an early start to see the sunrise at the summit. **Kula Lodge,** on Route 377 (878-2517), offers chalets with broad views of the island from its perch at 3,200 feet on the slopes of Haleakala. It also has a restaurant with great views. There are several B&Bs in the Kula area; contact **Bed & Breakfast Maui Style** (879-7865), or check the *HVB Accommodations Guide*. Because distances on Maui are not that great, you may also stay in Kahului or any of the West Maui resorts, returning to the mountain the next day or whenever you like.

Haleakala National Park

All of East Maui consists of the giant dormant volcano Haleakala (House of the Sun). Sleepy Hana, the Kula ranch country, and the resorts of Kihei and Wailea all lie on its broad slopes. It was at Haleakala, legend says, that Maui the demigod snared the sun, holding it captive until it agreed to move more slowly across the sky. The park's 28,655 acres reach from the highest point on Maui to the ocean, over 20 miles way. The park includes the entire crater of Haleakala, a massive, dormant volcano that last erupted in 1790. The present crater was caused by erosion rather than volcanic activity, but post-erosional eruptions have restored some of its volcanic appearance. Thirty-six miles of trails cross the crater and the park's coastal section, traversing barren cinder deserts, alpine shrublands, and lush tropical rain forests. If you followed the previous Hana Highway itinerary, you will have already visited Oheo, the Kipahula section of the park, so this part of the book will take you on a tour of the summit and crater sections of the volcano.

A unique feature of Haleakala is the silversword, a beautiful, rare plant that grows nowhere else in the world. A round bundle of silvery gray spikes, the silversword blooms only once in its five- to twenty-year life span—and then dies. The flowers begin to develop in May or June, reaching their peak in July or August. A silversword in bloom is an unforgettable sight. Its bloom, a center spike that can reach as high as 8 feet, is covered with dozens or even hundreds of yellow and reddish-purple flowers. Driven to the point of extinction by voracious herds of goats, the silversword has staged a successful comeback with the fencing of the crater and, thus, the elimination of the goats. Until recent years, it was necessary to hike into the crater to see any silverswords. Now some have been planted at park headquarters, along with the endemic Haleakala geranium, and a few silverswords have taken root in the summit area along the road just below the observation building.

Another rarity you can expect to see in the park is the *nene,* the Hawaiian state bird. The *nene,* an upland goose, is found only in Hawaii. Driven almost to extinction by hunters and animal predators, the bird is now protected and making a slow comeback with the aid of propagation stations, where young geese are raised and then released into the wild. One problem with the program is that *nene* raised in captivity have a low reproductive rate when released; scientists are currently trying to determine whether this is due to predation or some other cause.

If you spent the night in the Kula area, it will take between one and a half and two hours to drive to the summit. If you are starting from Kahului, allow at least two hours; from Kihei or Kaanapali, two and a half to three. If you are planning to take in sunrise at the summit, give yourself more time. Lots of tour buses will be doing the same thing, and there is usually a slowdown as they all line up at the park gate to pay the entry fee. Also, if you get behind the buses on the road, your speed will be reduced considerably, and it is often difficult and dangerous to pass on this very winding road.

Whether starting from Kahului or one of the West Maui resorts, you will begin your ascent of the mountain on Highway 37 since the roads from Lahaina and Kihei funnel into the Kahului area. Shortly after passing through the town of Pukalani (7.2 miles from Kahului), you will come to a well-marked fork in the road; bear left onto Highway 377. Six more miles will bring you to another well-marked fork, where you turn left again on Route 378. It is here that the long, steep switchback up the mountain begins, climbing nearly 8,000 feet in just over 20 miles. One authority has called this the steepest such gradient for motor vehicles in the world. Despite the grade, the drive is not difficult. The road is wide and fully paved, and the curves are banked. Drive slowly enough to enjoy the scenery, which gets better the higher up you venture.

Just about 11 more miles will bring you to the park entrance gate. The fee, good for a week, is $4 per car regardless of the number of passengers. Golden Age and Access Passports are honored. Shortly after the park entrance, a turnoff to the left leads to Hosmer Grove at 6,800 feet, where you'll find a picnic area, a campground, and the trailhead for a half-mile nature loop trail. The trail begins at the lower end of the parking lot, loops through a forest of introduced plants and trees, and returns to the picnic shelter. Many of the plants are labeled, and a trail guide, usually available at the trailhead kiosk, will help you to identify others. The grove was planted in 1910 by forester Ralph Hosmer, who introduced trees from around the world to see if they could be used to start a timber industry. From North America he brought several species of pine, as well as fir, spruce, and cypress. Sugi from Japan, eucalyptus from Australia, and even the deodar from the Himalayas can be found in the grove. Although most of the imported trees took hold, many of them do not grow as well or as fast as in their native lands. That, plus other economic considerations, prevented timber farming from becoming established on Maui.

After you return to the highway, another mile will bring you to park headquarters, where there are rest rooms and drinking water available, as well as park information, maps, and guidebooks. Three miles above park headquarters, in the middle of the fourth hairpin turn, you will see the turnoff for the Halemauu Trailhead, which is at 8,000 feet. *Nene* often hang out in the parking lot here. If you wish, you may hike one mile down the trail for a sweeping view of the crater and the Koolau Gap, where ancient lava flows once poured toward the sea.

There are two more overlooks, back on the highway, that are worth a stop for their views into the crater: Leliwi and Kalahaku. From Kalahaku, it is 2 miles to the large parking lot at the visitor center, on the crater's edge, at 9,745 feet. It is from this point that most people watch the sunrise, huddling inside the building for some protection from the frigid predawn temperature until the sun comes up. Farther up the road, near the actual summit, sits a better building, with large glass windows, from which you can watch the sunrise inside. (But better get there early, as the building fills up quickly.) This is Puu Ulaula, situated at 10,023 feet. The observatory structures at the end of the road, known collectively as Science City, contain Air Force, CAA, and University of Hawaii facilities, and are not open to the public.

From here, if conditions are right, the view is awesome. The islands of Hawaii, Kahoolawe, Lanai, Molokai, and the islet of Molokini are all visible in a sun-mirrored sea. On an exceptionally clear day, you can even see Oahu. The vastness of the crater spreads below you, 19 miles square and 2,700 feet deep. Some of the cinder cones that look so small from Puu Ulaula rise over 600 feet from the crater floor. The huge bowl that you see is not a true volcanic crater but an erosional depression, formed by rain and wind.

If you have the time and the inclination, you may experience the feel of the crater by taking the 5-mile round-trip down Sliding Sands Trail to Kaluu o ka O'o, the summit, at 8,200 feet, of one of the crater's cinder cones. Simply follow the signs that begin at Puu Ulaula. If you are interested in a longer hike, and have a nonhiker in the party willing to pick you up, refer to "Sliding Sands–Halemauu Trail" in the Day Hikes section of this chapter.

Places to Stay. The only accommodations on Haleakala are three cabins and two campgrounds within the crater, and the campground at Hosmer Grove. For information on those facilities within the crater, see the Backpacking Adventures section of this chapter. Hosmer Grove is a small, attractive, grassy area, with some large trees, a roofed, three-sided picnic shelter with grills, chemical toilets, and drinking water. Stays are limited to three nights per month, camping is free, and a permit is not required.

Maui's Leeward Beach Resorts

Although they don't quite qualify as "adventure" travel, few people who visit Maui will fail to spend some time at one or more of the fabulous beaches of its leeward shores. This section will therefore furnish a brief overview of this area, providing a basis for planning your own stay and a personalized exploration of this wonderful coast. Additional information can be found in the following sections: Snorkeling and Diving; Surfing; and Windsurfing.

The leeward beaches (and resorts) fall into two large groups: those on West Maui and those on East Maui. On West Maui, the long beaches of Kaanapali were the first to attract upscale tourist development, while Kihei, on East Maui, catered to those on a lower budget. Both areas grew rapidly, developers crowding the shoreline with hotels and condos, although Kihei managed to preserve several public parks on its oceanfront. As Kaanapali and Kihei became more congested, a new style of resort gradually appeared—Kapalua, north of Kaanapali, and Wailea, south of Kihei. Particularly at Kapalua, the emphasis is not on crowding the land with structures, but rather on using the structures to complement the land. Spread out and spacious, the **Kapalua Bay** and the **Maui Prince,** south of Wailea, give new definition and design to Hawaiian resort hotels, and the older resorts in the area are beginning to feel the impact. Although there are notable exceptions, Kaanapali in some ways now resembles a faded *grande dame* who is beginning to show her age, and the *cognoscenti* and the well heeled are migrating north to Kapalua, or south to Wailea. In response, the venerable Sheraton in Kaanapali closed its doors in 1995 for a multimillion-dollar facelift.

If you are staying in either Kihei or Wailea on East Maui, a good break from the beach is a drive south to the end of the road at La Perouse Bay, exploring as you go. Driving through Wailea, it is easy to get the impression that there is nothing to explore, as access to the shoreline is cut off by large hotel and condominium developments; however, public rights-of-way exist for all the major beaches in the area, required as a condition before county officials would approve development. This access includes parking, and in some cases rest rooms and showers. Watch for the blue-and-white access signs all along Maui's beachfront roads. In Wailea, the beaches of Keawakapu, Mokapu, Ulua, Wailea, and Polo are marked instead with signs bearing their names. These are all fine beaches, and are open for you to explore, swim, snorkel, or just laze.

About a mile south of Makena Landing a large cinder cone, 360 feet high, juts out into the ocean. This is Puu Olai, which divides two beaches that were favorite "hippie" watering spots in the late '60s and early '70s. Drive to the south side of Puu Olai and turn toward the ocean on the paved road through the *kiawe* trees, and park at the paved lot just in front of the beach. The long, wide beach stretching before you is Oneloa, more commonly known today by its hippie-christened names: Makena Beach and Big Beach. The beach is part of Makena State Park, to which facilities are gradually being added. The low, rocky cliff that serves as the beach's end is the south end of Puu Olai. You should have no trouble finding the short trail that leads up over the base of this wall to secluded Puu Olai Beach, or "Little Beach" in hippie times. You may encounter nudists here.

Leaving Oneloa, the road follows the rough shoreline of Ahihi Bay before it reaches La Perouse Bay, named for the French navigator who was the first Westerner to set foot on Maui. Unless you have a four-wheel-drive vehicle do not drive onto the rough lava road that continues past the bay. This barren, lava-covered landscape was the scene of the last volcanic eruption on Maui in 1790. A long portion of an *alaloa* begins at the end of the Jeep road, and you may want to explore part of it. But don't go too far unless you are prepared. There is no water and no trees, and the going is hot and rough.

North Coast to Iao Valley

If you are staying in West Maui, at Kaanapali, Kapalua, or somewhere in between, an interesting day's excursion is a circular tour of West Maui. The itinerary below begins and ends at Kaanapali and goes north, but you can start anywhere and go in either direction.

Leaving Kaanapali, turn off the highway as soon as you can onto Old Route 30, which runs closer to the coast and escapes the traffic. Passing clusters of condos and small hotels along the water, you'll finally reach Kapalua, probably the most tastefully developed resort hotel in the islands. The old road re-joins the highway just past D. T. Fleming Beach Park. Traffic drops off sharply here, but big cane trucks sometimes use the road, blaring their horns as they approach the curves. A mile up the road, atop a rise, you may see cars parked in a cane field to the left. This is the trailhead to Honolua Bay, one of Maui's major surfing spots. If the surf is up, stop awhile and watch the action.

Ups and downs and ins and outs begin in earnest now, as the road winds around Maui's ruggedly beautiful northeastern coastline. Not a single settlement disturbs the isolation until you reach the tiny town of Kahakoloa, a postcard-perfect example of a place that time forgot. Drive slowly on the *extremely* narrow, curving sections of road on both sides of Kahakoloa, where, if you meet another car, one of you will have to back up. After 4 more miles of winding turns, the road begins to straighten out, and then enters Wailuku.

After reaching Wailuku, turn right onto Highway 32 (Iao Valley Road) and proceed 3 miles through the valley to Iao Needle, a towering rock spire that is Maui's most famous landmark. The valley was the scene of the battle in which Kamehameha defeated the forces of the chief of Maui, bringing the island under his rule. On the drive in, watch for a sign pointing to a profile in rock of John F. Kennedy—a reasonably good likeness. Parking is usually difficult at Iao, and you may have to wait for someone to leave, or make several passes around the lot. After parking, cross the bridge and walk up to the lookout.

Returning to the main road, turn right on Highway 30, toward Lahaina. After about 13 miles, you will come to the small town of Olowalu, its only store visible on the right. Olowalu was the site of an infamous massacre of Hawaiian natives in 1790. An American sea captain, Simon Metcalf, seeking revenge for a stolen boat, lured the villagers beside his boat to trade, and then opened fire on them, killing more than eighty people. Outraged by the killings, the local Hawaiian chief captured another ship, this one under the helm of Metcalf's son, and killed the entire crew except for one man, Isaac Davis. Kamehameha captured John Young, the boatswain of the elder Metcalf's ship, and both Davis and Young eventually became trusted advisors to the king.

Behind Olowalu Store, a dirt road leads through the cane fields directly in front of the mountains. After about half a mile, watch for a platform along a cliff face on the right side of the road. This is the site of the Olowalu petroglyphs, which include figures of humans, dogs, and sails. Unfortunately, when I last checked the site in March 1994, a Danger: No Trespassing sign barred entry to the dirt road from the highway. Check at the store to determine the site's current status.

As you approach Lahaina, take the first exit to the town from the highway to get away from heavy traffic. This route will take you back to the water and through the old town. Lahaina, once the whaling capital and now the whale-watching capital of the islands, was also the capital of the Hawaiian kingdom for a short time. Today, even though Lahaina is a bit touristy, it still has a certain charm. The old part of town is much like it must have been in whaling days, except that sailors carousing through the streets searching for saloons and sex have been replaced by tourists looking for restaurants and T-shirts. Pause under the banyan tree, the largest in the islands, stop for a beer at the Pioneer Inn, and see the large Buddha at the Buddhist Cultural Park on Ala Moana Street, in the north part of town. Lahaina has a historic district with many interesting buildings, a replica of an old sailing vessel, and lots of shops, art galleries, and restaurants, all within strolling distance of each other.

Places to Stay. There are so many hotels and condominiums on the leeward coast that you will have no trouble finding something to fit both your mood and your pocketbook. I will mention only two; consult the *HVB Accommodations Guide* for further options.

The **Kapalua Bay Hotel** ([800]367-8000) sits on the land as lightly as a breeze. Luxurious and secluded, blending gently into Maui's loveliest waterfront parcel, its understated elegance sets the standard for Maui's most luxurious resorts. At the other end of the spectrum, both in posh and price, is the **Pioneer Inn** (661-3636), on the waterfront (*not* the beach) in the heart of old Lahaina. The hotel is noisy, rickety, and old fashioned, but staying there is like reliving history. A two-story wooden building (all rooms are on the second floor) surrounds a courtyard; the outside rooms share a long veranda from which to look down on the action in the streets below. Whenever I visit Maui, I have a hard time deciding whether to stay here or at Kapalua Bay.

Most B&Bs on the leeward coast are in East Maui, either in Kihei or in a hillside residential development called Maui Meadows. There is only one campground on the entire leeward coast, and it is privately run. **Camp Pecusa,** on a beach near Olowalu, about 6.5 miles south of Lahaina, offers tent sites in a small wooded area adjacent to a calm-water beach. There is a $5 per-person, per-night charge. For more information, call 661-4303.

Backpacking Adventures

Maui's two best backpack trips are both in Haleakala National Park. (For a description of the park, see Adventuring by Car, "Haleakala National Park," in this chapter.)

There are two options for overnighting in the crater: camping or staying in park cabins. Realistically, you probably only have one option, as the cabins are assigned on a lottery basis and are very difficult to obtain. To apply for a cabin reservation you must submit a written request three months in advance. For example, a request for any date in April must be received by park headquarters no later than January 31. If you are assigned a cabin, it will be for the exclusive use of you and your party. Your stay is limited to three nights, but only two consecutive nights may be spent in the same cabin. For reservations, write to Haleakala National Park, P.O. Box 369, Makawao, HI 96768, Attention: Cabins.

Another possible way to secure a cabin is by picking up a cancelled reservation. This can be done by calling park headquarters (572-9306) between 1:00 and 3:00 P.M. daily. You may ask about a cancellation within a specific time frame, but your best chance of getting a cabin is to accept whatever cancellation may be available. Cabin fees are $40 per night for one to six persons, and $80 per night for seven to twelve persons, and include firewood for the cooking stove that also provides heat for the cabin. Basic cooking utensils are provided, as are 12 padded bunks. You will need your own bedding and light source. Water, which should be treated before use, is piped into the cabin kitchen from a catchment tank in the rear of the cabin, and at spigots in the campgrounds. Other than this, there is no source of water anywhere in the crater. Pit toilets are located a short distance from the cabins.

If you would prefer the cabins but intend to make the hike regardless, you should plan to camp, since the crater's two campgrounds are colocated with two of the cabins. Then, if you are lucky enough to win the cabin lottery, you have the cabins; if not, you camp. A camping permit is required, and can be obtained free of charge at park headquarters. These permits are issued on a first-come basis between 7:30 A.M. and 4:00 P.M. on the day your hike is to begin. Since there is a limit of twenty-five people at each of the two campgrounds, you should arrive at headquarters as early as possible, especially if you plan to camp on summer weekends or major holidays.

The summit of Haleakala, where both trips begin, is at 10,023 feet, and the average elevation of the crater floor is 6,700 feet. Although rain is more common during the winter months, hikers must be prepared for rain and wind at any time of the year. Clouds sometimes roll into the crater, particularly in the afternoon, severely reducing visibility. At such times it is essential to remain on established trails, which are well marked and easy to follow. During good weather daytime temperatures are comfortable all year long; night temperatures average 50 to 32 degrees. Clothing for your trip should include rain gear and a windproof jacket. Boots are a much better choice than sneakers on the often rocky trails. You will also need sun protection—a brimmed hat, sunglasses, and sunscreen.

Hiking Inside Haleakala Crater (3 days, 20 miles; moderate to strenuous)

Maps: USGS topo quads—Kilohana, Nahiku. Earthwalk Press, Haleakala National Park Recreation Map. Haleakala Hiking and Camping Guide (free park handout).

This trip descends into the crater to explore its fascinating landscape. It allows for a leisurely three-day visit, overnighting at each of the two campgrounds in the crater, with a hike out on the third day. The trip can be made in two days if time is short. Your best bet is to enter the crater via Sliding Sands Trail and exit by way of the Halemauu Trail, which requires either positioning an extra vehicle at the Halemauu trailhead or arranging for a nonhiking member of your party to pick you up there. If neither of these is possible, you will need to enter and exit the crater via Sliding Sands. If you are lucky enough to snag a cabin, the itinerary is the same, as cabins are located at the two campgrounds you will use. For an early start,

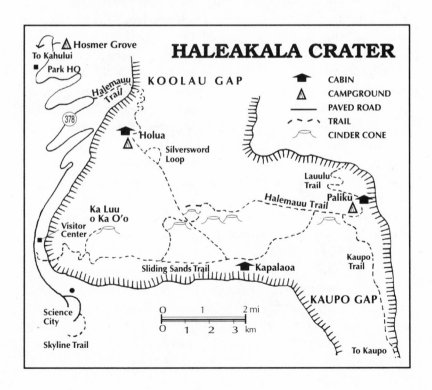

camp the night before at Hosmer Grove, a pretty campground just inside the park entrance at 6,800 feet. Facilities there include drinking water, chemical toilets, grills, and a small picnic shelter. A short nature trail loop begins at the campground. A permit is not required to camp at Hosmer Grove.

Day 1—Summit to Paliku Campground (9.8 miles, 5–6 hours). Pick up your camping permit at park headquarters, as well as a free map of the trails in the crater, and drive to the visitor center just below the summit, where you will find ample parking. Take a few minutes to enjoy the view of the crater from this spot; if you have time, you may also want to view it from the summit itself, a quarter-mile farther up the road. You enter Haleakala Crater on Sliding Sands Trail, which begins near the road at the right side of the parking lot as you face the crater. The trail descends, in a series of switchbacks, into a vast cinder bowl. Soon, to the left, a dark lava flow appears on the crater floor. The wide cut in the crater wall above the flow is the Koolau Gap, from which massive prehistoric eruptions flowed out of the crater and formed much of Maui's east side, including the Keanae Peninsula.

At the 2-mile point, take the half-mile side trip to Kaluu o ka O'o for a look into a cinder cone from its rim. As you continue your descent, two cinder cones, one behind the other, seem to grow higher the farther down you go. The one farthest from the trail is Puu o Maui, at 620 feet from the crater floor the highest cone in the crater. Start watching for silverswords; you should be able to see a few individual plants or small groups scattered about the landscape (see Adventuring by Car for information about this unique plant). After 4 miles from the start of your hike, the trail reaches the crater floor at an elevation of about 7,200 feet. Here an intersecting trail leads off to the left, toward three large cinder cones, and to Holua Cabin. Do not take this trail, but go straight ahead.

It is a 2-mile trek across flat desert terrain to the Kapalaoa Cabin. You may find the crater floor carpeted with evening primrose, an attractive, bright yellow flower. (Unfortunately, the plant is host to the Argentine ant, which is suspected of preying upon the pollinators of the silversword.) The cinder cones off to the left rise between 500 and 600 feet from the crater floor. At the cabin you may refill your water bottles and use the toilet facilities, but the cabin itself is for the exclusive use of those who have rented it.

Shortly after you leave Kapalaoa, the landscape begins to change. Although still dry and desertlike in appearance, more vegetation appears, including grasses and shrubs, and the trail winds through old *a'a* mounds. The walls of the crater then drop off sharply, revealing a huge expanse of blue, a dramatic meeting of sea and sky. This is the Kaupo Gap, and soon the giant volcanoes of the Big Island—Mauna Kea, Mauna Loa, and Hualalai—come into view almost a hundred miles away, across the Alenuihaha Channel.

The trail now crosses a large *a'a* flow which poured out of the north wall of the crater, and the verdant meadows of Paliku beckon in the distance. After passing to the left of a round, green hill, about two miles past the cabin, the Halemauu Trail comes in from the left, and you begin walking over an old *pahoehoe* flow. In another 1.1 miles the Kaupo Trail branches off to the right, and from this point it is only 0.3 miles to Paliku Cabin and Campground.

As you approach Paliku the environmental change is dramatic. Alpine shrubland will give way to green meadows, and trees dot the landscape for the first time. The reason for this astonishing change is simple: Most of the crater receives only about 20 inches of rainfall per year; the eastern tip, where Paliku is located, gets over 200. Unless you have the cabin, pitch your tent in the attractive, grassy campground. Water is available from a spigot in the campground, and you may use the pit toilet behind the cabin.

Paliku, at 6,380 feet, is almost 900 feet lower than Kapalaoa; this is the lowest elevation you will reach in the crater. The *akala*, the native Hawaiian raspberry, grows in profusion here. It is particularly abundant in the rear of the cabin and along the trail to the outhouse and the corral. You may also find *nene* here.

Day 2—Paliku to Holua Campground (6.3 miles, 4–5 hours). If the weather is good, and since this is a relatively short day with a modest 580-foot elevation gain, you may want to hike up the unmaintained Lauulu Trail, which starts behind the cabin's outhouse and reaches the crater rim in about 2 miles. A steeper, shorter trail, also unmaintained, ascends the notch in the crater wall behind and to the right of the cabin. Both trails offer sweeping views.

When you are ready to leave, depart the cabin by retracing yesterday's route. After 0.3 miles you once more come to the Kaupo Trail on the left. You'll soon lose the oasislike greenery of Paliku and return to the rock-and-cinder of the central crater. At 1.4 miles from Paliku you'll again reach the junction of the Sliding Sands and Halemauu trails, at which point you should bear right on the Halemauu. You'll cross the same *aʻa* flow of the previous day, closer to the crater wall, and you'll find more evening primrose carpeting the rocky meadows. After another 2 miles the trail reaches the first of two large cinder cones, and passes them to the north, hugging close to both. About halfway past the second cone you will reach Bottomless Pit, a volcanic hole which, at 65 feet deep, is not quite what its name implies. From here you have a spectacular view across the central part of the crater. The trail then strikes off northeast across the rocky cinder and lava desert.

Take the short detour to the right, on the Silversword Loop, which does not add any appreciable distance to your trip, and which is well worth the extra steps for the many silverswords clustered on both sides of the trail. At one time this was the only part of the crater where the plants survived, and there was an enclosure here to protect them from foraging goats. Today both the goats and the enclosure are gone, and silverswords grow elsewhere in the crater, but nowhere in such profusion as here. From the point where the loop re-joins the main trail it is less than a mile to the campground.

Holua Cabin is nicely situated on the rise from an old lava flow near the base of the Leleiwi Pali, the northwest wall of the crater. A grassy lawn and a picnic table are located in front of the cabin. The campground is situated above the cabin, on a rocky plateau, upon which also sits a three-sided, roofed stable for horses. If the horses are gone and the weather is bad, you may want to camp in the stable, although in April 1995 I found most of it walled in and the rest used to store construction materials. A pit toilet is located at the beginning of the campground, and water is available from a spigot on the trail between the cabin and the campground.

If you are making the trip in two days instead of three, continue on as described below. If you did not see *nene* at Paliku, you will almost certainly see them here. A small flock has taken up residence and will come honking around, hoping to be fed. Park authorities discourage this, not wanting the birds to become dependent on handouts. It's hard to ignore them, though.

Day 3—Holua to Halemauu Trailhead (3.9 miles, 3–4 hours). Before leaving Holua, take the time to explore a large lava tube just a short distance away. From the cabin proceed back in the direction of Paliku for about 150 yards, where you will find a circular pit on the left. Continue another 25 yards or so, watching for a faint trail on the right. Take this trail, which rises over mixed *pahoehoe* and *aʻa* lava, until it reaches a depression, where you will see the tube entrance. A sign warns of dropoffs and suggests bright lights. Although you have to stoop to enter the cave, once inside there is plenty of stand-up room. A metal staircase descends into the main part of the tube, which is best negotiated by going down backward, holding onto the railings.

Once down the stairs, proceed straight ahead, turning right and up around a large rock. After some climbing, you will reach a fork at which you bear left. At some point you will see a distant, small point of light. Upon reaching a second fork, bear left again, and you will begin to climb. You will exit from the second hole in the lava tube roof, where you will find yourself in the vicinity of the campground.

When you are ready to leave Holua, re-join the Halemauu Trail, which soon descends from the rise and strikes north toward the crater wall. About a mile from the cabin you will enter a small meadow and pass through a ranch gate. A series of switchbacks begins, bringing you to the rim of the crater a thousand feet above. As you begin to climb, a dramatic view of the western crater unfolds to your right and rear. The last part of yesterday's hike, and the first part of the first day's hike, appear like a giant relief map. Then, as you round one of the many turns, a whole new vista suddenly opens up: It sweeps across windward Maui and down Keanae Valley all the way to the sea, where the Keanae Peninsula thrusts into the blue Pacific. This spectacular sight is the Koolau Gap. After a final series of switchbacks, the trail settles down to a reasonably level three-quarter-mile stretch to the parking lot where it ends. You may see more *nene* there.

Day 3 (Alternate)—Holua to Haleakala Summit (7.4 miles, 4–

5 hours). If you are unable to arrange a pickup or position a second vehicle at the Halemauu Trailhead, you must return, from Holua, to the starting point of the hike, a climb of 3,000 feet. Begin by retracing yesterday's route, passing Silversword Loop. At a point 1.9 miles from Holua Cabin, the Halemauu Trail starts to traverse the left side of a large cinder cone, while another trail branches off to the right of the cone. Follow the trail to the right for 0.3 miles to a second trail that comes in at a sharp angle from the right. Make the sharp U-turn to the right and follow this trail around the right side of another cinder cone. In 1.3 miles the trail intersects Sliding Sands Trail, where you turn right again and begin the long haul to the summit.

From the Summit to the Sea via the Kaupo Gap (2 days, 18.4 miles; strenuous)

Maps: USGS topo quads—Kilohana, Nahiku, Kaupo. Earthwalk Press, Haleakala National Park Recreation Map.

This trip is one of the premier backpacks in the islands. It descends into Haleakala Crater, crosses its entire length from west to east, and then drops out of a huge gap in the crater wall to reach the sea far below. As mentioned earlier, it traverses so many climate and vegetation zones that one botanist called it the equivalent of hiking from Alaska to Mexico. The transportation arrangements for this trip are difficult, which is one of the reasons it is not attempted very often. If there are nonbackpacking members of your group, and you can talk them into it, they can drop the hikers at the summit of Haleakala and the next day drive to the small village of Kaupo on Maui's south shore to pick them up. If you are willing to add 7 road miles to the hike, they can pick you up at Oheo Gulch instead, where they can spend the day hiking and swimming while waiting for you. There is also a campground at Oheo in case you want to extend the trip.

If there aren't any nonhikers in your group, you can use two vehicles, positioning one at the trailhead 1.5 miles north of Kaupo, which saves you that much hiking distance. Drive the second car to the summit of Haleakala. The shortest route between Kaupo and Haleakala is south from the mountain through Kula and Ulupalakua Ranch, via Highway 31. But "short" is relative—we are talking 50 miles here—and the last section of the road is narrow and unpaved. The scenery, however, is wonderful (see Adventuring by Car in this chapter). It would be a good idea to combine this hike with a visit to Hana; that way, you can drive one way and back the other.

This hike can also be made in one long day, but before choosing this option make sure your knees are up to a 19-mile, 10,000-foot all-in-one-gulp descent.

Day 1—Summit to Paliku Campground (9.8 miles, 5–6 hours). Please see the preceding section for a description of this part of the hike.

Day 2—Paliku to Kaupo Trailhead (7.1 miles) or to Kaupo Store (Highway 31) (8.6 miles, 4–6 hours). Begin by retracing the 0.3 miles from the cabin to the intersection of the Kaupo Trail, turning left to begin your descent. The trail will drop steeply, in a series of narrow switchbacks, through shrubs, ferns, patches of woods, and small meadows. In front of you, sea and sky come together in a vast expanse of blue, and sweeping views of Mauna Kea and Mauna Loa on the Big Island appear far in the distance. As you go farther down the mountain, you enter a *koa* forest and then switch back down to a long, grassy meadow. After descending 3.5 miles, a sign at a gate tells you that the trail is entering private property (Kaupo Ranch). On the other side of the fence, the trail becomes a rough Jeep road for about 3 miles, passing mostly through steep brush and grasses. Pastureland begins near a wooden water tank, from which no water is accessible. From this point on the descent can become confusing, with forks and other tracks intersecting the route. Guide on a small settlement with a few scattered houses below. The Jeep road gives way to a trail, which can be heavily overgrown in spots, before finally ending up at a ranch gate at the settlement. If you have positioned a vehicle at the settlement, the hike is over; otherwise continue down the narrow, often grass–obscured road to Highway 31, just east of the Kaupo Store.

Day Hikes

SLIDING SANDS—HALEMAUU TRAVERSE: (11.3 miles, 4–5 hours; moderate to strenuous)

Maps: USGS topo quads—Kilohana, Nahiku. Earthwalk Press, Haleakala National Park Recreation Map. Haleakala Hiking and Camping Guide (free park handout).

This is the best day hike into Haleakala Crater, but it requires either pre-positioning a vehicle or arranging a dropoff at the Sliding Sands trailhead and a pickup at Halemauu trailhead. If you are unable to do this, you may undertake this hike by retracing your steps from Holua Cabin, and back up Sliding Sands Trail; this would increase the length of the hike to 14.8 miles. You can also make a 5-mile hike by going only as far as Ka Luu o Ka O'o. For the first part of this hike, please refer to Backpacking Adventures, "Summit to Paliku Campground," above. Use that trek as a guide until you reach the intersecting trail on the crater floor that leads to Holua Cabin. Pick up from here.

Take the intersecting trail, at the bottom of the crater, which leads off to the left toward the three large cinder cones (the trail climbs along the left side of the westernmost cone). After 1.3 miles it intersects a trail coming around the base of another cone. Make a very sharp left on this trail, taking it 0.3 miles to the Halemauu Trail. Continue north (left) on the Halemauu, following it for 1.6 additional miles, via Silversword Loop, to Holua Cabin. The picnic table in front of the cabin is a good spot for lunch, and water bottles can be refilled at the catchment tank behind the cabin. There are also pit toilets available. The cabin itself, however, is for the exclusive use of those who have rented it. You may well see *nene* here.

Please refer once again to the preceding section for the itinerary from Holua to the end of the hike at the Halemauu trailhead.

OHEO GULCH AND WAIMOKU FALLS: (4 miles round-trip, half day; moderate)

Maps: USGS topo quad—Kipahulu.

This varied half-day adventure includes hiking to two waterfalls, traversing a rain forest and a thick bamboo stand, and swimming up a small gorge to a third falls with a very pretty pool. Although

Oheo is part of Haleakala National Park, there is no road connection within the park between Oheo and the crater section of the park, and it is not practical to visit both sections in one day. Oheo lies on Maui's southeast coast, about 62 miles from Kahului and about 10 miles south of Hana. The site has rest rooms, picnic tables, and a campground, but drinking water is not available. Camping is free and does not require a permit, but it is limited to three days. For instructions on driving to Oheo—an adventure in itself—please see Adventuring by Car in this chapter.

There are several attractions at Oheo, the most prominent one being the series of pools descending the gulch; you will probably want to spend some time exploring these pools in addition to the hike to the falls. It is a good idea to make this hike in a bathing suit, or at least have one in your pack. The Adventuring by Car section in this chapter provides information about the pools.

The trailhead to the falls begins across the road from the Oheo parking lot. The trail ascends through a wooded area close to the west wall of the gulch, reaching Makahiku Falls Overlook in half a mile. From there a great side adventure is possible. At the overlook, watch for a trail, behind a dirt walk, that leads to the area at the top of the falls. From there you can swim upstream through a steep-sided gulch to a lovely waterfall and pool that few people have ever seen.

You can swim the gulch in two or three stints, depending on the water level of the stream, with short walks over gravel and stones in between the sections. The longest swimming distance is not more than 100 feet, and is well within the ability of an average swimmer. However, you should not attempt this trip if the stream is unusually high or swift, or if it has been raining. The stream can rise quickly and powerfully, and it is a long way to the bottom of Makahiku Falls.

After returning to the trail, the path leads through grasslands interspersed with guava and Christmasberry until it crosses another stream, a relatively easy rock-hop. Again, exercise caution if the stream is up, and turn back if it appears unsafe. Once across the stream, the trail enters a wet rain forest, crosses two more minor streams, and goes through a huge bamboo grove where the growth is so high and thick it almost blocks out the daylight. A short board-walk leads over a marshy stretch to a pool at the base of Waimoku, a lovely, "bridal veil" falls. The pool is not as deep as most, but it is still worth a dip.

POLI POLI SPRINGS STATE RECREATION AREA: This isolated park is situated at an elevation of 6,200 feet on the western slope of Haleakala. Its vegetation is atypical in that when it was refor-ested in the 1920s the trees planted were redwoods, cedar, Mon-terey cypress, and other mainland species. The forest is thick, tall, and beautiful, but it is not Hawaiian. It does, however, offer sweep-ing views, cool breezes, and an abundance of solitude.

Poli Poli is so remote from the rest of Maui that it requires an overnight stay in the area to enjoy its diverse hiking trails. Poli Poli has a small campground located in a redwood grove, and a cabin that must be reserved well in advance. Tent camping is free al-though a permit is required; there is a modest per-person charge for the cabin. For reservations and permits, contact the Division of State Parks, P.O. Box 1049, Wailuku, Maui, HI 96793; phone 243-5354. Although a conventional car can get you to Poli Poli if you drive with care, you will be happier in a four-wheel drive, especially if the upper road is wet—which is frequently the case. Also, a four-wheel drive will enable you to reach trailheads to which you would otherwise have to walk, thus allowing you more time to hike.

To reach Poli Poli Springs from Kahului, take Highway 37 through Pukalani to the *second* junction with Highway 377, about 17 miles. Make a hard left on 377, and drive for 0.3 miles, turning onto Waipoli Road on the right. (If there is no sign, Waipoli is the first paved road on the right.) The road, narrow and one-laned in most places, winds steeply uphill in a long series of switchbacks. After about 6 miles the pavement ends and the road levels out. Ruts and rock outcroppings require careful driving over the next 3.5 miles, where a fork to the right leads downhill to a picnic area, campground, and parking lot. The following three day hikes all be-gin from this area.

POLI POLI LOOP: (5-mile loop, 3 hours; easy to moderate)
Maps: USGS topo quads—Lualailua Hills, Makena. Poli Poli Springs Trails strip map in this section.

This loop provides an excellent sample of a unique island hiking area. It traverses stands of a variety of trees, among them redwoods, eucalyptus, cypress, cedar, and even plum trees. It is also a good introduction to island hiking for those short on time. This leisurely half-day hike utilizes four separate trails that together loop around the heart of Poli Poli Springs. Refer to the trail map in this section to plot the hike, as shown below.

The loop starts on the Poli Poli Trail, which begins at the parking lot and traverses a dense forest of cypress and cedar before intersecting the Haleakala Ridge Trail at about 0.6 miles. Turn right on the new trail, following it through a tall stand of eucalyptus and more cypress. In just under half a mile from the intersection, you'll be able to take a short side trip on the left trail that leads into a cinder cone. There is a small cave, used as a trail shelter, at the bottom of the cone. Returning from the cinder cone, turn right on the Plum Trail, which pops up quickly. There used to be lots of plums on this trail during the late summer, but the trees have suffered from the heavy shade of their bigger neighbors.

Ignore the Tie Trail, which enters from the right, and remain on Plum until the Redwood Trail intersects it, also from the right (1.7 miles from where you turned off the Haleakala Ridge Trail). Before you turn right on the Redwood Trail, go a little farther straight ahead (the Plum Trail has become the Boundary Trail) to see a lovely stand of tall fuchsias, and where you may see the native *apapane* and the Maui creeper flying among the blossoms. Once back on the Redwood Trail, it is 1.7 miles back to the picnic area, your starting point. En route you will pass an abandoned ranger cabin surrounded by hydrangea bushes, and later, just before the end, the state parks rental cabin.

SKYLINE TRAIL: (14 miles round-trip, 8 hours. Note: If a four-wheel drive vehicle is used to drive as far as the vehicle barrier, then it is 6.5 miles round-trip, 4 hours hiking time; moderate)

Maps: USGS topo quads—Lualailua Hills, Kilohana.

This trail is really a Jeep road that goes all the way from Poli Poli Springs to the summit of Haleakala by way of the mountain's southwest rift. The trail affords great views of Puu Kukui on West Maui,

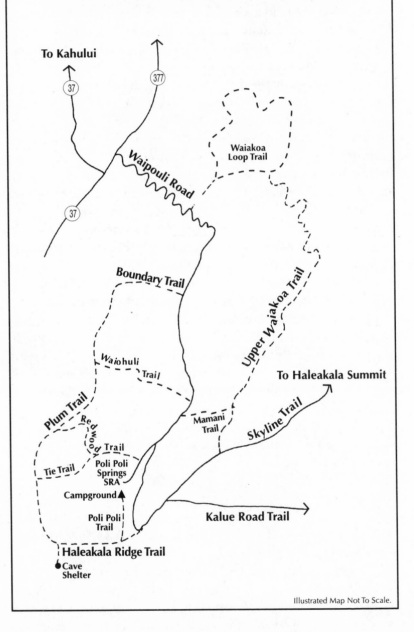

POLI POLI SPRINGS TRAILS

To Kahului

37

377

Waipouli Road

Waiakoa Loop Trail

Boundary Trail

Waiohuli Trail

Upper Waiakoa Trail

To Haleakala Summit

Plum Trail

Redwood Trail

Mamani Trail

Skyline Trail

Tie Trail

Poli Poli Springs SRA

Campground

Poli Poli Trail

Kalue Road Trail

Haleakala Ridge Trail

Cave Shelter

Illustrated Map Not To Scale.

the islands of Lanai and Kahoolawe, and the Big Island of Hawaii. There is an elevation gain of 3,800 feet on this hike.

Beginning in a deep cedar and redwood forest, vegetation starts to diminish quickly as you gain altitude—it disappears completely as the trail opens onto the volcano's cinder-covered upper slope.

From the picnic/campground area, return along the road that you drove in on, to the intersection with the Poli Poli Road, about 0.5 miles. Turn right (a left turn would take you back to the high-way), and after another half-mile you'll reach a hairpin turn in the road where the Haleakala Ridge Trail comes in from the right. Take time to enjoy the view of Kahoolawe, crescent-shaped Molokini, and the Big Island far in the distance. About a mile farther, you'll reach a fork in the road, where you'll bear left (the right fork is Ka-hua Road, which is the next hike, described below). The tall main-land trees will begin to disappear now, replaced by native trees and shrubs like *mamane, pilo, pukiawe* and *ohelo*.

At 3.7 miles a barrier across the road prevents further vehicle traffic; if you are driving, park off the road. You are at about 8,200 feet. Vegetation becomes sparse, limited to sporadic *pukiawe* and clumps of dry brown grass. A little farther on the vegetation will end altogether and you will be in the cinder world of upper Hale-akala. About 6.5 miles from the start you'll reach another vehicle barrier, where the trail joins a paved road that circles around Sci-ence City. Another mile on this road will bring you to the obser-vation building at the summit, and a little farther to the visitor center just below it. Return to Poli Poli Springs via the same route.

KAHUA ROAD TRAIL: (9 miles round-trip, 5 hours; moderate)
Maps: USGS topo quad—Lualailua Hills.

This is an open hike on Haleakala's rarely visited southwestern slope, with sweeping views from the summit to the sea. The trail is actually an old Jeep road that ends at a backcountry shelter.

From the parking area at Poli Poli Springs, follow the directions for Skyline Trail, above, to the fork in the road about 2 miles from your starting point. Turn right at the fork and you will be on Kahua Road, which ascends very gradually to about the 3-mile point, where it begins an almost level descent. The surroundings are mostly *aʻa* lava sprinkled with clumps of brush, ferns, and grass. Toward the summit you will see a line of cinder cones marching along the mountain's southwest rift zone; you will also catch a glimpse of the white buildings of Science City. Some 4 miles from the starting point the road crosses a *pahoehoe* lava flow and then reaches Kahua Shelter, where there is a pit toilet and a catchment water supply. The road continues for 0.5 miles past the shelter, where it ends at a small, grassy clearing.

You will now have reached the turnaround point for the hike. However, a rugged foot trail, marked by a metal pole, begins here and continues in an eastward direction for approximately another 3 miles. This trail brings an interesting change from the road, winding up and down through a series of gullies that becomes deeper and less arid the farther you go. Streams begin to flow, and vegetation becomes thicker. You may wish to explore part of this trail before you return to Poli Poli Springs, or you could plan an overnight at the shelter, allowing more time to explore this very isolated and fascinating area.

Snorkeling and Diving

While Maui's leeward coast is friendly to snorkelers and divers, the island's windward coast is not so hospitable. Leeward beaches are usually calm except for rare kona storms; the weather is fine, and most entries are easy. The windward coast, however, is rocky, with few beaches. Most of its shoreline is pounded by heavy waves, making entry and exit difficult. Generally the best snorkeling and diving are on the leeward side, and for that reason this section will concentrate mainly on leeward beaches. However, there are some good snorkeling and diving spots on the windward side that you should know about. If you are driving to Hana and would like to get wet, there are some great places for underwater action, but only if the weather and ocean cooperate. And there are a few really great windward dives for the adventurous and experienced diver.

Leeward Beaches—West Maui: Olowalu to Honolua Bay

OLOWALU (D/S): An excellent place to view scenery and marine life in shallow water, Olowalu is close to the road and easily accessible from a calm beach with little shore break. A frequently used entry point is a small patch of white sand at the remains of the Olowalu wharf. A long, shallow reef close to shore offers good snorkeling. Divers can swim farther out to deeper water, but depths here seldom reach much over 30 feet. It may be necessary to explore a bit, as some areas are very shallow and, hence, sometimes murky. But almost anywhere from the Olowalu Store south to Papalaua Beach is worth exploring. See Adventuring by Car in this chapter if you'd like to see the Olowalu petroglyphs, or for more historical information about the area.

BLACK ROCK (D/S): A stubby peninsula in front of the Sheraton Hotel, this is one of the best snorkeling and dive sites for beginners on Maui. The underwater terrain is black lava rock and coral, and lots of fish frequent the area as they are used to being fed by visitors. Small holes and crevices dot the wall, providing homes for eels and other sea critters. The easiest entry for divers is from the sandy beach adjacent to the peninsula. Snorkelers can enter there, too, or from along the rock itself, being careful of waves and swells. The protected cove is best for beginners, but better visibility can be had and more marine life will be found by following the rocky peninsula to the point. Depths average 20 to 30 feet. To reach Black Rock, drive about 3 miles north from Lahaina to the entrance to Kaanapali Resort. Turn left, and then bear right to the Sheraton, the last hotel in the complex. Black Rock lies just in front of the hotel. Be aware that public parking is very limited, however, and you may have to pay.

KAPALUA BAY (D/S): This is probably the prettiest and safest beach on Maui. A crescent of sand between two rocky arms, Kapalua is often calm when conditions are rough elsewhere. Snorkelers can explore either arm of the bay, while divers will want to follow the north arm to deeper water and then circle back. Close to shore the underwater terrain and activity are mediocre, but it gets better the farther out you go. The waters along either arm of the bay will probably not exceed depths of 40 feet. Access is from the south end of the beach, and the Kapalua Bay Hotel on the north end rents snorkeling equipment and offers guided dives, complete with all equipment. The smaller bay that lies immediately north of Kapalua, sharing its northern rocky arm, is another good snorkeling and dive spot. Driving north from Lahaina, turn off Highway 30 onto the coast road just after passing the Kaanapali Resort. Watch for the Napili Kai Beach Club (about 3 miles); make the next left turn after the club. There are a public parking area, showers, and rest rooms at Kapalua; a paved pathway to the right leads to the beach.

MOKULEIA BEACH (D/S): This out-of-the-way beach, frequented by those seeking to leave the crowds behind, is located at the bottom of a switchback dirt trail. The path to the beach is tricky to find. About half a mile after the new road joins the coast road (old Route 30), watch for a narrow dirt strip on the left. Cars parked along the strip will indicate that you are in the right place. Park and take the dirt trail down to the beach. Coral, lava, and sand comprise the sea bottom here. Snorkelers favor the eastern arm of the bay, and, when conditions are right, can swim all the way to Honolua Bay (see below). Divers can enter at the western point, either swimming along the shoreline or heading straight out to deeper water. Depths vary from 10 to 50 feet.

HONOLUA BAY (D/S): This popular site offers pretty coral reefs on both sides of a protected bay. Good coral formations swarming with reef fish can be found in 5 to 10 feet of water, after a short swim from shore. Hardy snorkelers can swim around the western arm of the bay to Mokuleia Beach, rest for a while, and then return. Others will want to poke around the long eastern reef. Divers will enjoy a tour along the east wall, where the water reaches a depth of 40 feet and where rays and turtles sometimes cruise. If the waves are up surfers will take over the eastern end of the bay, near the point, but the diving wouldn't be any good then anyway.

The beach itself is unattractive, consisting of boulders and stones, with a few patches of sand and a deteriorating concrete boat ramp. Though the water close to shore is often murky, visibility quickly improves the farther out one swims.

Access to the bay is somewhat difficult to find. Just past the Mokuleia Beach parking area, the highway descends and makes a sharp left turn at the bottom of a gulch. About 0.2 miles before the turn, a small dirt road heads toward the ocean. The road is not easy to spot, so drive slowly and watch for cars parked along the highway. The road is also in poor condition, so do not attempt to drive it: It is only a short walk through a forest of high trees to the beach and the concrete ramp. Honolua is a marine life sanctuary, so nothing may be removed from the water.

Leeward Beaches—East Maui: Kihei to La Perouse Bay

Although snorkeling and diving are possible from the three Kamaole Beaches in Kihei, better scenery and greater numbers of fish can be found farther south, in the Wailea area. All the beaches listed below have public access signs on the main road through the Wailea Resort.

MOKAPU AND ULUA BEACHES (D/S): These two pretty white sand beaches are separated by a rocky point. The underwater scenery consists of lava and patches of coral, and on most days lots of fish congregate here. Entry can be made from either side of the point; the usual procedure is to swim from one side to the other. Divers can follow the rocky point to deeper water, which will not reach much more than 40 feet. Equipment can be rented from a nearby hotel concession on the beach. Driving south on Wailea Drive, watch for the sign to both beaches just past the Stouffer Wailea Beach Resort. Incidentally, Ulua Beach was known as "Little Tarawa" during World War II, as it was used by the Marines as a training area for the bloody landing on that South Pacific island. Rest rooms and showers are available.

WAILEA BEACH (D/S): Less than half a mile south lies Wailea, a long stretch of white sand with a shallow offshore reef that extends south along the coast. A lava rock outcropping leads directly out from the parking lot walkway, providing a good entry point. More proficient snorkelers can follow the reef around a rocky point south to Polo Beach, perhaps arranging a pickup there. Divers can do the same, or opt to go straight out to explore the deeper sections of the reef, where the water reaches about 40 feet. Driving south on Wailea Drive, turn left at the sign for the beach about a quarter-mile past the Wailea Shopping Center. There are rest rooms and showers available.

NAHUNA POINT (D/S): This spot is noted for its caves, some of which are narrow enough to be dangerous. Turtles sometimes come to Nahuma—sometimes called "Five Graves" or "Five Caves"—and white tip reef sharks have even been seen resting on the bottom of the caves. Though the spot is primarily for divers, snorkelers can cruise around the rocks, but the caves are deep enough to require tanks. To reach Nahuma, drive 1.3 miles from Polo Beach, turn right on the dirt track, and park at the small cemetery. Take the path to the small cove and head straight out along the undersea wall, watching for the caves.

MAKENA LANDING BEACH PARK (D): The park consists of two small sandy beaches, both of them close to each other and to the road. The cliffs and offshore rocks to the south offer the best underwater terrain, with good topside views of Molokini, Kahoolawe, and Puu Olai. Depths range from 10 to 50 feet. The park offers rest rooms, outdoor showers, and limited parking. It is only a few hundred yards down the road from the turnoff to Nahuna Point. Makena was once the busiest port on Maui. In the mid 1800s it served the third-largest sugar plantation in the islands. When the plantation converted to a cattle ranch, the port became even busier shipping cattle to market. By the 1920s, however, most port activity had shifted to the better facilities at Kahului, and ships had stopped calling at Makena.

MAKENA STATE PARK (D/S): Oneloa Beach, also known locally as Makena Beach or "Big Beach," is a long, wide, sandy shoreline, under development as a state park. Its northern end is bordered by Puu Olai, a prominent cinder cone that juts out from the shoreline. Puu Olai can be seen from as far away as Lahaina, and is a good reference point. Enter the water at the end of the beach at the base of Puu Olai and swim out along the side of the cone. A sandy bottom, dotted with clumps of coral, leads around the point to Puu Olai Beach (Little Beach), tucked into the end of the cone, where you can exit and walk back to the starting point. The underwater landscape is somewhat more interesting for divers at the north end of Little Beach, but this requires hauling gear over a short but steep rocky trail from Oneloa. Depths at this area will average about 30 feet. Nudists frequent Little Beach. As of this writing, the parking lot and portable toilets are the only facilities in the park, which is about 4.5 miles past Wailea Shopping Center. Watch for a paved road leading to the right through *kiawe* trees (there was no sign on my last visit), proceed to the parking area, and follow the wide path to the beach.

AHIHI BAY (D/S): Although relatively shallow for divers, this area is more colorful than most. White sand, brown lava, multicolored coral and coral heads, and a scattering of narrow reefs decorate the sea bottom, the depth of which does not exceed 40 feet. Many varieties of fish are in abundance here. Less than a mile past the entrance to Makena State park (about 5.8 miles from the Wailea Shopping Center), you will reach a small bay with an old boat ramp close to the road. Enter the water at the ramp or anywhere nearby, and head straight out, or to the right or left.

LA PEROUSE BAY (D/S): La Perouse was named for a French sea captain who led the first foreign party ashore on Maui in May, 1786. After sailing from Hawaii, his ship disappeared, and he was never heard from again. Set in the middle of a stark lava landscape created by Maui's last volcanic eruption in 1790, the bay contains an interesting lava bottom that is often visited by large fish. Diving is best along the bay's western end, which is part of a marine conservation area. Depths range from 5 to 50 feet inside the bay.

Windward Beaches
The cautionary remarks in the first chapter of the book are worth repeating when discussing windward snorkeling and diving. These activities can be more dangerous here during adverse conditions

than on the leeward side, and should not be attempted during high surf or strong winds.

WAIHEE BEACH PARK (D/S): Located about 6 miles north of Kahului Airport on Highway 340, the park is part of a brown sand shoreline, with a long, wide, shallow reef just off shore. Depths range from only 2 to 20 feet as far as 800 yards offshore. The narrow beach is backed by a long grove of ironwood trees, providing an attractive, shady picnic area. Access is from a road on the left side of the Waiehu Municipal Golf Course parking lot. Entry is easy anywhere from the sandy beach. Rest rooms, showers, and picnic tables are available.

MALIKO BAY (D): This area is noted for the deep offshore crevices that provide shelter for the large turtles that can usually be seen here. The sea bottom is mostly boulders, with some coral in the shallow sections. Water close to shore can be murky due to runoff from the stream, but it is usually clear out by the dive site. The bay is on Highway 36, about 7 miles past the junction of Highway 37. After you cross the overpass, turn immediately right on the dirt road that doubles back under the highway and leads to the boat ramp. Enter the water at the ramp, snorkeling out along the right side of the bay until you reach the wash rocks. Drop down here and explore the area in front of the rocks, watching for those turtles and the large pelagic fish that often cruise by.

WAIANAPANAPA STATE PARK (D/S): A black sand beach provides an easy entry on this otherwise hostile shore. The center of the bay is mostly rock and sand, but there is a natural arch out on the right arm of the bay, which snorkelers will want to visit on calm days. Beautiful coral formations out along the far reaches of the low sea cliffs on the left will tempt divers. The terrain is exceptionally varied here, with coral-covered hills and lots of holes and cracks. Depths vary up to 50 feet. All the warnings about diving windward sites apply here; you should only dive or snorkel at Waianapanapa on the calmest days. Many facilities are available: rest rooms, showers, picnic tables, a campground, low-cost park cabins, and hiking trails. Also, be sure to visit the wet caves, and perhaps snorkel back in one of them (see Adventuring by Car in this chapter). The park is located on the Hana Highway (Route 360), about 2.5 miles before you reach Hana. Watch for the sign.

HANA BAY (D/S): I do not recommend you drive to Hana for either snorkeling or diving. But since you will probably be visiting Hana anyway, and if you feel you must put on a dive mask, Hana Bay and Waianapanapa (above) are about the only accessible spots. The left arm of Hana Bay (Kauiki Head) provides descent snorkeling and diving when the seas cooperate. Upon entering the ocean you'll find a finger reef, with good coral growth, and lots of fish circling the rocks. From Hana Beach Park, walk along the trail past the wharf, entering the water in the lee of the small island. Snorkelers should stay near to the shore, between the island and the wharf, where depths reach up to 16 feet. Divers can venture out to Twin Rocks, at a depth of about 50 feet with a sharp drop to deeper water seaward. Neither snorkelers nor divers should enter the water anywhere at Hana unless the seas are very calm. Rest rooms, showers, picnic tables, and a snack bar are available at the beach park.

The North Shore

There are three dive sites on the north shore that the experts say are the best dives on Maui: Nakalele Point, Honanana Bay, and Mokolea Point. I do not cover them here. All three are hard to find and hard to get to, all have tricky or dangerous entries, and all are far from help if it should be needed. If you would like to dive any of these places, I suggest you do so with a local dive club or someone who is familiar with them.

MOLOKINI ISLAND (D/S): Although not a shore dive location, I include this crescent-shaped jewel because it is worth paying to get to. Whether snorkeler or diver, you should consider a trip to this partially submerged volcanic crater. In the "old days," before tour boats started going to Molokini in droves, we would sail to Molokini, drop anchor, and hit the water. The first thing we always saw was sharks—lots of them. The really big guys would swim haughtily away, the medium-sized ones would come by to look us over, and the small ones would follow us around, swimming right up to the boat ladder on the way back. Nowadays, all the divers and snorkelers have made the sharks nervous, and they are a lot more scarce. But you still will see plenty of other fish at Molokini, and lots of coral and great scenery. And, if you are making your trip during whaling season, you may have the added bonus of whale-watching on the way out and back.

The usual dive boat to Molokini visits one of four locations. Talk to the operator in advance to see if he is going to the particular location you'd like to be. Snorkel boats generally anchor inside the crescent, in about 20 feet of water, where you'll find an abundance of coral and lots of fish. Dive boats anchor over either side of the crescent. The west side of the crater tapers off into a submerged reef with a dropoff to 100 feet, offering good scenery with a fair number of fish. The east side drops down in a series of ledges, where you have the best chance of seeing whitetip sharks resting in small caves or just cruising. Some boats drop divers off on the ocean-facing side of Molokini, a wall that drops almost 400 feet. Divers swim from one end of the island to the other, and the boat follows, picking them up at the other end.

There is no need for me to mention the many Molokini commercial operators here. They will be waiting for you on the waterfront at Lahaina or Maalaea, or you can check for a referral at your hotel.

Lanai Trips from Maui

There are no dive shops on Lanai. Even if you bring your own tanks to the island, you will have no way to refill them. The only dive operation is run by the Manele Bay Hotel, and it does not rent equipment or fill tanks. Although there are a few good snorkeling and dive spots accessible from shore (see the Lanai chapter), because of the tank refill problem the best arrangement for those wishing to dive Lanai is by boat from Maui—unless you plan to do extensive diving on Lanai, or plan to visit that island anyway. In this case it would make sense to use the Manele Bay Hotel dive operation.

Dive operators on Maui and the hotel make daily trips to sites off Lanai, choosing from among the locations below.

THE CATHEDRALS: This is by far the most popular Lanai dive, and if you plan to make only one dive on the island, this is the one you'll want to choose. A large cavern, with beams of light filtering through cracks in the roof, gives this site its name. Side chambers usually house eels, squirrel fish, and other denizens of dark places. There are tunnels, crevices, and connecting passages to explore, in depths ranging from 40 to 60 feet. Some boats bring snorkelers here, who can play around on the cavern roof. They will obviously not be able to enter the "church," but they will still have a good time.

You will get an even better deal if your dive captain includes *Second Cathedrals* (D) in the same trip. This is another large grotto, found in the base of a hollow rock pinnacle that rises to within 15 feet of the water's surface. It is possible to swim through one of several tunnels and exit the main cave from the rear. Marine life is similar to that of The Cathedrals, though depths reach to 60 feet.

SERGEANT MAJOR (D): This dive is named for the reef fish that swarm over this spot. Three separate ridges provide caves, one of which houses a long tunnel. Turtles are very often seen here; they seem to have no fear of divers, and will usually allow you to get quite close. Depths range to 50 feet. If time is a consideration, this spot is the nearest of the Lanai dives to Maui.

Knob Hill (D) is a massive lava rock on "legs," through which divers swim, amid arches and crevices in water up to 70 feet deep. Whitetip sharks can sometimes be seen resting inside caves here, while the reclusive lionfish often hides in the smaller recesses.

Lighthouse Reef (D/S) is another place where you are likely to see resting sharks. Two large lava tubes at the base of a wall, in about 60 feet of water, offer divers with lights a chance to look for lobster, shrimp, cowries, and other cave dwellers.

Shark Fin Reef (D/S) projects from the water like a huge dorsal fin. The "fin" rests atop a large coral-encrusted base where schools of reef fish swarm. Rays and *ulua* sometimes come by the seaward edge of the reef. Boats carrying only snorkelers often come here, and it is probably better for them than for divers.

MOLOKAI—MOKUHOONIKI ROCK (D): Some dive operators on Maui run occasional trips to this small island off the eastern tip of Molokai. This site is for the adventurous, experienced diver only. It features steep vertical dropoffs, coral ledges, and large schools of tropical fish. Depths range to 100 feet. The bigger open-water prowlers also frequent Mokuhooniki—barracuda, manta rays, and hammerhead sharks among them.

Surfing

Next to Oahu, Maui is the most popular island for surfers. From the power surf of Hookipa to the isolated beauty of Honolua and the friendly waves of Lahaina, Maui has something for everyone. Maui does, however, share one problem with the Big Island—distance. It's a long trip from Honolua to check out the surf at Honomanu. But for surfers who prefer Maui's distances to Oahu's crowds, it's worth it.

The Windward Shore

Except for one world-class spot, there is not much to lure surfers to this windy, rocky coast. Although local residents do surf here, choice spots are hard to find, have difficult access or require passing over private land, and are not worth the investment of a visitor's time for the quality of the waves.

The exception lies off shore *Hookipa Beach Park* (S/L/B), where the ocean forms a natural surfing arena. But there are two problems at Hookipa: wind and windsurfers. The sailboarders also consider Hookipa a world-class spot, a fact confirmed by their sheer numbers. When the wind is fierce, driving surfers to the beach, the sailboarders take over. Conversely, when kona conditions deflate windsurfer sails, the near-perfect waves create a paradise for surfers. It is the in-between conditions that cause the two kinds of boarders to clash. Although surfers generally rule the east end of the bay, known as *Pavilions,* and the sailboarders mostly control the western end, called *The Point,* domination of the middle of the bay is contested by both. Pavilions is the easiest and safest place to surf at Hookipa, and its rights can provide a fun time for intermediates. Better surfers can try their skills at the long or short rights at *Middles,* in the center of the bay, while true experts may dare the long lefts of *Lanes,* which perform only with a swell large enough to close out Pavilions. Hookipa is an all-year-round spot, with the strongest winds in the summer; kona or less windy days occur more frequently during the rest of the year. Hookipa is directly off Highway 36 about 3 miles east of the town of Paia, with the beach, parking areas, and surfing spots all clearly visible from the road.

About 18 miles east of Hookipa on the Hana Highway lies *Honomanu Bay* (S/L/B), protected from the trades by high walls. A dirt road at the apex of a hairpin turn leads from the highway to the mouth of a stream that empties into the bay. With calm winds and a decent swell, Honomanu's left walls provide experienced surfers with exciting rides in a dramatic setting.

Two more notable surfing spots on this shore are *Keanae Peninsula,* about halfway to Hana, where fast rights can get up to between 4 and 8 feet in winter, and *Hana Bay,* with easy lefts, 2 to 6 feet, breaking all year.

Much kinder to surfers is Maui's *Leeward Shore.* Here the offshore winds generally mean much cleaner conditions, and the waves are often more consistent. Summer is the best season at the following leeward spots.

Honolua Bay (S/B) has some of the best waves in the islands. Its long, curling walls can provide a surfing experience seldom equaled anywhere else. But because its swells are often blocked by other islands, Honolua is more of an event than a dependable source of surfable waves. Nevertheless, this is a premium spot, and when it's working it is crowded with experienced surfers wanting their share of the ride. If the waves or the crowds are too intimidating at Honolua, try *Honokohau* (S/L/B), the next bay north on Highway 30. Here beginners and intermediates can enjoy themselves on fun lefts and rights, long walls, and tubes, free from the crowds found elsewhere. Be aware, though, that when the waves build at Honokohau, strong coastal currents come with them, and it's time to head for the beach.

When conditions are flat everywhere else, *Lahaina* is one place where beginners to experts will usually be able to catch a wave. There are two surf spots at Lahaina, one on either side of Lahaina Harbor boat channel. The *Breakwater* (S/L/B), south of the boat channel and fronting the harbor breakwater, offers fast winter rights and hollow summer lefts. *Lahaina Harbor* (S/L/B), on the north side of the boat channel, offers rights at low tide and lefts when the tide brings enough water over the otherwise dangerously shallow reef. The only problem at Lahaina is that the waves are so good they bring out heavy crowds.

Other surfable spots south of Lahaina are *Olowalu, McGregor Point, Maalaea,* and *Kalama Beach Park.*

Windsurfing

Maui is Mecca for windsurfers, just as Oahu is for their surfboarding cousins. Both islands have a "North Shore" where the superstars of each sport congregate, and Paia, on Maui, is architecturally akin to Haleiwa on Oahu. Paia, a former plantation town now booming with surf sailors and the businesses that cater to them, calls itself the windsurfing capital of the world. Its location in the center of three of Maui's premier windsurfing spots gives it a good claim to that title. Wind conditions on Maui vary with the time of year. A typical recent year provided excellent short-board sailing 100 percent of the time in June, but only 53 percent of the time in February. But because of the diversity of sailing locations, on most days there will be some kind of sailing somewhere.

The North Shore

This is the heartland of Maui windsurfing, consisting of four adjacent sites. The trade winds, blowing down from the northeast, are funneled between two huge mountains, Puu Kukui on West Maui and Haleakala in the east. This creates a "venturi effect" that heightens wind speed as it rushes by the North Shore area and sweeps across Maui's isthmus. These strong winds, plus deep ocean swells, provide a dazzling variety of surf conditions, all within a 7-mile area. The North Shore offers a wide range of accommodations, hotels and condos in Kahului, and B&Bs, private rooms, and rental houses in and around Paia. There are two county camp-grounds right in the area: H. A. Baldwin Beach Park, only a mile from Spreckelsville; and Rainbow Park, just south of Paia.

Kanaha Beach Park, only half a mile from the Kahului Airport, is an ideal spot for windsurfing beginners and experts alike. Novices can learn water starts and practice jibing in calm, near-shore waters; intermediates can perfect their skills on the lower reef; and experts can tackle the high upper-reef waves of summer. On marginally windy days, most board sailors head for *Spreckelsville,* where the wind is usually 5 knots faster than anywhere else. Speed is the commodity here, especially in summer, when the winds are at their peak. Because of high winds and a shallow reef, Sprecks is not for beginners. To reach Sprecks from the intersection of the Haleakala and Hana Highways, continue toward Hana for 1.5 miles; turn left at the second road, then take the second right.

Hookipa Beach Park, on Highway 36, attracts expert sailboarders from everywhere, many of whom consider one of its breaks, *The Point,* one of the best windsurfing spots in the world. But board surfers like Hookipa, too, and many a contest is held between the two for control of the waves. Generally the break at the east end of the beach, know as *Pavilions,* belongs to the surfers, while *The Point* is dominated by sailors—everything else is fair game for both groups. Normally the high winds that appeal to sailors here force surfers to the beach, while low winds delight the surfers and send the sailboarders home. It is the in-between conditions that bring them both out on the same breaks. *Middles,* between Pavilions and The Point, is the most popular place for sailboarders, but The Point provides the best ride—and the most danger. It is a notorious cruncher of both equipment and bodies, dashing them against rocks and shallow reef. *Lanes,* the farthest west of the breaks, is only sailable when the swell reaches 6 feet or more, but then it provides a long left. This reef extends for some distance, affording good sailing and jumping for those who want to avoid the Hookipa crowds.

The last of the North Shore windsurfing areas, *Waiehu,* is normally sailable only when conditions are poor at other surfing spots. It is often good in winter north winds and occasionally during winter kona conditions. But when conditions are good at Kanaha or Hookipa, they are usually not good at Waiehu. Also, it is only sailable at medium or high tide. Waiehu is rarely crowded, unless sailing conditions are bad everywhere else.

The West Shore

This surfing area stretches from D. T. Fleming Beach Park in the north to Wailea Beach in the south. Windsurfing conditions on this long coastline can best be described as variable, and all levels of sailboarders, from novice to expert, will almost always find some kind of action at sea here. From D. T. Fleming Beach south to Kaanapali, strong trade winds blow from April to October, but it is necessary to paddle far enough from shore to pick them up, at which point they provide good downwind runs. South of Kaanapali, the trades are blocked by the West Maui mountains, and the light onshore breezes there are ideal for beginners and light wind sailors.

Lahaina offers four breaks. At the *Lahaina Shores Hotel* beginners and intermediates can practice in flat water directly off the hotel. *Lahaina Breakwater* has waves that can reach mast height with good tubes on north and south swells. Because of its dangerously shallow reef, this site should be sailed only at medium or high tides. *Lahaina Harbor*'s waves also produce good tubes, but it has a shallow reef and an additional hazard of boats leaving and entering the harbor. Both the breakwater and the harbor are popular surfing sites, and they frequently get heavy use by both types of boarders. Variable winds often blow at Lahaina's northern end, producing fast flatwater sailing. The parking lot in front of the *Chart House* Restaurant is the best place from which to launch, but watch for rocks and coral in this shallow start.

The enclosed nature of *Maalaea Bay* bounces the wind, and, together with shifting directions, permits windsurfing virtually year round. The trade winds, funneled between the West Maui Mountains and Haleakala, roar across Maui's isthmus and out to sea at speeds up to 35 knots, with an average of 24 knots. The bay has what many claim is the fastest breaking wave in the world. Speed sailing and high wind short-boarding are the activities here, restricting the area to expert sailboarders. Access is from Haywood Beach at the end of Hauoi Street, to the left of the boat harbor.

Kihei is the best place on Maui for the beginning windsurfer, although changing wind and surf conditions also attract more experienced sailors. Several sailboarding schools operate here, providing full equipment when it's needed. There are three popular windsurfing spots in the Kihei area, although the entire coast is sailable if launching spots can be found. *Ohukai Beach Park* (officially Mai Poina Oe Iau Beach Park) is normally suitable for beginners, but when gusty winds and south swells occur, the ocean there is better left to more experienced sailors. The next spot south, fronting the *Maui Sunset* condominium, is also for more experienced sailboarders due to its shallow reef. *Kalama Beach Park* has a break similar to Maui Sunset's, and beginners have easy beach access there. But again, it belongs to the experienced sailor when the wind and the swells are up.

Biking

Maui is the most popular bicycling destination in Hawaii. Heroic cyclists pedal from sea level to the top of Haleakala, a 10,023-foot climb—less heroic cyclists are hauled to the top in buses and bike down. There is the ride to Hana, the Mecca of island romantics. And there are West Maui's miles of lovely beaches with their views of the islands of Lanai, Molokai, and Kahoolawe across sapphire blue seas. But Maui is feeling some of the same development pressures that afflict Oahu. Each year seems to bring more traffic, more resort hotels, and fewer campgrounds. Maui has proportionally fewer camping places than any of the islands except Lanai. But what Maui does have is gorgeous scenery, magnificent coastlines, and fine weather—it's still a great place to ride.

Tour 1: the Road to Hana (51 miles, 4 days)

This is one of the best rides in the islands, cruising all of East Maui's beautiful windward coast. You will pedal around more than 600 curves, cross 56 bridges, and pass innumerable waterfalls, all the while surrounded by incredible scenery. This itinerary allows you

4 days: 2 days to reach Hana, 1 day to tour the area, and 1 day to return. Cyclists with strong uphill skills may opt for continuing around Maui from Hana rather than returning by the same route; this trip is covered in Tour 2.

Although it can be done, it would be a shame to ride the Hana Highway in one long day. There is so much to see and do along the way, so many places where you should get out of the saddle and explore or just enjoy, that you would miss much of the experience by rushing down the road. This does create a problem, though. There are only two places to camp along the route, H. A. Baldwin Beach County Park, which is too close to the tour's beginning, and Waianapanapa State Park, which is too close to its end. Camping is no longer permitted at Kaumahina State Wayside. The only alternative is to stay in the dormitory at the YMCA's Camp Keanae, a little more than halfway to Hana. Accommodations are limited, so it is best to reserve early. Contact the Maui YMCA, 250 Kanaloa Ave., Kahului, HI 96732; phone 242-9007.

You may have been told that the Hana Highway makes for relaxed cycling because the road is bad enough to restrict vehicle traffic and the big tour buses don't use it. While that is true, lots of tour *vans* do use the road, along with lots of tourists in rental cars determined to buy their "I Survived the Hana Highway" T-shirts. And while big *buses* don't use the highway, big *trucks* definitely do, bringing all kinds of supplies to Hana. Be alert at all times and stay well to the right of the road, especially on curves. Unless the "Halfway to Hana" roadside stand is open (which is not always the case), you will not be able to buy food until you reach town, and except for Camp Keanae and Puaakaa Wayside, there is no drinking water available unless you treat it. Secure your bike to an immovable object whenever you take any of the side trips on this itinerary.

Day 1—Kahului to Keanae (29 miles). Please refer to Adventuring by Car, "The Hana Highway–South Shore Loop," in this chapter for route information, points of interest, and side trips along the way. Information shown here is only that particular to bicycle travel.

At Twin Falls, you can either secure your bike to the fence or muscle it over the fence and continue to ride, but if you choose the latter option you will have to walk your bike over the last part of the trail. About 3 miles past Kaumahina State Wayside you'll reach Camp Keanae, on the left side of the highway, just before the road to the peninsula. This is your overnight stop. In addition to the dorms mentioned in Adventuring by Car, a "director's cabin" is sometimes available. It is simply two rooms and a bath, with only the most basic furniture. It is not worth the price unless you are traveling with a group that wants privacy. But when you reach Camp Keanae you will be more than halfway to Hana, with some of the best scenery awaiting you.

Day 2—Keanae to Hana (22 miles). Again, refer to Adventuring by Car for route information. There is no place to purchase food until Hana. Drinking water is available at Puaakaa State Park. Because this is a short day, take the side trip to Blue Pool on your way to Hana, rather than the following day. Be sure not to miss this lovely spot, which few people know about. If you are overnighting in town, you may also want to visit Waianapanapa State Park en route.

Day 3—Hana & Oheo Gulch. Follow the touring itinerary in Adventuring by Car. On Day 4, most cyclists, after spending Day 3 in and around Hana, will retrace their route on the Hana Highway. Cyclers in excellent condition with strong uphill skills may opt to continue around Maui's south shore to Kula (Tour 2 below). If you decide to do this, and are equipped to camp, you should arrange to see the points of interest close to Hana first, and then make the 10-mile ride to Oheo Gulch, where you can camp for the night. No fee or permit is required. There are rest rooms available, but water is available only from the stream and therefore must be treated before drinking. For a great adventure while at Oheo, you can hike to two waterfalls and swim to a third (see Day Hikes in this chapter).

Tour 2: Hana to Kula and Kahului via Kaupo (58 miles)

Continue to refer to Adventuring by Car for route information. This is a beautiful, wild, and virtually traffic-free ride, but you must be a strong uphill rider to enjoy this trip. Unless the Kaupo store is open, which is unlikely, once you leave Oheo there is no food or drink available until you reach the small store at Ulupalakua Ranch, 27 hard miles away. The 4.5-mile stretch of gravel road on both sides of Kaupo will slow you down, but you should have no other problems. Four miles past Kaupo, the road begins a steady 20-mile rise from sea level to 3,000 feet. When you reach Ulupalakua Ranch, you can take a well-deserved break and load up on drinks and snacks, but the uphill grind is not over. Another 1,200 feet must be gained in the next 6 miles before the long, glorious 15-mile descent through upcountry Maui, its green pastures rolling toward the sea.

It is also possible to make the entire Hana trip in reverse (Tours 1 and 2). This is particularly appealing if you plan to ride up Haleakala (Tour 3). From the top of the mountain to Nuu Bay, west of Kaupo, runs a fantastic 50-mile downhill roll.

Tour 3: Haleakala Summit (74 miles round-trip)

The road to the top of the mountain is the world's steepest paved road, rising over 10,000 feet in 37 miles. Only cyclists with lots of uphill experience and excellent endurance should consider this incredible climb. Those opting out of the uphill grind can still enjoy a thrilling descent of the mountain with one of the companies that lead groups of cyclists down the road on bikes with specially fitted brakes (see Biking Down Haleakala, below).

The normal starting point for the ride up the mountain is the intersection of highways 36 and 37, just southeast of the Kahului Airport. A prettier, less traveled route begins at the town of Paia, follows Baldwin Avenue southeast to Makawao, turns right on Highway 400 to Pukalani, and then left a short distance to Highway 377, the Haleakala Highway. If you are camping, H. A. Baldwin Beach County Park is less than a mile from Paia, a little over 3 miles from the airport. The last stores along the route are in Pukalani, 6 miles from the start; the last place to eat and fill water bottles is the Kula Lodge Restaurant, about 4 miles farther. There will be no more food at all, and no more water until park headquarters, a long, uphill 15 miles away. You will need warm clothing for this ride: A windproof jacket is necessary on the upper reaches of the mountain, and to protect you from the self-generated wind on the long roll down. Please refer to Adventuring by Car, "Haleakala National Park," for important route and other information.

The most obvious route down the mountain is the way you came up—a long, glorious ride. Most cyclists, whether heading toward Kahului or Paia, make it down in less than two hours. Hazards on the way, other than normal traffic, include cattle guards, which are trickier to ride over on the way down than on the way up, and your own speed, which you must constantly check by braking. Needless to say, your brakes must be in top condition for this downhill run.

Another descent possibility, especially if you intend to visit Hana, would be to do the previously described Hana to Kahului via Kaupo trip in reverse—an almost incredible 50-mile downhill ride through marvelous countryside and spectacular coastal scenery.

Tour 4: Haleakala Summit to Kahului via Skyline Trail and Poli Poli Springs State Recreation Area (32 miles)

Still another way to come down the mountain—if you have a mountain bike—is via the Skyline Trail. This little-known route follows a Jeep track from the summit along Haleakala's southwest rift to Poli Poli Springs, and from there a long, paved switchback road to Kula. This ride, which offers a completely new view of the mountain, is virtually free of traffic until it reaches Highway 37. A great round-trip can be had by coming up the Haleakala Highway then riding down the Skyline Trail. There is no water on this trip until Poli Poli Springs, and no food stores until Kula.

To descend by Skyline Trail, take the paved road from the visitor center toward Science City. Do not take the turnoff on the right to the Puu Ula Ula Overlook, but continue until you reach another intersection. Turn left; the road will take you around the south end of Science City. A little over a mile from the visitor center you'll reach a vehicle barrier across a Jeep track leading off the paved road to the left. This is Skyline Trail, and it should be marked by a sign.

As you descend across the barren cinder fields, you will begin to see the cinder cones of the southwest rift. As you drop lower, sparse vegetation, clumps of dry grass and *pukiawe*, begins to appear. About 3 miles from the first vehicle barrier you'll reach another, but the road on the other side is still too poor for anything but four-wheel-drive vehicles, and you will probably not meet any of them.

Vegetation becomes thicker now, and *mamane* trees begin to appear. Stay to the left, keeping to the main road when intersections with other trails appear. The road will gradually improve, and when you reach a major hairpin turn, stop and enjoy the views of Kahoolawe, crescent-shaped Molokini, and the Big Island far in the distance. Once you continue your journey, you will soon be surrounded by huge trees and a forest atypical of anything that normally grows in Hawaii. Redwoods, cedar, cypress, and eucalyptus dominate the landscape, all products of a reforestation experiment in the 1920s. Half a mile from the hairpin turn, a road to the left leads to a campground, a picnic area, and a state cabin. Pit toilets and drinking water are available here.

Unless you are stopping for the night, or need water, continue on the road, which now levels out, but watch for ruts and rock outcroppings. After about 3 miles the pavement begins, and the road descends in a long series of steep, short switchbacks. Although traffic is very sparse, you need to exercise care coming down this very narrow road, especially on the many blind curves. Once you reach Highway 377, make a short dogleg to the left to the junction of Highway 37, turn right, and begin the long roll to Kahului.

Tour 5: Biking Down Haleakala (37 miles)

If you do not want to ride up the mountain, you can still ride down, even if you don't have a bike with you. Four companies currently bus cyclists to the top of Haleakala and guide them down in groups. In addition to mountain bikes with special brakes, these guides provide full-face helmets, windbreaking jackets and pants, and gloves. The entire trip usually takes 8 hours, and meals are provided. A guide leads the group and a van brings up the rear. Frequent stops are made for picture taking, or to shed clothing, to use rest room facilities, or to allow traffic to pass. The trips have a good safety record, although some years ago a woman participant was killed when she fell underneath a truck. The following companies lead downhill tours as of this writing.

Cruiser Bob's
P.O. Box B
Paia, HI 96799
Phone: 654-7717

Mountain Riders
P.O. Box 6222
Kahului, HI 96732
Phone: 242-9739

Maui Downhill
333 Dairy Road
Suite 201E
Kahului, HI 96733
Phone: 871-2155

Maui Mountain Cruisers
P.O. Box 1356
Makawao, HI 96768
Phone: 871-6014

Tour 6: Circling West Maui (60 miles)

This is an excellent cycling adventure, revealing some of Maui's most rugged and isolated shoreline. The route wriggles and winds like a snake, up and down hills, in and out of gulches, and around lonely promontories. It provides spectacular seascapes and dramatic mountain vistas. There was a time when the road was so bad that only mountain bikers dared its perils, but it is fully paved now,

Cyclists get set for the 10,000-foot, 20-mile downhill roll from the summit of Haleakala to the sea. Photo by Richard McMahon.

and all cyclists can enjoy its scenic roller coaster. You may begin at any point on the circle, depending on where you are staying. But if you plan to complete the full trip you should ride in a clockwise direction as described here, so that you have the trade winds at your back when you cross Maui's isthmus. Again, please refer to Adventuring by Car, "Circling West Maui," in this chapter for a route description and points of interest.

This trip covers an unusually diverse 60 miles—some of it flat and fast, some of it hilly, twisting, and slow. It can be done in one long day, but not if you include the exploring recommended here. There are only two campgrounds along the entire route, one at Camp Pecusa near Olowalu, and Windmill Beach, near Maui's northernmost point. Pecusa offers tent sites on a first-come basis for $5 per person per night. There is no fee for camping at Windmill Beach, but a permit is required from Maui Land & Pineapple Company, phone 669-6201. Once you pass Fleming Beach Park, there is no food or water available until Wailuku.

Riding south from Wailuku, you cross the isthmus between East and West Maui on Highway 30, cane fields on your left, mountains on the right, and the wind at your back. Traffic can be heavy, and it will increase after Highway 380 joins from Kahului. After about 10 miles, you will round Papawai Point, the winds will cease, and you will be greeted by the still waters of the Auau channel, with its views of Kahoolawe and Lanai. A mile and a half later you ride through a tunnel and then cycle along the water and the sandy beaches south of Olowalu. You will continue to enjoy a relatively flat ride until well north of Kaanapali, where the old road comes back to the highway just past D. T. Fleming Beach Park. Here the roller-coaster soon begins. Take it slowly, and stop frequently to admire the stark, lonely beauty of this windswept coast. Walk out to the cliffs when you can, to watch the sea crash against the rocks below. Depending upon where you began your trip, make sure you ride into Iao Valley to see the Iao Needle.

Hunting

Pigs and goats are the only animals you may hunt in Maui, though Maui has the most liberal hunting rules of any of the Hawaiian islands. Maui has large public hunting areas, at which hunting is permitted year-round in all but one, and more than half of these have bag limits of two goats *and* two pigs per day, with no seasonal limit. Maui either has lots of pigs and goats, or wants to get rid of them—or maybe both. East and West Maui have populations of both animals, with heavy concentrations of pigs in East Maui's rain forests. Goats, although eliminated from the crater, still browse the slopes of Haleakala.

You may hunt nine kinds of birds on Maui: ring-necked and green pheasant, California Valley and Japanese quail, Chukar partridge, gray and black francolin, and spotted and barred dove. In addition, wild turkey may be hunted, but only on private land and with permission of the landowner. Unlike the hunting area for mammals, the public bird hunting area is limited to two adjacent sites at Poli Poli Springs State Park, which extends around to the southern slope of Haleakala. The season normally runs from the first Saturday in November through the third Sunday in January, on Saturdays, Sundays, and state holidays only.

CHAPTER FIVE

Molokai
Hawaii's Yesterday

MOLOKAI IS WHAT Hawaii must have been like a hundred years ago. With a sparse population, little development, and few roads, the island has changed less over the years than any of the others with the exception of Niihau—privately held and not open to visitors. Unfortunately, the changes that have taken place have been mostly detrimental to Molokai's population. Once a major pineapple producer, the island saw the end of pineapple operations in 1982, and with it the loss of its biggest employer. An ambitious plan to substitute tourism for pineapples foundered when only one of a planned six-hotel complex was built, mainly because the tourists did not come, at least not in the numbers that would justify continuation of the project. So Molokai remains relatively undeveloped.

In late 1994 Molokai Ranch, the island's largest landholder, announced grandiose plans to bring economic prosperity to the area. These plans include establishing the state's largest dairy; building a light industrial park and a housing development; and developing the island's eco-tourism industry—a current popular buzzword in tourism circles—which pleases ecologists and environmentalists

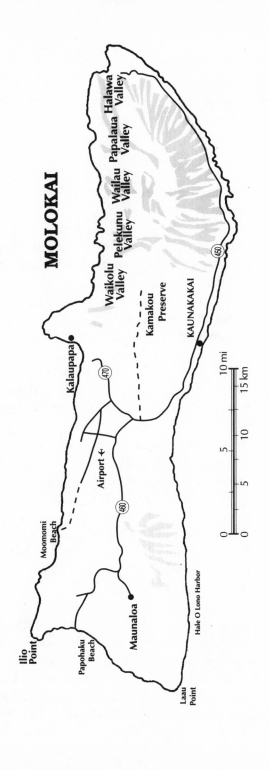

but remains an ill-defined concept. The residents of Molokai, however, remain skeptical: they have heard all this before.

A large portion of Molokai is inaccessible. Most of the western
third is owned by Molokai Ranch, and a good part of the eastern
third belongs to other ranchers. The central mountain spine can be
reached only by four-wheel-drive vehicle or on foot, and the precipitous north shore, with the world's highest sea cliffs, conquers
all but the most intrepid visitors. But there is high adventure on
Molokai for those who are willing to seek it.

Molokai is the fifth largest of the main islands, 38 miles long and
10 miles wide, encompassing 261 square miles. It was formed by
two volcanoes between 1.3 and 1.8 million years ago. A third, later
eruption created the peninsula where Kalaupapa settlement is located. The western half of Molokai is almost arid, receiving an average of only about 25 inches of rainfall per year. On the northwest
coast large sand dunes extend as much as 4 miles inland. Vegetation
is limited, tending toward scrub brush, grasses, *kiawe,* and other
drought- and salt-tolerant species. East Molokai, by contrast, receives plenty of rain. Lush green valleys, rippling streams, and the
highest waterfalls in the state make for spectacular scenery. Here,
Kamakou, the highest peak on Molokai, reaches 4,970 feet.

Molokai's population of roughly 6,700 contains a higher percentage of Hawaiians than any other place in the state, with the
exception of privately owned Niihau. There is no public transportation on the island, and hitchhiking is not legal.

Adventuring by Four-Wheel Drive

*Note: This section is designed to be used with a good road map at
hand, such as the full color topographic Map of Molokai and
Lanai, University of Hawaii Press, $2.95.*

I recommend that you use a four-wheel-drive vehicle for Molokai because there are some places you cannot safely go without
it. I am not suggesting that you use it to careen cross-country on the
island's inhospitable terrain, but rather to negotiate four-wheel-
drive roads and tracks where a conventional car would at the very
least have trouble—or not be able to go at all. A four-wheel drive
costs about double the rental of a conventional sedan, but you will

only need it for one of the two days, so you can switch vehicles at the end of the first day if you want to. In this section I will specify where four-wheel drive is needed. You may decide, after reading this portion of the book, to forgo seeing these places altogether, in which case a regular car will do just fine.

SUGGESTED ITINERARY: You will need two days for the itinerary outlined below, or more if you decide to add some of the other adventures described in this section and elsewhere in this chapter. While the starting point for each day is Kaunakakai, the first day will be spent exploring east, the second day going west.

Day 1—East Molokai (85 + miles), with a morning trip to Waikolu Lookout and Kamakou Preserve and an afternoon visit to Halawa Valley. You will need a four-wheel drive for the morning trip. Although this excursion will explore the eastern part of the island, you leave town driving west on Highway 46 for about 3.5 miles to a white bridge. Just before the bridge, a dirt road turns off to the right: Turn there, and the road will soon begin a gradual climb. Avoid the many side roads by bearing left on the main one. In a little more than 9 miles you'll reach a depression on the left side of the road. This is a "sandalwood pit," where natives measured out a shipload of wood during the days of the sandalwood trade between Hawaii and China in the early 1800s.

In another 0.8 miles you'll reach Waikolu Lookout, with its dramatic view encompassing Waikolu Valley from headwall to sea. There is a small picnic area and a campground here. A Jeep road continues beyond the lookout, but it becomes rough, rutted and very muddy, difficult even for four-wheel drive, especially in wet weather. There are, however, several interesting hiking trails here through native forest, including a boardwalked native bog and a lookout over Pelekunu Valley. See the Day Hikes section of this chapter if you are interested. In either case, return the way you came.

If you are feeling adventurous, and weather and road conditions permit, instead of retracing your route you can forge ahead, mostly bearing right, and find your way back down to the coast. Or you can turn around and take one of the several Jeep tracks that branch

off to the left of the main road, eventually leading back to Kaunakakai. But a word of warning: Some of these tracks lead to dead
ends and you may have to reschedule your afternoon activities. It
is important to have the USGS topo maps (Kaunakakai or Kamalo)
with you if you choose to try these routes.

For the afternoon portion of the trip, a four-wheel drive is not
necessary. Drive straight through town, going east on Highway 45.
Almost at once you will see a series of fishponds. These ancient
ponds, owned exclusively by the chiefs in old Hawaii, were used to
trap ocean fish for food, and to keep them alive until they were
ready for use. There were more of these ponds on Molokai than
anywhere else in the islands, and you will find more of them in the
17 miles east of Kaunakakai than anywhere else. As is the case elsewhere in the islands, they are no longer in use.

Almost 16 miles from town are the remains of the Iliiliopae
Heiau, one of the largest *heiau* in the islands. Watch for the Lady
of Seven Sorrows Church on the left side of the road. From the
church, clock 0.9 miles to a small bridge with white pipe railings.
Immediately after this bridge, a narrow dirt road turns left; the
heiau is situated at the end of this road on the left side. There is no
place to park here, so you might want to leave your vehicle off to
the side of the road and walk the half-mile to the *heiau*.

About 27 miles from Kaunakakai, the highway reaches a point
overlooking Halawa Valley, the only one of the four amphitheater
valleys of Molokai's north shore accessible by vehicle. The mile-
long descent is fairly steep on the narrow, but paved, road. The road
ends at a small county beach park, with a picnic pavilion, rest
rooms, and water that should be treated before drinking. Two
sandy beaches, both of them safe for swimming close to shore on
calm days, are located on either side of the bay. Two waterfalls lie
a short distance up the valley, one of them accessible by a 2-mile
trail, and the other by wading up a stream (see the Day Hikes section in this chapter). Retrace your route to Kaunakakai.

Day 2—West Molokai (36+ miles).
*Note: A four-wheel-drive vehicle is not necessary for this day's
exploration.*

Once again going west on Kaunakakai on Highway 46, turn off

on Highway 47 4.2 miles from town. Follow this road 5.5 miles to its end at Palaau State Park. The park has a large picnic pavilion with rest rooms (about 200 yards back down the road), and a rustic campground. Walk over to the Kalaupapa Lookout for a dramatic view of Molokai's north shore, the Kalaupapa Peninsula and the leprosy settlement made famous by Father Joseph de Veuster Damien, who served and eventually died there of the disease. Before Damien's time, people with the ailment were left to fend for themselves on the isolated peninsula. Although the disease is now controllable by medication, and the residents of the settlement are free to leave, about 100 persons with leprosy remain there voluntarily. Kalaupapa, a National Historic Park, is managed jointly by the State of Hawaii Department of Health and the National Park Service.

You may have heard of the mule ride down a precipitous trail to the settlement, which prompted the bumper sticker "Wouldn't You Rather Be Riding a Mule on Molokai?" Unfortunately, the mule ride stopped operating some years ago. But the 2-mile-long mule trail is still there, and it makes a great hike—better than before now that hikers don't have to dodge mules and mule droppings. The settlement can still be visited by advance permission; a fee is charged for the tour. See the Day Hikes section in this chapter for further details. If you prefer to fly in, Air Molokai and Island Air make daily flights into the settlement.

A short walk on a trail leading into the woods from the lookout following along the ridge line will bring you to the Phallic Rock, a large, explicitly realistic fertility symbol. Legend claims that in ancient times Hawaiian women made offerings here, if they wished to become pregnant or to insure safe childbirth.

Return to Highway 46, turn right, and drive about 10 miles to the turnoff for the Kalua Koi Hotel. When you reach the hotel continue left along Kalua Koi Road for about a mile to Papohaku Beach County Park. Papohaku is one of the longest and widest white sand beaches in the islands. The beach park, shaded by mature *kiawe* trees, is a good base camp from which to explore the beach. Rest rooms, outdoor showers, and drinking water are available here, and camping is permitted. No matter how inviting it may appear, though, *do not swim at Papohaku*. Strong offshore currents and a heavy shore break with a powerful backwash can occur at any time of the year. Even if you are only walking on the beach, watch for sudden waves that race quickly onto the shore; these are particularly dangerous to young children. If you want to swim, return to the hotel and ask for directions to the safer public swimming area.

Places to Stay. Kaunakakai is the most central place from which to explore Molokai. The **Pau Hana Inn** (553-5342) is an old favorite of people from Honolulu who run off to Molokai for the weekend. Its attractive waterfront location, and *lanai*/dance floor under a huge banyan tree, provide a real South Seas flavor at a moderate price. The moderately priced **Hotel Molokai** (553-5347), about 2 miles east of town, has very Polynesian decor, but its rooms are rather small. On the west end of the island, on Molokai's best white sand beach, is the **Kalua Koi** (552-2555), Molokai's premium hotel, priced in the moderate to expensive category. There are also several B&Bs in and around Kaunakakai. Check one of the referral services listed in the *HVB Accommodations Guide*. Two waterfront campgrounds are close to town, **Onealii Beach County Park** and **Kiowea Beach Park**. Although both are on the water and have beaches, swimming is poor due to shallow mud flats extending as much as a half-mile off shore. Both have rest rooms and water available.

Backpacking Adventures

Wailau Valley (16 miles round-trip, 9–12 hours each way; strenuous)

Maps: USGS topo quads—Halawa, Kamalo.

This adventure is a true wilderness trek, traversing Molokai's spine from south shore to north shore, crossing an uninhabited valley, and camping on an isolated beach. Except in the summer, it is usually unpopulated, providing a respite from people and their things. Wailau is the largest of the four amphitheater valleys on Molokai, its steep walls rising in some places to over 4,900 feet. Meaning "Many Waters" in Hawaiian, Wailau lives up to its name.

Papohaku Beach Park gives access to one of the longest and most deserted beaches in Hawaii. Photo by Richard McMahon.

Waterfalls pour over its sides, and its floor is crisscrossed by streams. Older, heavy forest covers the upper sections of the valley, but the remainder of the vegetation is mostly second-growth, with some open space remaining from former agricultural activity. Normally Wailau's beach is made up of boulders, but in summer a small sand beach usually forms on its western corner. Winter surf makes entry to the sea particularly dangerous, and often impossible, but it can be hazardous at any time of the year. There is little evidence of the flourishing community that once lived here except for some taro terraces. People began abandoning the valley in the early 1900s, and the tsunami of 1946 destroyed what remained of the village of Wailau.

Camping permits are required and can be obtained in advance from the Division of Forestry and Wildlife, P.O. Box 1015, Wailuku, HI 96793; phone 243-5352. The free permits are good for two nights, though longer stays may be permitted at the discretion of the Forestry Division. You can obtain a permit after you arrive on Molokai; however, the forestry office in Kaunakakai is only open on a part-time basis.

The Wailau Trail begins on the south shore of the island, climbs over the central mountain ridge, and then descends steeply to the valley floor where it follows Wailau Stream to the beach. The 8-mile trail, part of which crosses private property, is not maintained, which makes for a strenuous hike over rugged terrain. It begins at the Iliiliopae Heiau, 15.7 miles east of Kaunakakai on Highway 46. When you have driven about 14 miles, watch for The Lady of Seven Sorrows Church on the left side of the road. Proceeding 0.9 miles from the church, you will come to a small bridge with white pipe railings. Turn left immediately after crossing the bridge, onto the overgrown, one-way dirt road. The road ends in about half a mile, with a house on the right and a small wooden sign marking the trail on the left. Another sign, slightly farther on, reads "Wailau Trail, dangerous, 12 hours minimum, landowner assumes no liability." This is implied permission to use the trail, but if you want more formal permission, call Pearl Petro at 558-8113. As there is no parking area here the best course of action is to park your car somewhere along the highway and hike the half-mile to the trailhead.

The trail leads immediately to the *heiau*, then climbs 3 miles over fairly steep terrain, traverses a bog near the summit, and descends steeply from the ridge top at 2,800 feet. On reaching the valley floor it crosses the stream and follows its east bank to the beach, a distance of about 4.5 miles.

The last time I hiked this trail, the part from the top of the ridgeline to the floor of Wailau Valley was washed out in several places, making the going rough and dangerous. We also had to bushwhack along the stream before finding the trail again once we reached the valley floor. People who have hiked the trail more recently have said that its condition has not improved. If you can, be sure to get the latest information about trail conditions before you start out. Traveling with a group is the best idea: In March 1993 a lone hiker disappeared while hiking out of the valley.

One final note about Wailau: In the summer you are apt to find a fair number of campers strung out along the beach at Wailau and near the mouth of the stream. Many of these people arrive by boat, and some are prepared to spend the entire summer, illegal though it might be. They usually construct rickety, tarp-covered shelters and other eyesores, and comprise a noisy population. If you would prefer to avoid this situation, plan your trip for another time of the year when you are more likely to have the place to yourself.

Day Hikes

KALAUPAPA SETTLEMENT: (4 miles round-trip, 2–3 hours; moderate)
Maps: USGS topo quad—Kaunakakai.

This is the best hike on Molokai, providing striking views over the peninsula that houses the historic Kalaupapa Settlement; glimpses of Molokai's wild and isolated north shore; and an optional visit to the settlement itself before hiking back up the cliff. The trail is steep, though not dangerous. After all, mules carried tourists down the thing for years without mishap. If you are going to make the hike down the cliff, you should not miss visiting the settlement; however, *you must have prior permission to do so.* Unaccompanied sightseeing or wandering around anywhere on the peninsula is not allowed. Arrangements for a visit can be made by calling Damien Tours at 567-6171. Permission includes a $25 guided tour that offers a tour of the town, a bus trip to Father Damien's church, and a visit to a picnic area with spectacular views of the sea cliffs on Molokai's north shore. Hikers are picked up at the bottom of the trail once daily at 10:20 A.M., which means you should start down the trail no later than nine. Bring a lunch, as no food is available in the settlement. Persons under sixteen years old are not permitted to visit the settlement or to hike the trail.

To reach the trailhead, leave Kaunakakai going west on Highway 46 and turn off on Highway 47, 4.2 miles from town. Follow this road 5.5 miles to its end at Palaau State Park. Walk over to the Kalaupapa Lookout for a view of your destination and a peek at the dramatic sea cliffs of north Molokai, the highest such cliffs in the world. The trailhead to the settlement is not marked. To find it, return to your car and drive slowly back the way you came. At the first road to the left will be a stop sign and another sign warning unauthorized persons to keep out; a chain is sometimes stretched across this road. Leave your car parked on the side of the highway and walk down the road to the edge of the cliff. The trail begins here, on the east side of the communications building.

The trail is steep but wide, and great views of the peninsula and the cliffs will thrill you all the way down. This trail ends at a gray sand beach on the west side of the Kalaupapa Peninsula; a road at the eastern end of the beach leads into the settlement. If you have not made arrangements to visit the settlement you must end your hike at the beach, and after a rest and possibly a swim, proceed back up the trail.

KAMAKOU PRESERVE LOOP: (5-mile loop, 3–4 hours; moderate)
Maps: USGS topo quads—Kaunakakai, Kamalo. Kamakou Preserve Trails strip map in this section.

This trail is one of the best in the islands from which to view a native forest that has remained free from the intrusion of exotic species. A narrow boardwalk also traverses part of what is probably the oldest bog in Hawaii, and leads to a dramatic overlook into Pelekunu Valley. Because of the fragile nature of this ecosystem, it is important that boots and clothing be brushed free of seeds from other plants, and that hikers remain on the trail, road, and boardwalk at all times. Contact The Nature Conservancy on Molokai at 553-5236 for further information and possible restrictions. Also, you may not want to use your best boots for this hike: Conditions are usually wet and muddy on both the trail and the road, so you might, instead, want to wear an old pair of sneakers. They won't give you as much traction as the boots, but they won't carry five pounds of muck with you every step of the way, either, and they will be a lot easier to clean.

For driving instructions to the trailhead, see the directions to Waikolu Lookout (Day 1) in Adventuring by Four-Wheel Drive in this chapter. Refer to topo quad Kamalo, and the strip map in this book, to find—and stay on—the route. Park at Waikolu Lookout and continue along the road on foot for 0.2 miles to the Hanalilolilo Trailhead on the left side of the road. The trail climbs uphill along the rim of Waikolu Valley, which you will glimpse only rarely because of the dense native forest. *Ohia, hapuu,* and other native plants dominate the landscape. Pick your way carefully, as the trail is almost always wet, and knee-deep mud holes appear with some frequency. After 1.5 miles, the Hanalilolilo Trail ends at the same time it intersects the boardwalk over the Pepeopae Bog. Go left on the boardwalk, about 200 yards uphill, to a wooden platform with a fine view of Pelekunu Valley.

Retrace your steps on the boardwalk, continuing past the junction with the Hanalilolilo Trail. You are now in the heart of the bog, where dwarf *ohia* trees, sedges, mosses, and lichens grow in an undisturbed environment, as they have for thousands of years. In about another half-mile, the boardwalk ends at a Jeep track. Continue along this track, bearing right at all forks and intersections. The road, winding, heavily rutted, and muddy, traverses two gulches before reaching Waikolu Lookout 2.5 miles away.

HALAWA VALLEY WATERFALLS: (5 miles round-trip, 3 hours; moderate)
Maps: USGS topo quad—Halawa.

Tucked against the headwall of this beautiful ampitheater valley lie two lovely waterfalls, Moaula and Hipuapua. The most popular and easiest to reach is Moaula, with a pool at its base deep enough for swimming and plenty of rocks on which to sunbathe. Hip-

KAMAKOU PRESERVE

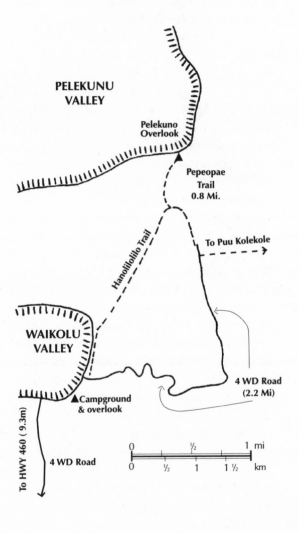

PELEKUNU
VALLEY

Pelekuno
Overlook

Pepeopae
Trail
0.8 Mi.

Hanolilolilo Trail

To Puu Kolekole

WAIKOLU
VALLEY

▲ Campground
& overlook

4 WD Road
(2.2 Mi)

To HWY 460 (9.3m)

4 WD Road

| 0 | ½ | 1 | mi |
| 0 | ½ | 1 | 1 ½ | km |

uapua, however, is the higher of the two, cascading 500 feet compared to Moaula's 250.

The trailhead is located at the end of Highway 45 in Halawa Valley, 28 miles from Kaunakakai. A small beach park is situated there, with rest rooms, a picnic pavilion, and water that must be treated before drinking. You may park in the vicinity of the beach park, but a better option might be to take advantage of the sign that points down the road to "Secure Parking." I don't know what the cost is but it is probably worth it: I have had my car broken into here.

The trail is not marked, but you begin by following a dirt road near a small church that leads back into the valley at a sharp left angle from the road on which you drove down. Follow this road for about half a mile to its end, where a path continues straight ahead. Follow this trail for about 150 yards, past two houses, where another trail turns sharply down to the stream at a gap in a stone wall. Take the path to the stream, at which point you may have to search for a crossing spot. The stream floods frequently, sometimes washing out the normal crossing point. The stream is not safe to cross if it is flooded and flowing rapidly, especially if it is raining. If it is high at this point in your trek, it will probably be worse on your way back.

After you cross the stream, you may have trouble finding the trail. If so, look for a stand of mango trees on the hillside beyond the low-lying stream bank. Head for the mangoes and you will soon find a clearly defined trail, about 50 feet above the valley floor. The trail heads upstream, crossing several old stone taro terraces, then parallels a water pipe. Two miles from the first stream crossing the trail crosses Hipuapua Stream, and shortly thereafter the trail forks. The left fork leads quickly to lower Moaula Falls and its large pool. The right fork, which becomes almost dangerously vertical, leads to Upper Moaula Falls, with its smaller, shallower pool.

To reach Hipuapua Falls, retrace your steps to Hipuapua Stream and rock-hop upstream for about 30 minutes. This is a strenuous but rewarding trek, as Hipuapua is twice the height of lower Moaula, and its pool, while not as big or as swimmable as Moaula's, has an interesting dumbbell shape.

Special Note: In May 1994, several residents of Halawa Valley, claiming that the trail to both waterfalls crosses their private property, barred public access to the falls. The state is working with the residents to try to settle the issue, and if necessary, the trail we be rerouted. However, as of May 1995, the matter had not been resolved. If you would like to hike to the falls, check the status of the situation with the Forestry and Wildlife Division, P.O. Box 1050, Wailuku, HI 96793; phone 243-5352.

Snorkeling and Diving

I do not recommend that you go to Molokai specifically to snorkel or dive. Most guide books on the subject do not even mention the island. The southern coast is mostly mud flats; the wave-battered, sea cliff–rimmed north shore is virtually inaccessible, and most of the eastern and western ends of the island are in private hands. But in case you plan to tour Molokai anyway, and are a die-hard diver or snorkeler, I have included the sites below, which are probably the best—if not the only—places that Molokai has to offer. Finally, do not plan to dive or snorkel here in the winter months, because the water is almost always too rough and murky during that time. And dangerous currents can be encountered at any time of year. Again, better diving can be had elsewhere.

KAWAKIU NUI AND KAWAKIU IKI BAYS (D/S): These two adjoining bays lie on the northwestern tip of Molokai. You will need a four-wheel-drive vehicle to reach either, but that will probably be your mode of travel anyway if you are adventuring on Molokai. If you are not lugging dive gear, and only plan to snorkel, you can hike to Kawakiu Nui in thirty minutes, so you will not need a four-wheel drive. But be aware that the gate to Kawakiu is locked when Molokai Ranch is running cattle in the area. Call the ranch at 552-2767 for information.

To reach the bays by car, drive west about 14 miles on Highway 46, turning right at the road to the Kalua Koi Resort. After 4.5 miles, turn right at the sign marked "Paniolo Hale," then continue straight for another half mile. (Do not turn left at the second "Paniolo Hale" sign.) You will find a small pavilion at which you should park if you don't have four-wheel drive. Otherwise, drive straight ahead, past the pavilion and onto the dirt road. Turn left when it forks, go through the gate, being careful to close it behind you, and continue to the Kawakiu Nui.

From the promontory where the road ends you will be able to see a small cove cut into the south arm of the bay. Enter the water there, and follow the rocks to the point, where there are some small caves and arches. You will see isolated mounds of coral on your route, as well as the usual reef fish. Either return the same way, or swim around the point, following it back on the other side and exiting on a small pebble beach. Really hardy divers can walk about 500 yards north to smaller Kawakiu Iki Bay, enter the water at its southern arm, round the point, and follow the wall back to Kawakiu Nui Bay, exiting on the beach. The underwater scenery is similar to the first dive. Depths in both areas do not exceed 30 feet.

MAKE HORSE BEACH (Pohaku Mauliuli) (S): This is a reasonably good snorkeling spot close to the Kalua Koi Hotel. Park in the hotel lot and walk north along the beach until it ends at a lava flow. Enter there and stay close to the rocks, where bottom depth ranges from 10 to 25 feet, then snorkel to Make Horse Beach. You should see plenty of reef fish. If you are wondering about the strange-sounding beach name, the "make" used here is not the English word, but the Hawaiian one, pronounced "MAH-*kay*," meaning "dead." The beach got its name when an old horse fell from the cliff and died on the beach.

PUU O KAIAKA (D): From the Kalua Koi Hotel, drive south to the public parking lot and public access to Kepuhi Beach. Divers can enter the water at the end of the path to the beach, and then swim along the submerged wall of the large hill that divides Kepuhi and Papohaku beaches. There is a large cave near the point, in about 30 feet of water, but you will need a light to explore it. The surge in and out of this cave can be powerful, even on seemingly calm days. Continue on around the point, exiting on Papohaku Beach, or return the way you came.

MOOMOMI BEACH (D): To my knowledge, this is the only accessible dive site on Molokai's lonely, windswept north shore. And whether you will be able to dive here depends on what is—and has been—going on weatherwise: I have been to Moomomi when it has been so scoured and battered by waves and wind that it was not even possible to get down to the water. Again, four-wheel drive should be your mode of transportation. To reach Moomomi, drive northwest from Kaunakakai on Highway 46 for about 6 miles and turn right on Route 481. After just over a mile, turn left on Farrington Avenue. At the end of the pavement, continue straight ahead on the dirt road until you reach a concrete foundation, the remains of a rest center. Park near the foundation and head for the beach. Select a good entry site near the eastern arm of the beach, and head for the point. The terrain and marine life is most interesting relatively close to the shoreline, where depths rarely exceed 30 feet.

MURPHY BEACH PARK (Jaycees Park) (D/S): Built by the Molokai Jaycees as a community service project, this park is a scant mile east of Waialua off Highway 46 on Molokai's east end. The offshore bottom is rocky and shallow, but the area beyond the reef offers good diving and snorkeling.

SANDY BEACH (S): About a mile and a half past Murphy's, this spot offers protected snorkeling in fairly shallow water (up to 20 feet), but it will be of interest mainly to beginners.

MOKUHOONIKI ROCK (D): This is a boat dive, but I mention it because it is the most exciting dive on Molokai. Lying off the eastern tip of the island, this site is for the adventurous, experienced diver. Depending on the section of the islet you dive, depths range from 20 to just over 100 feet. Mokuhooniki features steep vertical dropoffs, coral ledges, and large schools of colorful fish. The bigger open-water denizens also frequent the area, barracuda, manta rays, and hammerhead sharks among them. You will need to ask around if you want someone to take you to Mokuhooniki from Molokai;

otherwise, some dive operators on Maui come here when weather permits.

Surfing

Not many people come to Molokai to surf, but word is getting around: The island picks up both summer and winter swells, and people are beginning to notice. Although it does not have many surfing spots, and conditions are sometimes erratic, if the surf is up Molokai's fun waves and relaxed, hassle-free environment are a welcome contrast to Oahu's crowded surf. But you can forget about any nightlife on Molokai, and you will have to bring your board with you.

KAUNAKAKAI WHARF (S/L): Although the sea in this area is generally flat, surfable waves sometimes occur on the western side of the harbor's entrance channel. If you see local surfers out there you can give it a try; if not, don't bother.

POHAKULOA POINT (S/L/B): This rocky point of land, lying between two small bays, is a popular surfing area, offering friendly waves and easy surfing. It is about 23 miles east of Kaunakakai on Highway 45. Again, take your cue from local surfers.

HALAWA BAY (S/L): Another favorite local surfing area, Halawa Bay forms the seaward side of Halawa Valley, reachable by driving east to the end of Highway 45. There is a beach park at Halawa, with rest rooms, picnic tables, showers, and water that needs treating before you drink it.

KEPUHI BEACH (S/L/B/BS): The Kalua Koi, Molokai's most prestigious hotel, is located on this pretty white sand beach on the western end of the island. When the surf is up, conditions are good to excellent for experienced surfers, though heavy shorebreaks and powerful currents can occur during these times. To reach Kepuhi, take Highway 46 west from Kaunakakai for about 14 miles, to the Kalua Koi turnoff, which takes you to the hotel. The public beach access is on the south (left) side of the beach.

John Clark, in his book *The Beaches of Maui County,* lists Hale
o Lono and Kanalukaha Beach, and Kawaaloa Bay, as surfing
spots. The problem is that access to all these places passes through
private property, most of it restricted by locked gates barring entrance. If you really want to check these sites out anyway, try contacting Molokai Ranch; phone 552-2767.

Biking

An absence of traffic, sparse development, and great scenery combine to make Molokai a cyclist's dream. From a base in Kaunakakai three excellent tours are possible, each revealing a different
aspect of the island. In addition, for the mountain biker, there are
miles of forested and beach Jeep tracks to explore. Before starting
out on any of the three tours listed below, buy what food you need
for the trip and fill your water bottles. For route information, please
refer to Adventuring by Four-Wheel Drive in this chapter.

Tour 1: Kaunakakai to Halawa Valley (60 miles round-trip)

From town, ride east on Highway 45, which follows the coast for
the next 25 miles. You may have head winds most of the way, and
there are quite a few small grades as the road tops a rise and then
returns to sea level. About 25 miles from Kaunakakai the highway
begins a steady, stiff climb on a winding road until it reaches a point
overlooking Halawa Valley. The 2-mile descent on the paved road
is a fairly steep, narrow switchback. The road ends at a small beach
park, where there's a picnic pavilion, rest rooms, and water that
should be treated before drinking. Two sandy beaches, located on
each side of the bay, are safe for swimming on calm days if you stay
close to shore. Two beautiful waterfalls lie two miles up the valley
(see the Day Hikes section of this chapter). There is no campground
or other place to stay in the valley; the nearest campground is at the
Waialua Congregational Church, about 10 miles back toward Kaunakakai, but it is only rented to groups. For more information, call
558-8150. Once you get back up the switchback, the return to Kaunakakai is almost a coast. With the wind at your back, it almost
seems like it's downhill all the way.

Tour 2: Kaunakakai to Papohaku Beach (22 miles one way, including a 4-mile total side trip to Maunaloa)

This trip through west Molokai takes you to the widest and longest white sand beach on the island. There is an excellent campground there, and spending the night will give you the opportunity to explore Molokai's lovely and isolated western shore. If you make the side trip to Maunaloa, you will be able to replenish your food and drink supplies there.

Leave Kaunakakai heading west on Highway 46, passing a large coconut grove, and several churches, on the left. The road will begin to climb, and it will continue to do so for the next 5 miles to the airport. From there the grade lessens, but the road still runs noticeably uphill until its intersection with Kalua Koi Road, another 6 miles. The side trip to Maunaloa will allow you to replace food and water supplies, have lunch in a local restaurant, and browse in a couple of interesting local stores, including a kite factory.

Returning to Kalua Koi Road, you have a 5-mile glide down to the coast, the rolling plains of East Molokai unfolding before you. When you reach the Kalua Koi Hotel, continue left along Kalua Koi Road for about a mile to Papohaku Beach County Park, as described in Adventuring by Four-Wheel Drive. If you plan to camp and have a mountain bike, you can explore south and north of the beach park. Kawakiu Iki Bay, north of the hotel, is a particularly pretty spot (see the Snorkeling and Diving section in this chapter for directions). A note of caution: *No matter how inviting it may appear, swimming at Papohaku is dangerous almost any time of the year, due to heavy surf and strong offshore currents.* Swimming is safer at the hotel's public swimming area on the south side of the hotel, but even there, caution is advised.

Tour 3: Kaunakakai to Kalaupapa Lookout (7.5 miles one way)

Although relatively short, this trip is almost all uphill, and much of it is into a strong head wind. But it takes you into upland Molokai, with its spectacular view of Kalaupapa Peninsula and the massive sea cliffs of the north shore.

Leaving Kaunakakai, again to the west on Highway 46, turn off on Highway 47, a little over 4 miles from town. You will have been climbing for about a mile, and this turn continues the climb and brings you into the wind. Passing through the town of Kualapuu, you'll climb another 2.5 miles before the road levels out for the last mile, and then ends at Palaau State Park. Be sure to check Adventuring by Four-Wheel Drive for points of interest there. The return trip to Kaunakakai is a pleasant downhill glide.

Mountain Bike Tours

In addition to the above trips, mountain bikers have several other interesting options.

WAIKOLU LOOKOUT: (12 miles one way)
This trip takes you through Molokai's upland forest reserve and leads to a beautiful valley overlook (see Adventuring by Four-Wheel Drive in this section for the route description and other information). You will make an altitude gain of 3,200 feet, most of it on an 8-mile stretch of dirt road. This is a hard climb, suitable only for bikers with good uphill endurance. The road may be impassable for bicycles if it has been raining in the mountains. The Jeep road continues beyond the Waikolu Lookout, but it can be rough, rutted, and very muddy. If weather permits, you can make an exploratory descent as outlined in Adventuring by Four-Wheel Drive.

NORTHWEST COAST: Several Jeep roads meander northward toward the coast from Farrington Highway in Kualapuu. Used mostly by fishermen, some of them lead to isolated ocean overlooks, coves, and beaches. The area is rocky and windswept, and high sand dunes back the beach toward the western end.

SOUTHWEST COAST: This long unpaved coastal road begins 2.5 miles west of Kaunakakai, branching left off Highway 46. You may need to explore several branches of the road before finding the right one, and even then it is possible to run into a locked gate. But if the gates are open, you'll have a great level ride along 9 miles of isolated, empty beach. This coast can also be reached via Jeep road from Maunaloa, again depending on whether the gates are open. You might check with Molokai Ranch; phone 5 5 2-2627 for access information.

Hunting

Goats, pigs, and axis deer are the three animals you may hunt on Molokai public lands. In addition, for a fee, Molokai Ranch will permit you to hunt eland, blackbuck antelope, and Barbary sheep on its property. Check with the ranch at P.O. Box 8, Kaunakakai, HI 96748; phone 5 5 2-2741 for the latest information, including fees. There is no public hunting allowed in West Molokai; all the hunting areas are located east of Highway 470. Bag limits for goats and pigs are as liberal as on Maui—two per day of each—but the season is more restricted depending on the area, and there is no hunting at all on Molokai except on weekends and holidays.

A special permit, obtained by public drawing, is required to hunt axis deer, and the limit is one animal per season. The season normally runs for nine consecutive weekends, ending the last Sunday in April. Bag limit is one animal per season. Applications for the public drawing can be obtained by contacting the Division of Forestry and Wildlife, 1151 Punchbowl Street, Honolulu, HI 96813; phone 587-0166.

The Nature Conservancy, which maintains stewardship over Pelekunu Valley and its fragile ecosystem, ran into a buzz saw of opposition from animal welfare groups and hunters when it attempted to control feral pigs in the valley by using snares. To the animal welfare groups the procedure, which inflicted a lingering death on the pigs, was painful and cruel. To hunters it was a waste of good meat. As a partial solution to the problem, the Conservancy opened the valley to Molokai-resident pig hunters on a selective basis.

You may hunt 10 kinds of bird on Molokai: ring-necked and green pheasant, California Valley and Japanese quail, Chukar partridge, gray and black francolin, spotted and barred dove, and wild turkey. Except for wild turkey, the season normally lasts from the first Saturday in November through the third Sunday in January, weekends and holidays only. For those wishing to hunt wild turkey, the season comprises the first three weekends in January. Although situated in the same general location, the public bird hunting area is more restricted than that for mammals.

Kayaking the North Shore

The pioneer of Hawaiian kayaking is Audrey Sutherland, whose books *Paddling My Own Canoe* and *Paddling Hawaii* are the classic guides to the subject. This remarkable, gutsy lady first tackled— alone—the daunting north shore of Molokai in 1962. Her "own canoe" consisted of a mask, snorkel, fins, and a waterproof pack, which she towed as she swam along one of the world's roughest seacoasts. Since then Sutherland has graduated to inflatable kayak, making 18 solo trips down Molokai's formidable shoreline as well as kayaking in Ireland, Scotland, France, Norway, and the South Pacific. Lately she has turned her attention to British Columbia and Alaska, paddling over 9,000 miles, doing in those cold subarctic waters what she used to do in these warm subtropical ones. But in either Hawaii or Alaska, she remains the undisputed authority on offshore inflatable kayak adventuring.

The northeastern shore of Molokai can be a very hostile place. An onshore wind blows almost continuously, sending 10- to 25-foot waves crashing against the world's highest sea cliffs. No one (except Audrey Sutherland) would consider swimming in these waters, and even boaters treat this coast with great respect. On a scale of 1 to 6, this is a class-5 paddle (open ocean, high winds, choppy seas, surf breaking on rocky shores). Yet kayakers in hardshells, foldups, and inflatables ply this coast every year during the summer months, mostly without mishap. In spite of Audrey's success, I do not recommend that you kayak this coast alone. It is too isolated, and you are too far from help, with no way to get it should you need it. The best way to make this trip is with a kayak club or similar group. The group leader will normally make logistical arrangements, and the group itself will usually include people who have made the trip before—they know where the dragons be. A club that makes at least one annual trip to Molokai is Hui Waa Kaukahi, P.O. Box 88143, Honolulu, HI 96830.

If you have rough sea and surf landing experience, there is no reason why you and a partner cannot organize a trip without a kayak group. If you decide on this plan Sutherland's *Paddling Hawaii* is a valuable planning tool. I would recommend two single boats rather than a two-man kayak: For flexibility, carrying capacity, and emergencies, two kayaks are better than one. June, July, and early August are the best months for this trip: The winter surf is far too dangerous, and in spring and fall conditions are unreliable. You will need to bring *everything* with you that you need, except water, but you must bring a means of purifying that. Also, be sure to bring a mask, snorkel, and fins. They function more as necessities than recreational items on this trip, especially for coming ashore (see below). If you plan to rent a kayak, you must do so in Honolulu, as there is no place to rent one on Molokai. The rental firm with the largest kayak selection is Go Bananas, 732 Kapahulu Avenue, Honolulu, HI 96816; phone 737-9514.

Halawa Bay–Waikolu Valley (water distance 14 miles; 3 to 5 days)

Maps: USGS topo quads—Halawa, Kamalo, Kaunakakai.

This trip calls for a put-in at Halawa Bay and a take-out at Waikolu Valley, from which you will then hike about a mile to Kalawao Park, which is within the boundary of the Kalaupapa Settlement. *You must have advance permission to enter the settlement,* and you must also arrange for transportation from Kalawao to the settlement's airport for a flight out. Permission to enter Kalaupapa and transportation to the airport can be arranged by calling Damien Tours at 567-6171, and they can also arrange a tour of the settlement—well worth the modest charge—at the same time. Air Molokai, phone 521-0090, has daily service to Kalaupapa from Honolulu, and also from the Molokai airport. At this writing, fares were $55 one way to Honolulu and $20 one way to Molokai Airport. Island Air also has two flights a day to both places, but at higher fares. Because only small planes can service Kalaupapa, luggage space is limited (see below for information on transporting kayaks). Currently Air Molokai allows 40 pounds per passenger, with a 25¢ per pound surcharge over that limit—providing there is room on the plane for the extra baggage. There is no road to Kalaupapa, and the only land access is a steep, 2-mile trail that descends the cliff behind the peninsula. The mule ride down the trail has been discontinued. If you are in good hiking shape, it is possible to backpack your gear up the trail, and then taxi (by prior arrangement) down to Kaunakakai.

As you can see, these logistical problems rule out hardshell kayaks on this trip—there is no convenient way to get them out from Kalaupapa. Folding boats are heavy, 40 to 80 pounds, and they can be damaged by the rough-water, boulder-beach landings that must be made. That leaves inflatables. Weighing from 25 to 40 pounds each, small enough to pack for flights, and with the resiliency to bounce rather than break on rough, rocky shores, an inflatable is the best choice for this trip.

SUGGESTED ITINERARY: The itinerary below assumes that you take four days for the trip, overnighting at Hakaaano, Wailau, and Pelekunu, with a layover day at each valley. This is a water distance of 14 miles. Without the layovers, however, the trip can be made in three days. For kayaking in these waters, the USGS topographic maps are more useful than nautical charts, since it is *land* features that you will be guiding on. Water depth and navigational hazards are of secondary interest, as your craft will not draw enough to be affected by underwater shoals. You should remain relatively close to shore on this trip, but well away from shore swells and breaks. For your stop at Pelekunu, it will be necessary to inform The Nature Conservancy's Molokai office of the number of persons in your party, the date you will arrive, and the length of your stay (553-5236).

Day 1—Halawa Valley to Hakaaano (4 miles). You'll want to start as early as possible from Halawa, to beat the head winds that begin to build up by midmorning. Drive to the beach park at the end of the road in the valley, and put in over the sand. Depending on the conditions, you might also put in on the opposite side of the bay. If waves are breaking in the entrance, you will have to time your exit between sets. Once you have cleared the bay and turned left, you have a mile to paddle before you round Lamaloa Head. Here, a left turn will put you on an eastern course for the rest of the journey. You will now pick up a tailwind that will remain with you for the rest of the trip. Sheer 1,200-foot cliffs and blue water comprise your world for the next two miles to Puaahaunui Point, the tip of a small, relatively flat *hala-* and brush-covered peninsula.

Less than a mile farther on, you'll reach Hakaaano Peninsula, your first stop. Paddle around to the lee side to come ashore. This is a boulder-beach landing that can be handled in two ways. The first option, if the surf is not too rough, is to run the boat up on the rounded rocks, jump quickly ashore, and haul the boat out. The other method is to disembark in waist-deep water and guide the boat in through the surf. In either case you should have a line fixed to the bow that you can hold or loop over your shoulder so that the boat does not get away from you. You will also need protective footwear. Dive booties and reef walkers are okay, but the best choice is felt sole tabis (*limu tabi*), available in local fishing supply stores in the islands.

On the west side of the peninsula you will see a lean-to and some other improvements constructed by a local fisherman who camps here on his fishing trips. Please do not disturb anything. Water, which should be treated, is available at the cliff falls. You may camp in the immediate vicinity, or, if it is very windy, you can find shelter inside the tree line to the east. Once you have set up camp, take the afternoon to explore Papalaua Valley on the other side of Keanapuka, the big arch to the west. You can wade through the arch unless the tide is in; then you may have to swim partway. Despite its narrowness and steep sides, taro was once grown in the valley, and you will still see traces of terracing. Papalaua Falls, up at the head of the valley, drops in a 1,200-foot cascade, and by rock-hopping through and around the stream you can reach the pool at the base of its last 80-foot drop. If you are still feeling adventurous and have the time, you can swim around the cliff on the west side of Papalaua Stream to Kikipua Peninsula, where there are rock remains of ancient Hawaiian houses, taro terraces, and a *heiau*.

Day 2—Hakaaano to Wailau Valley (3.5 miles). As you leave Hakaaano the next morning, you may want to paddle through Keanapuka. Once you pass Papalaua and round Kikipua Point, another 1.5 miles brings you to Lepau Head, followed by the Wailau Valley. Unless the surf at the sand beach on the west side of the valley is very calm, come ashore at the boulder beach at the mouth of

the main stream. Wailau is the largest of Molokai's north shore valleys. It once had a sizable settlement, including a school. The lure
of city life caused its population to dwindle steadily, and by 1920
the last resident had left. Officially no one lives there now, although
a few semipermanent residents seem to have established themselves. And in summer, as you will see, quite a few people set up
encampments on or near the beach, staying anywhere from a few
days to a few months. The Wailau Trail begins at the beach, follows
the stream back to the head wall of the valley, and then climbs over
the valley rim and down the south side of the island. It is thus possible to hike in and out of the valley, trail conditions permitting (see
the Backpacking Adventures section of this chapter). Use the afternoon to explore the valley, and be sure to look for the good swimming holes along the stream.

Day 3—Wailau Valley to Pelekunu Valley (4 miles). About a mile
after putting back in at Wailau, you'll pass Waiehu, a small peninsula. Shortly thereafter you will be paddling beneath the world's
highest sea cliff—3,450 feet. Over the next three-quarters of a mile,
four spectacular waterfalls pour over its face, dancing in the wind
before plunging into the sea. There is a turbulent stretch of water
as you pass between Kaholaiki Bay and Mokohola Rock, 0.4 miles
seaward of the bay's two points. You'll now turn into Pelekunu Bay,
along its eastern wall. Like Wailau, the best landing on this boulder
beach is near the mouth of the stream, which is on the eastern side
of the beach.

Pelekunu is now uninhabited, although it, like Wailau, once had
a fair-sized settlement, including a school, a church, and a post office. But by 1931 the people were gone—like those of Wailau—to
the towns. Very few people visit the valley today. It has become a
preserve under the management of The Nature Conservancy, which
limits access. On the west wall of the bay you can see what remains
of a derrick that was once used by boats supplying the valley; they
were unable to load and unload across the rough beach, especially
in winter surf. An old Geological Survey shack also once stood in
this location. It is also possible to swim about a third of the way out
along the eastern arm of the bay, come ashore at an indentation in
the cliff, and climb to a beautiful overlook of Kaholaiki Bay.

Day 4—Pelekunu to Waikolu Valley (4.2 miles). Just after you leave Pelekunu Bay you may encounter another area of turbulence as you paddle between Mokumanu Rock and the shoreline cliffs. When you round Pahu Point into Haupu Bay, you will see a house on the cliff above. The private home of a Molokai family, this is the only permanent structure on the entire coastline until Kalaupapa. There is a lava tube cave, into which you can paddle, in the cliff beneath the house. As you paddle toward the inner bay, you'll come to a cluster of small, rocky islets with a bay behind them, a lava beach, and a waterfall. If water and wind are calm, and they usually are, this is a great place to play around and simply enjoy your boat and the scenery; the eastern portion of Haupu Bay provides a respite from the wind. Be wary, though, of rock falls from the cliffs if you go ashore.

On the first point of land after leaving Haupu Bay, you'll come to Kapailoa, a tunnel through which you may paddle, but only if the surge leaves you plenty of room. The light inside the tunnel is the same translucent blue seen in Capri's Blue Grotto.

Continuing eastward, and rounding Kukaiwaa Point, you may encounter more rough water. Take note of the Huelo sea stack, with its covering of *loulu,* Hawaii's only native palm.

Once you pass between Okala Island and Leinaopapio Point, turn left and head for the shore at Waikolu, where reduced wind and calm water should ensure a relatively easy landing. You will have to hike about a mile from this point, over the stone and pebble beach and up a rise, to Kalawao Park, where your prearranged transportation should meet you. It is possible to avoid most of the walk along the beach from Waikolu by coming ashore at the beginning of the Kalaupapa peninsula, just below Kalawao, but this is at the expense of a rough landing through pounding surf. Entry into Waikolu Valley is not permitted as it is a watershed for the Kalaupapa Settlement.

If you would like to do more kayaking in the islands, see "Kayaking the Na Pali Coast" in this book (page 338), and by all means be sure to read the island-by-island kayaking trip descriptions in Audrey Sutherland's *Paddling Hawaii.*

CHAPTER SIX

Lanai
Looking for an Identity

U NTIL THE FALL of 1992, Lanai was considered little more
than a large pineapple plantation. Even among Hawaii residents, Lanai was the least popular of the islands, attracting mainly
hunters, fishermen, and a few scuba divers. In 1992 the Lanai Company, a subsidiary of Dole Food Company, which owns virtually
the entire island, ceased all pineapple production on Lanai, causing
a severe dislocation in the small population of 2,200, and its mostly
agricultural-oriented workforce. The company has now opened
two luxury hotels on the island, golf courses have been built, workers have been retrained, and the character of the island has begun
to change, albeit slowly. Dole has grand plans for expensive homes
on the golf courses, which, if approved, will change things even
more. Tourism is increasing, but not to the degree expected by the
resort planners, who had hoped to attract an affluent crowd. Apparently there are not as many rich people out there as the planners
expected—or at least not that many willing to come to Lanai. Not
all Lanai residents are pleased with what is happening to their island, but they need the work.

The smallest of the inhabited main islands, except for privately

LANAI

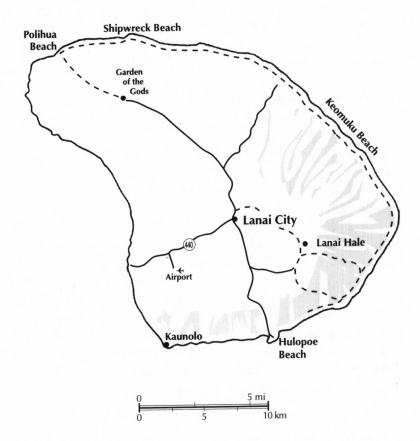

Polihua Beach

Shipwreck Beach

Garden of the Gods

Keomuku Beach

Lanai City

Lanai Hale

440

Airport

Kaunolo

Hulopoe Beach

0   5 mi

0   5   10 km

held Niihau, Lanai is 18 miles long and 13 miles wide, and encompasses 140 square miles. The island is a shield volcano, between 1.3 and 1.8 million years old. At 3,370 feet, Lanaihale is Lanai's highest point. Lanai is one of the dryest of the main islands, because it lies in the wind shadow of Maui, which restricts its rainfall. You will become acutely aware of this dryness as your vehicle churns up the dust on Lanai's former plantation roads. There is no public transport on the island and hitchhiking is illegal, but no one will bother to stop you from doing it if you can manage to get a ride in Lanai's sparse road traffic.

Adventuring by Four-Wheel Drive

Note: This section is designed to be used with a good road map at hand, such as the full-color topographic Map of Molokai and Lanai, University of Hawaii Press, $2.95. You should also have USGS topo quads Lanai North and Lanai South. These are provisional maps; please note that all contour intervals and elevations are in meters.

Unless your adventuring is limited to driving from luxury hotels to golf courses, a four-wheel-drive vehicle is almost essential for getting around Lanai. Without superior traction and a low gear ratio you will be limited, for the most part, to the three paved roads radiating from Lanai City: Highway 44 west to Kaumalapau Harbor; the same road north to the beginning of Shipwreck Beach; and Highway 441 south to Hulopoe Beach. There is so much more to a Lanai adventure than can be experienced from these roads. Shown below are three full-day driving adventures on Lanai, all originating from Lanai City. Should you be staying at Manele Bay, the third day's itinerary can be modified.

MUNRO TRAIL–KEOMUKU SHORELINE LOOP: (22 miles)

Weather permitting, this should be your first four-wheel adventure on Lanai. The Munro Trail is a Jeep track that leads along a forested ridge to Lanaihale, at 3,370 feet the highest point on the island. At Lanaihale, you'll then descend a steep trail to the eastern shore of the island, exploring its isolated beaches as you make your way north. Finally you'll connect with Highway 430 and return to

Lanai City. If it is raining, or if the uplands are covered in fog, save this trip for another day and head for a coastal area, where the weather will probably be better.

To reach the trailhead, start at a point on Keomuku Road (Highway 430) just in front of the Koele Lodge, one of Lanai's two resort hotels. (You can get a strip map from the hotel's activity desk that shows the route.) From there, drive about 1.25 miles, turning right onto the tree-lined, paved road. You will pass a cemetery on the right, and then, less than half a mile on the left, is a sign for the start of the trail. The trail traverses an area reforested in the early 1900s by naturalist George Munro in order to restore Lanai's watershed, which had been destroyed by years of overgrazing. Munro replanted the area with eucalyptus, ironwoods, and Norfolk Island pine, all of which now cover the long ridgeline behind Lanai City. On a clear day, five of the main islands of the Hawaiian chain may be seen from various points on Lanaihale.

The trail begins in a grassy area and passes through a series of small gullies, shaded by tall eucalyptus trees, before starting uphill near Maunalei Gulch. This was the scene of a 1778 massacre of islanders during a war with a chief from the island of Hawaii. Once on the ridge, the trail continues along the ridgeline until it reaches Lanaihale, about 5.5 miles from the original starting point. About 1.2 miles past the summit, watch for a trail leading off to the left with a sharp turn; this is the Awehi Trail, and it is a steep, rugged descent. You will need to be in both low transfer case and low gear, as well as four-wheel drive, to complete this route. Although it is less than 3 miles to the coast, it will seem much longer.

Upon your arrival at the shoreline, turn left on the dirt road that runs along the coast—taking advantage of the turnouts to the narrow beach for views of Maui and Molokai—and to enjoy some isolated beachcombing. Although much of the beach along this stretch is mud flats, you will find sandy sections where you can take a dip. The water here is almost always calm. About 3 miles up the road is Club Lanai, which entertains tourists who arrive by boat from Maui with swimming, snorkeling, biking, and other activities. Club Lanai does not cater to visitors from Lanai, but you will be welcome at their all-you-can-eat-and-drink buffet lunch. Less than

2 miles farther up the coast is the deserted village of Keomuku, marked only by a small abandoned church. Though it is hard to envision, a sugar plantation once existed at Keomuku. The road continues to follow the coast through a forest of *kiawe* and ironwood trees until it joins paved Keomuku Road (Highway 430), about 5 miles from the church. From there, return to Lanai City.

Even this coastal part of the trip should not be made in wet weather. Despite its level grade, even four-wheel-drive vehicles can get mired down in the mucky pools that form in the middle of the dirt road, lasting for days after a heavy rain. If you prefer a shorter, or less rugged, trip, instead of taking the Awehi Trail you can continue down the Munro Trail, returning to Lanai City via Hoike Road and Route 440 (Manele Road).

MORNING: KAUNOLU VILLAGE, AFTERNOON: HULOPOE BEACH:
(32 miles round-trip)

An important archaeological site, Kaunolu Village offers both an interesting visit to one of the most significant places in ancient Hawaii and a real four-wheel drive experience. The ruins of this fishing community are situated at the bottom of a steep, rocky Jeep track on Lanai's south shore. A favorite vacation and fishing spot of Kamehameha, the site is also associated with other Hawaiian chiefs. A trail runs through the former village, where signs are posted at important locations including Kahekili's Leap, a vertigo-producing cliff from which young chiefs reputedly plunged into the sea to prove their manhood.

To reach Kaunolu, take Highway 44 southeast from Lanai City to Kaupili Road (unmarked), which lies just past the airport (about 3.4 miles from Lanai City). Turn left and proceed another 2.2 miles along a former pineapple (dirt) road to a turn on the right, which soon becomes a Jeep road, then a very steep, rocky Jeep road. You will need to be in four-wheel drive and low transfer case for this precipitous descent, but it is not dangerous if you proceed slowly and with care. When you have finished exploring at Kaunolu, return to the pineapple field road (3.3 miles) and turn right (left would take you back the way you came). After 2.7 miles, this road intersects paved Manele Road (Highway 440), where you can turn right and proceed downhill to Hulopoe Beach.

Hulopoe Beach is a beautiful crescent of white sand on Lanai's south shore. Local residents sometimes refer to it as "Manele Beach," although this is properly the name for a small beach at Manele Bay, which lies immediately east of Hulopoe and has a small boat harbor. An ancient fishing village existed at Manele Bay, and some of its ruins can still be seen. A grove of *kiawe* trees backs the beach, as does the Manele Bay Hotel. A campground, the only one on the island, is also located here. For a permit, contact Koele Company, P.O. Box L, Lanai City, HI 96763; phone 565-7233. Offshore, on the east side of the bay, a lava shelf contains colorful coral formations, which, unfortunately, were damaged by Hurricane Iniki in 1992. Hulopoe is almost always safe for swimming except when the surf is high. The bay is part of a marine life conservation district, which restricts fishing and boating activities—signs will let you know what is permitted. A short walk along the lava reef that borders the left (east) side of the bay will bring you to Puu Pehe Cove, a lovely small pocket of white sand with a prominent sea stack offshore. Snorkeling is excellent here, especially along the rocks on the right side of the beach, and swimming is usually safe.

After you return from Hulopoe Beach, be sure to visit the Luahiwa Petroglyphs. Located about 2 miles south of Lanai City via Highway 440, Luahiwa has some excellent examples of ancient Hawaiian rock carvings on clusters of boulders. From Hulopoe, it is 4.9 miles to (unmarked) Hoike Road, which angles in from the right. Take this road for about a mile, to the dirt road that crosses it, and turn left, watching for signs to the petroglyphs. They can be hard to find, since signs are sometimes knocked down or removed, so it is best to ask directions locally. A formal trail to the site is planned, which will solve the problem.

GARDEN OF THE GODS–POLIHALE–SHIPWRECK
BEACH LOOP: (29 miles)

The Garden of the Gods is a pretentious title for this small patch of eroded rock and soil that has been augmented by people placing rock cairns all over the place. In spite of what you may hear, all of the cairns are of recent origin. Garden of the Gods is accessible about 6.6 miles northwest of Lanai City via dirt road through the former pineapple fields. Again, the best starting point is Keomuku Road in front of the Koele Lodge. Head north on Keomuku (the lodge will be on your right) for about half a mile, turning left on the road that runs between the lodge's stables and its tennis courts. At the crossroads turn right, and then stay left whenever you come to a fork. Once you reach an ironwood forest, the Garden of the Gods is about 1.5 miles farther on.

From there it is about 4.5 miles straight ahead to Polihua Beach (when you come to a fork in the road, bear right). This long white sand beach is totally isolated from the rest of Lanai, and is a wonderful place to be completely alone. But resist the temptation to swim here. A strong offshore current often has the force of a fast-flowing river, and your next stop could be Tokyo. When you are ready, continue along the Jeep track, which now follows the shoreline heading east (the ocean is on your left), to Shipwreck Beach. Be careful that you don't lose the Jeep track here. Wind and high waves sometimes obliterate the trail; if that is the case, stop and go forward on foot until you find the track again and are satisfied that it is safe for driving. Even four-wheel-drive vehicles can get stuck in the sand, and you don't want that to happen way out here. If you cannot find the Jeep track, or if it crosses soft, deep sand, it is best to turn around and retrace your route.

Shipwreck Beach is one of the best places in Hawaii for beachcombing. It has miles of driftwood in all sizes and shapes and even glass net floats and paper nautilus shells sometimes wash ashore. Two major shipwrecks lie on the reef just offshore, and the remains of smaller vessels are scattered over an 8-mile stretch of coastline. There is not much chance to snorkel or swim here due to the shallow offshore reef, but you can poke around in the water if you have reef walkers or other suitable footwear. Snorkeling can be good out on the edge of the reef itself if the water is clear. The road follows the shore closely, and you will have good views of Molokai across the channel. Except for occasional *kiawe* trees there is not much shade on this coast, so this can be a hot, dry trip. After Shipwreck

Shipwreck beach extends for nine miles on Lanai's north shore and is one of the best places for beachcombing in Hawaii. Photo by Richard McMahon.

Beach, the Jeep track ends at Highway 430, which takes you all the way back to Lanai City.

Backpacking Adventures

The population of Lanai centers almost exclusively around Lanai City; the rest of the island is virtually uninhabited. As mentioned earlier, Lanai is almost entirely owned by Dole Food Company, so the company is, of course, able to set many of the rules that govern activities on its property. Unfortunately for backpackers, Dole does not permit visitors to camp anywhere on the island except in one location, Hulopoe Beach. (As far as I know, Dole does not patrol the mountains or the beaches looking for unauthorized campers. But rules are rules.) While this is admittedly a lovely spot, it is of little use to backpackers or hikers interested in exploring other parts of the island. Residents of Lanai, on the other hand, are allowed to camp almost anywhere in the wilderness—in the forests, on the mountains, or along the beaches. With the possibility in mind that you may know someone on the island, or that Dole may someday change its policy, I have included some suggestions for backpacking below. One drawback on all of these trips is lack of water. There is virtually no surface water on Lanai—you will have to pack your own.

MUNRO TRAIL: (10.5+-mile loop; moderate)
Maps: USGS topo quads—Lanai North (Provisional), Lanai South (Provisional).

Please see the previous section, Adventuring by Four-Wheel Drive, for a description of this trail. There are many good, flat places to camp near the summit of Lanaihale, including one with a picnic table. From here, you may continue along the Munro Trail as it descends to the center of the island, and then return to Lanai City. Or, for a longer, more challenging trip, you can descend to the east coast via either the Naha or the Awehi trails. The Awehi Trail is described in the previous section. To take the Naha Trail, watch for the point where the Munro Trail makes a hairpin turn to the right, about 2 miles from Lanaihale. Continue on a straight path, and within 200 yards the trail will begin its descent to the left. Unless you plan a long hike—over 30 miles—arrange for someone to pick you up along the road. A good rendezvous spot would be Club Lanai, about 5.7 miles from the end of the pavement on Route 430.

SHIPWRECK BEACH TO POLIHUA BEACH: (10 miles one way; easy)
Maps: USGS topo quad—Lanai North (Provisional).

Shipwreck Beach is one of the best places in Hawaii for beachcombing. There are tons of driftwood in all sizes and shapes, and even those Japanese glass balls used as net floats sometimes wash ashore. There are claims that paper nautilus shells have also been found. Two major shipwrecks lie on the reef just off shore, and the remains of smaller vessels are scattered over an 8-mile stretch of beach. This is, however, a dry, hot hike. Shade is sparse, and sun protection is essential.

To reach the starting point for the hike, take Highway 430 from Lanai City and proceed north to the coast, about 8.3 miles. Turn left on the dirt Jeep track that follows the shoreline westward, and park. This is the beginning of Shipwreck Beach. For a description of Shipwreck Beach, and Polihua Beach, your destination, see Adventuring by Four-Wheel Drive, the previous section. There are plenty of great spots to put up a tent at Polihua, but remember, there is no water. The next day (or whenever) retrace your steps to Shipwreck Beach.

If you have a nonhiking companion, you can eliminate backtracking along Shipwreck Beach. Have your companion drive the backpackers to Garden of the Gods (above), from which you can hike the 4.5 miles down to Polihua Beach. After overnighting at Polihua, hike eastward along Shipwreck Beach to Route 430, where a companion can pick you up.

Day Hikes

The two day hikes listed below cover the same ground as the backpacking trips described in the previous section. Please refer to that section for information on these hikes.

MUNRO TRAIL TO LANAIHALE: (11 miles round-trip)
This hike follows the trail as far as Lanaihale, and then returns the same way. There is no water available.

SHIPWRECK BEACH: (up to 16 miles round-trip)
On this hike you may go the full 8 miles to Polihua Beach before returning, or you may turn around at any intermediate point. This is a hot hike, with no accessible drinking water, and sun protection is required.

Snorkeling and Diving

As mentioned earlier, there are no dive shops on Lanai; the only dive operation is run from the Manele Bay Hotel, but this does not help shore divers as the hotel will not fill or refill tanks, and their equipment is not rented out but used only in connection with their own dive program. Unless you intend to do extensive diving on Lanai, it is not necessary to plan a stay on the island to dive there. Daily tours from Maui make trips to Lanai's best sites (see Snorkeling and Diving in the Maui chapter of this book). The Manele Bay Hotel operates combined snorkeling and dive tours to these same sites, using several catamarans and a large inflatable. All equipment is provided, but divers who bring their own receive a 10 percent discount. (If you have everything but tanks and a weight belt, you'll still get the discount.) The advantage in diving directly from Lanai is quick transportation to the dive sites compared to the trip over from Maui. For example, The Cathedrals, Lanai's most popular site, is practically in front of the Manele Bay Hotel. It is not necessary to stay at the hotel to take advantage of its tours, but on Lanai you don't have many other options. Listed below are snorkeling and dive sites accessible from shore.

HULOPOE BEACH (D/S): This is the best place to snorkel on Lanai as well as the best shore dive. Entry and exit are easy from the beautiful sandy beach. There used to be lots of pretty coral formations in shallow water along the east side of the bay, but in September 1992, Hurricane Iniki caused considerable damage to the shallower coral and it is now necessary to snorkel farther out. For divers the scenery is even better, with crevices, arches, and more coral becoming apparent in the deeper water. You'll see many different kinds of reef fish in all areas, while turtles can sometimes be seen on the west side of the bay.

A walk of about a quarter of a mile out along the lava reef on the east side of the bay will bring you to the pretty, small sandy beach known as Puu Pehe Cove (D/S). Snorkeling and diving are good there, though snorkeling is best along the rocks of the western arm of the cove. Divers can explore either arm of the cove, or head toward the large sea stack off its eastern arm. The Hulopoe beach park at the bay provides rest rooms, showers, picnic tables, and a campground. Hulopoe is one of the few places in the islands where you can camp right at a dive site. But it is a marine conservation area, so nothing may be disturbed. To reach Hulopoe from Lanai City, take Manele Road all the way to its end.

MANELE BAY (D/S): This is the only public boat harbor on the island; there is also a beach park. Though not attractive for swimming, the area provides reasonably good snorkeling and diving. Check for more information locally. To get to Manele Bay, proceed as for Hulopoe, but turn left instead of right to reach the boat harbor at the end of the road.

KAUMALAPAU HARBOR (D): This harbor was constructed to ship fruit from Lanai's pineapple fields to Honolulu. But since island pineapple production has ceased, the harbor receives only occasional use. The breakwater at its north end affords a good wall dive, which drops as much as 90 feet to a sandy bottom. You can explore several caves and holes on the way down. There is less coral than you will find elsewhere, but large ocean fish can often be seen, and the dropoff is dramatic, with good visibility. To reach Kaumalapau from Lanai City, take Kaumalapau Highway past the airport, to the highway's end at the harbor. Enter on the outside of the breakwater, anywhere after you pass the large storage tanks.

KAUNOLU BAY (D/S): A very steep, rutted, rocky Jeep road leads to this ancient site, now a National Historic Landmark (see Adventuring by Four-Wheel Drive in this chapter for directions to the site and other information). Kaunolu is a difficult place to reach, so combine your dive with a tour of the village, which has signs marking the various points of interest. Snorkelers can investigate the rocks close to shore, while divers can explore either arm of the bay. If you enter on the far side of the lava rocks on the west side of the bay, you can swim out to the point, cross a pretty coral reef, and exit onto the boulder beach. On the east side, enter from the beach, rounding Palaoa Point, with its lighthouse, then following the east wall of the point before returning to exit back on the beach. If you are careful with your air, you might be able to combine both trips.

SHIPWRECK BEACH (S): This long, deserted shoreline extends about 8 miles from the end of Keomuku Road (44) north to Polihua

Beach. The beach gets its name from the many vessel groundings, accidental and deliberate, that have occurred there. The beach is littered with driftwood and remnants of past wrecks. A shallow reef extends about 200 yards seaward. Snorkeling is possible on the outer edge of the reef almost anywhere along this coast, but the water can be murky and choppy due to wind conditions. But if you plan to do some beachcombing here (the best activity for this coastline), it certainly won't hurt to bring your mask and snorkel along. It is also advisable to wear some kind of reef walkers to protect from sharp coral and urchins while searching for snorkeling spots.

Surfing

Nobody comes to Lanai to surf. Just about the only boards in the water belong to local residents, and you won't see very many of them—but it's all the surf they have without hopping a flight to another island. If you are visiting Lanai for other adventures, and get the feeling that you must go out and catch a wave, the places below will at least allow you to get wet.

For practical purposes there is only one surfing spot on Lanai, *Hulopoe Beach* (S/L/B). To reach Hulopoe Beach from Lanai City, take Route 441 south to the end of the road. There are rest rooms, picnic tables, showers, drinking water, and a campground at Hulopoe. Lanai residents sometimes also surf at *Lopa Beach* or *Polihua Beach,* both of which are accessible only via four-wheel drive. Lopa requires a long drive on a bad road just to see if the surf is up. It is about 2.5 miles south of Club Lanai. Polihua, in addition to having difficult access, is a treacherous place to be in the water.

Biking

I do not recommend that you come to Lanai specifically for bicycle riding. True, the island's very light traffic is a boon to cyclists, but in every other aspect cycling is better on the other islands. Lanai's paved roads, not particularly interesting to ride on, lead in three directions from Lanai City: The first runs through former pineapple fields to a commercial harbor, while the second road leads to the dry and empty north coast—great for beachcombing, but difficult to ride on, even for mountain bikes. Only the third road reaches an attractive destination—a lovely beach with a major resort hotel—but the road also passes through miles of empty fields. All three thoroughfares drop steadily downhill from Lanai City's 1,800-foot elevation, requiring a long slog back up. Also, there is only one small campground on Lanai; and of the island's three hotels, two are luxury class and quite expensive while the third, with only eleven rooms, is usually full.

For those determined to spin their wheels on Lanai anyway, I suggest referring to the Adventuring by Four-Wheel Drive section in this chapter, modifying the trips as desired. The following comments should help in planning your ride. Other than the luxury hotel and campground at Hulopoe Beach, there is no food or water available anywhere outside Lanai City.

MUNRO TRAIL–KEOMUKU SHORELINE LOOP: Only mountain bikers should consider this trip, and it would be best not to take the Awehi Trail to the eastern shore unless you are willing to walk your bike down most of this rugged, very steep trail. You can, instead, continue down the Munro Trail, returning to Lanai City via Hoike Road and Route 440 (Manele Road). If you want to ride the Keomuku shoreline, you can get there later by using Highway 430.

I do not recommend you ride even a mountain bike down the very rocky trail to Kaunolu Village.

Any bike can handle the easy dirt road to Garden of the Gods, but I do not recommend continuing with the Polihale–Shipwreck Beach Loop, even with a mountain bike. Cyclists can reach Shipwreck Beach from Lanai City via Highway 430, which also provides access to Keomuku Beach. The Jeep tracks on both of these beaches are best ridden on mountain- or similar fat-tire bikes. But watch out for *kiawe* thorns, which can puncture a tire as efficiently as any nail.

Hunting

The good news about hunting on Lanai is that almost half the island is a public hunting area. The bad news is that there is very little to hunt. Unlike the other islands, there are no feral goats or pigs on

Lanai. The only two animals you can hunt there are mouflon and axis deer. Unless you hunt with a bow and arrow, both require a special permit obtained only by winning a public drawing. Hunting is good on Lanai for the mouflon, a prized trophy animal. The mouflon season is short, four days, and usually takes place on the four Sundays of August. The first two Sundays are bow and arrow only, no permit required, and the last two are for special permit holders using rifles, shotguns, or bows. The limit is one mouflon per season. During the 1994 season more than 150 mouflon were taken; about half of the hunters on Lanai bagged one during the four-day season. Hunting mouflon on Lanai will become more popular in the future, now that the animals are being eradicated on Mauna Kea on the Big Island.

The axis deer season normally runs for nine consecutive Sundays, ending the last Sunday in April. Bag limit is one animal per season. Archery season comprises two Sundays prior to the regular season. Applications for the public drawing can be obtained by contacting the Division of Forestry and Wildlife, 1151 Punchbowl Street, Honolulu, HI 96813; phone 587-0166.

You may hunt eleven kinds of birds on Lanai: ring-necked and green pheasant; Japanese, California Valley and Gambel's quail; Erkel's and gray francolin; spotted and barred dove; and wild turkey. The hunting area is the same as that for the mammals. Except for wild turkey, the season normally lasts from the first Sunday in November through the third Sunday in January, Sundays and holidays only. For wild turkey, the season takes place on the first three Sundays in January.

CHAPTER SEVEN

Oahu
Where the People Are

I F ONE THING can be said to be wrong with Oahu, it is the
amount of people on the island. Even though it encompasses only
10 percent of the land area of the islands, Oahu must support over
80 percent of the state's population. More than 840,000 residents
and 100,000 tourists crowd the island every day, most of them in
the Honolulu/Waikiki corridor on Oahu's southeast corner. Traffic
on the H1 Freeway crawls along in Los Angeles–style gridlock, and
not only during rush hour. Hotels, condominiums, and office buildings destroy views and block trade winds. Bodies carpet the beaches
of Waikiki, Ala Moana, and Hanauma Bay, making it difficult to
see even the sand. Admittedly, these conditions don't bring "adventure" to mind for many people. Except for shopping adventures, adventures in fine dining, and nightlife adventures, Oahu is
perceived as a playland for those who want comfort and convenience, all of it close at hand.

Yet only a few miles from the heart of Honolulu, the crowds,
cars, and construction disappear, and the wilderness takes over.
Three-quarters of the island is rain forest, rugged mountains, uninhabited valleys, and deserted beaches. The forests are as lush, the

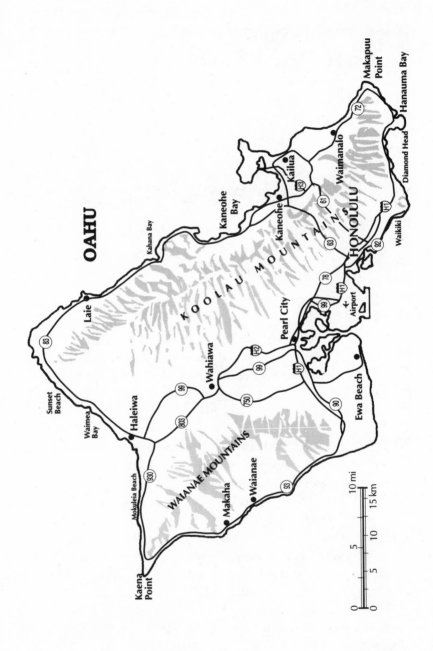

mountains as silent, the valleys as pristine, and the beaches as empty as any on the outer islands—you just have to know where to go.

The third largest of the main islands, Oahu was formed between 2.2 and 3.4 million years ago when two volcanoes joined together in the sea. The island is 44 miles long, 30 miles wide, and 594 square miles in area. Mount Kaala, 4,020 feet high, is Oahu's highest point. After tourism, federal spending—mostly for defense—contributes the most money to the island's economy. More than sixty thousand military personnel are stationed on Oahu. All services are represented: the Navy at Pearl Harbor, the Army at Schofield Barracks, the Air Force at Hickam, and the Marines at Kaneohe. While these are the major installations, there are still others elsewhere on the island. For years the mainstay of Oahu's economy, sugar, under the pressure of countries with cheaper land and lower costs, saw its last harvest in early 1996. The miles of waving green cane fields, so familiar to residents and millions of past tourists, are no more.

Oahu's regularly scheduled bus system serves virtually the entire island and runs every day of the week. Free timetables are available at satellite city halls (see Appendix II), and bus maps and guides can be purchased at a reasonable cost at newsstands and book stores. For bus schedules, times, and route information call 848-5555. Luggage is limited to what will fit in your lap, so the bus is not a good choice going to or from the airport unless you have little or no luggage. Also, metal frame backpacks are prohibited on most bus routes. Several reasonably priced limousine services run between the airport and most major hotels. Hitchhiking is legal, but only if you're standing at a bus stop.

Adventuring by Car

Note: This section is designed to be used with a good road map at hand. The best one for Oahu comes in two parts: Oahu Reference Map #1 (Honolulu, South Shore, Central Oahu), and Map #2 (Windward Coast, North Shore, Leeward Coast), James A. Bier, Publisher. They can be purchased at bookstores, newsstands, and many other places. The map of Oahu in the University of Hawaii

Press series may be used for more general planning, where detail is not needed.

It is a bit difficult to meet the challenge of adventuring by car on Oahu. Although there is plenty of adventure on Oahu, the island is just too built up for much of it to be accessible by car. For the most part your car can take you to places where adventures begin, but you will usually have to park in order to partake of any of them. But there are some adventures, set forth below, that can at least be enjoyed *close* to your car.

During your time on Oahu you will most likely stay in Waikiki, visit most of Honolulu's points of interest, and take a tour around the island by car. This section will only deal with your car tour of the island. Honolulu's points of interest are well known, mentioned in many other guides and free handouts, and really don't qualify as "adventures." However, before we move on to the round-island tour, I'd like to fill you in on some lesser-known aspects of the routine tour highlights that will enhance your overall experience of the island.

WAIKIKI BEACH: By now you have probably discovered that the famed beach, hemmed in by huge hotels, is quite narrow in most places, and very crowded. Fort DeRussy, an R&R center for military personnel, lies between the Hilton Hawaiian Village and the Outrigger Hotel. It has the widest sand beach in Waikiki, and is open to the general public, as are its spacious, grassy picnic grounds backing the beach. Fort DeRussy is also home to the U.S. Army Museum, housed in a former coast artillery battery.

DIAMOND HEAD: Everyone is familiar with this famous Waikiki landmark, but many people are unaware that an easy trail leads through tunnels and staircases to a former military bunker on its peak, where you can find great views of the city and the coastline. The trail begins inside the crater, which you enter via a tunnel from Diamond Head Road. Parking is available at the trailhead.

ARIZONA MEMORIAL: While here, don't fail to tour the *USS Bowfin,* a World War II submarine moored nearby.

HANAUMA BAY: When you visit this, Oahu's premier snorkeling spot, take time out from feeding the fish to walk around the right side of the bay to see the Witches Brew, a cauldron of wind-whipped water and crashing waves just a few minutes from the beach. Then go around the left side of the bay to the Toilet Bowl, a small pool separated from the open sea by a rock ledge. Wave action causes the water in the pool to flush in and out. Care should be taken at both of these spots, though, as drownings have occurred.

MAKAPUU LIGHTHOUSE OVERLOOK: If you have the time, and would welcome a little exercise and about an hour's break from driving, this 2-mile round-trip on a paved road leads to a magnificent lookout. After leaving Sandy Beach, the highway begins to climb toward Makapuu Point. In about 1.2 miles you will note a road, barred by a gate, turning off to the right. There is a shoulder pulloff, and there is normally room to park. Ignore the No Trespassing sign, which no longer applies. The road winds uphill, affording dramatic views of the rocky coast below, until it reaches a platform overlooking the Makapuu Lighthouse and a glorious seascape spreads out before you. You can see Kaohikaipu and Manana (Rabbit) Island and Makapuu Beach Park, and a long expanse of the windward coast unfolds in a panorama of green mountains and blue sea.

If you have an hour or so more to spare, you can climb down to the Makapuu tidepools. Here, when the swells are up, you will see as many as six blowholes, two of them higher and more spectacular than the Halona Blowhole, a major tourist attraction mentioned below. Even when they are not spouting water, a respectable roar rises from these blowholes as the swells enter the caves beneath them. On calm days you can explore and swim in any of several tidal pools scooped out of the plateaulike reef at the base of the cliff.

To reach the Makapuu tidepools you take the same road as you would to the lighthouse. After about 0.8 miles, the road makes a sharp left turn at the top of a sea cliff. Four stone pillars, each about two and a half feet high, appear on the right. Continue along the road, about 0.4 miles, until you reach the beginning of a line of similar pillars, also on the right. A path begins here that leads down to the tidepools. A white arrow, painted on the road surface, points to the path, but it is easy to find.

The descent to the pools will take about 30 minutes, but you need not go all the way—in fact, you may not be able to if the ocean is particularly boisterous. Boots are best for this rocky trail, but jogging shoes will do. Ordinary street shoes are apt to get scuffed. It is possible to return via a trail at the base of the cliff, which you will see heading right as you face the sea. In this event, you would come out on a flat plain where the cliff ends, and return to your parking area via a dirt road.

Around Oahu by Car (100 miles round-trip)

The following itinerary suggests starting in Honolulu, crossing the Pali Highway to the windward side of the island, driving north along the coast to the north shore and Haleiwa, and then returning to Honolulu via Wahiawa and the H2 and H1 freeways. You can just as easily drive this route in the opposite direction, except that the sun is in a better position for picture taking in the morning along the beautiful and photogenic windward coast. An early start from Honolulu gives you morning highlights on the cliffs all the way up to the windward coast. The trip can be made in one day, although if you are going to take advantage of the adventures along the way it would be better to stop overnight en route. I also assume that you will visit Honolulu's southeast shore on another day. Its attractions, such as Hanauma Bay and Sea Life Park, can take up a day in themselves, especially if you're sightseeing along the way at places such as the Halona Blowhole and Lanai Lookout.

Begin your drive by taking the H1 Freeway to the Pali Highway. About 2.5 miles after entering the highway, watch for Nuuanu Pali Drive on the right. Turn off on this road for a scenic drive through a small rain forest. The road will rejoin the highway in about 1.5 miles; watch for the turnoff to the Pali Lookout in approximately 1.3 miles. Park and walk over to the windy lookout for a sweeping view of windward Oahu. Please note the cliff to your left (as you face the ocean): This is the one over which Kamehameha's warriors forced the remnants of Oahu's army, driving them to their deaths on the rocks below and bringing the island under Kamehameha's domination.

Return to the highway and continue through the tunnel to its windward side. After the hairpin turn (about 1.5 miles from the tunnel) move into the left lane so that you can turn left on Highway 83 (Kamehameha Highway) toward Kaneohe. After passing through the congested center of town, the highway hugs the coastline along beautiful Kaneohe Bay, the only true lagoon in the Hawaiian Islands. The highway intersects Kahekili Highway and turns right, where it continues to follow the sea. At this point you may wish to make a short detour to the Byodo-In Temple, a replica of an eleventh-century Buddhist temple in Kyoto, Japan. If so, turn left instead of right and proceed 1.7 miles to the entrance to the Valley of the Temples Cemetery on the right, and follow the signs to the temple. There is an admission charge. As you continue north, you will see some of the most striking mountain and ocean scenery in all the islands. Drive slowly and stop often, looking up toward the-ever-changing green cliffs. Turn off the highway at Kualoa Regional Park. After you park your car, gaze up at the mountains and Mokolii Island (Chinaman's Hat), which lies a quarter-mile offshore. Kualoa was one of the most sacred locations in ancient Hawaii, and a Place of Refuge. (See the Adventuring by Car—National Park to Kailua–Kona—section on the "Hawaii" chapter.) When the sailing canoe *Hokulea* returned from its first trip to Tahiti in 1976, a feat accomplished without modern navigation instruments of any kind, Kualoa was chosen as the place for its ceremonial landing.

Here is one spectacular adventure you can undertake from your car. At low tide it is possible to wade to Mokolii Island, and then climb a trail to its summit. Even if the tide is not so low, you may wade a good part of the way and swim the rest, though nonswimmers should not attempt a crossing even at low tide. Unpredictable holes and crevices on the sea bottom can put a wader temporarily under water. There is a tiny beach, not visible from the shore, on the ocean side of the island. Even if you don't want to tackle the trip to the island, Kualoa is a great place just to get wet and break for lunch. There are rest rooms, showers, drinking water, picnic tables, and a campground.

Once you have started on your way again, watch for Swanzy Beach Park on the right. Shortly thereafter you'll reach the Crouching Lion, a realistic rock formation above the road near a large restaurant of the same name. As you round a curve to the left Kahana Bay comes into view, with its lovely tree-lined crescent beach. Behind the beach, Kahana Valley State Park offers an 8-mile loop trail through an undeveloped valley. Check at the visitor center for maps and information. About 3.5 miles from Kahana you will come to Sacred Falls State Park. If at all possible, you should stop and take this 5-mile round-trip walk to a very pretty waterfall and its equally lovely pool. The pool, a great spot for a swim, is typical of dozens of such lovely pools throughout the islands, most of which are much harder to reach.

The trail starts on a dirt road, and, after about a mile, enters a forest of *kukui,* guava, and mountain apple trees interspersed with ginger and *ti.* Following the stream, first on one side then the other, the trail reaches the falls after another mile. Hawaiian legend claims that the 80-foot-high falls and its pool are sacred to Kamapuaa, the demigod half man–half pig and sometime-lover of Pele, the goddess of fire. You should not take this trip if it is raining. As the many warning signs proclaim, the trail is subject to flash floods, and people have died here.

On the road once more, you'll soon pass the Polynesian Cultural Center, which requires a full afternoon and part of an evening to see properly. If you want to, you can break for the day and visit the center the following day. The Rodeway Inn, a moderately priced motel with a swimming pool, is adjacent to the center. More luxurious digs, at the Turtle Bay Hilton Hotel, are available about 6 miles farther up the road. Just pass the lodge, at the Laie Shopping Center, a side trip right on Anemoku Street and right again on Naupaka will bring you to Laie Point, a wild, rocky promontory pounded by waves.

Leaving Laie Point, you will pass Brigham Young University's Hawaii Campus, and the Mormon Temple off to the left. Next comes Maleakahana State Recreation Area on the bay of the same name. The beach is beautiful and virtually empty, and you can wade to another island, this one a bird sanctuary, offshore (see Oahu's Empty Beaches, in this chapter). The small, quiet town of Kahuku was once the hub of a large sugar plantation, and you will pass an old sugar mill, now trying to survive as a tourist shopping stop, on the right. Farther along, also on the right, you will see the abandoned ponds of a large aquaculture venture, which for years raised fresh- and saltwater prawns and shrimp on the former cane land. After going through several owners, the operation finally failed in 1994.

If you turn in at the entrance to the Turtle Bay Hilton Hotel, you can hike to Kahuku Beach, another of Oahu's empty beaches. Leaving the hotel you will see a series of windmills in the hills to your left, including the world's largest wind generator (if it's still there). Constructed to augment the islands' electric grid with wind-generated power, the project has so far not proven financially successful. From the Hilton, it is 3.6 miles to Sunset Beach, one of Oahu's most famous surfing sites. Unless the surf's up, there is little point in stopping here (although the tour buses do). Parking is difficult, and there is not much to see unless there are surfers in the water. Another 2 miles brings you to Shark's Cove and Three Tables, two of the north shore's most popular snorkeling and dive spots. Above the Foodland store, on the road to Pupukea, is the Puu O Mahuku Heiau, a state monument but now really little more than a pile of rock. It takes imagination to visualize the priests' huts and altars that once stood on this spot, but the view of the coastline is excellent.

Shortly past Foodland, round the bend to Waimea Bay, scene of some of the biggest waves in the state during the winter months. Only the most experienced surfers dare to ride these monsters, which stop traffic all along the highway as drivers gape and stare. Yet in summer, Waimea can be a lake, with children playing in the surf and a sailboat or two floating peacefully at anchor in the bay. The waves only break at Waimea when the surf is higher than 18 feet, and this only happens two or three times a year, between November and March. Behind the bay is Waimea Falls Park, a pretty, botanically groomed valley with a large waterfall and a pool. There is an admission charge.

After you've passed through the quaint town of Haleiwa, make the second right off the traffic circle (actually almost a straight line through the circle), and at the intersection of Farrington Highway, turn right. The road will soon reach the coast at Mokuleia Beach, another long, almost deserted beach (see Oahu's Empty Beaches, later in this chapter). Drive by Dillingham Airfield, where glider rides are available, and shortly after passing the YMCA's Camp Erdman you'll reach the paved road's end. From there a badly eroded and rutted four-wheel-drive road continues for about a mile, until a barrier prevents further vehicle traffic into Kaena Point Natural Area Preserve. This is a wild, lonely, windswept place, wonderful for shoreline exploration. The *ohai,* one of Hawaii's rarest native beach plants, is slowly struggling to make a comeback here.

Although there is no road connection from here to leeward Oahu, a railroad once ran from Honolulu along the leeward coast, around Kaena Point, and then all the way to Kahuku. It ceased operation in 1948. Without either road or rail, you have no choice but to return along the coast the way you came. This time, do not turn at the intersection in Waialua, which would bring you back to the traffic circle, but go straight on through, up the tree-lined road past Schofield Barracks army post, on to the H2 and then H1 freeways back to Honolulu. If you get an early start you may want to drive to the leeward side of the island, the coast you could not reach from Kaena Point. If so, after passing Schofield Barracks, turn right on Highway 750 (Kunia Road), following it about 9 miles to the H1 Freeway. Go west on H1 toward Waianae.

THE LEEWARD COAST: Conditions on the leeward coast differ markedly from the rest of the island. The climate is dry, almost arid, and the vegetation reflects it. With only 17 inches of annual rainfall, salt-tolerant grasses, cactus, and *kiawe* trees predominate. The hills close to the shoreline are mostly brown, rather than the luxuriant green of the windward side of the island. But the uncrowded white sand beaches, deep blue water, and nearly constant sunshine provide Oahu's best environment for water sports and recreation. A friend of mine in the hotel industry once told me that if Waikiki were being built today, it would be located here. Yet the coast is mostly undeveloped and economically depressed, and it's apt to remain that way. People with lower incomes need an affordable place to live, and the leeward area comes close. Houses are more modest than elsewhere on the island; there are few restaurants and bars, and almost no tourist attractions. But the weather is fine, the beaches are wonderful, and the water is crystal clear—and local residents want it to stay that way.

For information about the leeward coast, please see the Biking section of this chapter, bearing in mind that the itinerary shown there will be the reverse of yours.

Backpacking Adventures

Backpacking on Oahu is limited by the lack of good backcountry overnight campsites. Although there are more than thirty campgrounds on the island, only two are wilderness sites that connect with interesting scenic trails. Though there are dozens of fine trails that are worlds removed from Honolulu, few of them are suitable for camping. Even on these it is often difficult to find a level spot on which to pitch a tent, or the treks are too short to make backpacking worthwhile. Fortunately the two sites mentioned below will allow you to get away from it all with your tent, sleeping bag, and stove. One is located in the Koolau Mountains, the other in the Waianae, giving you a choice of two very different environments.

Kuaokala Trail–Peacock Flat Loop (10-mile loop, 2–3 days; moderate)

Maps: USGS topo quads—Kaena, Waianae.

Located in the Waianae Mountains on the northeastern tip of Oahu, this hike combines forested trails, open ridges, and dramatic views of Oahu's north shore and the leeward coast. It requires a free camping permit, obtainable from the Division of Forestry and Wildlife, 1151 Punchbowl Street, Honolulu, HI 96814; phone 587-

0166. There is no water on this hike, except that which may be flowing from two or three intermittent streams.

Day 1—Trailhead to Peacock Flat (4.5 miles). To reach the trailhead from Honolulu, take the H1 Freeway to its end near Makakilo, at which point it becomes Farrington Highway. Continue along the leeward coast on Farrington to the end of the pavement at the beginning of Yokohama Beach. On the right you will see the access road to the Kaena Point Satellite Tracking Station and a gatehouse, at which you may have to show your permit. Proceed up the access road about 2 miles, turning right at the T intersection and then passing left around the administration building. After another half-mile, you'll reach a dirt lot on the right, where you can park. A rectangular CONEX container, used as a small office, sits on the edge of the lot, and will help identify it. The trail begins across the paved road from the parking lot, and is marked by a Na Ala Hele state trail sign.

The path follows a wooded ridgeline, and soon reaches the rim of Makua Valley, which it then follows. Just about 3 miles from the start, after a short, steep climb, the Kuaokala Trail ends at a dirt road. Turn left on this road, which leads away from the rim of Makua Valley. You will soon reach a four-way junction at which you turn right onto the Mokuleia Firebreak Road. This road ends at another paved road on the left, which takes you past an abandoned Nike (anti-aircraft artillery) site. After curving through a gulch, the road reaches Peacock Flat, marked by a dirt road that intersects it from the right. This is your camping spot. A roofed picnic pavilion, enclosed on two sides, and a composting toilet are the only facilities. There is no water. If you find a boisterous Boy Scout Troop at the site, your camping permit allows you to camp anywhere you choose, except in the Pahole Natural Area Reserve, which begins about half a mile farther down the dirt road.

Day 2—Layover: Mokuleia–Makua Rim Loop (5.5-mile loop). If you have only two days for this hike, and you get an early start, this loop can be made in the afternoon, after you have set up camp. Or it may be taken as part of a longer return trip on your second day.

Starting from the dirt road leading into Peacock Flat, hike south-

east, away from the Nike access road. The dirt road will turn into
the southern end of the Mokuleia Trail. A little over a mile from the
campground, you'll reach an open clearing with a trail shelter, at
which point a short spur trail leads from the clearing to the Makua
Rim Trail. Turn right, and follow the Makua Rim back to the Nike
site, then to the campground.

Day 3—Return Loop (4 miles). From Peacock Flat, retrace your
route to the Mokuleia Firebreak Road. Follow the road as it travels
the crest of the Waianae Mountains back to your car. You will pass
the intersection of the Kealia Trail and come to several forks: At the
first two forks, bear left; bear right at the third; and bear left and
down at the fourth (near the gatepost).

This hike can be done as a traverse, rather than a loop, if you can
arrange transportation. From Peacock Flat you can descend either
on the paved road (Peacock Flat Access Road), which is closed to
vehicles, or by way of the Kealia Trail, which comes out on the west
end of Dillingham Airfield. The Mokuleia Trail has no access from
the highway, except by special permission to certain authorized
groups. If you attempt the hike in this manner, it is a long way from
the dropoff to the pickup points. Since the road does not go around
Kaena Point, the pickup requires a trip clear around the Waianae
Range, a distance of about 56 miles.

Wahiawa to Laie—Across the Koolau (19 miles, 3 days; strenuous)

Maps: USGS topo quads—Waipahu, Hauula, Kahuku.

This is an exciting adventure that crosses the Koolau Mountains
from the middle Oahu plain to the windward coast. It begins on the
Schofield–Waikane Trail, traverses a 7-mile section of the Koolau
Summit Trail, then descends via the Laie Trail. You will need to
either position two vehicles at the trailheads, or arrange dropoff
and pickup. If you cannot do this, you can overnight at the summit
shelter and return the way you came.

The Koolau Summit is an 18-mile trail that begins at Pupukea
on the north shore and follows the ridge of the Koolau Mountains
to about the middle of the range. Many other trails lead up to join
the Koolau Summit as it winds its way southeast. Some of these

trails are closed or overgrown, but others provide some of the best hiking on Oahu. The Summit Trail is not for everyone; sections of it are frequently overgrown, often muddy, and sometimes covered with a dense mist that restricts visibility. The weather can be windy, rainy, and cold—but it can also be warm, sunny, and beautiful, with views unparalleled anywhere else on the island. Even on the sunniest days, however, you might find long stretches of mud on the trail. The Koolau receives so much rain that parts of the trail never fully dry out. The Poamoho Shelter, near the southern end of the trail, consists of a roof, a floor, and four walls—no furniture, no toilet, and a water catchment tank that is in disrepair, though it usually does contain water. (If not, you can get water from the small stream about a quarter-mile back down the Poamoho Trail.) The state has plans to renovate or rebuild this deteriorated structure in the future. One note: Because this is a summit trail, there is little water along the route, except for small, stagnant pools. Water can be obtained from streams downslope of the trail, but it is a good idea to bring along an emergency supply. All water along the route must be treated before drinking.

A permit is required for hiking the Schofield–Waikane Trail, and may be obtained from the Directorate of Facilities Engineering, U.S. Army Support Command, Fort Shafter, HI 96858. A permit is also required for use of the trail shelter, and is available from the Division of Forestry and Wildlife, 1151 Punchbowl Street, Honolulu, HI 96813; phone 587-0166. Please keep in mind that you may only hike the Schofield–Waikane Trail on weekends and holidays because it is located in a military maneuver area. This requires that you begin your hike on a weekend, but you may exit onto the Laie Trail any day of the week. No permit is needed for the Laie Trail.

Day 1—Schofield–Waikane Trail to Poamoho Shelter (7.5 miles). To reach the trailhead from Honolulu, take the H1 Freeway to the H2 cutoff; then take the H2 to the Wahiawa Exit. Turn right at California Avenue, following it about 3 miles to the entrance to Schofield Barracks East Range, at the end of the road. Enter the gate in the chain-link fence and make an immediate left onto the dirt road, which leads through several training sites. Proceed on the road toward the mountains until it reaches an open, grassy area just before a forest. You can park in the dirt lot, on the right, that is backed by a grove of eucalyptus trees. Continue on foot along the road for about a mile to where it makes a sharp turn back toward town. The trail begins at the apex of this turn, branching off to the right of a small mound of earth.

You can reach the exit trailhead by returning to California Avenue, then taking a right on Kamehameha Highway following it to Haleiwa and along the coast past Waimea Bay and Kahuku to Laie. Turn right at Naniloa Loop in the north end of town, and take the second exit, for Poohaili Street, off the loop. Drive almost to the last house on the street and park. Do not go past the informal gate marked by posts on both sides of the road, where there may or may not be a chain to prevent you from driving farther. Park on the side of the road.

After you return to the Schofield–Waikane trailhead, half a mile from a start is a fork in the trail where you bear right and go up a ridge. The left fork goes down to the Kaukonahua Stream, which has good swimming holes in both directions. (If you are returning by this same route, instead of exiting by the Laie Trail, this would be a good side trip for a cooldown after the hike.) The trail then follows the ridgeline, mainly on the right side, for about 3 miles, and then climbs to the ridge top itself for most of the remainder of the hike. Many native plants grow in this upper section, including *ohia, kopiko, uke, olapa, naupaka,* and *ohelo*. There are sweeping views in all directions, including back to the Waianae Mountains. The trail then skirts the right side of a summit peak and reaches the *pali,* where it intersects the Summit Trail. From here a dramatic view of the windward coast unfolds. Turning left (north), it is about 1.5 miles to the Poamoho Shelter, your overnight stop.

Day 2—Poamoho Shelter to Laie Trail Intersection (7 miles). Don't be surprised if it takes you an entire day to complete this seemingly short hike along the Koolau Summit Trail. Although the distance is not great, the going is usually slow due to the condition of the trail. It may be muddy, narrow and hard to follow in others, and possibly overgrown. Bad weather will slow you down even more. On the other hand, if you are in luck and the weather is good you will reach your campsite early, and you'll have time to enjoy the great panoramic views.

After hiking the first half-mile you will reach the Poamoho Trail, intersecting from the left. Continue along the ridge on the Summit Trail, paying careful attention to the route. It is possible to take a false trail, or to occasionally lose your way if you are not observant, or if visibility is low. The trail makes frequent ups and downs, but any major drop off of the trail to one side of the ridge or the other will alert you to a wrong turn. If you're feeling uncertain about your location, retrace your steps until you feel confident you're on the correct route. When you estimate you are approaching the 6-mile point, stay alert for the intersection of the Laie Trail on the right, identified by a small bowl in the summit ridge. A pole sticking out of the top of a small pit marks the top of the Laie Trail, along which you have great views of the windward coast and the north shore. Look for a flat dirt clearing, a good spot to pitch your tent.

Day 3—Laie Trail to Laie Town (6 miles). After leaving the bowl in the summit, you'll pass through a gulch, wade through thick *uluhe,* and enter a wet forest. In many places the trail is narrow and slippery, and you may encounter overgrown sections. There are usually small washouts, requiring careful passage. Despite all of this, this part of the hike presents an eerie, beautiful landscape, particularly if morning mists are infiltrating the trees. About halfway down the Laie, watch for a short side trail on the left that leads sharply down to a small waterfall and its shallow pool. The main trail will then make a relatively level traverse lined with strawberry guava trees, at the end of which it enters a grove of Norfolk Island pine. Exiting the grove, the trail becomes an eroded dirt road that descends along a mostly bare ridge until it flattens out, passes an old pump house on the left, crosses a small concrete bridge, and passes between two gateposts that may have a chain strung between them. Your car or pickup will be parked along the dirt road here.

Day Hikes

Not too many years ago Oahu could have easily held its own with the outer islands as far as adventurous day hikes were concerned. However, development and land use restrictions have taken their toll. The spectacular Haiku Stairs (Stairway to the Sky), a nearly vertical 2,400-foot ascent of the Koolau cliffs, has been lost to vandalism, deterioration, and construction of H3, one of the most expensive and unnecessary freeways in the nation. The Makapuu–Tom Tom Trail has been severed by a radar installation atop the cliffs, its Waimanalo end vanishing in the scrub behind a housing development. Castle and Waikane trails, both of which offer breathtaking climbs to the Koolau summit from the windward side, are closed because their owners are reluctant to deal with possible hiker injury liability claims in our increasingly litigious society. Other trails and climbs have had their access cut off by new housing developments. Despite this discouraging scenario, however, there are still many excellent day hikes on Oahu—more than on any other island—they are just not quite as adventurous. And many of them lead through forests and valleys to fantastic views and panoramic overlooks. The Makiki/Tantalus/Manoa Trail Complex, for example, contains fifteen interconnected trails traversing rain forests, bamboo jungles, scenic ridges, and a major waterfall, yet it is only minutes from Honolulu.

If you plan to do extensive hiking on Oahu, *The Hiker's Guide to Oahu*, by Stuart M. Ball, Jr. (University of Hawaii Press), is the best, most complete book on the subject available. If you prefer hiking with a group, the Sierra Club hikes a different Oahu trail every Sunday; visiting hikers are welcome. The group meets at 8 A.M. at the Church of the Crossroads, 2510 Bingham Street, on the lanai facing the Bingham Street parking lot. Outer island chapters of the club also schedule weekend hikes. For information, contact them directly. The Hawaiian Trail and Mountain Club also welcomes visiting hikers on Sunday outings. Usually tackling more rugged hikes than the Sierra Club, the club meets on the mountain side of the Iolani Palace at 8 A.M. The Hawaii Nature Center offers moderate hikes on Saturdays, for which advance telephone sign-up

(955-0100) is required. Commercial companies also offer guided hiking trips—consult the guest services staff at your hotel or the free airport handouts for more information or referrals.

Below are some of the best hiking adventures on Oahu. There are others, but I have tried to select those that can be enjoyed with a reasonable amount of safety. Falling 2,000 feet off a sheer cliff due to crumbly rock is an adventure you don't need. But there are no guarantees. After all, you can be killed crossing the street in Waikiki.

OLOMANA: (5 miles round-trip, 3–5 hours; strenuous)
Maps: USGS topo quads—Mokapu, Koko Head.

From most points of view, this prominent peak on Oahu's windward side seems almost unclimbable. Rising to an elevation of only 1,643 feet from the Maunawili plain, Olomana—standing alone, independent of the Koolau Range to its rear—seems higher. Though Olomana is often called the "Matterhorn of Oahu," climbing to its main peak is actually easier than it appears. A trail leads all the way to the summit, although climbers must tackle a sharp rock face just below the top. This hike is not for acrophobes. Verbal permission to cross private land is required and can be obtained from the Royal Hawaiian Country Club at 532-1440, or the Y. Y. Valley Corporation at 261-1437.

To reach the trailhead from Honolulu, take the Pali Highway (Route 61) north through the tunnel, which leads to the windward side of the island. Three stop lights past the tunnel turn right on Auloa Road and then make an almost immediate left onto a road that runs parallel to the highway. Park off the road before it becomes a bridge. Once you've walked across the bridge, turn right with the paved road, soon passing a guard shack. About 0.4 miles after the shack, watch carefully for a white trail sign on the left. It is off the road about 20 yards, in a heavily wooded area, and hard to see. Take the trail uphill to a dirt road, and turn left, following the road until it reaches the ridgeline. A trail will head off to the right through an ironwood grove, straight up the Olomana ridgeline. Two tricky places, one of them the rock face mentioned above, have cables to provide some security. Once on the summit of the main peak you'll have a spectacular, 360-degree view of the southern part of windward Oahu.

The hike to the second peak is a bit stickier than the climb so far, though still reasonable. The third peak, which pierces the sky like a green fang, has a very narrow ridge approach, with sheer dropoffs on both sides. The climb is made more dangerous by unstable and crumbly rock along the route. Most climbers are happy to settle for either the first peak, or the first two.

WAIMANO–MANANA TRAILS LOOP: (14.5 miles, 7–9 hours; moderate to strenuous)

Maps: USGS topo quads—Waipahu, Kaneohe.

The Waimano and Manana are two parallel trails, each leading to the Koolau summit along separate ridgelines. The two are joined by a connecting trail along the summit ridge, a fantastic traverse though it can be dangerous in rain, fog, or high wind. *I do not recommend taking this trail if fog or mist interferes with visibility.* The loop described here requires either two vehicles, one positioned at each trailhead, or a dropoff at one and a pickup at the other. If you cannot arrange this, return the way you came; it will still be a great hike. The itinerary below hikes up the Waimano and down the Manana, though it can just as easily be done in the reverse. The top of the Waimano Trail is about 300 feet lower than the Manana, so that the connecting trail, in this case, is also uphill.

To reach the trailhead from Honolulu take the freeway to Pearl City (Exit 10). Bear right on Moanalua Road to its end at Waimano Home Road. Turn right, and proceed 1.7 miles to the security post at the entrance to Waimano Home. Park outside the fence. To position a car at the end of the Manana Trail, proceed as above to Waimano Home Road, but instead of following it all the way, turn left when you reach Komo Mai Drive and follow that street to its end. Park anywhere you can find room.

The Waimano trail begins on the left side of the fence at an old trail registry and a Na Ala Hele trail marker. The well-maintained trail passes through several vegetation zones and affords fine views of the Waianae Mountains, Pearl Harbor, and the windward coast. For much of its 7 miles the trail follows an old irrigation ditch, with tunnels and dams along the way. The grade is relatively easy, rising gradually over long ridges and moderate switchbacks. At the beginning the trail divides into lower and upper trails, with the lower portion re-joining the upper one after about a mile. Along the lower elevations the trail is lined with strawberry guava, and mango trees dot Waimano Valley to the left, with some of the larger ones eventually reaching the trail. At this point in your trek you'll pass through a *koa* forest, interspersed with several clumps of royal palms, and a large eucalyptus grove. About two-thirds of the way, *ohia* trees take over, with tree ferns (*hapuu*) seeking shelter in their shade. Unlike most trails in the Koolau, the Waimano gets wider as it nears the summit, and the final mile to the summit ridge is relatively open, with ferns, such as *uluhe*, predominating. From the summit a sweeping view of Kaneohe Bay unfolds, all the way from Chinaman's Hat to the Mokapu peninsula.

The connecting trail to Manana begins on the left. Stay as far back from the edge of the *pali* as the trail allows, and *watch your step*. Low-lying ferns can sometimes hide a free ride to Waihee Valley, more than 2,000 feet below. After about a mile, you'll reach a large prominent knob, the starting point for the Manana Trail. The 6-mile route starts out in the usual stunted growth of the Koolau summit, but the vegetation increases as you descend, and the trail in fact becomes heavily forested, with occasional open and grassy areas. This trail is steeper than the Waimano, and the going is rougher, with more ups and downs. About a mile and a half from the summit, you'll come to a flat, elevated clearing with a good all-around view. A walk through the long, open area of grass and young trees leads to a eucalyptus forest, and in about a mile you'll reach a narrow, paved road marked by a water tank. Another half-mile will bring you to your car.

MAAKUA GULCH: (6 miles round-trip, 3–4 hours; moderate)
Maps: USGS topo quad—Hauula.
Maakua is more like a very narrow, almost vertical-sided canyon, than a gulch. Its steep walls come so close together near its end that you can touch them both with your outstretched arms, and the

sun has difficulty shining in. A stream flows through the gulch, and although the trail begins by following it (and crossing it thirteen times), the streambed itself eventually becomes the trail. The hike ends at a small pool through which you will probably need to swim to reach the larger pool, which is fed by a pretty waterfall. A rope on the right of the falls will allow agile (and trusting) hikers to ascend to the top of the falls, where there is another pool and a continuation of the gulch and stream, but no trail. Maakua Gulch is subject to flash floods, and its narrow confines would be a nasty place in which to be caught by one. It is best not to take this hike in the rain, or following several days of heavy rainfall.

To reach the trailhead from Honolulu, take the Likelike Highway (Highway 63) north through the tunnel to its intersection with Highway 83 (Kahekili Highway). Turn left on 83 and continue another 17 miles to Hauula Beach Park on the right. Turn left on Hauula Homestead Road, just after the park, proceeding 0.2 miles to Maakua Road, a dirt road on the right. Park on Maakua, or in the small dirt parking area on the right, and you will see a wood sign for "Hauula Trails" straight ahead. Walk left at the chain (to prevent access to vehicles, not people) stretched across the dirt road. You will come to a Na Ala Hele sign for the Hauula Loop Trail on the right, and another for the Papali Maakua Ridge Trail on the left. Continue straight down the road, which widens where it turns into Maakua Gulch and continues into the woods.

Snorkeling and Diving

More than 800,000 people live on Oahu. Add to this up to 100,000 tourists on any one day, and its sounds like a pretty crowded place. Yet Oahu's waters, like its forests, offer escape from people as well as everyday routine. There always seems to be plenty of room for divers and snorkelers. With the exception of Hanauma Bay (mentioned later), once you're in the water, you will not feel pressured by others; divers will rarely make contact with any but members of their own party. If Oahu is the only island that you will have a chance to visit, take heart; there are many fine snorkeling and diving sites to enjoy.

The South Shore

This is the most crowded part of Oahu. It is where most residents live, and where almost all the hotels are. South shore beaches can be crowded, but the crowds diminish at the water line. Although there are better dive sites, the south shore has one thing going for it: It can be dived almost any time of the year, except during periods of south swells. Conditions are particularly good in the winter months, when diving is problematic or impossible elsewhere.

ALA MOANA BEACH PARK (D/S): Directly across from Ala Moana Shopping Center and west of the Ala Wai Yacht Harbor, Ala Mona is a popular and usually crowded park. It is best to enter the water from the end of the sandy arm that extends out from the park itself. Swim straight out, passing through the second opening (counting from the left) in the rock jetty. Angle to the right, to stay out of the way of boat traffic from the yacht harbor. The underwater scenery is surprisingly good here, considering the bottom is rarely more than 20 feet deep and considering things are so built up on shore. You will find coral patches, trenches, ledges, and various reef fish. Facilities include rest rooms, showers, water, and picnic tables.

SANS SOUCI BEACH (S): From Waikiki drive east on Kalakaua Avenue, passing the aquarium. Watch for the Natatorium War Memorial on the beach side; there is a parking lot for Sans Souci Beach just past the memorial. Snorkelers can enter the water from the beach and swim out to the reef, cruising along its edge. A channel cuts through the reef to the hotel south of the beach. Beginners will enjoy the shallow water close to shore, while more experienced snorkelers will find the scenery gets better the deeper they go.

KOKO KAI BEACH PARK (D/S): A small, undeveloped park at the edge of Portlock, a high-priced housing area, Koko Kai is little more than an entry area for divers and snorkelers. To reach the park, leave Honolulu driving east on H1, continuing on after it becomes Highway 72. After you pass the Koko Head shopping center (about 5 miles after the end of the freeway), the next road to the right will be Lunalilo Home Road. Turn right, then left on Poipu Drive, right on Hanapepe Loop, and right again on Hanapepe Place; keep going until you hit a dead end. Parking is difficult, and you will probably have to park somewhere back on Hanapepe Loop. Enter the water anywhere from the flat lava ledge along the water's edge. The best snorkeling is to the right, with coral formations and coral heads in depths ranging from 15 to 30 feet. Divers swimming left will find coral heads and a dropoff to 80 feet about 150 yards off-shore. Exits can be difficult here: Either wait for a swell and kick hard to raise yourself onto the ledge, or look for footholds in the ledge and remove your fins and climb out, timing your movements to coincide with the swells. Currents can be strong here any time of the year.

HANAUMA BAY (D/S): This is indisputably the best snorkeling spot on the island, but it is overcrowded any day of the week, and even worse on weekends. Everybody feeds the fish here, which tends to cloud the water. Ecology groups, city officials, and other concerned citizens are seeking ways to reduce the impact of its own popularity on Hanauma Bay. Restrictions on tour buses, taxis, and dive groups have already been put into place, and more can be expected. Hanauma may be the only "No Smoking" beach in the country. Your best chance here, whether you want to dive or snorkel, is a very early morning visit. If you can be ready to leave Hanauma by 10 A.M. you should miss the crowds—and you might even get a parking place. Non-residents pay a $5 entry fee.

To reach Hanauma, leave Honolulu driving east on H1, continuing on after it becomes Highway 72. About 6 miles after the end of H1 you will see a sign for the bay. After parking, stop and enjoy the sweeping view of this volcanic crater that has opened one of its sides to the sea. You will see a shallow, inshore reef running the length of the beach and extending seaward 200 yards or more. This is the place where the most fish are because it's where they are fed, and where most of the beach's visitors will congregate. The coral reef here is mostly dead, but there are interesting passages winding through it that can be clearly seen from your viewing point. The water here tends to be murky, suitable mainly for beginning snorkelers or those who want to be surrounded by fish. Depths do not exceed 10 feet. Beyond this shallow, inner reef you will note that the water changes from light green to blue as it gets deeper, reaching depths of 15 to 70 feet. In these deeper waters, the coral is alive and prettier, there are fewer fish—and there are far fewer people. Experienced snorkelers prefer the scenery and the comparative solitude out here, and this is the only place at Hanauma for divers.

Once you have the lay of the land, descend the rather steep paved walkway to the beach. If you plan to snorkel on the inner reef and/or feed the fish, you can set down on the beach and enter anywhere. Those wishing to snorkel beyond the inner reef can also enter the water here, making a passage through the reef. A better way is to walk to the south end of the beach, then take the path leading between the water and the rocky wall, and enter the water over the rocks at a convenient spot. Do so before you reach the rough water area known as the "Witches Brew." Divers should take this same route. Snorkelers should avoid the "Witches Brew," but can explore along both walls of the bay as well as the far side of the inner reef. Divers, of course, have more flexibility. The "Witches Brew" has little effect under water, and the bottom has lots of trenches, holes, and coral to explore. In the deeper water, toward the entrance to the bay, bigger fish, including rays and sharks, can sometimes be seen. Rest rooms, showers, and water are available at Hanauma, and there is a snack bar.

LANAI LOOKOUT (D): The main attraction at Lanai is a wall dive, descending about 60 feet, right along shore, with abundant coral, ledges, and caves. The lookout is the first paved turnout after Hanauma Bay. Park and pick your way over the rocks on the right side of the lookout until you see the small cove below. The last part of the climb down is steep, but the entry is an easy step off the rocks. The underwater scenery is great in either direction as long as you stay close to the wall. A heavy surge is common at Lanai Lookout, so only experienced divers should dive here.

HALONA BLOWHOLE (D): To the right of this popular tourist attraction is a small sandy beach fronting a narrow, rocky cove. A path leads from the right side of the blowhole parking lot to the beach. Enter and exit directly from the beach. If you dive to the right you will find trenches and ledges encrusted with coral, and a plateau rising from the sea bottom with lots of cracks and holes to explore. Depths average 30 feet, with deeper spots in some of the trenches. The Halona Blowhole is just off Highway 72, about 1.5 miles past the entrance to Hanauma Bay. Again, frequent surge restricts this area to experienced divers.

The North Shore

Diving on Oahu's north shore is mostly a summer activity. In winter the area is host to some of Hawaii's biggest waves and most famous surfing tournaments. However, there are also many calm winter days, when snorkeling and diving conditions are excellent. Check the weather, and when the surf's up, don't dive.

WAIMEA BAY (D/S): Since this is the place where the biggest surfing waves in the state come rolling in, it should be obvious that snorkeling and diving should be attempted only on the calmest days. The large rock close to shore on the left side of the bay (there will be lots of people jumping from it) has a submerged tunnel at its end that snorkelers can swim through. You can then explore the rocky shoreline; or divers can investigate the rocky off-shore islets. Snorkelers can also swim along the right side of the bay. Depths at Waimea range from 10 to 35 feet. To reach Waimea from Honolulu, take H1 and H2 to Wahiawa, Highway 99 to Haleiwa, then 83 northeast to the bay. Rest rooms, showers, water, and a few picnic tables are provided.

THREE TABLES (D/S): Three flat rocks, sometimes awash but always visible, give this site its name. An attractive sandy beach fronts the rocks, providing for easy entries and exits. Snorkeling is excellent around and between the "tables," with lots of coral, crevices, and even a close-to-the-surface arch through which even snorkelers can swim. One of the tables has a small tunnel running through it. Divers reach even more varied terrain by swimming farther out to find trenches, coral hills, and more arches. The bottom slopes gradually off the tables from 20 feet to about 60 feet farther out. There are plenty of fish, eels, and even lobsters in the nooks and crannies in the deeper waters. Immediately after rounding Waimea Bay, watch for Three Tables on the left. It, and Shark's Cove, described next, are both Marine Conservation areas.

SHARK'S COVE (D/S): This is probably the most popular shore dive on Oahu after Hanauma Bay. You will not find as much marine life here as at other places; the cove's main attraction is its profusion of crevices, ledges, and caves, particularly around the right side of the cove. Divers can even enter one of the caves from a surface pool in the reef behind the shoreline and can swim out to the sea. Cave-diving experience is necessary here; divers have lost their lives by becoming wedged in these caves. Also, be aware that you'll need a light to explore the larger caves. In case you're worried, the place is apparently misnamed, as sharks are rarely seen here. Entry and exit are normally at the entrance of the cove, where small pockets of sand sometimes accumulate, but it is also possible to walk out along the reef to the right, jump off, and swim back to the cove. Depths range from 10 to 40 feet along the reef, and reach 60 feet farther off shore. Shark's Cove is about 0.4 miles northeast of Three Tables.

MOKULEIA BEACH PARK (D/S): Though this park is generally more interesting for snorkelers, divers will still enjoy this very chopped up and jumbled area—if they don't mind a shallow dive. And divers who don't mind a long swim can explore the offshore reef with its many ledges and caves. Unfortunately, poor visibility can be a problem here any time of the year. Depths vary greatly over the reef, and even at the dropoff, the bottom is usually only 30 feet deep. To reach the park from Honolulu, take H1, then H2 to its end, where it becomes Highway 99, then 803 to Waialua. At the junction right before Waialua, bear left on Highway 930 toward Kaena Point and the beach park. Facilities include rest rooms, water, showers, picnic tables, and a camping area.

The West Shore

Like the south shore, conditions are favorable here most of the year. But whereas summer is the time for caution on the south shore, it is winter here that brings the big waves that have made Makaha world famous. The area has some of the island's finest beaches, clearest water, and best weather. The West Shore is less populated than the south coast, and there are fewer people on the beaches and in the water. Diving is popular on this coast because of the good conditions year-round and the excellence of the shore's many dive sites.

KAHE POINT BEACH PARK (D/S): Clear water and a white sand bottom studded with coral heads greet divers and snorkelers in shallow water here. Then a colorful coral reef begins, extending well out to sea. The depth of the reef rarely exceeds 20 feet, even 300 yards or more from the shore. Many varieties of fish congregate on this reef, making it an excellent place for beginning snorkelers and divers. Divers comfortable with long swims may explore a 60-foot dropoff about 400 yards from shore, where there is a good chance to spot turtles. Most of the shoreline of the park is a low, rocky sea cliff, which can make entry with tanks difficult. A small sandy cove at the north end of the park is the best entry and exit for divers. To reach the park from Honolulu, take H1 all the way to its end, where it becomes Highway 93. About 3 miles farther on, a large electric power plant looms on the right; the beach park is on the left. Rest rooms, showers, picnic tables, water, and a campground are available at the park.

NANAKULI BEACH PARK (D/S): Conditions are similar here to those at Kahe Point, except that easy access to the water is afforded over a sandy beach. The shallow reef does not extend as far offshore here, probably 100 to 150 yards in most places. Again, it is necessary to swim out over a sandy bottom before reaching the reef. Nanakuli is about 1.8 miles past Kahe Point. Facilities include rest rooms, showers, water, picnic tables, and camping.

POOHUNA POINT (D): This small black rock peninsula juts out into the water just south of Makua Beach. Its flat surface, almost level with the ocean, allows easy entry into about 20 feet of water. Exit can be made here also, or if the tide has come up, on the sand at Makua Beach. From the point, divers should head directly out to sea to find caves, trenches, and ledges in waters that reach to about 60 feet. The area is heavily dived, but there is still a surprising amount of sea life. Poohuna Point is off Highway 93, north of the town of Makaha. After passing the town, watch for a sign announcing the beginning of Kaena Point State Park. Half a mile past the sign, turn left onto the dirt road that leads to the ocean. You should be able to see the peninsula.

YOKOHAMA BAY (D): Flanked by a fairly long sandy beach that offers entry over a wide area, Yokohama provides access to a seldom-visited lava and coral floor replete with ledges, small caves, and an abundance of holes. Most of the marine life here consists of larger fish and critters that hide in dark places. Entry can also be made from Pukano Point, a rocky entrance just before the paved road leading up to the satellite tracking station. Because of the bay's uneven bottom, depths vary from 10 to 40 feet. The bay is at the end of the pavement on Highway 93. Rest rooms and showers are available at the south end of the beach.

The Windward Shore

There is good diving on this coast, but most of it requires a boat. If you are interested in boat diving here, Moku Manu Island, parts of Kaneohe Bay, and the reef and lobster cave at Crouching Lion are all worthwhile spots. It is possible to make a shore dive from Makapuu Beach Park, swimming right along the high cliff, but there are not too many days when the seas permit it. A snorkel trip along the southern half of Goat Island (Mokuauia Island) can be made from Maleakahana Beach; it's a fun trip, but the coral formations are routine and the sea is shallow enough for people to wade to the island at low tide.

SNORKEL AND DIVE BOAT TRIPS: Dive shops are located pretty much throughout Oahu. Most operators, regardless of their location, dive the leeward coast more frequently than the others because of the reliable conditions found there most of the year, and the many good dive sites. Windward dive shops are your best bet if you want to dive the windward shore, but they also organize trips elsewhere, wherever the weather and water are good. A popular location is the wreck of the Mahi, a sunken minesweeper in about 95 feet of water off the leeward shore. There is also a sunken Corsair fighter plane from World War II nearby. Other boat dives along the leeward shore include Makaha Caves, Keeau Corner, and Twin Caves at Maili Point. The Yellow Pages, your hotel, and lots of free airport handouts can provide you with lists of current dive operators.

Surfing

There is no question about it: Oahu is the best place to surf in Hawaii. If you are coming to the islands for surfing, this is where you want to be. Oahu's unique location puts it in the best position of any island to receive both winter and summer swells, with no intervening islands to break them up or a continental shelf to slow them down. Oahu has a greater number of surfing spots than the other islands, with more wave variety. No matter how bad conditions may be at one spot, you can almost always find the surf up elsewhere on the island. Even the ambiance changes from place to place. Surfing cosmopolitan Waikiki is so different from riding the waves on the laid-back north shore that you might think you're on different islands.

That said, there is a flip side to surfing Oahu. Most of the well-known surf spots on the island are crowded, especially when conditions are right. And long-time surfers at the most popular spots are adept at crowding out and intimidating newcomers and the less experienced with a mixed bag of tricks guaranteed to make them feel unwelcome—if not downright threatened. At famous breaks, when the real experts are out in force, there is no room for anyone else. At those times the average surfer has no choice but to retire to the beach and watch the action, or seek out a less premium location.

There are more surfing locations on Oahu than can be mentioned here. One authority cites ninety-six of them—and there are probably more. Listed below are some of the best-known surfing spots on Oahu. They include locations suitable for all levels of surfers, beginners through experts, but conditions are changeable at all of them. Surfers must know their own abilities and limitations, and abide by them. For people who are just learning to surf, well-known big wave surfer Bobby Owens recommends the following locations, which provide a round-the-island experience: on the south shore, *Queens;* on the leeward shore, *Waianae Army Recreation Center;* on the north shore, *Alii Beach (Haleiwa);* and on the windward shore, *Bellows Beach.*

The South Shore

This is where surfing began. Hawaiians were surfing the waves off Waikiki years before Westerners even heard of such a sport. And despite surfing's worldwide popularity today, Oahu's south shore is still renowned as one of the world's best summer surfing areas, thanks to consistent offshore winds and rolling south swells breaking on nearly ideal reef configurations.

Diamond Head, Cliffs (S/L/B) and *Lighthouse* (S/L) comprise two side-by-side spots in the shadow of Oahu's most famous landmark. Although best in summer, unlike most other south shore spots they are both surfable year round. Cliffs is consistent enough to offer 2- to 3-foot waves when there is nothing anywhere else. Short left and right breaks provide variety for beginners to experts. Such is not the case at Lighthouse, however, where fast, powerful rights and a shallow reef require advanced skills. Both spots can be accessed from Diamond Head Beach Park.

Around the corner from Diamond Head, the famous Waikiki surfing spots extend 2 miles in front of the world's most well known beach. Their graceful, rolling waves delight the eyes of surfers and tourists alike, and they are as much a part of a Waikiki postcard as Diamond Head. Of the almost two dozen surfing spots found here, the following four offer some of the finest summer surfing to be found anywhere.

Almost directly in front of the Royal Hawaiian Hotel, *Populars* (S/L/B) has something for surfers at all levels of skill. It offers long rights with nice walls and easy peaks. But living up to its name, it can be very crowded, especially when the surf is up. *Canoes* (S/L/B), the next break toward Diamond Head, with its gentle lefts and rights, is a good spot for beginners and intermediates, but it can be crowded with tourist canoes and tourist (read: never been on a board before) surfers. *Queens* (S/L/B) is in the heart of Waikiki, directly off Kuhio Beach Park, and for many surfers this is what south shore surfing is all about. With its clean, long performance rights off a small peak, Queens will produce waves when every other spot on Waikiki is flat. Unfortunately, you can count on crowds here. Another spot with consistent surf is *Publics* (S/L/B), off the Natatorium, which has some of the prettiest of Waikiki's waves. Long lefts provide a great ride, but coral heads and a shallow reef restrict this spot to experienced surfers only.

Another surfing area geographically still part of Waikiki extends from the Ala Wai Boat Harbor south to the Hilton Hawaiian Village Hotel. The breaks listed below are all close together. From north to south, *Ala Moana* (S/L), just south of the boat harbor channel, breaks left and is the most crowded wave. *Rock Pile* (S/L) breaks right and left on a shallow reef. *Inbetweens* (S/L) breaks right, but needs a decent-size swell. *Kaisers* (S/L/B), probably the best of the four areas mentioned here, has long lefts and short rights. Although technically outside the boundary of Waikiki, *Tennis Courts* (S/L/B) deserves mention as a spot with a nice, consistent, lined-up wave. Located straight out from the tennis courts at Ala Moana Beach Park, the spot offers long rights, short lefts, and a safe wave.

The Leeward Shore

Hot, sunny days, dry weather, and miles of white sand beaches characterize Oahu's west coast. Although best in winter, the surf breaks all year round at most leeward spots, and offshore winds shape rideable waves year round. *Tracks* (S/L/B), located just past the Kahe Point power plant, offers close-to-shore rights and lefts, the rights predominating in winter and the lefts rolling in with summer's southwest swells. Although Tracks is surfable for beginners and intermediates, they will often be crowded out by knowledgeable regulars. If this happens, the best thing to do is to move northward, where there is a series of breaks offering short but satisfying rights.

While *Maili Point* (S/L/B) attracts all classes of surfers, and everyone can have fun there, beginners should venture out only on the calmest days. During periods of big swells Maili can be a dangerous place for all but the most experienced surfer. Normally strong, fast lefts, the waves here frequently shift without warning, and strong currents and a shallow reef add to the problem. But when Maili conditions smile, everyone has a great time. The break is located between Hookele Street and Maili Stream, while additional breaks can be found northward toward Nanakule.

Makaha (S/L/B/BS) is the surfing jewel of the leeward shore. It is here that big-wave surfing got its start. To the early pioneers of the big ride, Makaha was Mecca. This is where the world championships evolved, and big wave surfers still have a lot of attachment to it. Despite its awesome reputation, intermediates through experts can enjoy themselves at Makaha, where the size of the waves determines who is going to ride the long rights and small lefts. On good days, even beginners can ride the close-to-shore waves. The surfing area is off the north end of Makaha Beach Park. It is without dispute the best surfing spot on the leeward shore, and one of the best in the islands.

The North Shore

When winter swells begin to roll in, the eyes of world surfing shift to Oahu's north shore. Renowned tournament competitor Bobby Owens calls the north shore "the Aspen of surfing." But just as Aspen is more than skiing, the north shore is more than surfing. Each locale has its own unique character and ambience, and each its own life off the slopes or the waves. But despite the fun, without skiing Aspen would be just another obscure cow town, and the north shore would be just a sleepy country community dozing in the sun. Both have become centers of activity, though with very different results.

While Aspen has developed massively to accommodate the crowds, the north shore stubbornly refuses to yield to the pressure of growth. "Keep the country *country*" is the cry that rings from

Mokuleia to Kahuku every time a new construction project is proposed. And it usually works. The crowds get bigger every year, traffic comes to a standstill on the single road, and parking lots overflow onto every inch of highway shoulder. Yet the north shore is not much bigger today than it was in the 1970s. True, a bypass has been built to speed traffic past Haleiwa (causing mixed emotions among the merchants of the town), two small shopping centers have sprouted, and a few new restaurants have opened. But there is still only one hotel, a handful of B&Bs, and an assortment of dingy dens that stack sleeping surfers as high inside as their boards are stacked outside. In sum, the north shore keeps attracting more people while doing little to accommodate them. Whether things remain as they are—or whether the dam will eventually burst under the pressure of surfers and the people who come to watch them—remains to be seen. Meanwhile, the surf rolls on.

The first waves a traveler sees on his or her way down through the pineapple fields of Wahiawa are those of *Haleiwa* (S/L/B), home to surfing's World Cup. Located off Haleiwa Alii Beach Park, this can be a fun spot—with the right conditions—for all levels of surfers. When the surf is low, beginners can improve their techniques on the gentle, white water reforms on the inside, while the experts will be happy to take on the fast, powerful lefts found on the outside. As wave height escalates, strong currents and a dangerously shallow inner reef exert increasing influence, forcing all but the most masochistic out of the water.

Located almost midway between Papailoa Road and Pohakuloa Way, *Laniakea* (S/L/B) is a gold mine for intermediate and advanced surfers alike. With most of its waves under 5 feet, Laniakea provides generally consistent rights and lefts, lined up over a large, flat reef. But the real Laniakea comes alive several times a year during the winter season, when a pure north swell of 6 feet or more arrives. Then Laniakea is transformed into one of the longest, down-the-line right-handers on Oahu. When this happens, surfers from all over the island will be there.

Chun's Reef (S/L/B) is another spot where fun takes priority over daredevil performance. By north shore standards, Chun's is a soft, easygoing, forgiving wave. It offers long rights and short lefts from several different peaks. With no dangerous reefs or currents lying in wait, Chun's is a favorite spot for the ladies, older surfers, beginners who want to perfect their technique, and those who just enjoy the sport.

It's a horse of a different color at *Waimea Bay* (S/L/B/BW/BS). There the true monsters of winter are tackled by the very few hardcore big-wave riders willing to accept the challenge. No one but an expert belongs in the water when Waimea is booming at 20+ feet—and that can be just the beginning. Breaks of this size normally only occur two or three times a year, but when they do, everything else stops.

The tubes at *Banzai Pipeline* are legendary, and so are the crowds. Only surfers with advanced skills should consider "The Pipe," as the waves stand up steep and hollow over a dangerous reef. When they begin to build over 6 feet, it is time for all but the experts to head for the beach. Watching Pipeline break on a good day is one of the great spectacles in surfdom. You can reach the

Breakers pound the beach at Waimea Bay. Photo by Richard McMahon.

Pipeline by walking west (toward Haleiwa) from *Ehukai Beach Park* (S/L/B/BW/BS).

Rocky Point (S/B) offers excellent north shore surfing for intermediate and advanced surfers. Fast rights and hollow lefts provide great rides as long as the swells remain between 5 and 8 feet. The downside here is that this is often one of the most crowded spots in the area, and the reef lurks just a few feet below a hard-breaking wave. Rocky Point is located between Ehukai Beach Park and Sunset Beach.

Sunset Beach (S/L/B/BW) is the classic surfing spot on the north shore and surfing's Triple Crown is held here every year. Sitting right off the highway, Sunset is a magnet for every vehicle going by, and traffic slows to a crawl as drivers check out what's happening. One of the things that makes Sunset so attractive is that it is not fickle. It works on lots of different swell directions, making it a great day-to-day surf spot. Despite its postcard-perfect appearance from the beach, Sunset is not for novices. It has steep, shifting peaks, strong rip currents, and a shallow inside reef. In the world of big-wave surfing, Sunset Beach is considered one of the most challenging and physically demanding breaks. Even experienced surfers paddling out on a good day will often find fifty to sixty surfers in the water, and every wave claimed. If that happens, relax and enjoy the action from the beach, or seek out a less crowded spot.

The Windward Shore

An almost continuous shallow reef breaks up the swells before they reach the beach on the windward coast, and the offshore trades rarely allow clean conditions. But kona winds can bring perfect waves. One advantage to windward surfing is that it gets you away from the crowds. Windward waves tend to break farther off shore than other areas, requiring surfers to paddle farther out. Although mostly a winter surfing area, some windward spots break all year round. Portuguese man-of-war, usually arriving in bunches, can be a problem in windward waters; check the beaches for blue blobs before venturing out.

Seventh Hole (S), off the Kahuku Municipal Golf Course, offers up a great, isolated adventure in surfing. Its powerful lefts and short rights, when combined with a relatively windless day and a 6-foot swell, will more than satisfy experienced surfers. The break here is about a quarter-mile off shore. To reach Seventh Hole, turn off Kamehameha Highway onto Puuluana Street in Kahuku, bear left at the fork, and continue past the golf clubhouse to the small parking area. *Goat Island* (S/B) offers a series of left slides with deep, smooth tubes when the winds are low. The break is on the south side of the island, which is accessible from Malaekahana State Recreation Area. Because of the constant trade wind swell, "Goats" is a popular summertime spot, especially when the south and north shores are flat. *Laie* (S/B), also called *PCC* because it lies off shore of the Polynesian Cultural Center, shows one of the prettiest waves on this coast—if you can see it. Access is by public trail about a quarter-mile north of the McDonald's, a somewhat roundabout trek. When conditions are right, long, hollow lefts, short rights, and an absence of crowds are your rewards for making this trip.

A little over half a mile south of the Cultural Center is *Pounder's Beach,* a well-known bodysurfing spot with a crunching shore-break. Bodyboarders love to play here too. A mile and a half north of Kualoa Regional Park lies *Kanenelu Beach* (S/L/B), which has waves for beginner and intermediate surfers all year long. Its right walls and occasional lefts provide fun without fear of reefs and overpowering waves. Try Kanenelu during the summer, when the south shore has a flat day, or in the winter, when north shore waves are more than you bargained for. South of Kaneohe Bay, *Kailua Beach, Lanikai Beach,* and *Bellows Beach* are good year-round spots for beginners. *Makapuu Beach* is Oahu's premier bodysurfing and bodyboarding spot. Other board surfers are not permitted in the beach area, but they are allowed around the rocky point toward Waimanalo. Beginners should be wary any time the surf starts to build, and fins are always a good idea at Makapuu. Because of its long, rocky shelf, only experienced board surfers should tackle the right tubes around the point. Not really part of the windward shore, though it is just around the corner from Makapuu, *Sandy Beach* is another favorite bodysurfing and bodyboarding location, with hardboard surfers working its eastern fringe. Some of the most powerful waves anywhere slam the shore at Sandy, and injuries are common among those who don't take them seriously.

Windsurfing

Oahu has some of the world's best windsurfing sites. Considering the number of people on the island, Oahu windsurfing lanes are generally uncrowded. A good deal of this is due to the extended nature of Oahu's windsurfing areas like Kailua Bay and Mokuleia, and the general lack of competition between sailboarders and surfers for the same sites (except at Diamond Head and Backyards). Oahu probably surpasses Maui in the variety of its wind and surf conditions; the island is kinder to the beginning and intermediate windsurfer while still providing experts with all they could ask for. The five areas listed below are the main windsurfing spots. Experts need look nowhere else, but beginners and intermediates can find other friendly areas, particularly along the windward coast where onshore winds protect them from being blown out to sea. Sailboards can be rented at Waikiki, and lessons are offered, but this is a crowded area in which to learn the sport, and sailboarders will find themselves competing with surfers, canoes, and swimmers for the same piece of surf.

Kailua Bay has been called the perfect family windsurfing vacation spot. With 4 miles of protected bay, a long sandy beach, an offshore reef, and close-in islands, Kailua offers more windsurfing variety than any other area in the islands. From beginner to expert levels, Kailua has something for everybody—easy beach starts and flat water for novices; wave riding, jumping, and speed runs for the advanced sailboarder. Offshore cruisers can sail north to Moku Manu Island, almost straight out to the Mokolua, or south as far as Waimanalo Beach, or even Rabbit Island with its beautiful mountain and shoreline scenery all the way.

Beginning sailors will do well to limit their forays to Kailua, the best place in Hawaii to learn the sport. Kailua Town has windsurfing shops (rentals, sales, instruction), and an abundance of restaurants, but no hotels. Families on extended vacations usually rent houses or condos (though there are not many of these in Kailua either); others take rooms in private homes or B&B's (see the *HVB Accommodations Guide*).

Diamond Head is a favorite spot for experienced sailboarders. It is also a great place to watch acrobatics as wave sailors go through their repertoire of jumps and loops, especially when the winds are easterly. Of the three breaks, the center one, *Cliffs,* is ridden the most often. *Lighthouse,* the westernmost reef, provides the longest ride, although it ends on a shallow note. Both of these breaks are long-time surfing sites, and surfers are almost always present. Although most of them ride the rights, leaving the lefts for windsurfers, they sometimes end up on the same wave, and the sailor must be prepared to yield the right-of-way.

Mokuleia Beach Park is an excellent place for the experienced sailor to get completely away from the crowds. One of Oahu's most isolated yet accessible beaches, Mokuleia can make the boardsailor feel that the entire ocean belongs to him. The wind is more consistent here than anywhere else on the north shore. Depending on wind and wave conditions windsurfers can slalom, sail downwind runs, or jump the waves. But when the waves reach 6 feet or more, it's time to head for the beach. Long stretches of Mokuleia are fronted by rocky ledges, requiring care for launches and returns. There are no accommodations or restaurants in Mokuleia.

Until the sailboarders came, *Backyards* was a popular north shore surfing spot—for many surfers, it is still a favorite. Nowadays surfers ride the waves on glassy, low-wind days, and the sailmen take over the break when the wind picks up. At other times, except for an occasional interloper from either camp, surfers stay out of Backyards, and in exchange sailboarders do not sail into Sunset Beach if surfers are there. Backyards is strictly for experts. Some of the biggest waves in Hawaii roll in here, along with 12- to 30-knot winds. This is considered one of the most exciting wave-jumping locations in the islands. On a north swell it is possible to ride one of these hollow monsters all the way to Sunset Beach. The downside at Backyards is its extremely shallow reef and strong currents. To find the Backyards launch site, turn off Kamehameha Highway just east of Sunset Beach, onto any side street. **The Turtle Bay Hilton Hotel** is two miles east, and a small number of rooms in private homes is available in the Sunset area. Several small eateries are nearby; the **Proud Peacock** is an excellent, moderately priced restaurant at Waimea Falls Park. There is also a snack bar at Backyards.

Laie is a good spot for novice and intermediate sailboarders, except during high winter swells. Hukilau Beach and the beach fronting the Polynesian Cultural Center are the best places for beginners, although the latter is also a surfing spot. Intermediates can launch from Temple Beach or Malaekahana State Recreation Area, where surfers can often be found riding the break south of Goat Island. Laie Bay is a fine cruising spot, with beautiful coastal and mountain views. **The Rodeway Inn,** phone 293-9282, is a motel adjacent to the Cultural Center and several vacation cottages are located nearby. Malaekahana has an excellent state campground. Several small eating places are located in the shopping centers of Laie, Hauula, and Kahuku.

Biking

Most people coming to Hawaii for a cycling vacation do not bother with Oahu, but instead go immediately to one of the outer islands. They may be making a mistake. Admittedly traffic conditions are better off Oahu, and all the other islands do have dramatic places to visit. But Oahu has lovely valleys, majestic mountains, and beautiful coastlines, all of which are more accessible to bicycles. Cyclists who choose to tour Oahu will not be disappointed.

Biking on Oahu is a paradox. It is a perfect model of good news and bad news. The good news is that Oahu has some of the most scenic and enjoyable bike excursions to be found anywhere. The island has lots of good campgrounds—most of them free of charge—conveniently located for the cyclist. It has many points of interest, some of them world famous, which make a bicycle tour interesting as well as good exercise. Now for the bad news: urban sprawl, heavy traffic, few bike paths, and narrow shoulders on many roads. Unless you live and bike in a major city and have good urban traffic skills, cycling in and around Honolulu is more frustration than fun. But the rest of the island is conducive to bike touring—and it is beautiful.

The cycling tours described below are shown in four geographic segments, allowing cyclists to make their own daily itineraries. Many bikers will want to take a trip around the island, and the tours are arranged in that order. Campgrounds and other overnight accommodations are indicated, allowing flexibility along the route.

Tour 1: The Southeast Coast, Waikiki to Waimanalo Bay (18 miles)

Maps: Oahu Reference Map #1 (Honolulu, South Shore, Central Oahu), and Map #2 (Windward Coast, North Shore, Leeward Coast), James A. Bier, Publisher. These can be purchased at bookstores, newsstands, and many other places.

This is the shortest of the four tours, but it passes many major points of interest where you will want to spend some time. It begins at Kapiolani Park, at the south end of Waikiki, and ends at Waimanalo Bay State Recreation Area. Food and water can be replenished at Hanauma Bay if you go down to the beach. From Kapiolani Park take Kalakaua Avenue in the direction of Diamond Head. After passing the Aquarium, the Natatorium, and the Outrigger Canoe Club, the road bears left and intersects Diamond Head Road. Turn right, and the road will climb slightly for about a mile as it makes its way between the base of Diamond Head and the sea. Stop at the overlooks to Diamond Head and Kuilei Cliffs Beach parks to watch the windsurfers offshore.

About half a mile from Kuilei Park you'll come to a fork where you'll bear right onto Kahala Avenue. At this point you are only about 0.7 miles from the tunnel that enters Diamond Head Crater. An easy trail, which starts inside the crater, leads through tunnels and staircases to a former military bunker on the crater's peak, affording great views of the city and the coastline. If you decide to make this side trip take the left fork, a continuation of Diamond Head Road, to the tunnel entrance. Parking is available at the trailhead where you can secure your bike to a railing or a tree.

If you do not make the side trip, take the right fork, Kahala Avenue. Continue through the upscale suburb of Kahala, watching for Kealaolu Avenue on the left (if you come to Waialae Beach Park you have gone too far). Turn left on Kealaolu, and in about 0.7 miles you'll reach the intersection of Kalanianaole Highway (Route 72), where you'll turn right. This heavily traveled road follows the shoreline along scenic Maunalua Bay. The paved shoulder to the right of the white line is generally wide enough for comfort, except where there's construction, but you will have to share the shoulder with joggers and buses pulling over.

Soon after you pass Maunalua Beach Park the road begins to climb for almost a mile until it reaches the entrance to Hanauma Bay on the right. This is Oahu's premier snorkeling spot, as you will see from the crowds on the beach. If you stop here, refer to the Adventuring by Car and Snorkeling and Diving sections in this chapter.

The nearly 2-mile downhill run from Hanauma Bay to Sandy Beach is a narrow, winding road with lots of tourist traffic. This can be a risky stretch for cyclists, as cars make sudden turns into pull-outs at Molokai and Lanai lookouts and the Halona Blowhole. Go slowly and exercise caution on all turnouts and curves. Sandy Beach is also one of the major bodysurfing spots on Oahu; its mile-long beach is also frequented by bodyboarders, sand sliders, and sun worshipers. After you leave Sandy, the road begins to climb toward Makapuu Point. In about 1.2 miles you will note a road barred by a gate, turning off to the right. Ignore the "No Trespassing" sign, which no longer applies. Pass your bike around the gate, and the one a short distance farther on. The road winds uphill for about a mile, but on the return you'll have a delightful downhill, without the worry of vehicle traffic. For more information about this excursion, and a side trip to the Makapuu tidepools, refer to Adventuring by Car, Makapuu Lighthouse Overlook, in this chapter.

Back on the highway, the road will round Makapuu Point; if you did not take the ride up to the lighthouse lookout, stop at the pull-out on the right for a similar (if not quite as spectacular) view. A downhill glide will bring you to Makapuu Beach, the most popular bodysurfing beach on the island. It lies in a beautiful setting at the base of towering cliffs from which hang-gliders launch into space. There is a county campground here, just north of and adjacent to the beach, with its own separate entrance. (Before you decide to stay here, see below.) Just past the beach is Sea Life Park, a major aquatic attraction featuring an undersea coral reef exhibit and performing sea critters. The road then follows the shoreline to Waimanalo Beach Park, which offers access to one of the finest sandy beaches on Oahu. Though there is a county campground here, only a mile farther down the road is one of the island's nicest campgrounds, at Waimanalo State Recreation Area. It has the same access to the three-mile-long curving beach, lapped by gentle waves and backed by ironwood trees. After overnighting here, you can retrace your route or continue north by linking up with the next tour.

Tour 2: The Windward Coast, Kaneohe to Malaekahana Bay (24 miles)

This is the prettiest bike ride on Oahu, and the easiest. The route follows the coast, and has dramatic views of the mountains and the sea all along the way. It begins on the windward side at the junction of the Likelike Highway (Route 63) and Kamehameha Highway (Route 83). If you are continuing from the first tour, remain on Kalanianaole Highway until it intersects the Pali Highway (Route 61), turn left, and ride 1.8 miles to Kamehameha Highway on the right. (The sign will point to Kaneohe.) Turn right, and continue to the intersection of the Likelike Highway. If you would prefer a less traveled (though longer) route, turn off the highway at Keolu Drive, and, with the aid of a map, select a route through Enchanted Lake, Kailua, and Kaneohe.

If you are coming from Honolulu you may use either the Likelike Highway or the Pali Highway to reach the island's windward side. While both of these routes are dramatic rides, they have heavy traffic and present some hazards. Good urban traffic-riding skills are required. Of the two routes, the Likelike is more direct, offers spectacular views of the cliffs during the windward descent, and has a decent shoulder most of the way. Due to traffic, I recommend walking your bike on the sidewalk through the Wilson Tunnel. The Pali Highway affords the opportunity to stop at the spectacular Pali Lookout, but the road has a much narrower shoulder and a long, downhill U-turn after you exit the tunnel. Whichever route you take, there are ample stores to replenish your food and drink along the way.

Once you have arrived at the junction of routes 63 and 83, take Kamehameha Highway north through Kaneohe. From here, please refer to Adventuring by Car, picking up the itinerary in Kaneohe town and ending at Malaekahana State Recreation Area. The mostly coastline route is flat, steady but not oppressive with traffic. This is one of the most delightful rides in the islands; the cliff and mountain views on your left are breathtaking. Malaekahana State Recreation Area is the perfect place to stop for the day. The secluded campground, one of the best in the islands, lies directly on the beach, and is shaded by mature ironwood trees. The beach is beautiful and virtually empty, and you can wade to an offshore island (see Oahu's Empty Beaches, later in this chapter).

Tour 3: The North Shore, Malaekahana to Kaena Point (28 miles)

The north shore is home to Hawaii's biggest waves, and a second home to surfers from all over the world who come here to try their skills. This is a one-road-wide community, stretching 18 miles from Turtle Bay to Mokuleia, of some 11,000 persons. The north shore is resistant to change, and *very* resistant to development. People from other parts of Oahu call the north shore "the country," as in bumper stickers that demand "Keep the country *country*." Residents obviously want this area of Oahu to stay the way it is; whether it does remains to be seen.

You will find ample food and water along the way during this trip. Again, you have a flat ride that hugs the shore most of the way. The mountain scenery is nowhere near as dramatic as that of the previous day's ride, but the coastal scenery is more breathtaking. Once more, please refer to Adventuring by Car for a suggested itinerary and points of interest.

If you backtrack less than 0.2 miles from Sunset Beach, you'll find the Comsat Access Road, which heads up into the green hills behind the coast to a mountain bike wilderness criss-crossed with Jeep tracks and trails. Motorized dirt bikes and All-Terrain Vehicles also use this area, and much of it is a military maneuver zone, off limits except on weekends. A new, paved bicycle path, separate from the highway, begins half a mile before you reach Sunset, on the ocean side of the road. It runs about 2.5 miles to Shark's Cove and Three Tables, the north shore's most popular snorkeling and dive spots.

After passing the sugar town of Waialua, traffic decreases sharply. About 2.5 miles from the Waialua High School, watch carefully for the palm tree farm on the left, obvious because of the palms planted close together in neat rows right up to the highway. At the beginning corner of this farm a paved road heads straight back toward the mountains: This is the Peacock Flat Access Road, which climbs to the upper reaches of the Waianae Mountains. The paved portion of this road goes as far as a wilderness campground at Peacock Flat, where it then connects to a series of Jeep tracks and trails that will keep mountain bikers happy for days. By using the Mokuleia Firebreak Road and the Satellite Tracking Station Road it is possible to descend from Peacock Flat to the leeward side of the island, ending up at Yokohama Beach (see Backpacking Adventures in this chapter).

Not too far from Peacock Flat Access Road, Farrington Highway reaches the coast at Mokuleia Beach, another long, almost deserted sandy beach (see Oahu's Empty Beaches, later in this chapter). This great ride offers up fantastic views, with some of the island's highest mountains on the left and a dramatic shoreline on the right. You'll pass Dillingham Airfield, where glider rides and parachute jumping are available, and Camp Mokuleia and Mokuleia Beach Park, both of which offer camping. Shortly after passing the YMCA's Camp Erdman, at which you can also find camping facilities, the paved road ends.

At this point, if you are planning to continue with Tour 4, you may wish to stop for the night at any of the three campgrounds. Camp Mokuleia (phone 637-6241) and Camp Erdman (phone 941-3344) offer cabins and limited meal service. If you opt for returning to Honolulu, continue on to explore Kaena Point, as explained below.

From the end of the pavement, a badly eroded and rutted Jeep track continues another 2.5 miles to Kaena Point. This is a mountain bike road, but touring bikes can navigate the road with careful going. Watch the seaward gulches for the remains of small bridge abutments, all that is left of a railroad that used to run from Honolulu around Kaena Point, and then as far as Kahuku. A mile before the point a barrier prevents further vehicle traffic into Kaena Point Natural Area Reserve. (If you do not plan to proceed with Tour 4, you may prefer to secure your steed to the fence and proceed on foot; otherwise you need to muscle it over the fence.) This is a wild, lonely, and windswept place, wonderful for shoreline exploration. The *ohai,* a rare beach plant found nowhere else in the world, is struggling to make a comeback here. The dunes and vegetation in this area are recovering from years of damage from dirt bikes and All-Terrain Vehicles. It is very important that you stay on the road with your bike, thereby not contributing to the damage. Go as far as the toppled concrete lighthouse. From there you'll have a sweeping view of the leeward coast to Makua Valley, Yokohama Beach, and beyond.

Tour 4: The Leeward Coast, Kaena Point to Kahe Point Beach Park (19 miles)

Before deciding to take this trip you should be aware that the dirt road from Kaena Point to Yokohama Bay on the leeward side of the island is in poor condition, and contains washouts. The last time I checked, these washouts could be navigated by walking your bike, but there could be more by now, and no one is currently charged with repairing this abandoned road. If you encounter a washout that you cannot get around, you can—if you have a mountain bike—still get to the leeward coast by retracing your route partway and taking the Peacock Flat route mentioned earlier. Otherwise you must return to Honolulu via Waialua and Wahiawa.

If you've made it this far when you round Kaena Point be sure to take the lower road. The upper road, which appears in better condition, dead-ends at a former military gun platform. Almost immediately you'll pass through a cut in the rock, made to level the railroad grade. About 0.2 miles from here, you'll see a small cave entrance on the left of the trail; this entrance leads to an inner chamber about 50 feet in diameter. As you continue farther, you will find more bridge abutments as well as some splintered railroad ties. The coastline is stark and dramatic, although often marred by derelict vehicles pushed off the road onto the rocks below.

Pavement begins at Yokohama Beach, and for the next 3 miles you will continue to cycle through Kaena Point State Park, which ends at the large open cave on the left side of the road. The lovely green valley about 2 miles from the start of the pavement is Makua, a military training and impact area closed to public entry. Three miles past the cave you'll see Makaha Beach Park, world famous for its big surfing waves.

South of the town of Waianae traffic picks up and the road widens. You'll ride through the modest carbon-copy communities of Maili, Lualualei, and Nanakuli, with the mountains on the left and an almost continuous stretch of white sand beach on the right. Your tour ends at Kahe Point Beach Park, where you may choose to camp; there are also campgrounds at Nanakuli, Lualualei, and Keaau Beach parks. Because of several acts of violence against campers in the past year or so, many people advise tourists against camping along the leeward coast. Camping at a place where other campers are located, and camping close to them, should prevent any problems, however. It is probably not a good idea to camp at an isolated campground such as Keaau if you are the only one there.

Hunting

The only animals you may hunt on Oahu are goats and pigs—not a problem because these are pretty much the only animals on the island. The only other wild animal you'll find on the island is the rock wallaby, introduced when a pair escaped captivity in 1916. A small wallaby colony clings to survival in the upper reaches of Kalihi Valley. They are rarely seen, stay close to home, and mind their own business. You cannot hunt them.

Current bag limits for pigs and goats are one of each per day; there are no seasonal limits. In one hunting area both animals can be hunted daily, year round, which is annihilatory as far as the goats are concerned—there will probably not be goats for many more years on Oahu. Pigs, however, are doing well, and should be around awhile.

The dwindling goat population is now limited to the northwest section of the Waianae Mountains, while pigs can be found both in the Waianae and the Koolau, and in the plateau between the two. Once when I stopped on the side of the H2 Freeway to check a tire, a pig went galloping by, thoroughly confused by all the traffic. And I have a neighbor on the north shore who swears he saw a pig come down from the mountains, cross the highway, take a swim in the ocean, and then go back up into the hills (I still don't believe it). Hunting on Oahu is pretty much a local affair, because of all the people, traffic, and development, visiting hunters do not often choose to hunt here.

Six kinds of birds may be hunted on the island: ring-necked pheasant, green pheasant, Japanese quail, Erkel's francolin, spotted dove, and barred dove. (I don't know why anyone would hunt the last two—they are as ubiquitous as sparrows are in more populous areas, and relatively scarce in the wild. They both frequent my lawn and I wouldn't think of shooting, or eating, either of them.) There are only two bird hunting areas on the island, both in the northwest corner of the Waianae above Kaena Point. The bird hunting season is generally November through January, weekends and holidays only, and bag limits are liberal. By the way, if you happen to run across a big, bluish-green bird with a large tail, it is not a mutant form of Hawaiian pheasant but a peacock. Quite a few have escaped from various private small zoos and parks over the years and they have settled in the hills above Kaena Point. In spite of the fact that this is a bird hunting area, you cannot shoot them.

Freshwater Fishing

Many tourists are surprised to learn that there are opportunities for freshwater fishing in Hawaii. Practically speaking, only Kauai and Oahu offer this sport. A fishing license is required (see the section on fishing in How to Use This Book). There are two places for freshwater fishing on Oahu, as described below.

NUUANU RESERVOIR: You can fish the reservoir three times a year; announcements of these dates are published in area newspapers. A lottery is held and special permits are issued, though presently, all persons applying for a permit can be accommodated. Fishing dates and times are determined by the number of people who apply for permits. You may catch channel catfish, Chinese catfish, and talapia (sunfish) here, but please note that fishing is from shore only.

LAKE WILSON: Fishing is permitted here year-round, but you need a special entry permit that can be obtained when you purchase your fishing license. Both shore and boat fishing are permitted. The following fish can be caught in Lake Wilson: small- and largemouth bass, tucunare (see Freshwater Fishing in the Kauai chapter for information about these three fish), channel and Chinese catfish, pongee (snakehead), bluegill, and talapia.

Oahu's Empty Beaches

Oahu is perceived by most people to be an overpopulated island, its beaches overrun with tourists, and an unpleasant place for those who prefer to escape the crowds. Yet Oahu has beaches as deserted as those on any outer island—and they are far easier to get to on Oahu. Listed below are four beaches that are no more than an hour's drive from Honolulu; yet you could stroll them for a mile or more without encountering another person. They represent miles of undeveloped sandy shoreline, most of it as pristine as the day the island rose from the sea. Only time will tell if they are destined to remain that way.

KAHUKU BEACH: Located on Oahu's northernmost tip, this wild and isolated series of beaches (Kaihalulu, Hanakailio, Keawaawaloa, and Kahuku Golf Course beaches) blend together and form one long beach that stretches more than 5 miles without the intrusion of civilization. You can easily walk all five of those miles without meeting another soul. Oahu's only nudist club was once located here. The beach begins on the east side of the Turtle Bay Hilton Hotel, rounds Kahuku Point (the northernmost point on Oahu), and finally merges with Malaekahana Bay to the south (see below). At first the shoreline is backed by a long grove of ironwood trees, and there is a trail just inside the tree line that is used by the hotel as a bridle path. Upon rounding Kahuku Point, however, the ironwoods gradually retreat from shore and the beach becomes mostly open and windswept. Although sandy, much of the beach has a rock outcropping at the shoreline, making water entry and swimming difficult, especially if the surf is up—a frequent condition here. Swimming anywhere along this shore should be attempted with care, if at all. The sea is often rough, the winds strong, the currents unpredictable. You are a long way from help if you get in trouble. But this is a great place for a shoreline hike.

To reach Kahuku Beach from Honolulu, Take the H1 Freeway, then the H2 Freeway to its end at the junction with Route 99. Continue on 99 to Haleiwa, then follow Highway 83 about 10 miles northeast along the coast to the entrance to the Turtle Bay Hilton Hotel. Turn right on the Hilton entry road and proceed to the gate for the parking area. Just before the gate, on the right side of the road, is a turnoff to a public parking lot. Park and follow the path at the end of the lot toward the beach, turning right at the shoreline away from the hotel grounds.

MOKULEIA BEACH: Even though a road runs along most of its 6-mile length and some houses dot its shores, Mokuleia is almost as deserted as Kahuku. Except for a few pockets, such as a county beach park and a YMCA camp, beachgoers on Mokuleia are few and traffic is sparse—the road dead-ends at Kaena Point Natural Area Reserve. Other conditions are also similar to Kahuku: The sandy beach is mostly fronted by beach rock, waves pound the shoreline, and strong, unpredictable currents lurk off shore. But small sheltered coves, where entry to the water is possible, can be found, and close-to-shore swimming is usually safe. Even so, this is primarily a beachcomber's and fisherman's beach, proferring stunning sea and mountain vistas.

To reach Mokuleia, follow the directions above, but upon reaching the end of the H2 Freeway, continue straight ahead, toward Waialua, at the junction of Highways 99 and 803. Proceed through Waialua on Farrington Highway (Route 930) to Mokuleia Beach Park, where there are parking, picnic tables, rest room facilities, and a campground. From there you may walk the beach for 3 miles or more in either direction. Or, if you're looking for a wilder, even more isolated coast, you can continue to drive to the end of the paved road, where a rough Jeep track and a rocky shoreline lead toward Kaena Point.

MALAEKAHANA BAY: Because of its proximity to the town of Laie and the state recreation area at its south end, this mile-long crescent-shaped beach on Oahu's northeast coast may not be as deserted as the previous two. But on most days, Malaekahana is still a marvelous, almost empty beach in a lovely setting. The sandy beach is not wide, but ironwood, beach almond, and sea grape trees form a pretty backdrop, and they are so close to the shore that you need only move a few feet to go from sun to shade. Mokuauia, a flat island lying close off shore, is a sanctuary for seabirds. Known locally as Goat Island, it has several small beaches of its own; you can wade out to it most of the time, especially at low tide. You are permitted to walk around the fringes of the island, but not inland, where you might disturb nesting birds. Swimming at Malaekahana is almost always safe, except during periods of high winds and rough surf. The offshore bottom is a combination of rock and sand, and coral rubble rolls back and forth in the shore break. The water is shallow for a good distance offshore.

To reach Malaekahana from Honolulu, take the H1 Freeway to the Likelike Highway (Route 63). Proceed north on the Likelike, through the Wilson Tunnel and down to the junction on the left with Kahekili Highway (Route 83), about 2.5 miles past the tunnel. Follow Route 83 along the coast for about 22 miles to the entrance of the Malaekahana State Recreation Area. Park in either of the area's two parking lots and walk to the beach, which lies just over the grassy, wooded knoll. There is a nice campground at Malaekahana.

A smaller, more accessible beach can be found at Waialee, about a mile and a half from famed—and crowded—Sunset Beach. Backed by the University of Hawaii Research Farm, Waialee sits well off the highway, protected from direct access; yet Waialee is only a few minutes' walk from a popular beach pullout. In 1993 a

Hawaiian monk seal came ashore here to give birth, and mother and offspring remained undisturbed and mostly unknown for several weeks until they decided to return to the sea.

To reach Waialee, drive northeast from Sunset Beach for just over a mile, watching for a curve in the highway to the right at an ironwood grove. As the road arcs, you will see a parking area behind a low rock wall on the left side of the road, with a small islet offshore. Park and walk around the small point on the left as you face the ocean. You will see an empty, curving beach, fronted in many places by beach rock. If you walk along this beach for 2 miles, you will come to Sunset Beach.

CHAPTER EIGHT

Kauai
Rain Forests and Waterfalls

IN JANUARY 1778 Captain James Cook came ashore at Waimea,
on Kauai's southwest coast, and became the first Westerner to set
foot in the Hawaiian Islands. When he returned to winter in the
islands after failing to find a northwest sea passage through North
America, he went to the southern end of the island chain. His successors following in his wake. Trading vessels and entrepreneurs of
all stripes came to Hawaii, Maui, and Oahu, but they rarely ven-
tured to Kauai. Because of its distance from the other main islands,
Kauai was slower to come under Western influence. Even Kamehameha, the chief who united all the islands, was unable to conquer
Kauai, and the island finally came under his control, peacefully, in
1810.

But Kauai wasn't completely out of the mainstream. Missionaries from New England came ashore at the same time as they did
on the other islands. Sugar, for years the mainstay of Hawaii's economy, got its start on Kauai, and the original plantation is still producing. Although today the future of sugar grows bleak on other
islands, it remains relatively healthy on Kauai. The island is now
growing coffee and macadamia nuts, both of them heretofore Big

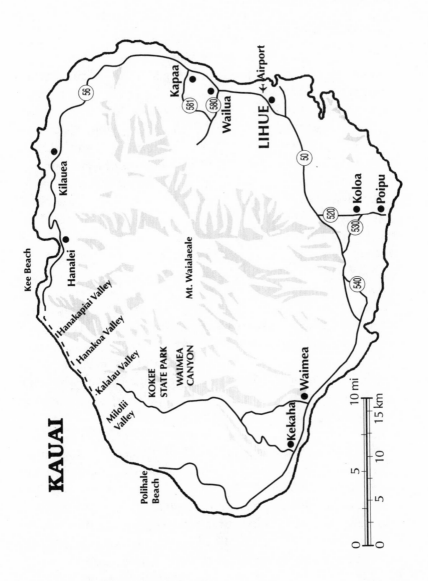

Island commodities. As you would expect, Kauai's 51,000 residents are employed in tourism, agriculture and government services.

The fourth largest of the main islands, Kauai is almost circular, about 33 miles long and 25 miles wide, and encompasses an area of 558 square miles. Formed from a single shield volcano, its caldera was once the largest in the islands. At 5,243 feet Kauai's highest point is Kawaikini, a remnant of the caldera as is its close neighbor, Mount Waialeale. The oldest of the inhabited islands, at somewhere between 3.8 and 5.6 million years, Kauai has been molded into a place of great beauty by the forces of wind, rain, and sea. Kauai receives more rain than the other islands, accounting for the lushness of its vegetation and its nickname: "The Garden Isle." Luxuriant rain forests and fertile green valleys are "watered" by streams and waterfalls plunging from Mount Waialeale, one of the wettest spots in the world. With an average annual rainfall of 451 inches, Waialeale outdid itself in 1982 with a record 665 inches of rain. Yet only a few miles away, Waimea Canyon, the "Grand Canyon of the Pacific," is almost as dry as its Arizona namesake.

Kauai does have a county bus line. The Iniki Express (formerly Kauai Bus), phone 241-6410, runs hourly from Lihue in both directions, Monday through Saturday, during daylight hours (roughly 5 A.M. to 6 P.M.). Buses leave Lihue (Kukui Grove) for Hanalei (east) on the hour, and for Kekaha (west) 15 minutes past the hour. Hitchhiking is permitted, but you must stay off the paved section of the road.

Many tourists consider Kauai the most beautiful of all the islands, and they keep coming back year after year. Hollywood, too, keeps returning to Kauai. Over the years at least twelve films have been made on the island, including *South Pacific, Jurassic Park,* and *Outbreak.* Yes, Kauai is beautiful, but all this beauty does not render it immune from disaster. In 1982 Hurricane Iwa battered the Hawaiian Islands, and although there was destruction all over the state, Kauai was hardest hit. Hotels and condominiums in Poipu Beach were gutted, and the damage island wide was estimated at $234 million. Trails in Kokee State Park were so covered with felled trees that some of them did not open for five years—one never reopened. But, after months of reconstruction and years of regrowth, the island was finally back on its feet and as beautiful as ever.

Then came September 11, 1992. On that day Kauai was struck by Hurricane Iniki, one of the worst storms ever to hit the Hawaiian Islands. Winds gusting up to 160 miles per hour, lashing rain, and monster waves smashed into the island. Over a thousand homes were destroyed, and several thousand more were damaged. Electric power and telephone service were lost for weeks, and air travel was disrupted. Perhaps even more devastating for an island dependent on tourism, every hotel on the island was damaged so severely it had to shut down. Rental car fleets were decimated, and hundreds of tourists, along with many of Kauai's residents, were stranded in crippled hotels or emergency shelters.

This time Kauai's recovery was slower and more painful. Though residents attacked the damage—estimated at nearly $2 billion—with vigor, even by the middle of 1995, five major hotels had still not reopened. One of them, the Westin Kauai Lagoons, the showpiece of the island, was thrown into bankruptcy. (It may be just as well: Grecian statuary, Venetian gondolas, and live African animals are hardly images of Hawaii.) The hotel is now struggling to reopen as a combination hotel/condominium.

Once more, much of the damage has been repaired, the vegetation is growing back, and Kauai is again open for business. But to those who know the island well, the scars are still there. There is still plenty of adventure to be found on Kauai—but everyone hopes it won't come in the form of another hurricane.

Adventuring by Car

Note: This section is designed to be used with a good road map at hand, such as the full-color topographic Map of Kauai, University of Hawaii Press, $2.95.

This itinerary divides Kauai roughly in half at Lihue, allowing one day to explore the island west of the town and a second day to venture east and north. This is workable, not only using Lihue as a starting point but anywhere from Poipu to Kapaa. If you are staying in Princeville, or points west of Poipu, you will need to modify the itinerary accordingly.

THE WESTERN HALF: (110 miles, round-trip)

From Lihue, drive southeast to Rice Street toward Nawiliwili Harbor, following the road as it passes Nawiliwili Beach Park, the harbor, and Niumalu Beach Park. About half a mile from the park you will come to a lookout over Alakoko Fishpond, one of the largest and best-preserved fish ponds in the islands. Tour guides are fond of referring to it as the Menehune Fishpond, attributing its construction to a race of mythical little people that supposedly lived in Hawaii prior to the arrival of the Polynesians. There is no evidence to indicate that the pond was created differently from any other, or that the *menehune* themselves ever existed.

Continue on Hulemalu Road until it reaches Highway 50 and then turn left. After about 5 miles you will come to the turnoff to Koloa and Poipu, where the road passes through the famous eucalyptus "tree tunnel," which, sadly, was stripped of its charm by Hurricane Iniki. The trees are recovering, but the "tunnel" will take years to grow back. On a happier note, the small town of Koloa was the location of the first sugar mill in Hawaii, and the plantation is still in operation.

Poipu Beach and its hotels were devastated by Iniki, but the area has recovered well, although as of mid-1995 two of its major hotels were still closed. Those who remember what the shoreline looked like before the hurricane will notice the difference. From Poipu it is possible to drive to secluded Mahaulepu Beach, which most tourists at Poipu never see. White sand beaches and coves shaded by ironwood stands make up this 2-mile stretch of beautiful, isolated shoreline, only a few miles—yet worlds away—from the hotels and condos of Poipu. Swimming, surfing, snorkeling, and fishing can all be enjoyed here. To reach Mahaulepu, you will need to use the McBryde Sugar Company's cane roads. Take Weliweli Road east from Koloa Town, until you reach the McBryde Sugar Mill. Continue past the mill on the cane road for about 1.3 miles, then bear right on the road leading toward the coast. Before leaving the Poipu area, be sure to take the short drive to the Spouting Horn, a blow hole accessible by taking the first left turn after leaving Poipu en route back to Koloa.

Nomilu Fishpond, one of the most unusual ponds in the islands, should be your next stop. It sits behind a small beach, at one place separated from the sea by a strip of land only 200 feet wide. The pond, fed by freshwater springs, sits at the bottom of a former volcanic cinder cone. Its water is brackish, however, and its level rises and falls with the tides, indicating an underwater connection to the sea. To reach this privately owned fish pond, begin at the intersection of Poipu Road and Route 53 in Koloa, heading toward Poipu. Proceed for 0.9 miles and turn right onto the dirt cane road. Mark the point, and at 4.4 miles turn left, following the road straight to a low sea cliff overlooking the water and the pond.

After visiting the pond and its small beach, return to the cane road, turn left, and, after about 4 miles, rejoin Highway 50 at Eleele, with Hanapepe just across the bridge. Another 6 miles brings you to the ruins of Fort Elizabeth. Built by a Russian naval officer in 1815, the fort stands as a reminder of czarist attempts to gain a foothold in the islands. A statue of Captain James Cook stands across the river on the seaward side of the road, near the spot where the great Pacific explorer first came ashore in the Hawaiian Islands in January 1778.

Just before the outskirts of town, one of the two roads leading to Waimea Canyon joins the highway on the right. This is Waimea Canyon Road. On my last visit I noticed that the road sign had been removed, perhaps indicating that authorities prefer that tourists use the second, clearly marked, route about 3 miles farther on, in Kekaha. My preference is for the first road, however, as it follows the rim of the canyon from its beginning. If there is no sign, ask locally for Waimea Canyon Road, making it clear that you want the road that leads up from the town of Waimea. If you'd like some variety, you can return via the other road.

After passing a string of houses, the road begins to climb, and there are several unofficial pullouts of which you should take advantage to watch the canyon unfold. Another 6.3 miles will bring you to a junction with the road from Kekaha, and about a mile and a half farther on you will note a sign for the Kukui Trail on the right. This is a steep trail that descends 2.5 miles to the canyon floor, but the Iliau Nature Trail, just before the trailhead, makes a short, interesting loop only a few steps from the road. There is a small picnic pavilion here, and the trailhead is also a good place to take photos of the canyon. If you are interested in hiking this trail, see the Day Hikes section of this chapter.

Waimea Canyon Lookout is the first of two official turnouts where you can view the canyon. From the lookout, it is easy to see how Waimea got its nickname: the "Grand Canyon of the Pacific." Both canyons were created by erosion, and for those who have seen the Grand Canyon in Arizona, the resemblance is striking, even if the Hawaiian canyon is on a less imposing scale. Watch for more unofficial lookouts as you continue your drive up the canyon rim, particularly at a sign marked Waipoo Falls, where you can view a distant stream drop over the rim of the canyon to the floor below.

Puu Hinahina is the second official lookout over the canyon, where goats can sometimes be seen and heard on the cliffs below. Be sure to visit the smaller Niihau Lookout, also located here, for a good view of the private island of Niihau and its smaller sister, Lehua. Closed to visitors for years, Niihau supports a small ethnic Hawaiian community engaged primarily in ranching and fishing. The island is still closed to all but its residents and their guests, but it is now possible to take a helicopter tour of the island, landing for a short stop at an isolated Niihau location.

From Puu Hinahina it is 5.2 miles to Kokee Lodge in Kokee State Park, where you will find a museum, a snack bar, a gift shop, a large picnic area, cabins, and a campground. This is a good place to stop overnight, especially if you began your trip from Princeville or somewhere else on the north shore. Although you can check at the lodge for cabin vacancies or cancellations, it is best to reserve well in advance, as the cabins are very popular. Write to Kokee Lodge, P.O. Box 819, Waimea, Kauai, HI 96796, or call 335-6061.

Kokee State Park's 4,345 acres of upland forest provide an important habitat for native plants and birds. Since most of the park is at an elevation of 4,000 feet, the average temperature is 60 degrees Fahrenheit, so nights can be cool. The park has more than 35 miles of hiking trails, and to really experience this different (i.e., cool weather, upland forest) aspect of Hawaii you should try to make at least one or two short hikes. Waipoo Falls, a portion of the Pihea Trail, or, if you have more time, the Awaawapui Trail, are good choices. See the section on Day Hikes in this chapter for more information.

While visiting the lodge and the museum, you will probably see many roosters and chickens in residence, cadging food from tourists. These birds are "jungle fowl," former domesticated birds that escaped from the population established since the original Hawaiians arrived over a thousand years ago. Although the ones you see at Kokee appear to be opting for civilization again, most of them still reside deep in the forest, and you will hear roosters crowing on the most isolated trails. The birds have survived only on the island of Kauai, where the mongoose, natural enemy of ground-nesting birds, was never introduced.

Less than 2 miles past Kokee Lodge sits the Kalalau Valley Lookout, with its awe-inspiring view over the beautiful, isolated valley at the end of the 11-mile Na Pali Coast Trail. The green, rocky spires and distant waterfalls seem more a part of a mythical land of enchantment than a populated island—but then again Kalalau is not so far from all that. The best chance for a good view is in the morning, before the afternoon clouds begin to gather.

After the valley lookout, the road continues for a short distance to Puu o Kila, another lookout over the valley. On a clear day you may be able to see the summit of Mount Waialeale, although you may have trouble identifying it because it is a relatively flat, rather than prominent, peak. From this lookout, a rough Jeep road continues until it turns into the Pihea Trail, which enters the Alakai Swamp from the north. The Jeep road is all that remains of an abandoned plan to build a connecting route between Kokee and Kauai's north shore—fortunately, conservation and ecological interests have prevailed, so the road will probably never be built.

When you are ready to leave Kokee (if you came up Waimea Canyon Road), take the road to the right at the intersection of the two access routes, which will bring you to Highway 50 at the town of Kekaha. Turn right onto 50 and continue northwest, driving by portions of a 15-mile-long white sand beach that reaches from Kekaha to Polihale. After passing Barking Sands Pacific Missile Range Facility, the road turns toward the mountains. A small sign will direct you left onto a dirt road that winds through the cane fields to

Polihale State Park. There you will find one of Hawaii's widest and longest white sand beaches, dramatically framed by high ridges to the north. This is a good place to swim when the water is calm, and there are rest rooms, showers, picnic pavilions, and a campground. This is as far as you can go by road, thus ending your exploration of western Kauai.

THE EASTERN HALF: (104 miles, round-trip)

Just before leaving Lihue to the north on Highway 56, Route 583 turns off to the left for Wailua Falls, where the Wailua River plunges 80 feet to a beautiful tropical pool lying upstream of the Fern Grotto (see below). Return to Highway 56, and just before crossing the bridge over the Wailua River you'll find a right turnoff to the Wailua Marina, where boats ply the river to the Fern Grotto, a vault cave with hundreds of ferns sprouting from the ceiling and walls. This trip is very touristy, but the cruise is pleasant and the cave is pretty.

Back on the highway, as soon as you cross the bridge over the Wailua River, the first road left goes to Opaekaa Falls. While here, cross the road from the parking lot for a good view of the Wailua River and the boats making their way to the Fern Grotto. This is also the road to the trailhead up the Sleeping Giant (Nounou Mountain), a low ridgeline that resembles a reclining man when viewed from the highway near Kapaa. About 12 miles north of the Wailua Bridge you'll come to Koolau Road on the right. Watch for a fruit stand, which marks the beginning of the road, on the right just off the highway. Turn here if you would like a peek at the lush, rural Hawaii you will not see from the highway, and for a side trip to lovely Moloaa Bay. The road will rejoin the highway in about 3.5 miles. Another 3.5 miles brings you to the road to Kilauea Point, with its lighthouse and seabird sanctuary. There is a small admission charge at Kilauea, well worth it for the view of the coastline and of hundreds of birds flying and roosting on the sea cliffs and the rocky island off shore. You may even see chicks nesting in the foliage along the walkway.

Once back on the highway, watch on the right for the dirt road just before Kalihiwai Road. (Practically speaking, it will probably be necessary for you to drive as far as Kalihiwai Road, turn around where it is safe to do so, and then take the first dirt road to the left.) You will reach a small unpaved parking lot, where a trail leads down to Kauapea Beach, also called Secret Beach because so few people know of it. Kauapea, a long, wide, sandy beach stretching all the way to the west side of Kilauea Point, is backed by low sea cliffs. The beach has a wild, isolated beauty, and is usually pounded by high surf, especially in the winter months. Swimming is not recommended unless the water is very calm. You are very likely to find nudists here.

A few miles farther down the highway you'll reach the entrance to Princeville, a large hotel/condominium complex, its golf course boasting the most spectacular oceanfront scenery in the islands. Just past the entrance is a pullout on the left for a lookout over Hanalei Valley. The green taro paddies stretching along the river double as a waterbird sanctuary. After crossing the bridge over the Hanalei River, look carefully at the green fields to your right. This is Hanalei Garden Farms, which maintains a herd of 300 bison—the Great Plains "buffalo" are thriving on the lush Hawaii pasturelands.

The sleepy town of Hanalei hasn't much to offer other than a home for Puff, the Magic Dragon, but you may want to drive down to the old wharf for a view of the town's graceful bay. Also, there are some interesting mission buildings on the left just as you leave town. Most of the missionaries who first arrived in Hawaii built homes that were copies of their old houses in New England. Their small windows, low ceilings, and lack of sun protection made them hot and stuffy. The mission at Hanalei was one of the few to incorporate Polynesian architecture into its construction. A high hip roof, which extends to cover a wraparound veranda, provides cooling shade for the entire house.

From Hanalei the road narrows and crosses several one-lane bridges as it closely follows the coast, providing wonderful views of several small bays and beaches. One of these, Lumahai, is especially pretty; it was the setting for the movie *South Pacific*. You can reach Lumahai by parking off Highway 56 just after the end of Hanalei Bay, where the road goes uphill and turns left. You will see other cars parked in the vicinity, and since Hurricane Iniki stripped the trees, Lumahai is visible below. A narrow path descends to the beach.

About 2.5 miles farther on, you'll come to a wide cave in the cliffside on the left of the road; to the right is Haena Beach County Park, a good place to picnic or camp. Less than a mile beyond on the right is a parking area, where you can leave your car and take a short hike uphill to Waikapalae Wet Cave, a deep, water-filled lava tube where you can swim if you are so inclined. If you have a waterproof flashlight and a face mask or goggles, you can explore the rear of the cave, including a second chamber that requires swimming a short distance underwater. Less than half a mile down the road is Waikanaloa Wet Cave, so close to the highway you can see its water-filled interior without leaving your car. The cave can also be an interesting place to swim if the water is clear. The highway ends at Kee Beach, its small lagoon protected by a reef close off shore. This is a great place to swim, snorkel, or just laze in the sand. Rest rooms, drinking water, and outdoor showers are available. The platform in the rocks to the left of the beach is an ancient hula site. It sits near the ruins of a *heiau* dedicated to Laka, the goddess of the hula. In the past, on important occasions Hawaiians would throw blazing firebrands from the 1,200-foot cliff behind the beach. Until a few years ago, the practice was perpetuated by pushing the coals of a huge bonfire off the cliff on the Fourth of July.

The parking lot at Kee is also the start of the 11-mile-long Kalalau Trail that ends at Kalalau Valley, which you saw from the overlook in Kokee State Park. This is an ancient Hawaiian trail used to connect the different valley communities of the north shore, all of which have now been abandoned by their former inhabitants. This is probably the most spectacular hike in the islands. If at all possible, hike along the trail as far as Hanakapiai Beach, a marvelous white sand oasis in a junglelike setting. You can make the round-trip in about 2.5 hours, but don't make the mistake of attempting it in street shoes. Jogging shoes are normally okay, but you'll slip if parts of the trail are muddy. If you have half a day, see Day Hikes, later in this chapter, for a trip to Hanakapiai Falls. If you are pressed for time, at least go as far as the first turn in the trail, which reveals the entire Na Pali Coast in all its splendor as well as a great look back at Kee Beach and its submerged reef. You may see schools of porpoise and, during the winter months, whales.

Another way to see the Na Pali coast is by boat. Several companies offer daily boat trips, usually originating from the Hanalei River outlet. Captain Zodiac, an outfit that uses bouncing motorized rubber rafts, has an office on the main street in Hanalei, phone 826-9371. More comfortable, conventional boats also ply the coast.

Backpacking Adventures

Kalalau Trail (3 days, 28 miles round-trip, including side trips to two waterfalls; strenuous)

Maps: USGS topo quad—Haena. Earthwalk Press Recreation Map, Northwestern Kauai.

This is the best, most popular backpacking trip in the islands. The dramatic views on the way to your destination—and the stunning scenery that surrounds you after you get there—make for a truly unforgettable experience. There may be more beautiful beaches than those found at Kalalau and its sister valley, Honopu, but if they exist, I haven't found them yet. Kalalau's broad white sand beach, with its backdrop of towering rock spires, is graced by a lovely waterfall directly on the shore. And Honopu, its beach divided by a rock archway and its lush, dark valley protected by a cliff, is as mysterious as it is beautiful.

This coast is aptly named—*Na Pali* means "the Cliffs." All along this coast sheer rock walls plunge into the sea or stand guard over silent, green valleys. The 11-mile-long coastal trail to Kalalau winds its way over and around the cliffs, sometimes snaking along heart-stopping dropoffs, other times pushing through lush, wet forests. The Kalalau crosses three major streams and many smaller ones, and passes through five valleys and numerous gulches. There are many ups and downs before the trail finally ends at Kalalau Beach. The trail follows an ancient Hawaiian route mapped out in the days when Na Pali valleys were alive with fishing and farming communities. The people are gone now, their house plots and taro

patches consumed by the forest, but Kalalau's beauty remains. Today the area is protected by Na Pali Coast State Park, comprising
6,500 acres of Kauai's most spectacular landscape.

Sun protection is necessary on the trail, especially on the more
exposed second half. A wide-brimmed hat is best, supplemented by
a sunblock. Rain and wind protection are important too, particularly on the first part of the trail. Do not let rain at the trailhead
dissuade you from making the trip—unless the streams appear
flooded. By the time you reach Kalalau you will be on the drier side
of the island, and the weather may be fine. Boots are the best footwear for this hike, but I have made the trip comfortably several
times in thick-soled, strap-on sandals. One advantage to wearing
sandals is not having to walk in wet boots after a stream crossing,
but they are not for everyone. Running shoes work all right if you
are used to backpacking in them, but they will not grip as well as
boots on slippery surfaces. I have even seen hardy souls making this
trip barefoot!

The hike can be made in one day, but it will be more rewarding
if you can spend two days going in, allowing for a more leisurely
pace and for side trips to two lovely waterfalls on the way. The two-
day trip is described below. If you are making it in one day you will
probably need to eliminate the trips to the two waterfalls.

You must have a permit to camp at Kalalau or either of the two
campgrounds along the way. These permits are free and can be obtained from the Division of State Parks, 3060 Eiwa Street, Lihue,
HI 96766; phone 241-3444. To minimize impact on the valley and
the trail, the state parks office issues camping permits for only sixty
persons per day at Kalalau, or anywhere along the trail. In recent
years the hike has become so popular that all permits for the summer months are often gone by June, and permits for holiday periods
usually go quickly. You should apply for a Kalalau permit as far in
advance as possible; you must supply information such as the
names of all persons in your party, and their Social Security numbers or a photocopy of a piece of ID, such as a passport or driver's
license.

A maximum of five days is allowed in the park, and no two consecutive nights may be spent at either of the campgrounds on the

way in. This allows for several combinations. You could, for example, hike in and out in one day and have five nights in Kalalau. You could camp along the trail on the way in and out, giving you three days in the valley. Or, as the itinerary below describes, you could camp on the way in, spend up to four days in the valley, and hike out. Whichever you choose, this excursion will be one of your most memorable experiences.

Day 1—Kee Beach to Hanakoa Valley, with a side trip to Hanakapiai Falls (10 miles, including 4 miles round-trip to the falls). The trail begins at the end of Highway 56, north of Hanalei at Kee Beach. The trail starts uphill at once from the sign at the trailhead. Some of the stones paving this path are part of the original ancient trail. After half a mile, the trail turns a corner and the entire Na Pali coast is revealed in a postcard-perfect setting. This is a place to stop and stare—if you don't have a camera, you'll wish you did. Schools of porpoises can sometimes be seen in the water far below, and if you are hiking in the winter months, you might be lucky enough to spot a few whales.

The trail makes its way in and out of gulches, crossing several small streams and alternating between forested and open areas in which more views of the Na Pali cliffs appear. The trail will climb as high as 400 feet before dropping to sea level again. After about 1.7 miles, you will get a glimpse of a lovely small white-sand beach, Hanakapiai, where the trail begins its descent toward both the beach and the valley of the same name. (If you are hiking during the winter months, there may not be any beach. Winter surf takes the sand out to sea, then the summer surf brings it back.)

The trail reaches sea level at Hanakapiai Stream, about 100 yards upstream from the beach and 2 miles from the trailhead. If the water level is not too high a series of rocks will allow you to rock-hop across the stream, aided by a fixed rope suspended over the water. If the stream is high it is sometimes easier to cross down at the beach, where the stream diffuses and loses some of its force. Do not cross if it appears dangerous to do so, especially if it has been raining. If you have difficulty here, there are two more streams along the way where the crossings will probably be worse.

Once across the stream, you may be tempted to cool off with a dip at the beach. If so, heed all the signs and use caution. Do not swim if the surf is up, and watch for currents: People have drowned here. If you do decide to swim, it is safest to remain inside the shore break. After you have had your fill of the beach, find the sign for Hanakapiai Falls, taking care that you don't proceed on the coastal trail by mistake. The trail to the falls starts up the valley, following the stream, while the coastal trail, which you will rejoin later, begins to switch back up the cliff.

The path follows the stream and enters a deep forest, in which huge mango trees appear in groups of two or three. If it is early summer you may be in for a feast, but you will have to settle for fallen fruit; blossoms set only on the highest parts of the trees exposed to the sun, making the fruit unaccessible. After three-quarters of a mile, you'll reach a stand of high bamboo and a picnic shelter. The remains of a rock chimney to the left of the shelter are evidence of a failed attempt to grow coffee in the valley. Interestingly, coffee is once more being grown on Kauai, replacing some sugar acreage. Once you've passed the shelter, you'll see some abandoned taro terraces as the path passes through several of them.

At about 0.3 miles from the picnic shelter you will cross the stream again; though the stream is wider here, you should still be able to rock-hop your way through it. (You will cross the stream two more times.) Watch for colored ribbons tied to tree branches to aid in finding the trail again on the other side of the stream. The forest will become wetter, with mud likely in low places. In fifteen minutes or so the trail will narrow and turn sharply uphill, making its way along the side of a small ridge. Here you get your first view of the falls. *Watch your footing carefully.* From here to the end of the trail it is narrow and often wet, and a slip could land you in the stream 15 or more feet below. The trail will descend over a steep short face that you will need to get down, after which you'll cross the stream one last time. From this point it is about 5 minutes to the falls, which plunge 120 feet to a deep pool. Even though the water is cold, don't miss the rare chance to swim behind the falls, prop yourself up on the rocky ledge, and gaze at the world through a veil of falling water.

To return to Hanakapiai Beach from the falls, rejoin the Kalalau

Trail. This will be the last time you will stand at sea level until you reach Kalalau Valley. In a series of switchbacks, the trail begins a steep ascent up to 800 feet, the highest point on the route. You will recognize the point by a large rock on the seaward side of the path. If you go around this rock you will be confronted by a sheer drop, where waves crash against the cliff 800 feet below. Incidentally, if someone tries to tell you that a Hawaiian princess once leaped from this spot because her father refused to allow her to marry her lover, don't believe it.

From here the trail descends through huge sisal plants, some with spires the size of telephone poles. Sightings of these plants, a desert import run wild, will become more frequent as you continue toward the drier side of the island. You'll hike through Hoolulu and Waiahuakua valleys, two of several "hanging" valleys on the coast. (A hanging valley is one that does not descend to the sea, such as Hanakapiai, but instead ends in a cliff, with a stream cascading into the sea far below.) Finally, a turn in the trail will reveal a wide, amphitheater-like green valley. This is Hanakoa, and in less than half a mile you'll reach a dilapidated shack on the left. You are now 4 miles from Hanakapiai Beach and 6 miles from the trailhead, at an elevation of 500 feet. You will not want to stay in the shack; boards are missing from the roof and the floor, and it is usually surrounded by garbage left by goat hunters and hikers. But there is a small clearing directly on the other side of the trail from the shack, and a short trail from the clearing leads down to a delightful pool with a small waterfall and even a "Tarzan rope" from which to swing out and drop into the pool. Don't fail to stop and take a dip—even if you don't make like Tarzan.

The best campsites are on the other side of Hanakoa Stream. There is no rope here to assist your crossing, so proceed cautiously. You may get your feet wet, as rock-hopping usually only takes you across parts of the two forks of the stream, which come together here. Again, do not cross if the water is too high—a backpacker was swept to his death here several years ago trying to cross the flooded stream. After you've crossed the stream, the trail will border a series of old taro terraces, now hosts to wild coffee trees. Their flat surfaces make good campsites. Mosquitoes are usually abundant in Hanakoa, and it rains frequently, so you would be wise to put up your tent. As always, water from the stream should be boiled or treated before use.

Day 2—Hanakoa to Kalalau Beach, with a side trip to Hanakoa Falls (6 miles, including a 1-mile round-trip to the falls). Your second day starts with a short trip to Hanakoa Falls. The trail begins at a wooden sign about 30 yards from the stream crossing, in the vicinity of your campsite; you may have spotted it the previous day. The first part of this trail can be confusing, and it is possible to make one—or even two—false starts. Unfortunately these instructions can be confusing also, unless you read them carefully. If ribbons are on the trail, they will help to solve this problem.

After passing through several taro terraces, the trail crosses the *west* fork of Hanakoa Stream, follows it downstream about 20 feet, then turns away from the west fork and proceeds along the west bank of the *east* fork. The bank is steep and the trail is narrow, and often wet. If you find yourself following the west fork of the stream, it is best to go back and start over. Hanakoa is a bridal veil falls, not as high or as powerful as Hanakapiai, and its pool is not as large, but it is a lovely spot and because of its seclusion you are almost sure to be alone.

Once you return to the main trail and round the turn leaving Hanakoa Valley, the change in landscape is sudden. The lush vegetation is now mostly gone, replaced by shrubs, sisal, and grasses. The trail has reached a region protected from the moisture-laden trade winds, and the forest has given way to open gullies and eroded slopes. Streams are fewer, and water is less available. The trail is much more in the open now, winding around ridges with dizzying dropoffs to the sea. Acrophobes may have difficulty negotiating this part of the hike. The trail makes one last climb to the saddle of Puukula (usually called Red Hill) at 500 feet, and Kalalau finally appears, its beach beckoning below.

You will need to descend Puukula's eroded and crumbling slope slowly—a trial with the end of the trail so close. You will then cross Kalalau Stream, again assisted by a fixed rope. Once across, be sure to turn right toward the beach, not left toward the valley. The campground is on the beach; camping is not allowed in the valley.

(You can explore the valley later, as outlined below.) The trail now traverses a thinly wooded area on the shoreline, ending at Kalalau's magnificent beach.

There is much here to choose from when it comes time to select a campsite. The first sites provide the most privacy, but they are farthest from the water supply. Wooded sites farther on afford both, but tend to harbor mosquitoes. Most hikers prefer to camp as close as possible to Hoolea Falls, which drops almost directly on the beach and serves as the community water supply and shower. It is also possible to camp on the sandy beach, but be sure to pitch your tent far enough inland to avoid having the tide as a bed partner. Another option is a large sea cave in the cliff, just beyond the waterfall, right on the beach. This cave provides protection from sun and rain, and, if you don't mind the lack of privacy, you won't even need a tent. The cave cannot be used in winter, however, as it is usually filled with water. One danger associated with the cave is that goats on the cliffs above often knock rocks down in front of

Kalalau Beach, at the end of the 11-mile Kalalau Trail. Photo by Richard McMahon.

the entrance. These rocks make a pattern in the sand, and it is important to move through this "impact zone" without loitering. Also, keep in mind that rock avalanches sealed two previously camped-in caves west of this one in the 1980s.

Day 3—Exploring Kalalau Valley (4–6 miles). Actually, this excursion need not take place on Day 3. Depending on your own schedule you may take Day 3 to kick back and enjoy the beach. Or you could go up the valley over the course of a morning or afternoon, shortening the visit as you see fit.

Return to the trail just before Kalalau Stream, which leads up the valley. Within half a mile you will reach a clearing with sweeping views of the valley and its fluted, green spires. Back in the forest the trail passes over former taro terraces, groves of large mango trees, and guavas. You'll even find an orange tree if you look carefully. As the trail proceeds you'll cross a small stream, and later on another, where the water forms a shallow pool, christened "Little Pool" by the generation of hippies who made Kalalau their home in the 1970s. Two miles from its start the trail reaches a double pool surrounded by rock ledges, named "Big Pool" by the same free spirits. Big Pool is deep enough for diving, but check your landing zone first to avoid any submerged surprises.

On your return you may want to hike to Waimakemake Falls, about a mile off the main trail on your right as you return. The side trail, which is somewhat difficult to spot at first, lies between Big Pool and the last stream crossing, about 10 minutes back from Big Pool. Look for it branching right in an area of prominent taro terraces. Once you find it, the trail is not difficult to follow; in fact, ribbons may be posted to help you find your way.

Another adventure, this one for confident swimmers, is a visit to the isolated beach at Honopu, the next valley west of Kalalau. There is no trail to Honopu; its only access is by boat or a five- to ten-minute swim from Kalalau. Honopu has a lovely beach cleft into two parts by a dramatic stone arch, and a small waterfall almost as pretty as the one at Kalalau. There is something mystical and unearthly about Honopu; maybe that's why it was chosen as a location for the "lost world" part of the film *King Kong* some years ago. (Others have evidently felt the same way, as Honopu has been nicknamed "Valley of the Lost Tribe." But despite the Indiana Jones name, there never has been a lost tribe in Hawaii, or any "tribes" at all, for that matter.)

A calm morning is necessary for the swim to Honopu, and the earlier you go the better. There is sometimes a westerly-flowing current along the beach, and it gets stronger in the afternoon. A reasonably good swimmer should have no trouble with the current any time of the day, except in rough water, but the earlier you make the return swim, the easier it will be. To begin the swim, walk as far west as you can on Kalalau Beach, until you reach a very large rock slide. (Prior to the slide in 1987, swimmers started out for Honopu through a double entrance cave, which was buried by the 1987 avalanche.) You should soon be able to see the beach at Honopu. Walk as far as you can or strike out from shore, depending on how long a swim you want to make. Once ashore you may be tempted to climb the arch or the small cliff that seals off the beach from the valley. If you do, remember that Hawaii's volcanic rock is soft and crumbly—it doesn't take much for it to break loose. And if you fall, help will be a long time coming.

Another way to experience the Kalalau trail is to take a Zodiac raft one way and then hike the other. Captain Zodiac, in Hanalei (phone 826-9371), makes trips to put parties ashore (or pick them up) at Kalalau once a day from mid-May to mid-September. The Zodiac trip offers a spectacular tour of the coast, including a few runs through a sea cave or two, and ends with a thrilling dash up the beach at Kalalau as the craft and its crew try to stay ahead of a dumping wave. The cost is $60 one way for you and your backpack. Additional luggage will incur an extra charge. You must have a camping permit in your possession before you board the boat. The Zodiacs cannot land on the beach in rough water, so if you plan to go to Kalalau by sea you should be prepared to add an extra day or two to your trip, just in case.

Waimea Canyon (21 miles round-trip, 2–3 days; moderate)

Maps: USGS topo quads—Waimea Canyon, Kekaha, Hanapepe. Earthwalk Press Recreation Map, Northwestern Kauai.

This is a unique trip that takes you from the mouth of Waimea Canyon, along the canyon floor to its center, and then along a narrow side canyon. It ends at an isolated campsite with two great pools, one below the other, each with its own waterfall. The trail follows the Waimea River for most of its length, fording it nine times. It climbs very gradually from sea level to about 1,600 feet at Lonomea Camp, the camping destination.

Scenery on this trip is dramatic. The trail—beginning on a rough four-wheel-drive road and becoming a trail for the last third of the trip—is framed by canyon walls almost all the way, and topped by a deep blue sky. The trail is not difficult, unless the last part has become overgrown and in need of clearing. You should not attempt this hike if the water is high enough at the first ford to make the crossing difficult. Rain upcountry sometimes causes flooding of the Waimea River, and if the crossing is hard here, it will probably be worse upstream. You are never far from water on this trip, but it should be treated before drinking. You will need a permit to camp in the canyon, which can be obtained from the Division of Forestry and Wildlife at the State Office Building, 3060 Eiwa Street, Room 306, Lihue, HI 96766; phone 241-3433. No open fires are permitted and you must pack out all garbage and trash.

Day 1—Waimea Town to Lonomea Camp (10.5 miles). From Waimea, turn right on Menehune Road (between the police station and the small shopping center). After two miles, you will reach a dirt parking lot on the right, where the road makes its first ford of the river. If you are driving, park in the lot and cross the ford. You'll soon reach a sign-in station for hunters and hikers. (Please reclose any gates that you pass through on this hike, and do not attempt to cross any of the rickety suspension bridges you will see. They are no longer safe.) You will ford the river four more times in the first hour of the hike.

After crossing the fourth ford (be sure to count the first one back at the parking lot) the road forks, and the right fork crosses the river. Do not cross here, but take the left fork and the road soon passes over a large black pipeline. Shortly after the pipeline, the road forks again, where you may go either way, as the roads quickly converge. The road then makes a twenty-minute climb and follows along the west bank of the Kekaha Ditch. The ditch is part of an irrigation system bringing water from the upper reaches of the Waimea River and the Koaie Stream to the cane fields along the coast. To your left, the canyon walls tower into the sky. After following the Kekaha Ditch for about a mile and a half, the road descends once more to the river, makes two more crossings, and reaches the Mauka Powerhouse and its suspension bridge, where you'll make the eighth crossing.

Once across, you'll continue north on a faint path between the river and a cabin and stable compound, keeping the cabin on your left. Soon after the cabin, the path crosses a small stream and widens to road width for a short distance. At the point where this widening ends is a deceptive trail on the right, leading to the river. Do not take it, but look to the left and take a second trail, which leads upward and straight ahead. The trail soon follows the base of a rocky cliff, and then turns into a rough road as you reach Wiliwili Camp. There you will find a picnic shelter and pit toilet. This is also the start of the Kukui Trail, which goes from here up to the canyon rim. Take a break here for lunch and to cool off in the pool about 100 feet downstream. You can usually swim here, but even if the water is low, it will still be deep enough to enjoy a soak.

With the river on your right, proceed north on the road, which rises steeply after crossing a dry, rocky streambed and quickly intersects another road at a T. Bear right and downhill here, but where the road crosses the river, you must remain on the west bank. You'll then navigate a narrow path cut into a rock face, with green pools of water about 50 feet below. Proceed carefully here—portions of the trail are wet and slippery, and acrophobes may have difficulty. After the rock face, the trail once more becomes a dirt road. About half a mile from Wiliwili Camp you will reach a ford where a sign formerly indicated your crossing point. In mid-1995, all that remained was a washed-out wood panel nailed to a tree, but it is still a good reference.

Shortly after crossing the river, the road passes Kaluahaulu Camp, which consists of a pavilion and a table. After the camp, at the point where the road appears to cross a large stream, watch for the beginning of the Koaie Canyon Trail, marked by a path leaving the road and heading uphill on the right. The trail winds its way above the east bank of Koaie Stream, climbing gradually and framed by the sheer walls of Koaie Canyon. There are great views whenever the trail breaks out of the mostly *kukui* forest. A little less than a mile from the crossing you will pass another picnic shelter, this one called Hipalau Camp. From there, the trail becomes rougher and can be more difficult to follow. Proceed slowly, taking care not to lose your way. Another mile and a half through *kukui* and other trees will bring you to a long stand of coffee trees and then to Lonomea Camp. There you will find a pavilion with a picnic table, and a pit toilet nearby. Best of all are the two wonderful pools and their waterfalls, promised earlier.

Day 2—Return to Waimea Town. Retracing your steps will not be boring, as you will discover new aspects of the canyon as you hike back down. However, you may vary the trip by exiting the canyon via the Kukui Trail, which begins at Wiliwili Camp, if you can arrange transportation. This is a strenuous 2.5-mile hike, climbing 2,000 feet over a steep ridge and a series of switchbacks. See the Day Hikes section later in this chapter for a description of the route. I recommend a good soak in the pool at Wiliwili before the long uphill grind. Many hikers dunk themselves, clothes and all, before starting up.

Day Hikes

NUALOLO–AWAAWAPUI LOOP: (10.5-mile loop; moderate to strenuous) *Maps: USGS topo quads—Haena, Makaha Point. Earthwalk Press Recreation Map, Northwestern Kauai.*

This day hike is so spectacular that I have named it one of the best adventures in the Hawaiian Islands. Beginning in an upland rain forest, it breaks out into the open on dry ridges leading to the Na Pali cliffs, providing awesome views into two of Kauai's hanging valleys. It reaches the farthest point of any trail above the Na Pali coast—more than 2,000 feet over a cobalt blue sea—and the entire coastline comes dramatically into view. The final portion of the hike is along the highway. If you are able to either arrange a pickup or position a car at the Awaawapui Trailhead, you will save 1.3 miles of walking on the road. There is no source of water on this hot, strenuous hike, unless an intermittent stream is running, so carry plenty of water with you. The last 3 miles on the trail are almost all uphill.

The hike begins at the Nualolo Trailhead, on the west side of Kokee Road, about 50 yards south of the ranger cabin at Kokee Lodge. The trail is wide at the start, where it penetrates a deep upland rain forest with a fair number of native plants. The intrusion of introduced species will soon become apparent as passion fruit and banana poka vines entangle trees and other plants. Blackberry bushes also grow along the trail, and although all three fruits are welcome edibles, they endanger the forest by crowding out or strangling native species.

After passing through a meadow of high grass the forest begins to thin, and the trail starts to descend, steeply enough in places to require you to hold on to branches and roots. Soon the almost bare ridges of the northwest coast will come into view. Following one of these ridges, the trail breaks into the open, and before long you'll be able to see the islands of Niihau and Lehua to the northwest.

Continuing its downhill course, the path negotiates a set of dirt steps cut into an eroded ridge, and the Cliff Trail enters from the right. Go straight, and a few more steps will lead you to a breathtaking view of Nualolo Valley. You may see helicopters, as small as dragonflies, flying up the valley far below. The trail continues along the west rim of the canyon until it reaches a point overlooking the whole Na Pali coast, the entire blue Pacific Ocean at your feet—another fantastic view! At this point you have dropped from about 4,000 feet at Kokee Lodge to 2,234 feet.

Retrace your route to the Cliff Trail, which joins the Nualolo with the Awaawapui Trail 2.2 miles away. A short way up the Cliff Trail you will reach a small picnic pavilion in a pretty meadow—a good lunch stop. On the other side of the meadow, the trail enters the forest again and begins to rise. This is the *only* section of the trail where you *may* find a source of water, an intermittent stream at a small waterfall. But don't count on it—and if there is water, treat it before using it.

After a short, level traverse, the Cliff Trail joins the Awaawapui Trail. Do not turn right for the return leg yet as there is one more great view in store. Turn left and proceed to the Awaawapui Lookout, making sure you reach the point where iron railings mark a vertigo-producing drop into Awaawapui Valley far below. The sheer valley walls here make for an incredible sight. To the left of the Awaawapui Lookout is a different view into Nualolo. If you are not acrophobic, you can walk onto the short, narrow, eroded ridge jutting out into Nualolo, where the world drops away on both sides and to your front. You are at an elevation of 2,900 feet.

The final 3.1-mile leg on the Awaawapui Trail is almost all uphill, switchback at first and then a broad trail. It is forested all the way, cutting through one of the last dry mesic forests left in the islands. The last mile is festooned with various kinds of ginger on both sides of the path. When you reach the parking area at the trailhead, it will be another 1.3 miles down the road to your right to the lodge, unless you have arranged a pickup.

PUU O KILA LOOP: (11.5-mile loop; moderate)
Maps: USGS topo quad—Haena. Earthwalk Press Recreation Map, Northwestern Kauai.

This very pretty hike starts and ends at Kokee Lodge. It begins with a walk on a dirt road, follows the banks of a lovely stream, traverses a portion of the Alakai Swamp, traces the spectacular headwall of Kalalau Valley, and finally meanders through an attractive forest dotted with plum trees.

From the ranger station, walk west along the highway to Camp 10 Road, the first dirt road on the right, just over a tenth of a mile. Proceed on Camp 10 Road for 3.5 miles to Kawaikoi Camp, making sure to stop at Alakai Picnic Area for a dramatic view of Poomau Canyon. (If you have a nonhiker in your party, you can shorten this hike by having him or her drive about 1.5 miles to the sign on the road that advises four-wheel drive only beyond that point. If you have a four-wheel-drive vehicle, your driver can take you all the way to Kawaikoi Camp, lopping 3.5 miles off your trek.)

Enter the gate in the fence at Kawaikoi Camp and walk to the far end of the grassy field, on the right side near the stream. There you will find a trail sign reading "Pihea Trail, 3.75 miles to Puu o Kila." The trail follows the left side of Kawaikoi Stream for about

0.7 miles, at which point another sign points right to the Kawaikoi Stream Trail. If the stream is not high, you may want to cross and add this 1-mile round-trip loop to your hike. The trail continues along the stream bank, passing a covered picnic table beside a swimming hole. This is a good spot for lunch and a dip.

Beyond the picnic area, the trail crosses a small stream and begins a moderate switchback ascent until it reaches a boardwalk intersection with the Alakai Swamp Trail. Cross the intersection, remaining on the Pihea Trail, which also becomes boardwalked at this point. You'll now hike through typical Alakai Swamp vegetation: ferns, mosses, *hapuu,* and *ohia* trees. After about half a mile the boardwalk ends and the trail begins to climb a small knoll—prepare for mud here. Atop the knoll you will suddenly find yourself on the rim of Kalalau Valley, with its magnificent view all the way to the sea. The trail will follow the headwall of the valley, ducking in and out of the forest for more views on the way to Puu o Kila, a stone platform overlook at the end of the road.

From the overlook, proceed along the paved road for about half a mile, watching carefully for the Kaluapuhi trailhead on the left. It was unmarked in 1994, but the trailhead is easy to spot due to its width and the sharp back angle at which it joins the road. If you are hiking in the late spring or early summer, you will find fruit-bearing plum trees in abundance. Picking is regulated, so check with the ranger station before your hike. After a level walk of 1.9 miles, you will rejoin the highway, at which point you'll have another 1.6 miles to go before you get back to the lodge.

ALAKAI SWAMP TRAIL TO KILOHANA LOOKOUT:
(13 miles round-trip; moderate to strenuous)
Maps: USGS topo quad—Haena. Earthwalk Press Recreation Map, Northwestern Kauai.

This is a real swamp, in which you are guaranteed to get wet and muddy—even on the driest of days. The Alakai receives several hundred inches of rainfall annually. Its 30 square miles of wilderness has been invaded by few introduced plants, and native species, adapting to the wet conditions, have proliferated. The Alakai is also a haven for native birds; here they are safe from predators and protected from mosquito-borne avian malaria by the 4,000-foot altitude.

The state Forestry Division is slowly boardwalking the swamp to prevent damage to its fragile ecosystem. This makes hiking easier and faster, but somehow it's just not as much fun as in the pre-boardwalk days, when the soggy trail snaked through strange plants in a misty world where sinking up to your knees in muck at least half a dozen times per hike was the norm. The boardwalk takes much of the mystery and adventure out of the whole experience. But if you hike the Alakai before the boardwalk is finished, you will still have a real swamp experience.

The swamp is one place where you may not want to wear boots; when your feet sink into the mud they are hard to pull out (either with boots or without), and they will be a mess to clean. Nor do you want to wear thongs or sandals: Thongs will pull off and disappear as you extract your feet from the muck, and sandals will not protect your feet from "pungi stake" branches or plant stems lurking in the mud. An old pair of running shoes, preferably high-topped, is fine—but make sure that they're shoes you don't care about. A good hiking stick will come in handy for probing soft spots before taking what could be that fateful step. A compass and the topo map sheet for the area should be part of your emergency equipment. If you get lost in the swamp, they will be essential for finding your way out of it.

The Alakai trailhead is located on the Camp 10 Road, directly opposite the Alakai Picnic Area. Follow the directions for the preceding hike as far as the picnic area (including suggestions for shortening the trip with a vehicle). The beginning of the trail is dry, and almost as wide as a small road. The forest here, which consists of small *ohia, hapuu* fern, and other plants, shrubs, and trees, provides overhead cover, even though the *ohia* are stunted from the wet soils. Upon reaching the boggy area, the trail narrows and the boardwalk begins. After 1.2 miles, you will reach the intersection of the Pihea Trail, which is also boardwalked at this point. Turn right, and the trail will soon descend in a series of boardwalk steps to a stream in a deep gulch. After this point, you can look for the boardwalk to end at any time.

Crossing the stream, the trail climbs out of the gulch and begins to traverse a flat, boggy plain. Trees and large ferns thin out considerably, and brush and swamp grasses predominate. The swamp is at its wettest here, and it is not unusual to occasionally sink in the muck up to your knees—or even higher. Watch your step, trying to avoid the obvious deep spots, and test doubtful areas before putting your full weight on any forward foot. (That stout hiking stick will come in handy here.) To add to your difficulties, the trail becomes hard to follow, the foot trace disappearing for long stretches. Watch for the stakes that mark the trail, as well as poles from an abandoned telephone line that generally follow the route. One word of caution: A heavy mist often lies over this section of the swamp. If it is thick enough to prevent you from seeing the trail-marking stakes, it is best to turn back; you will see nothing from the lookout, and you will be in danger of getting lost. Should that happen, your map will tell you that you need to head west and slightly south to intersect the Pihea Trail, and your compass will keep you on that heading. It will be a slow, miserable slog without a trail to guide you. The best course of action is not to let that happen. People have disappeared in the Alakai.

About 2.3 miles from the intersection with the Pihea Trail, you will reach Kilohana Overlook, with its view over Wainiha Valley stretching to the sea near Hanalei. (It's supposed to be a great view, but I can't vouch for it; I have been there three times and it was so foggy I didn't see anything.) Return to the starting point of the hike by the same route.

WAIPOO FALLS–KUMUWELA TRAIL LOOP: (6.1-mile loop; moderate) *Maps: USGS topo quad—Waimea Canyon. Earthwalk Press Recreation Map, Northwestern Kauai.*

This hike takes you to two small waterfalls, one of which features a delightful tropical pond; provides sweeping views of Waimea Canyon; and finally winds along Kumuwela Ridge in Kokee's upland forest. It begins and ends at Kokee Lodge. A shorter, 3.4-mile version of the same hike will take you to Waipoo Falls, and then back again by the same route.

From the lodge proceed south on Kokee Road (Highway 550)

for about 1.3 miles, to the junction of Kokee and Halemanu roads opposite the entrance to the NASA Tracking Station. Halemanu Road joins from the left, making a very sharp turn that almost bends back toward the direction of the lodge. The dirt road drops steeply, then makes a sharp turn to the right. At about 0.6 miles another, smaller dirt road branches off to the right, ending 0.2 miles farther on in a small clearing used as a parking lot. A nonhiker can drive you to this point in a conventional vehicle in good weather, but a four-wheel drive is safer if it has been raining, or if the road surface is wet.

From here follow the sign for the Canyon Trail, and make the very short side trip on the Cliff Trail to a canyon overlook. Return to the Canyon Trail, which descends through the forest into a small gulch. When you reach the Black Pipe Trail intersection, stay on Canyon Trail by bearing right and downhill. The trail will soon break out into the open on the rim of Waimea Canyon, where you can look across and see people at the Puu Hinahina Overlook. After a short distance, the trail will once more descend into a gulch, where a sign will lead you to the left to Falls Number 1. Falls Number 2, which you'll visit later, is just a short distance farther down the trail.

At the first falls you will find a lovely pool surrounded by wild ginger. This is a wonderful place for a dip. The second falls is where Waipoo actually flows over the canyon rim, cascading 800 feet to the floor below. There are several small soaking pools there. When you are ready to resume the hike, cross the stream where the trail begins to climb through high grass into the forest. It will reach another lookout into the canyon before turning north, where it ends at Kumuwela Road, a little over a mile from the falls. Continue north on Kumuwela Road for about half a mile to the Kumuwela Trailhead on the left. Take the trail, which climbs over a small rise and then drops to Kokee Stream after about 0.4 miles. It does not cross Kokee, but it does cross a small tributary stream, which may or may not be flowing. In another 0.4 miles, the trail ends but continues as a dirt road, which then crosses Kokee Stream. Soon after the crossing, Waininiua Trail branches off to the right. Remain on the road for 0.2 miles, turning left at its intersection with another dirt road, then right at another within 100 yards. Another 0.6 miles along this road will bring you to Highway 550, across from Kokee Lodge.

WAIMEA CANYON RIM TO CANYON FLOOR:
(5-mile round-trip; strenuous)

Maps: USGS topo quad—Waimea Canyon. Earthwalk Press Recreation Map, Northwestern Kauai.

This is a dramatic hike that takes you to the bottom of the canyon via the Kukui Trail, offering up wonderful views of the canyon en route, and culminating in a dip in a refreshing pool at the bottom. The Kukui Trail is steep, dropping 2,240 feet in 2.5 miles. The trailhead is located 7.5 miles north of the town of Waimea on Waimea Canyon Road. There is a small pull-off parking area alongside the road at the wooden trailhead sign.

After leaving the road, the trail is level for a short distance, passing the Iliau Nature Trail (a half-mile loop) and a small picnic pavilion. Immediately after you leave the pavilion, the trail switchbacks down through a wooded area and then breaks out onto a long, eroded ridge with great views of the canyon, especially from the lookout with the small, rough bench. About 1.5 miles from the start of the trail, watch for the sharp left turn that will bring you out onto an eroded, rust-colored ridge that slopes sharply downhill. The trail becomes poorly defined here, and some side trails may cause confusion. Stay as near as possible to the crest of the ridge, watching for the white mileposts that mark every quarter-mile, some of which can be seen from fairly far off.

At the end of the ridge, the trail enters a forest and once more becomes easy to follow. There is a danger of making a wrong turn about half a mile after entering the woods. There a dry streambed intersects the trail, and many hikers mistake it for the trail itself. Both are rocky at the point, and about the same width. Be alert for this, and be sure to bear right, checking as you go to make sure you are on a path. (If you have chosen correctly, the trail will be rocky but well defined.) As you near the bottom of the canyon you will pass several giant sisal plants just before you reach a small picnic pavilion with a pit toilet nearby. This is Wiliwili Camp, at the bot-

tom of Waimea Canyon. Cross the rough Jeep road between yourself and the river and go over to the bank and walk about 100 yards
downstream, where you will find a nice pool. Lying on your back
in the pool and staring up at the walls of the canyon is an experience
not to be missed. You can usually swim in the pool, but even if the
water is low it will be deep enough to enjoy a soak. You may wish
to stay wet, or at least wet your T-shirt before you tackle the hot
climb back up the trail.

POWERLINE TRAIL: (9 miles one way; moderate)
Maps: USGS topo quads—Waialeale, Hanalei.

This trail is actually an abandoned Jeep road crossing northeastern Kauai from south to north (our itinerary, but the hike can
just as easily be completed in reverse). It provides a unique opportunity to explore this seldom seen and little traveled interior part of
the island, and affords dramatic views of distant waterfalls. It begins by climbing a ridge and then dropping partway into Hanalei
Valley, following the valley north almost to its end. The trip works
best either by positioning a car at each end, or arranging a dropoff
at one end and a pickup at the other.

From Lihue, drive north on Highway 56 eight miles to Highway
580, which begins on the left immediately after crossing the Wailua
River bridge. Continue about 7 miles past the turnoff to Opaekaa
Falls, to the end of the road at the Keahua Arboretum parking lot.
If the stream permits, you can cross and drive another quarter-mile
to a turnout on the right, where a large silver postal box serves as
a hunter check-in station. The trail (road) begins here. If you are
positioning a second car at the trail's end, continue to drive north
on Highway 56 to the Princeville Airport (29 miles from Lihue).
One mile past the airport, turn left on Pooku Road, and drive past
the stables to the end of the pavement, about 1.8 miles. The road
continues here as the Powerline Trail.

Upon returning to the southern end of the trailhead, you'll find
that the road is overgrown and rutted at first; the going does get
better after it begins to pass a series of powerline towers. *Ohia* and
guava are prevalent, and *uluhe* grows along the banks on the sides
of the road. As the trail climbs, there are great views to the north

and northwest. At 2.5 miles from the trailhead, an open spot in the road serves as a point from which you can see two beautiful waterfalls, Kapakanui on the left and Kapakaiki on the right. Another half-mile brings an even more sweeping view as you reach the ridgeline. Hoary Head and Nounou Mountain appear to the south, and a whole new vista opens up to the west. Views vie with forest passages as you continue north, and the trail will eventually reach an elevation of more than 1,800 feet before it begins its long, gradual descent.

About 7.3 miles into the hike, you'll begin to see the Hanalei coastline as well as quick snatches of the Hanalei River through the trees. In another half-mile you might want to start looking for waterfalls. You should be able to see Namolokama Falls to the west, although you may need a break in the vegetation to find it. There should be several long, thin falls coming off Hihimanu, the large triangle-shaped mountain to the west. The trail will then pass through guava, *hau,* and *uluhe,* and you'll soon find another postal box moonlighting as a hunter check-in station. A short distance later you'll reach pavement, and the end of the trail.

HANAKAPIAI FALLS: (8 miles round-trip; moderate)
Maps: USGS topo quad—Haena. Earthwalk Press Recreation Map, Northwestern Kauai.

This hike traverses one of the prettiest parts of the Na Pali Coast Trail, arrives at lovely Hanakapiai Beach, and then takes you through a verdant valley before ending at a high waterfall with a deep, swimmable pool at its base.

For the route and other information about this hike, please refer to the Backpacking Adventures section of this chapter, and turn to the first part of the Kalalau Trail trip, which duplicates this hike.

Snorkeling and Diving

Due to Kauai's topography and its position in the sea, much of its diving and snorkeling is more seasonally dependent than that on the other islands. Kauai is the island with the most rainfall, and three rivers and many streams carry runoff into the ocean, causing murky conditions and adversely affecting coral and other marine life in many areas. A good portion of the island's coastline is in private hands, making access difficult, and its western shore—so divable on Hawaii, Maui, and Oahu—does not have many good snorkeling sites. Yet there is some very good diving on Kauai.

The South Shore

Divers and snorkelers will be able to practice their sports pretty much any time of the year on Kauai's south shore—definitely not the case for the rest of the island. Fortunately, these conditions coincide with some fine sites, so that no matter when you visit Kauai, you should be able to get in some good snorkeling and diving.

POIPU BEACH PARK (S): If you visited this park before Hurricane Iniki in 1992, you will have difficulty recognizing it—this is a very different beach today. Much of the shoreline has been altered. Tide pools have been filled and coral buried under tons of sand moved onshore by giant, windswept waves. And the change extends to the landscape beneath the waves: In some places the underwater scenery is still the same; in other places it is entirely new. But the fish still come to Poipu.

KOLOA LANDING (D/S): The sea is almost always calm at Koloa, making it one of the most popular shore dive sites on Kauai. Although Koloa is primarily a dive site, snorkelers will enjoy the landing also due to the schools of tame reef fish expecting handouts, and the beautiful coral formations set off by the brilliant white sand. Easy entry and exit are provided by a concrete boat ramp. Swimming to the left, divers can follow a long coral reef out to depths of about 50 feet; to the right there are better coral formations and abundant marine life. Depths at Koloa average 25 to 30 feet.

To reach the landing from Lihue, drive west on Highway 50 to Poipu Road, then turn left and drive through the famous "tree tunnel," which is no longer a tunnel thanks to Hurricane Iniki. Continue through Koloa toward Poipu, then take the right fork toward Spouting Horn, making the first left on Hoonani Road. In about 0.2 miles you will come to a paved road in poor condition on the right, which will take you to the landing.

KUKUIULA SMALL BOAT HARBOR (D): Two very colorful coral reefs—and the loads of tropical fish swimming around them—are the main attractions here. Entry and exit can be made from a point along the right side of a path to the breakwater: Just follow the breakwater and the reef that extends from it. Across a break of sand another reef appears on the right, extending from the Spouting Horn across the bay.

To reach the harbor, drive south from Koloa toward Poipu, and turn right toward Spouting Horn. The harbor is off the road about half a mile before the Spouting Horn parking lot. Facilities include rest rooms, showers, and a picnic pavilion.

MAKA O KAHAI POINT (D/S): This off-the-beaten-path adventure is worthwhile as much for its above-water scenery as that below. In fact, the diving alone would not be enough for me to recommend that you take all the trouble to get here. Though larger fish frequent the area, and turtles often come in to munch, the undersea terrain is not out of the ordinary. (Of course, in Hawaii, that still means it's pretty good.) But the point's main feature is Nomilu Fishpond, one of the most unusual such ponds in the islands (see Adventuring by Car in this chapter for directions and a description of the area). Enter the water on the west side of the point, preferably at the small beach. Head either left, to explore the point, or right along the rocky shoreline. Snorkelers will normally be in 20-foot depths, while divers will average 40 feet or even 60 feet farther off the point.

The Windward Shore

This coast, which runs roughly from Lihue north to Anahola Bay, is exposed to year-round northeast trade winds that slacken only during periods of kona winds. The coastline offers no topographical protection, such as bays or inlets, to block the force of the trade winds. Sites that would otherwise be good are not divable due to seas beaten to a froth by constant winds. In addition, much of this coast is private property. Some good dive spots can be accessed only by private cane roads, most of which prohibit private vehicles. It makes no sense to risk a charge of trespassing, or collision with a huge cane haul truck, to dive at any of them.

AHUKINI STATE RECREATION PIER (D): I debated whether to include this site, since it is so seldom divable. But those who dive Ahukini swear by it. With an abandoned pier on the south arm of Hanamaulu Bay, the area is swept by the trades, which normally batter the surf onto the shore. The water at Ahukini is also subject to murky conditions due to runoff from Hanamaulu Stream. But on calm days, and when kona winds blow, knowledgeable divers still head for Ahukini. A boulder bottom, rarely more than 30 feet deep, teems with so many fish it has been likened to an aquarium. To reach the site, drive east from Lihue on Ahukini Road (the airport road). The road doglegs around the airport, and ends at the pier parking lot.

Enter the water either from the ledge on the rocky shore by the state park sign, or continue on, park in the lot, and enter in the vicinity of the jetty. The dive area is on the seaward side of the jetty. If the water is a little rough, you can enter on the protected side of the jetty and swim around. If it's really rough, you shouldn't be diving.

ANAHOLA BEACH COUNTY PARK (D/S): This park sits near the eastern end of Anahola Bay, where protection from the trades usually affords calm conditions. A good assortment of reef fish swims among the coral patches resting on a broken, irregular sea bottom. The large boulders and rocks begin once you head out from Kahala Point, the eastern arm of the bay. Depths here vary from 15 to 30 feet. To reach the park, drive north on Highway 56, through Kapaa, turning right on Anahola Road. Follow the signs to the beach park and drive to the far end and park. Select an entry as close to the rocky point as possible and snorkel along the rocky shore; divers can go out around the point. Rest rooms, showers, drinking water, picnic tables, and a campground are located in the beach park.

There are two other places on this coast where snorkeling and diving are reasonably good, when conditions permit. Nukolii

Beach Park and Lydgate State Park are both off Highway 56, between Lihue and Wailua.

The North Shore

Summer months offer the best conditions on Kauai's north shore, as winter swells and waves pound the shoreline and make the water murky. However, there are good days in the winter, too—when the surfers are complaining about the north shore, it's time to grab your tanks.

HAENA (TUNNELS) (D/S): This is the best diving site on the north shore. Entry is from a beautiful sandy beach, and the first dropoff is only 30 feet from shore. The reef is shaped like a giant fishhook, with a lovely lagoon inside the "hook." Snorkelers and beginning divers should head right, exploring the inner wall of the reef within the lagoon. There are lots of cracks and small lava tubes to poke around, and trenches in the reef can be easily viewed by a snorkeler on the surface—and there are plenty of fish. Depths inside the reef range from 15 to 50 feet farther offshore. More experienced divers can swim left, exiting through the natural channel, and then turn seaward, following the reef's outside wall. At depths of 50 to 60 feet you'll find plenty of ledges, caves, and interconnected passages. In addition to the usual marine life, whitetip sharks can sometimes be found resting in the caves, and there might be some turtles.

To reach Haena Point drive 8.3 miles past the entrance to Princeville on Highway 56, watching for a dirt turnoff on the right. You can usually spot it by an overflow of cars parked along the road, especially on summer weekends. If you reach Haena Beach County Park, with its prominent cave on the right, you have gone too far. Double back just over 0.2 miles, and park, if there is space, in the informal lot in the trees. Take care not to box yourself—or anyone else—in. Entry can be made directly in front of the parking area. Rest rooms, showers, water, and picnic tables are available at Haena Beach Park, and you may camp here with a county permit. You may have to park at Haena if there is no space at Tunnels.

HAENA (CANNONS) (D): A wall dive with underwater scenery and marine life similar to Tunnels, this site is 0.35 miles past Haena

Beach Park. A trail leads down to the water just before a house that sits behind a prominent chain-link fence. You should be able to see a cut in the coral reef that fronts the sandy beach; enter the ocean through this cut. (Be sure to exit through the same cut in the reef.) A dropoff begins in about 20 feet of water and plunges to 50 feet. Swimming left along the wall will bring you to a large arch and many small caves. Facilities, as described above, are back at the beach park.

KEE BEACH AND LAGOON (D/S): This pretty beach and visible near-shore reef is at the end of Highway 56, past Haena Beach Park. Kee Beach is as far as you can drive on Kauai's north shore. A nice, sandy beach leads into a small lagoon, which is protected by the reef. Only beginning divers will be happy inside the reef, but this is a good place for snorkelers, especially on the left side of the lagoon, where there are pretty coral formations and a fair variety of fish. Depths range from 10 to 20 feet along the inside of the reef, while depths of 30 to 40 feet outside the reef will tempt divers. There is much more sea life there, and many small caves, ledges, and holes. A cut in the reef, normally visible form shore, allows divers to swim through to the outer ocean beyond. Unfortunately the sea is often rough at Kee, preventing access to the area beyond the reef. If you can't dive, take a hike up the Kalalau Trail, an 11-mile coastal trail that passes through some of Kauai's most beautiful valleys (see Backpacking Adventures, earlier in this chapter, for details).

SNORKEL AND DIVE BOAT TRIPS: One of the best trips on Kauai is a snorkel excursion off the Na Pali Coast. This is a "two-for-one" bargain, because, in addition to snorkeling in a relatively pristine location, you get a beautiful tour of this dramatic coastline. At last count there were two operators in Hanalei who offered this trip; refer to the Yellow Pages (under "Diving" or "Scuba") for specific operators.

Oceanarium, a deep dive to three spectacular pinnacles on the north shore, is one of the few dives where you can see black coral. Dive shops on the south shore offer visits to such places as General Store, Oasis Reef, and Sheraton Caves, all excellent sites. For a unique adventure, Bubbles Below (6251 Hauaala Road, Kapaa, HI 96746; phone 329-9348) offers weekly trips to almost virgin territory off the coast of Niihau, the "Forbidden Island." These excursions are all-day adventures on a 33-foot dive boat, with food, beverages, and three tanks included.

Surfing

It is a little known fact that Kauai probably has the second most consistent surfing waves after Oahu. Surfing on Kauai tends to be low key because that's the way local surfers like it. They are protective of their island and their surf spots, and the last thing they want is to see their waves become as crowded as Oahu's. So far they are succeeding: Although Kauai's major surfing areas are well known, and some get quite crowded, they are not overrun. Surfing Kauai is still a relaxing experience in a tropical paradise with friendly people. If you are tired of the hassles and *huhu* of Oahu, Kauai is your island—as long as you respect the local surfers and the local waves.

POIPU BEACH: The most popular summer surfing area on the island, Poipu was devastated by Hurricane Iniki in 1992; it is still not completely back on its feet. Famous surfer landmarks like the Beach House Restaurant and Brennecke's were closed for almost a year. Two major hotels, both them gutted by the storm, still had not reopened in late 1995. And there has been some major geographical facelifting along the shoreline. People who remember Poipu Beach Park before the hurricane won't recognize the place today. But the surfers are back, and so are a lot of the facilities. And the waves are as good as ever.

There are six surfing spots at Poipu, three on the Poipu side of Waikamo Stream and three on the Lawai (east) side. Those on the Lawai side are the most popular; all of them are visible from the Beach House Restaurant, on the ocean side of Lawai Road. For experienced surfers, *Longhouse* (S/L/B) has long, hollow lefts and some rebreaking rights, while *Centers* (S/L/B) offers fast rights, except when southeast swells pump up the lefts. *Acid Drop*'s (S/L/B) steep, hollow, short rights and shallow reef also mark it for experts only. On the Poipu side of the stream, *First Break* (S/L), half a mile from shore, needs a 6- to 8-foot south swell, but the site offers good waves for experienced surfers. *Waiohai*'s hollow left tubes are best surfed at high tide due to its shallow reef. *Brennecke*'s, roughly in front of the restaurant of the same name, is a bodysurfing beach with a powerful shorebreak.

Pakalas, also known as *Infinities* (S/L/B), raises one of the best waves in the islands, a very fast left that usually separates into three peaks, each one successively farther from shore. When conditions are just right, the three peaks come together for a 250-yard—or longer—ride. A sharp, shallow reef on the east and numerous coral heads on the west make Pakalas a risky place to surf at low tide. The sea is often rust brown at Pakalas from silt washing into the bay from Mahinauli Gulch. Pakalas breaks all year, but it is best in summer. You can reach it by following the short trail from the small bridge about 4 miles west of the highway bridge in Hanapepe. Look for cars parked along the street just after you cross the bridge.

Polihale (S/L/B/BS) lies at the end of the road on Kauai's western shore. Polihale offers relative solitude, and right and left breaks all year. The beach also serves up dangerous currents at any time, which increase in power with the height of the waves. Polihale's summer surf is good for beginners and intermediates, but winter's more powerful waves are strictly for the experienced surfer. To reach Polihale, take Highway 50 past Barking Sand Pacific Missile Range, staying with the highway as it turns toward the mountains. Turn left into the cane field at the sign for Polihale, and follow the signs to the beach. There is an excellent state campground here, which requires a permit (see Appendix II).

Tunnels (S/L/B), although a popular winter surf spot, has a critical wave that breaks right on a sharp, shallow reef. The ride is usually quick: a few seconds in the tunnel and it's over. You should not consider surfing here unless you have extensive tube-riding experience over shallow reefs. Tunnels can be reached by a right-of-way about a quarter-mile east of Haena Beach Park. Lack of parking may require that you leave your vehicle at Haena's parking lot and walk down the beach to Tunnels.

Not many surfers are aware that in winter, *Hanalei Bay* (S/L/B/

BW) has one of the best right-hand reef breaks in the world. Its three takeoffs, *Impossibles, Flat Rock,* and *The Bowl,* are great surfing spots in their own right, but on those rare days when they connect, they provide a phenomenal experience. And, when the powerful 20-foot boomers roll in, Hanalei provides the ultimate big-wave challenge. Intermediates through experts will find thrills at Hanalei, but the waves are almost always crowded. Turn off Highway 56 in Hanalei toward the ocean, and take Weke Road to Hanalei Beach Park, next to the old pier.

Another surf spot on the west side of the bay is *Waikokos* (S/L/B), which offers fine, hollow lefts when the swell is up and the winds are down. You can reach Waikokos from Waikoko Beach, just before the highway turns uphill toward Lumahai Beach.

Anahola (S/L/B), also called *Unreals,* or *Gas Chambers* when the swell is up, breaks all year, and its fast, hollow rights are best with kona winds. But Kahala Point affords some protection from the trades, and although they are sometimes bumpy, rideable waves are more frequent here than elsewhere on the windward shore. A shallow reef requires caution. Turn seaward off Highway 56 toward Anahola Beach Park, and drive east on the dirt road that parallels the beach until you can see the surf breaking.

Kealia (S/L/B) is another windward spot that breaks all year and provides good surfing from right and left beach breaks on kona days. *Coco Palms,* right off its namesake hotel, is an excellent body-surfing spot all year round. *Ammonias* is a small spot off Nawiliwili Park that offers gentle summer waves for beginners.

Windsurfing

Kauai would be a much better place for sailboarding were it not for the island's beach access problems. Much of the north shore is barred by steep cliffs and a rocky shoreline, and miles of beaches on the south shore are inaccessible because they are fronted by private land. Another problem is that since, for some reason, windsurfing has been on the decline on Kauai, three windsurfing equipment stores have closed in the last few years. Visiting sailboarders usually head for Maui or Oahu, as have even local sailboarders. But don't let any of that stop you from coming to Kauai to windsurf. It is a beautiful island, and if you are looking for low-key sailboarding, this is the place to be. At least one instructor was still doing business in mid-1995: Windsurf Kauai has been in business for eleven years, offering lessons and rentals. Lessons are given at Anini Beach (see below), and cost $60 for a three-hour session that includes all equipment. You can contact Windsurf Kauai at P.O. Box 323, Hanalei, HI 96714; phone 828-6838.

Anini Beach, just east of Princeville, is probably Kauai's most popular windsurfing spot. Its reef-protected shallow lagoon and sandy beach, and the virtual absence of a shore break, make it an ideal place to learn the basics of the sport. But Anini is not just for beginners. It will satisfy all the requirements of more experienced sailboarders, and when it's really windy even experts can be challenged. Anini has an excellent county campground (see Appendix II), and there are hotels and condos in Princeville. Restaurants are located in Princeville and Hanalei. Two other popular beginner areas are *Nawiliwili Bay* and *Port Allen,* on the south shore. Both offer protected waters and moderate winds. For the more experienced sailor, there are *Salt Pond Beach County Park* and *Mahaulepu Beach,* both of which are also popular surfing spots. Salt Pond has a spacious county campground, and several small restaurants nearby. On the north shore, the prevailing conditions at *Tunnels* restrict sailboarding to the experts a good part of the time. Tunnels lies right off Haena Beach County Park, which allows camping. Camping is also offered a short distance away at the YMCA's Camp Naue (phone 246-9090), which also has dormitory facilities. A snack van is usually parked in the Haena parking lot.

Biking

It was not so long ago that there were no traffic lights on Kauai. Traffic that sparse may have been one of the reasons why Kauai became the second most popular cycling destination in the islands after Maui. But the main reason has to be that Kauai is such a beautiful place to ride. There are few locations anywhere that can compare with a coastal cruise along the island's north shore beaches, or a dramatic ride along the rim of Waimea Canyon. Kauai has traffic lights now, and traffic is anything but sparse, but the beauty is still there. Listed below are three bike tours of the island, plus additional itineraries for mountain bikers.

Tour 1: Lihue to Kee Beach (38 miles)

This trip takes you along the east shore of the island, and then along the north shore to the end of the road. Traffic is apt to be heavy at the beginning of the trip, particularly in the congested area between Lihue and Kapaa, but it will thin out considerably after that. Several side trips (you may want to cycle some of them on the way out and some on the way back) are included on this on this itinerary, adding to the trip's mileage. There is a gradual grade between Kapaa and Kilauea, and several small hills afterward. There is no problem with food and drink along the way, except that there are no stores after Hanalei. Please refer to Adventuring by Car, Day 2, in this chapter for the trip itinerary, side trips, and points of interest.

If you plan to overnight on this trip, hotel and condo accommodations are available in Princeville. There are a few B&Bs in the Princeville-Hanalei area, and campgrounds are located at Haena Beach County Park (only a mile from the end of the trip) and at Anini and Anahola Beach county parks. A YMCA campground, Camp Naue, is near Haena.

Tour 2: Lihue to Polihale State Park (38 miles)

This is a far different trip from the previous one, taking you now around the dry side of the island. It is nowhere near as lush, particularly as you near the western shore. There are a few hills between Lihue and Waimea, but after that the road is relatively flat all the way to Polihale. Drinking water is available in Polihale, but the last place to buy munchables is Kekaha. Please refer to Adventuring by Car, Day 1, for route information and points of interest, but do not go up the road to Waimea Canyon; that is the next day's tour. Polihale has an excellent campground, directly on the beach and secluded from the rest of the beach park, with sweeping views of the ocean and the cliffs. There are no hotels, but there may be some B&Bs in the Waimea Area. Check the *HVB Accommodations Guide*.

Tour 3: Waimea Canyon and Kokee State Park
(44 miles round-trip)

This is a dramatic ride offering marvelous vistas, but it requires strong uphill skills and endurance. The road climbs from sea level to 4,000 feet in about 17 miles, with the steepest part of the tour in the first 6 miles or so. There is no food or water along the way, but water is available at Kokee, and there is a snack bar at the park lodge. Please see Adventuring by Car—The Western Half—earlier in this chapter for route information and points of interest, and see below for campgrounds in the Kokee area.

Mountain Biking

KOKEE STATE PARK: At Kokee there are many miles of dirt roads and Jeep tracks providing access to out-of-the-way overlooks, streams, and picnic areas with almost no vehicle traffic. To find these roads, purchase the inexpensive Kokee Trails map, which shows not only trails, but all of the park's dirt roads and tracks, at the park museum. In addition to the state campground at the main section of the park, three more campgrounds are located along these roads, with free permits required from the Division of Forestry and Wildlife, 3060 Eiwa Street, Lihue, HI 96766; phone 241-3433.

Another mountain-biking opportunity in the Kokee area are the many Jeep roads that branch off the highway westward toward the Na Pali cliffs. Most of these follow long ridgelines, and some lead to scenic lookouts over the ocean. If you prefer to explore Kokee with a group, Outfitters Kauai (P. O. Box 1149, Koloa, HI 96756; phone 742-9667) offers a combined biking/hiking adventure along these back roads and trails, visiting lookouts and Waipoo Falls. Outfitters furnishes bikes, helmets, and lunch for a cost of $78 per person, as of this writing.

WAIMEA CANYON: If you don't mind walking your bike over the rough spots and fording the same stream eight (or more) times, the 15-mile round-trip along the bottom of the Waimea Canyon, starting from Waimea Town, is a unique and picturesque trip. With a Forestry and Wildlife permit you can overnight at Wiliwili Camp.

For directions to the trailhead and a description of the route, see the Backpacking Adventures section in this chapter, but do not go beyond Wiliwili Camp.

POWERLINE TRAIL (9 miles): The Powerline Trail in northeastern Kauai is another fine mountain-bike tour, again, if you don't mind walking your bike over the rough spots. For a description of the route see the Day Hikes section of this chapter.

Hunting

You may hunt pigs and goats on Kauai, but what sets the island apart from the others, at least for avid hunters, is that it is the only island where you can hunt black-tailed deer. Public hunting areas cover a fairly large part of the island, but with a few minor exceptions hunting is only permitted on weekends and state holidays. One of the most notable exceptions is a year-round, daily archery-only unit on the Na Pali coast in the Hapakapiai and Hanakoa areas. I used to admire the archers I saw heading off into the Na Pali coast wilderness to bring down their prey the old-fashioned way. But after I started hiking in the area myself, I concluded there was not much sport involved when a goat just steps out of the woods ten yards away and stares at you. I must admit, though, that never stopped me from sharing a hunter's kill simmering over an outdoor fire at the old Hanakoa shack. Because they are voracious vegetation eaters, the goat population needs to be controlled, especially on this coastline, where erosion is a major problem.

A special permit, which is available through public drawing, is required to hunt black-tailed deer. The season is normally held on the five weekends preceding the last full weekend in October. Bag limit is one animal per season. Applications for the public drawing can be obtained by contacting the Division of Forestry and Wildlife, 1151 Punchbowl Street, Honolulu, HI 96813; phone 587-0166.

You may hunt eight kinds of birds on Kauai: ring-necked pheasant, Japanese quail, Chukar partridge, barred and lace-necked dove, and gray, black, and Erkel's francolin. The season normally lasts from the first Saturday in November through the third Sunday in January, weekends and holidays only. The public bird hunting area is more restricted than that for mammals.

Freshwater Fishing

Kauai is the only place in Hawaii where you can fish for trout. Three other game fish can also be caught here. A fishing license is required (see the section on fishing in How to Use This Book). In addition, fishing in reservoirs or ponds on private lands requires permits from the landowners, as explained below.

RAINBOW TROUT: Anyone who knows anything about trout would not expect them to survive in a semitropical environment; the cool streams in Kokee State Park are the only place in the islands where they have been successfully introduced (though a commercial trout farm exists on the Big Island). Although the waters are cool enough to ensure survival, they are not cold enough to promote spawning, so the state must restock the fish from the mainland on an annual basis. The largest trout catch recorded on Kauai was 5 pounds 10 ounces, but most trout are much smaller than this, on average around 8 ounces.

Trout season begins the first Saturday in August and continues daily for the next sixteen days. After that, fishing is allowed only on weekends and holidays until the last Sunday in September. To fish the best parts of the streams in Kokee, you need a four-wheel-drive vehicle, although good fishing can often be found at Puu Lua Reservoir. It's best to check directions to these locations when you get your license; as in most places, the farther you get from the beaten path, the better the fishing will be. Many of the streams are small, their banks heavily overgrown with thick vegetation. Casting room is limited so you can fly fish in only a few spots, generally along Koaie and Waialae streams. Standard lures work well where you can use them (Kawaikoi, Waialae, and Puu Loa Reservoir), but along many of the streams, the overgrown banks will restrict you to bait like earthworms and salmon eggs. Bag limit is 7 trout per day, each of them not less than 10 inches.

LARGEMOUTH BASS: These game fish are found mainly in the reservoirs of the sugar plantations and are usually smaller than their mainland cousins, but they will give you just as big a fight. The record catch on Kauai stands at 8 pounds, but you are unlikely to see anything over 3 pounds (most weigh in at a pound or two). Because the reservoirs are on private land you will need a permit from the land's owner, in addition to your fishing license.

Anglers who wish to fish for largemouth bass and tucunare (peacock bass) will need special permits to access reservoirs and streams on private land, in addition to a state fishing license. These can be obtained from:

[Lake Waita]
Secretary
Lihue Plantation Co.
P. O. Box 751
2970 Kele Street
Lihue, HI 96766
Tel: 245-7352

[Tanaka Pond]
Secretary
McBryde Sugar Co.
P. O. Box 8
Eleele, HI 96705
Tel: 335-5111

Fishing season for bass, as with all other fish except trout, is year-round. The most popular place to fish for bass on Kauai is Lake Waita, a 460-acre reservoir near the town of Koloa. Another favorite spot is Tanaka Pond, near Wailua. Check when you buy your fishing license for other spots. As far as lures are concerned, whatever works for you at home will work in Hawaii. Bag limit is 10 bass per day, large- or smallmouth or a mixed catch. Fish must be not less than 9 inches apiece.

SMALLMOUTH BASS: The smallmouth is found mainly in streams feeding from the Wailua River's drainage system. Although the largest recorded catch on Kauai is 3 pounds 11 ounces, the average fish is much smaller, usually 9 to 12 ounces. One place to find smallmouth bass is on the north fork, and part of the south fork, of the Wailua River. As far as lures go, Mepps spinners work well, but some local fishermen say live crayfish are the best bait. Please see Largemouth Bass, above, for bag limits.

TUCUNARE (Peacock Bass): Not really a member of the bass family, this import from South America inhabits the plantation reservoirs along with the largemouth bass; you will also need a permit from the plantation to fish for it. (Please see Largemouth Bass for more information on obtaining these permits.) The tucunare is an aggressive fish, and will fight hard when hooked. The record catch on Kauai is 8 pounds 13 ounces, and fish up to 3 pounds are not uncommon. The same lures that work for bass are good for catching tucunare, though one expert recommends a bright orange or red sinking crankbait. Bag limit is 3 fish per day, each of them not less than 12 inches.

Kayaking the Na Pali Coast

Few adventures in the entire state of Hawaii—and indeed in the world—can compare with a kayaking trip down the Na Pali coast. A downwind paddle past stunning scenery, with stops at fascinating sites, it is an unforgettable experience. The 15-mile water distance can be paddled in anywhere from one to five days; and you should definitely take the full five if you have the time. The Na Pali is one of the most beautiful coasts in the islands. For a wilderness area, it is also highly traveled. On land, you will catch glimpses of hikers high up on the cliffs, negotiating the 11-mile long trail to Kalalau. At sea, you will meet motorized Zodiac rafts and other, more conventional craft taking tourists back and forth. In the air, helicopters whirl by, whisking visitors into otherwise inaccessible valleys. Yet despite all this activity, a kayak trip down this spectacular coast qualifies as a real wilderness adventure. True, you will put ashore at places where people are, but you will also land where others cannot go—no trails for hikers, no landings for larger boats, and no pads for helicopters. And, for most of the time, you will be alone with the sea and the cliffs.

If you have offshore kayaking experience you should have no trouble making this trip, with a similarly qualified partner. If there are just two of you, you might want to consider two separate boats rather than a two-man kayak. For flexibility, carrying capacity, and emergencies, two kayaks are better than one. If you prefer to go with a group, you might contact Hui Waa Kaukahi, P. O. Box 88143, Honolulu, HI 96830.

Audrey Sutherland's *Paddling Hawaii* is a valuable planning tool for this trip, best made in June, July, or early August. Winter surf is too dangerous, and in spring and fall conditions are unreliable. You must bring everything with you that you need except water, and you must have a means of purifying that. Make sure also that you bring mask, snorkel, and fins. You will visit prime snorkeling spots. A good idea, too, is a line that you can tie from yourself to your kayak, so that you can tow it behind you and not have it blow away in the wind as you snorkel over some offshore reefs. The line will also help in pulling your boat ashore.

If you plan to rent a kayak for this trip, you can do so in Kauai, which gives you the opportunity to use a high-performance hard shell boat without the hassle of shipping it by barge from Honolulu. Kayak Kauai (P. O. Box 508, Hanalei, HI 96714; phone 826-9844, or toll free: (800) 437-3507) rents Scupperpros and Dolphins for $120 a week, and Zuma Twos for $200 per week. Daily rates are also available. This operation will provide free pickup at the Princeville Airport, transport you and the kayak to the Haena Beach put-in for $8, and pick you up at Polihale for $40. You can leave excess baggage with them ($3 per day), and they will deliver it to you at Polihale.

You will need camping permits for your overnight stays on this trip. Camping on the Na Pali coast is limited to a total of five nights in any one consecutive thirty-day period. Within this five-night maximum, however, you are allowed only one night at Hanakapiai, five nights at Kalalau, and three at Milolii.

SUGGESTED ITINERARY: The itinerary below suggests that you take advantage of all five nights as follows: one night at Hanakapiai, three at Kalalau, and one at Milolii. If time is short, you could eliminate the third night in Kalalau. A permit can be obtained at the Division of State Parks, 3060 Eiwa Street, Lihue, HI 96766; phone 241-3444. You will need to specify how many nights you wish to spend at each location, and furnish some sort of ID for each member of your party. It is important to request your permits as far in advance as possible; the state limits the number of permits it will issue for Na Pali, and often all permits for the summer months are gone by early June.

For kayaking in these waters, the USGS topographic maps are more useful than nautical charts since it is land features that you will be guiding on. Water depth and navigational hazards are of little interest, as your craft will not draw enough to be affected by underwater shoals.

Day 1—Haena Beach County Park to Hanakapiai Beach (3 miles). Maps: USGS topo quads—Haena, Makaha, Kekaha.

If you wish to get an early start, you may camp, with a county permit, at this attractive park. From your put-in at Haena it is 1.4 miles to Kailiu Point, with Kee Beach just on the other side. Kee is a fine beach and a good snorkeling spot when the water is calm. If you want to stop, do so at the extreme east end of the beach. Kayaks are not permitted in the small lagoon between the beach and the reef, nor are they permitted to come ashore anywhere on the main part of the beach. The platform in the rocks to the left of the beach is an ancient *hula* site. It sits near the ruins of a *heiau* dedicated to Laka, the goddess of the *hula*. There used to be a house, used for scenes from the TV mini-series, *The Thornbirds*, next to the *hula* site. Kee is also the start of the 11-mile Kalalau Trail, which ends at Kalalau Valley.

Resuming the trip, another 1.5 miles will bring you to Hanakapiai Beach, its lush, green valley sweeping out behind it. This is your stop for the night. You should be able to get ashore on the sandy beach without too much difficulty, although a frequent dumping surf on the steep shore may necessitate careful timing of the wave sets. Hanakapiai Stream often pools behind the beach, flattening the sand, which in turn reduces the shore break. Your best bet is to just pick your spot and paddle in. Spend the afternoon exploring the beach and the valley, or hike the 2 miles to Hanakapiai Falls, with its great pool. Be sure to swim behind the falls and sit up on the ledge behind the wall of water. See the Day Hikes section of this chapter for a guide to exploring the valley and directions to the pool.

Day 2—Hanakapiai to Kalalau Valley (5 miles). About a mile after leaving Hanakapiai, you'll reach a sea cave with a waterfall guarding its entrance. The water is coming from a stream exiting hidden Hoolulu Valley. If the sea is not too rough you can paddle under or around the falls and into the cave. Another, much larger cave appears about half a mile farther down the coast. This one you can paddle all the way through, again, sea conditions permitting. A shaft of light penetrates the roof of the cave, and a waterfall flows through it here. Since tour boat operators like to come full bore through this tunnel, it is a good idea to have one kayak guarding the entrance while the other is going through. Shortly beyond the cave you will see Hanakoa, the largest valley on the coast until Kalalau, its waterfall pouring over a cliff and into the sea. On the other side of Hanakoa, vegetation thins out considerably as you turn almost imperceptibly into the drier side of the island. The Kalalau Trail is visible more often now, lower down and no longer hidden by thick forests and deep valleys. Finally, a long, sandy beach backed by towering green spires comes into view: You have reached Kalalau.

Kalalau's beachfront is long enough to give you several landing options. Much of the shore break here is plunging, with a steep dropoff. Look for places where the sand levels out and the waves tend to run up on the beach. Pick out the best of these, time the wave sets, and paddle hard for shore. Spend the rest of the day selecting your camp, getting established, and exploring this magnificent beach. Take a dip in the ocean, then relax and watch the sunset. The next day you should reserve for exploring the valley, and the following day you can paddle or swim to neighboring Honopu, which many feel is the most beautiful beach in all the islands. For information on selecting a campsite, exploring Kalalau Valley, and visiting Honopu, see the Backpacking Adventures section earlier in this chapter.

Days 3 and 4—Kalalau to Milolii Beach (4 miles). About 0.7 miles after you pass Honopu you can paddle into a cave where the ceiling has fallen in, forming an island in its center. This is actually a collapsed lava tube. A little over a mile farther, and you'll reach Nualolo Kai, a half-mile-long beach bordered by steep cliffs at both ends. A ladder once existed at the eastern end of this beach, affording entry to Nualolo Valley (Nualolo Aina). Small settlements of Hawaiians existed at both of these locations, the beach dwellers providing the products of the sea and the valley dwellers the fruits of the land. The remains of the settlement can be found behind the eastern end of the beach, and snorkeling is excellent on the edge of the reef fronting this section of the beach.

About a mile west of Nualolo Kai you will see Milolii Beach, recognizable by a cabin, several shelters, and a water tank at its western end. There are channel markers to guide you through the reef to the beach. Milolii is the most "civilized" of the campgrounds on the Na Pali coast. In addition to the above, it has pit toilets, and running water and showers with water warmed by sun-heated pipes. A mile-long trail leads up Milolii Valley to a waterfall situated in a narrow, chute-like chamber, its sheer walls soaring up to the sky. It is an eerie place. The trail begins near the water tank and generally follows the stream. A small falls along the trail provides a pleasant sit-down shower. As you proceed up the trail you'll pass taro terraces overgrown with *koa haole*, which will soon give way to *kukui* trees and some Java plum. The valley, not wide to begin with, narrows sharply toward its head, where an 8-foot waterfall feeds a small pool. Climbing around this falls brings you to the chamber described above, where a 100-foot falls drops down a steep face. Watch out for falling rocks.

Day 5—Milolii to Polihale Beach (3.4 miles). The final leg of your voyage lacks some of the dramatic impact of the previous days. The sea is calmer, the wind lower, the scenery not as stunning, and there are no more valleys, caves, or tunnels to pique your interest. In fact, the only dramatic thing remaining might be your landing at Polihale. From Milolii to Polihale the dry cliffs march on your left. You pass valleys too small and too high up from shore to see into, until, finally, the vast white sands of Polihale come into view. With luck you may be able to simply run your boat up on the beach. More likely, however, you will have to make a surf landing, and there is a possibility of your being dumped. Pack and secure your gear accordingly. If you plan to camp, try to come ashore south of the beach park (look for tents), so you won't have to haul your gear so far. Otherwise, watch the surf, pick the best place and time, and go for it. There is an excellent campground at Polihale, off by itself and away from the beach park proper. It has its own rest rooms, drinking water, showers, picnic tables, and grills, plus a great oceanfront view.

If you are short of time, or would prefer not to go ashore to explore and camp, Outfitters Kauai (P.O. Box 1149, Koloa, HI 96756; phone 742-9667) offers a one-day kayak tour, as described above, of the entire coast between mid-May and mid-September. It involves about six hours of paddling time, plus a lunch stop at Milolii. Outfitters furnishes Scupperpro kayaks and provides transportation to the put-in at Haena and the take-out at Polihale. Cost is a reasonable $125. If you are not in Hawaii during these months and would still like to go on a kayak trip, they offer full-day and half-day tours on the south shore all year round.

Finally, if you would like to do more kayaking in Hawaii, be sure to see the island-by-island kayaking trip descriptions in Audrey Sutherland's *Paddling Hawaii*.

Suggested Reading

The following books will provide you with additional information about subjects covered in this book. There are many other good books about Hawaii that you might enjoy reading or that you might find useful. All but one of the books on this list are soft cover, and many are pocket size, making them easy to carry in jackets or packs. They are most likely to be of interest to adventurers, hikers, and other outdoor enthusiasts.

General

Shoal of Time, by Gavan Daws. University of Hawaii Press, Honolulu, 1974. One of the best histories of the Hawaiian Islands, told in a relaxed, readable style.

Feathered Gods and Fishhooks, by Patrick V. Kirch. University of Hawaii Press, Honolulu, 1985. The origins and development of ancient Hawaiian history and culture as revealed through archaeological evidence. Illustrations. (Hard cover)

A Hawaiian Reader, edited by A. Grove Day and Carl Stroven. Mutual Publishing, Honolulu, 1984. Selections by thirty authors writing about Hawaii, including Robert Louis Stevenson, Mark Twain, and Jack London.

Myths and Legends of Hawaii, by W. D. Westervelt, selected and edited by A. Grove Day. Mutual Publishing, Honolulu, 1987. An abridged, pocket size version of the classic reference.

Hawaiian Petroglyphs, by J. Halley Cox and Edward Stasack. Bishop Museum Press, Honolulu, 1970. Descriptions and locations of sites throughout the islands.

Hidden Hawaii, by Ray Riegert. Ulysses Press, Berkeley, 1993. A good, easy-to-read travel guide to the islands.

Adventurer's Hawaii, by Peter Caldwell. Taote Publishing, Honolulu, 1992. A book of beautiful color photographs of some of the most out-of-the-way places in the islands, with interesting and informative commentary.

Paddling Hawaii, by Audrey Sutherland. The Mountaineers, Seattle, 1988. The definitive guide for kayaking the coasts and rivers of all of the Hawaiian islands. Provides detailed itineraries and information on types of kayaks, paddling techniques, appropriate gear, packing for trips, safety rules, and more.

Six Islands on Two Wheels, by Tom Koch. Bess Press, Honolulu, 1990. Describes several cycling itineraries on the main islands.

Surfer's Guide to Hawaii, by Greg Ambrose. Bess Press, Honolulu, 1991. A comprehensive guide, entertainingly written in surfer's language. Authoritative, detailed information is provided in the text as well as in informative icons for each surfing area.

Diving and Snorkeling Guide to the Hawaiian Islands, by Doug Wallin. Gulf Publishing, Houston, 1991. Nice illustrations, but short on directions to diving and snorkeling locations. Seems to be the only book on the topic currently in print.

Hawaiian Hiking Trails, by Craig Chisholm. The Fernglen Press, Lake Oswego, OR, 1989. A listing of forty-nine of the more popular hikes on all the islands, with good maps.

Camping Hawaii: A Complete Guide, by Richard McMahon. University of Hawaii Press, Honolulu, 1994. Detailed information about more than 120 campgrounds and inexpensive wilderness cabins. Includes background information about the geography, history, culture, flora and fauna of the islands as well as descriptions of hiking trails, points of interest, and activities at each campground.

Flora and Fauna

Hawaiian Coastal Plants, by Mark Merlin. Oriental, Honolulu, 1986.

Hawaiian Forest Plants, by Mark Merlin. Oriental, Honolulu, 1980.

Trees of Hawaii, by Angela Kay Kepler. University of Hawaii Press, Honolulu, 1990.

Ferns of Hawaii, by Kathy Valier. University of Hawaii Press, Honolulu, 1995.

Hawaiian Seashells, by Stephen Quirk, Betsy Harrison and Jerry Kringel. Boom Enterprises, Honolulu, 1972.

Hawaiian Reefs and Tidepools, by Ann Fielding. Oriental, Honolulu, 1985.

Hawaiian Reef Animals, by Hobson and Chave. University of Hawaii Press, Honolulu, 1990.

Hawaii's Fishes, by John P. Hoover. Mutual, Honolulu, 1993.

Hawaii's Birds, Hawaii Audubon Society, Honolulu, 1986.

Hawaiian Reptiles and Amphibians, by Sean McKeown. Oriental, Honolulu, 1978.

A Field Guide to the Mammals in Hawaii, by Sandra and Charles van Riper III. Oriental, Honolulu, 1982.

Hawaii

Beaches of the Big Island, by John R. K. Clark. University of Hawaii Press, Honolulu, 1985. A fascinating, readable guide to all of Hawaii's beaches, with maps, photos, historical information, and cultural anecdotes. Other books in the series, covering the beaches of Maui, Molokai, Lanai, Oahu, and Kauai are listed below.

Hawaii Trails, by Kathy Morey. Wilderness Press, Berkeley, 1992. A good guide to sixty hikes and strolls on the Big Island.

Trailside Plants of Hawaii's National Parks, by Charles H. Lamoureux. Hawaii Natural History Association, Volcano, HI, 1976.

Volcanoes of the National Parks in Hawaii, by Gordon A. MacDonald and Douglas H. Hubbard. Hawaii Natural History Association, Volcano, HI, 1982.

Volcano Watching, by Robert and Barbara Decker. Tongg, Honolulu, 1984.

Maui

The Beaches of Maui County, by John R. K. Clark. University of Hawaii Press, Honolulu, 1989. See *Beaches of the Big Island,* above.

Haleakala: A Guide to the Mountain, by Cameron B. and Angela Kay Kepler. Mutual, Honolulu, 1988. A small, useful guide, with many color photographs.

Maui's Hana Highway, by Angela Kay Kepler. Mutual, Honolulu, 1987. (Same as above.)

Maui Trails, by Kathy Morey. Wilderness Press, Berkeley, 1991. More than fifty hikes and walks are described.

Molokai

Molokai, by O. A. Bushnell. University of Hawaii Press, Honolulu, 1975. A fictional, but accurate, account of the conditions in the early days of the leper colony at Kalaupapa.

Paddling My Own Canoe, by Audrey Sutherland. University of Hawaii Press, Honolulu, 1978. A classic, true story of one woman's solo journeys on Molokai's north shore, swimming with a pack in tow, and in a small inflatable kayak. Much more than an adventure tale, the book is a life statement.

Oahu

The Beaches of Oahu, by John R. K. Clark. University of Hawaii Press, Honolulu, 1977. See *Beaches of the Big Island,* above.

The Hiker's Guide to Oahu, by Stuart M. Ball, Jr. University of Hawaii Press, Honolulu, 1993. The best guide to hikes and trails on the island. Detailed descriptions of fifty-three of Oahu's finest day hikes, by one of Hawaii's most knowledgeable veteran hikers. Includes excellent route maps of each hike.

Kauai

Beaches of Kauai and Niihau, by John R. K. Clark. University of Hawaii Press, Honolulu, 1990. See *Beaches of the Big Island,* above.

Kauai Trails, by Kathy Morey. Wilderness Press, Berkeley, 1992. A good guide to sixty-two hikes and strolls on Kauai.

On the Na Pali Coast, by Kathy Valier. University of Hawaii Press, Honolulu, 1988. An informative, easy-to-read guide for hikers, kayakers, and others interested in exploring the Na Pali coast. Includes a mile-by-mile description of the Kalalau Trail as well as points of interest on a sea journey down the coast.

Useful Addresses and Phone Numbers

National Parks

For backcountry camping and cabin permits and general information, write or call:

Hawaii Volcanoes National Park, HI 96718; phone 967-7311.

Haleakala National Park, Box 369, Makawao, HI 96768; phone 572-9306.

State Parks

Camping permits may be obtained at any state park office for any island. Write or call the Division of State Parks, at one of the offices below:

Hawaii—P. O. Box 936, Hilo, HI 96720; phone 933-4200.

Maui & Molokai—P. O. Box 1049, Wailuku, HI 96793; phone 243-5354.

Oahu—P. O. Box 621, Honolulu, HI 96809; phone 587-0300.

Kauai—3060 Eiwa Street, Lihue, HI 96766; phone 241-3444.

County Parks

Camping permits may be obtained by writing or calling the Department of Parks & Recreation at the addresses below:

Hawaii—25 Aupuni Street, Hilo, HI 96720; phone 961-8311.

Maui—War Memorial Center, Wailuku, HI 96793; phone 243-7389.

Molokai—P. O. Box 526, Kaunakakai, HI 96748; phone 553-3204. Camping permits can also be obtained from the parks office on Maui.

Kauai—4280A Rice Street, Bldg. B, Lihue, HI 96766; phone 241-6660.

Oahu—650 South King Street, Honolulu, HI 96813; phone 523-4525. Free bus schedules may also be picked up here.
Camping permits and bus schedules may also be obtained at any of the satellite city halls listed below:

Ala Moana—Ala Moana Shopping Center—phone 973-2600
Fort Street Mall—1000 Fort Street Mall—phone 532-2500
Hauula—54-316 Kamehameha Highway—phone 293-8551
Kailua—302 Kuulei Road—phone 261-8575
Kalihi—Palama—2295 North King Street—phone 832-2900
Kaneohe—46-018 Kamehameha Highway—phone 235-4571
Wahiawa—830 California Avenue—phone 621-0791
Waianae—85-555 Farrington Highway—phone 696-6371
Waipahu—94-144 Farrington Highway—phone 671-5638

Division of Forestry and Wildlife

Camping permits for areas under Forestry control and hunting information may be obtained at the following:

Hawaii—1648 Kilauea Avenue, Hilo, HI 96720; phone 933-4221.
Maui, Molokai—P. O. Box 1050, Wailuku, HI 96793; phone 871-2831.
Oahu—1151 Punchbowl Street, Honolulu, HI 96813; phone 587-0166.
Kauai—3060 Eiwa Street, Lihue, HI 96766; phone 241-3433.

Interisland Airlines

Aloha Airlines—484-1111
Hawaiian Airlines—838-1555
Mahalo Air—833-5555

Commuter Airlines

Air Molokai—521-0090
Island Air—484-2222

Bus Schedule Information

Hawaii—Hele-On Bus Service; phone 935-8241.
Maui—Trans Hawaiian (shuttle only from airport to Kaanapali area); phone 877-7303.
Oahu—The Bus; phone 848-5555.
Kauai—Iniki Express; phone 241-6410.

Index